The Sciences Po Series in International Relations and Political Economy

Series Editor, Christian Lequesne

This series consists of works emanating from the foremost French researchers from Sciences Po, Paris. Sciences Po was founded in 1872 and is today one of the most prestigious universities for teaching and research in social sciences in France, recognized worldwide.

This series focuses on the transformations of the international arena, in a world where the state, though its sovereignty is questioned, reinvents itself. The series explores the effects on international relations and the world economy of regionalization, globalization (not only of trade and finance but also of culture), and transnational flows at large. This evolution in world affairs sustains a variety of networks from the ideological to the criminal or terrorist. Besides the geopolitical transformations of the globalized planet, the new political economy of the world has a decided impact on its destiny as well, and this series hopes to uncover what that is.

Published by Palgrave Macmillan:

Politics in China: Moving Frontiers
edited by Françoise Mengin and Jean-Louis Rocca
Tropical Forests, International Jungle: The Underside of Global Ecopolitics
by Marie-Claude Smouts, translated by Cynthia Schoch
The Political Economy of Emerging Markets: Actors, Institutions and Financial Crises in Latin America
by Javier Santiso
Cyber China: Reshaping National Identities in the Age of Information
edited by Françoise Mengin
With Us or Against Us: Studies in Global Anti-Americanism
edited by Denis Lacorne and Tony Judt
Vietnam's New Order: International Perspectives on the State and Reform in Vietnam
edited by Stéphanie Balme and Mark Sidel
Equality and Transparency: A Strategic Perspective on Affirmative Action in American Law
by Daniel Sabbagh, translation by Cynthia Schoch and John Atherton

Moralizing International Relations: Called to Account
by Ariel Colonomos, translated by Chris Turner
Norms over Force: The Enigma of European Power
by Zaki Laidi, translated from the French by Cynthia Schoch
Democracies at War against Terrorism: A Comparative Perspective
edited by Samy Cohen, translated by John Atherton, Roger Leverdier, Leslie Piquemal, and Cynthia Schoch
Justifying War? From Humanitarian Intervention to Counterterrorism
edited by Gilles Andréani and Pierre Hassner, translated by John Hulsey, Leslie Piquemal, Ros Schwartz, and Chris Turner
An Identity for Europe: The Relevance of Multiculturalism in EU Construction
edited by Riva Kastoryano, translated by Susan Emanuel
The Politics of Regional Integration in Latin America: Theoretical and Comparative Explorations
by Olivier Dabène
Central and Eastern Europe: Europeanization and Social Change
by François Bafoil, translated by Chris Turner
Building Constitutionalism in China
edited by Stéphanie Balme and Michael W. Dowdle

Building Constitutionalism in China

Edited by
Stéphanie Balme
and
Michael W. Dowdle

palgrave
macmillan

BUILDING CONSTITUTIONALISM IN CHINA

First published in 2009 by
PALGRAVE MACMILLAN®
in the United States—a division of St. Martin's Press LLC,
175 Fifth Avenue, New York, NY 10010.

Where this book is distributed in the UK, Europe and the rest of the world, this is by Palgrave Macmillan, a division of Macmillan Publishers Limited, registered in England, company number 785998, of Houndmills, Basingstoke, Hampshire RG21 6XS.

Palgrave Macmillan is the global academic imprint of the above companies and has companies and representatives throughout the world.

Palgrave® and Macmillan® are registered trademarks in the United States, the United Kingdom, Europe and other countries.

ISBN: 978–0–230–60032–4

Library of Congress Cataloging-in-Publication Data

Building constitutionalism in China / edited by Stéphanie Balme and Michael W. Dowdle.
p. cm.—(Sciences Po series in international relations and political economy)
Based on an international conference on "Constitutionalism and Judicial Power in China" at Sciences Po (CERI) in Paris in December 2005—Preface.
Includes bibliographical references and index.
ISBN-13: 978–0–230–60032–4 (alk. paper)
ISBN-10: 0–230–60032–8 (alk. paper)
1. Constitutional law—China—Congresses. I. Balme, Stéphanie. II. Dowdle, Michael W.

KNQ2069.B85 2008
342.51—dc22 2009002720

A catalogue record of the book is available from the British Library.

Design by Newgen Imaging Systems (P) Ltd., Chennai, India.

First edition: October 2009

10 9 8 7 6 5 4 3 2 1

Printed in the United States of America.

CONTENTS

CONTRIBUTORS

Stéphanie Balme is Senior Research Fellow at Sciences Po, Paris (CERI & Chair MAPDP) and Visiting Professor at the Tsinghua University School of law.

Michael W. Dowdle is the former Chair of Globalization and Governance at Sciences Po, Paris and a Visiting Associate Professor of Law at the National University of Singapore School of Law.

Fu Hualing is a Professor of Law at the Hong Kong University Law School.

Keith J. Hand is an Associate Professor of Law at the University of California Hastings College of the Law.

He Xin is an Associate Professor of Law at the School of Law, City University of Hong Kong and a member of the New York University Law School's Global Faculty.

Ji Weidong is a Professor of Law at Kobe University and Dean of the Leo KoGuan Law School of Shanghai Jiao Tong University.

Randall P. Peerenboom is a Professor of Law at La Trobe University, an Associate Fellow at the Oxford University Centre for Socio-Legal Studies, and Director of the Oxford Foundation for Law, Justice and Society China Rule of Law Program.

Eva Pils is an Assistant Professor of Law at the Chinese University of Hong Kong Faculty of Law.

Glenn D. Tiffert is a Ph.D. candidate at the University of California Berkeley History Department.

Tong Zhiwei is a Professor of Law and former Dean at the Shanghai Jiaotong University School of Law, and Director of the Institute of Constitutional and Administrative Law.

Pierre-Étienne Will is a Professor at the *Collège de France*, Chair of History of Modern China, and Director of the *Institut des Hautes Études Chinoises*.

Xiaohong Xiao-Planes is University Professor at *l'École des Hautes Études en Sciences Sociales* (EHESS) and holds the Chair in Chinese History at *l'Institut National des Langues et Civilisations Orientales* (INALCO).

Yu Xingzhong is an Associate Professor of Law at the Chinese University of Hong Kong Faculty of Law.

Zhu Suli is a Professor of Law and Dean of the Beijing University Law School.

ACKNOWLEDGMENTS

This book is the product of three years of investigation into China's constitutional option. It stems from earlier research into the development of constitutionalism and rule of law in socialist countries in the post–cold war world. This led to an international conference on "Constitutionalism and Judicial Power in China" that we convened at Sciences Po (CERI) in Paris in December 2005. This conference, which was organized with the help of our friend Pasquale Pasquino, brought together fifteen prominent scholars from China, Europe, and the United States. It also benefited immensely from the participation and support of two Grand Justices of the French Constitutional Council: M. Pierre Joxe and M. Olivier Dutheillet de Lamothe. We are particularly appreciative of M. Dutheillet's subsequent visit, along with that of his colleague, Grand Justice Guy Canivet, in 2008 to the Tsinghua University Law School, in order to discuss important constitutional issues related to China.

Additional thanks go, first and foremost, to Professor Mireille Delmas-Marty, who initiated Franco-Chinese legal cooperation in the 1980s and is still pursuing her unique pedagogical approach to rule of law developments in China. Most recently, she has been engaging both Chinese scholars and Chinese authorities in debate of law and globalization. She has been a great inspiration for this research project. Judge Wang Yaqin and her colleagues from various jurisdictions in China provided invaluable assistance in facilitating Stéphanie's long and intrusive fieldworks in Southern and Western China. Our thinking about this issue has also benefited from constant intellectual exchanges with Judge Jean-Luc Quinio, head of the Franco-Chinese judicial cooperation program of the French Embassy in Beijing, and Antoine Garapon, General Secretary of the *Institut des Hautes Études sur la Justice* (IHEJ) in Paris.

This project was also nourished by cross-cultural discussions with local Chinese students (especially Yang Lihua, Xu Mengxi and Liao Xiaoxi) and the informal yet growing "*faluren*" (*law people*) Internet discussion group that Stéphanie set up with Glenn Tiffert.

Finally, we would like to acknowledge the vital contribution of the following institutions: Sciences Po (especially Christophe Jaffrelot, Miriam Périer, Catherine Honnorat, Francis Vérillaud, Alessia Lefébure, Gérard Grunberg and Bruno Latour); the Cultural Services of the French Embassy in China (especially Alexandre Ziegler, Donatienne Hissard, and Christine Cornet); the Chinese University of Hong Kong; and the Tsinghua University Law School (especially Wang Chenguang, Wang Zhenmin, Wang Yaxin, Cheng Jie, Chen Weizuo, Yu Lingyun, Shen Weixin, and Zhang Han).

* * *

Chapter 12, "Citizens Engage the Constitution: The Sun Zhigang Incident and Constitutional Review Proposals in the People's Republic of China," by Keith J. Hand, is adapted from Keith J. Hand, "Using Law for a Righteous Purpose: The Sun Zhigang Incident and Evolving Forms of Citizen Action in the People's Republic of China," *Columbia Journal of Transnational Law* volume 45 (2006), pages 114–195. We are grateful to the *Columbia Journal of Transnational Law* for their permission to publish this adaptation.

Chapter 13, "Rights Activism in China: The Case of Lawyer Gao Zhisheng," by Eva Pils, is adapted from Eva Pils, "Asking the Tiger for his Skin: Rights Activism in China," *Fordham International Law Journal* volume 30 (2007), pages 1209–1287.

Chapter 14, "Virtual Constitutionalism in the Late Ming Dynasty," by Pierre-Étienne Will, is adapted from Pierre-Étienne Will, "Le contrôle de l'excès de pouvoir sous la dynastie des Ming," in Mireille Delmas-Marty and Pierre-Étienne Will, eds., *La Chine et la Démocratie* (Paris: Fayard, 2007), pages 111–157.

Stéphanie Balme, Beijing
Michael W. Dowdle, Singapore
June 2009

CHAPTER ONE

Introduction: Exploring for Constitutionalism in 21st Century China

Stéphanie Balme and Michael W. Dowdle

I. China's "Constitutional Option"

> Of the plausible scenarios for China's future, the possibility of a new constitutionalism has been taken seriously by only a few Western specialists. Yet the constitutionalist scenario gains credibility from the improbability of the alternatives.
>
> (Nathan 1996, 43)

Andrew Nathan argued this in 1996. Fifteen years later, and notwithstanding the ups and downs of mainland China's political and legal evolution, the evolutionary pull of this "constitutional option" has become clear. But despite the recent explosion of interest in comparative constitutionalism, and the massive interest in China's prospects for rule of law and democratization, the dynamics and possibilities of China's constitutional potential remain as unexplored today as they were in 1996. This book seeks to fill this gap, by examining the developmental possibilities of China's emergent constitutionalism. It shows how, despite considerable weakness and deficieny, constitutionalism is fast becoming an important component of political dynamics in China. Through its chapters, it explores how this constitutional potential has come about, and how it manifests itself in such a seemingly inhospitable political environment.

In this introductory chapter, we critically examine the various ways that one might approach the issue of "constitutionalism" in present-day China.

These include the analytical lenses of judicial power, political jurisprudence, popular constitutionalism, and envisioning the state. We argue that these lenses should not be viewed, as they too often are, as stand-alone analytic constructs, but as interrelated conceptual frameworks whose power lies in their collective interplay. Part 2 then describes how the chapters to this volume explore and expose such interplay in China's present constitutional environment. What we find in China, we believe, is a transitional constitutionalism whose future success is by no means certain, but whose dynamics and possibilities are significantly more interesting and robust than generally is recognized at present.

A. Constitutionalism and Judicial Power

Constitutionalism is often closely associated with—and even conflated with—the judiciary's power and effectiveness in enforcing constitutional norms (what Americans generally call "judicial review"). Following Martin Shapiro and Alec Stone Sweet (2002), we might refer to this model as that of "judicial power." This is perhaps the most common way that constitutionalism is evaluated. But this court-led model of constitutional development is actually incomplete. As we shall see, it presumes a constitutional system that is already relatively mature—in which a notion of rule of law is already embedded firmly enough in the constitutional culture to give special and deontological status to both "the law" and the courts' particular and unilateral explications of that law. And for this reason, it does not by itself provide an accurate description of what happens in younger and more emergent constitutional cultures, like that of China.

Of course, the judiciary is important to constitutionalism. We see this in the close association we draw between constitutionalism and what we call "rule of law"—an association that dates back at least to Chief Justice Marshall's famous line in *Marbury v. Madison* (1803, 177) that American constitutionalism had resulted in "a nation of laws, not men." This conflation was then famously taken up by Albert Venn Dicey (1981), who argued that "rule of law"—what today we would call "judicialization"—was the essence of English constitutionalism. The general syllogism that underlies this association goes something as follows: "constitutions are phenomena that are regarded as laws; law is a phenomeon that is enforceable by courts; therefore constitutions must be phenomena that are enforced by courts; and therefore constitutionalism is principally a product of judicial power."

Nevertheless, our understanding of the relationship between constitutionalism and this particular vision of judicial power needs to be qualified by two important caveats. First, even in the most effective constitutional system, significant aspects of constitutional structure are invariably nonjusticiable.

Of course, the United Kingdom's "unwritten constitution" is the paradigmatic example of this. But it is not unique. The Dutch Constitution is also not justicially reviewable (Ten Kate and Van Koppen 1994). And while the Swedish Constitution has long allowed judicial review in theory, even after 200 years the Swedish courts are yet to avail themselves to this power in practice (Walsh 1987). In both Japan and Italy, courts occasionally engage in judicial review, but the governments have claimed authority to ignore their rulings (Volcansek 1990). In India, which has enjoyed a particularly robust practice of judicial review, some suggest that this practice in fact has had only marginal effect on the actual development of India's political and constitutional order (Cassels 1989). Even in the United States, which may revere the practice of judicial review more than any other country, large tracts of the Constitution are nevertheless affirmatively rendered nonjusticiable. This includes, most notably, much that concerns its Montesquieuian separation of powers, which has been removed from the courts' purview by the political question doctrine.

Beyond this, the practice of judicial review is particularly rare in new and emergent constitutional systems like that of China. In the United States, judicial review did not become an accepted constitutional practice until the 1880s, almost one hundred years after the constitutional system itself came into being. France's Constitution did not articulate such a practice until 1958, and the resulting Constitutional Council was only able to gain independent effectiveness and widespread political credibility through its historic decision of July 1971, some eighty years after the Third Republic introduced constitutional stability into France's political system (Pasquale 1998). With the exception of South Africa, practices of judicial review have played little catalyzing role in the "third wave" of democratic transitions that occurred in the late 1980s and early 1990s (Dowdle 2002, 25–26).

Moreover, when courts do exercise judicial review in emergent constitutional systems, they are ultimately as likely to weaken as strengthen such systems. The infamous *Dred Scott* case (1856), whose decision did much to provoke a civil war, provides a paradigmatic example of this in the American context (Fehrenbacher 1978). Similarly, judicial efforts to assert constitutional supremacy in South Africa in the 1950s and in India and Korea in the early 1970s resulted in political crises that curtailed the development of constitutionalism and judicial independence in those countries, as did judicial efforts to exert constitutional discipline in Russia and Peru in the 1990s, and the Philippines and Thailand in the decade thereafter (Schmemann 1993; *The Economist* 2007; Pangalangan 2004; Montlake 2008).

One of the reasons why a focus on judicial power causes us to overlook the delicacy and complexity of judicial involvement in constitutionalism, particularly in emergent constitutional systems, lies in the metaphors we use to explain the source of this "power." In constitutional thinking, judicial power is closely associated with the notion of judicial independence: the latter being regarded as a necessary condition for the former. But this metaphor of "independence" is problematic from the perspective of how constitutions actually operate. At its heart, a constitution is an innately *cooperative* phenomenon. But the metaphor of "independence" cloaks the cooperative dynamics upon which a Constitution vitally depends for its effectiveness. It causes us to frame our analyses of court contributions to constitutionalism by seeing courts as (ideally) insular institutions operating (ideally) in their own self-contained universes. When in fact, the courts' constitutional effectiveness is actually found in its interactions with other institutions rather than in its isolation from them.

In the United States, for example, the courts' judicial power depends vitally on the cooperation of other constitutional actors, and the cooperation of the society as a whole. Even in a robust democracy, a judiciary's inherent status as the Constitution's least dangerous branch makes it a poor candidate for enforcing constitutional norms against noncooperative political actors. "Mr. [Chief Justice John] Marshall has made his decision, now let him enforce it," the American President Andrew Jackson purportedly said in 1832, in response to the American Supreme Court's decision in *Worcester v. Georgia* (Brands 2006, 462) Abraham Lincoln famously (or infamously) seems to have ignored the constitutional pronouncements of the courts during much of his tenure as president of the United States (Abraham 1998, 116–117). More recently, in *Planned Parenthood of Southeastern Pennsylvania v. Casey* (1992: 865), Justice Sandra Day O'Conner would again remind us that:

> [T]he Court cannot buy support for its decisions by spending money and, except to a minor degree, it cannot independently coerce obedience to its decrees. The Court's power lies, rather, in its legitimacy, a product of substance and perception that shows itself in the people's acceptance of the Judiciary as fit to determine what the nation's law means and to declare what it demands.

This is not to claim that courts are unimportant players in the dynamics or emergence of constitutionalism. Rather, the point is that the complexity of the courts' role in constitutionalism and its emergence is not adequately captured by existing concerns about judicial power stemming from judicial independence. The power and effect of courts are found, not in their independence, but in their interdependence. Our understanding of the full constitutional effect of the courts therefore requires a much more thorough mapping of their actual interactions with the rest of the constitutional system than a focus on judicial independence encourages. This means, that while judicial power is indeed important, maybe even vital, to constitutional dynamics, it is not a particularly good place to *start* a constitutional analysis. Judicial power comes from, and makes sense only in the context of, the courts' place within and interactions with the larger constitutional structure. It is to this larger structure that we must first look if we are to understand China's "constitutional option," and the courts' possible contributions to that option.

B. *From Judicial Power to Political Jurisprudence*

We can get a better understanding of the relationship between constitutionalism and judicial power in China by looking at another political feature that is generally associated with constitutionalism, namely that of democracy. Conventional wisdom generally conflates constitutionalism with democracy. And indeed, it is the Chinese leadership's infamous resistance to democratization that leads many to question the relevance of constitutionalism to China's present-day political dynamics or to its potential for political development.

However, constitutionalism's actual relationship with "democracy" is quite contentious, at least insofar as Anglo-American constitutionalism is concerned. Historically, Anglo-American constitutionalists have actually tended to present constitutionalism as an *alternative* to democracy, rather than as an articulation of democracy. This opposition is clear in the writings of the American founders, whose "constitutionalism" was motivated by what might best be described as a fear of the alternative, "democratic option" they saw in America's emerging political and economic pluralism (Wood 1993, 252–255). A very similar fear was behind Dicey's intellectual reinvigoration of a distinctly constitutional order in England (Schneiderman 1998; Tulloch 1977). Relatedly, many have recently argued that in the context of today's European Union (EU), the "constitutional option" represented by the now rejected *Draft Treaty Establishing a Constitution for Europe* (2003) was premature precisely because it would stifle the necessary, ongoing democratization of the new, distinctively transnational, European polity that the EU had itself brought into being (Christodoulidis 2003; Wilkinson 2003).

It is in this tension between constitutionalism and democracy in which the distinctive relevance and importance of the courts and their judicial power to constitutionalism lies. This is most seminally articulated by Dicey himself. To Dicey, it was precisely the courts' insulation from majoritarian, populist, and democratic politics that recommended them as the most appropriate guardians of England's constitutional wisdom (Schneiderman 1998). This appeal is well rehearsed in the United States as well—perhaps most famously in Justice Stone's famous claim in *United States v. Carolene Products Co.* (1938: 152–153 n.4) that one of the defining constitutional roles of the courts lay in their distinctive ability to protect "discrete and insular minorities" from majoritarian tyranny (see also Lusky 1982). It is also apparent in Ronald Dworkin's famous distinction between "principle" and "policy" in the context of America's constitutional order (Dworkin 1977, 14–45).

By contrast, in continental Europe, courts seem to have played a lesser role in constitutionalism, precisely because of a more pronounced preference for a political (as opposed to juridical) form of dispute resolution. French constitutionalism, for example, vests much less constitutional authority in its courts than does that of the US or India. At the same time, many see French constitutionalism as much more affirmatively "democratic"—at least in the "deliberative" sense—than its American-inspired counterparts: France's Rousseauian conception of sovereignty has always been understood as a democratic state power beyond and above the reach of its unelected judiciary. It is precisely because of the Rousseauian preference for politics over juridification that French constitutionalism, and perhaps continental European constitutionalism more generally, has refused to give its courts and judges the same say over constitutional principle that American judges enjoy (Corrado 2004, 2–7).

Indeed, in the context of China, it is precisely in the Chinese leadership's infamous resistance to democratization that the real motor for China's present-day constitutionalization seems to lie. Chinese resistance to democratization appears to have encouraged authorities to advance "rule of law" (and associated law reform) as political-legitimacy substitutes for democratization (Peerenboom 2007a). This shifting of political focus to "the law" has in turn pushed demand for political reform into the legal arena, and more precisely onto constitutionalism—that area of the law where law and politics seem most fully to overlap. It is not accidental that the first appearance of a distinctly public discourse of constitutionalism in China has occurred with regards to issues that have a distinctively legal shape to them: such as in the use of administrative detention, or in the protection of property rights. The language of constitutionalism allowed those seeking to resist governmental and party actions and policies in these areas to frame their resistance as being in alliance with the state's own ongoing efforts to define itself through law. And obviously, through litigation, the courts provide very convenient fora through which such arguments can be advanced.

For this reason, in China—perhaps more so than anyplace outside of the United States and India—the courts despite their well-known constitutional infirmities have paradoxically become major vehicles for expressions of political reform. This is most clearly manifested in the emergence during the early 2000s of the "rights-protection movement [*weiquan yundong*]"—a direct product of court-focused, litigatory resistence strategies pioneered by rural activists in the 1990s (Yu 2004a). This is a movement comprised of a growing network of lawyers, legal scholars, and grassroot social activists who, by using a discourse of constitutionalism-as-law as mobilized through processes of administrative litigation, may be the most effective domestic voices for political reform operating in China today (see the chapter by Eva Pils later in this volume; see also Fu and Cullen 2008).

In this sense, China presents us with an interesting twist to the relationship between constitutionalism and judicial power. Consistent with the general observations that underlie the judicial-power visions of constitutionalism, the courts in China have indeed assumed a defining role in the emergence of a Chinese constitutionalism. But it is a role that is not explained by the traditional metric of judicial power, that of judicial independence, because the courts, as is well recognized even in China, are simply not independent—only rarely are they able to withstand interference from outside their walls. But they nevertheless feature as the constitutional forum of first resort to persons advancing political reform. Why might this be the case?

In beginning to answer this question, we might note that there is a distinctly expressive aspect to the courts' contributions to constitutionalism in present-day China. As we implicated above, constitutional litigants in China appear to be using courts, not simply or even primarily to win disputes, but as fora in which they can frame their disputes in legal-constitutional terms (see especially Dowdle, chapter twelve in this volume, and Pils, chapter fourteen in this volume). We might say that litigants and constitutional activists are using the distinctive discursive dynamics of litigatory interaction, not so much to win cases, but to advance a kind of "jurisprudence" for constitutional-political reform (see also Lee 2007). By jurisprudence, in this context, we mean that complex web of interconnected normative ideas and social expectations that give meaning, identity and legitimacy to a nation's political-legal, and in this case constitutional, environment (cf. the chapter by Pierre-Étienne Will on the constitutional "jurisprudence" of the late Ming dynasty).

Because it operates in the realm of social *meaning*, this metaphor of "jurisprudence" is—consistent with Anglo-American understandings of the constitutional role of courts—somewhat insulated from the raw pluralist proceduralism of electoral democracy (Ackerman 1991). But at the same time, the fact that it operates within the realm of a distinctly *social* meaning also highlights the interdependence that binds this particular jurisprudence to the norms and expectations of a wide range of political actors, hence our characterization of this particular kind of constitutional jurisprudence as distinctively "political" (compare with Shapiro 1981).

C. Constitutionalism and the Beijing Olympics? From "Top-down" to "Popular" Constitutionalism

Of course, the above argument assumes that China's leadership elite's interest in rule of law is authentic. But many skeptics dismiss this interest as disingenuous: they argue that elite appeals to "rule of law" serve merely as rhetorical window dressing whose principal intent is simply to perpetuate the Chinese Communist Party (CCP)'s existing totalitarianism. In particular, for example, some would point to the leadership's behavior leading up to the 2008 Summer Olympics (which also coincided with the 17th Party Congress) as support for this claim. And indeed, the Chinese political system did slip into a much more invasive and controlling gear during the run up to these games.

But in fact, the legal reform agenda was actually very active even during the Olympics period. In the Spring of 2008, the Supreme People's Court reclaimed the right to review any case in which a death sentence (or suspended death sentence) was imposed, and tightened restriction on the use of capital punishment more generally, even in the face of considerable public and political opposition. Amendments to the Law on Lawyers were passed that offered some improved protections for lawyers from political interference in their work (although at the same time, however, imposing other forms of political supervision). Animated public discussion attended the passages of the Labor Dispute Mediation and Arbitration Law and the Labor Contract Law. In June of 2008, right before the Olympic Games, the Supreme People's Court reopened public discussion on China's new Property Law (*Zhonghua Renmin Gongheguo Wuquan Fa* 2007)—a discussion that had recently provoked unprecedentedly public and contested constitutional discussion both among China's political elite and among the ordinary citizenry—by inviting public comment on its draft implementing rules for that law. The work report that the president of the Supreme People's Court, Xiao Yang, delivered to the National People's Congress during March 2008 was particularly open and critical about the present state of China's judiciary and the urgent need for reform. And in little more than a month after the closing of the games, Beijing University law professor He Weifang (2008a, 2008b) engaged in a public and contentious debate with members of the Supreme People's Court (including the chief judge) about the proper role of judges in a rule-of-law system (see *Dongfang Zaobao* 2008; Wang Shengjun 2008).

As to what actual intent underlies the leadership's appeals to rule of law, we of course cannot say. But what we can say, however, is that even if intended as hollow political incantation, the simple fact that China is appealing to a rhetoric of "rule of law" (whether *fazhi* or *yifa zhiguo*) clearly affects social understandings and expectations. It provides a new set of social meanings against which government and political behavior is judged by the society as a whole. In this way, the repeated official discourse on rule of law, whether heartfelt or not, has an effect of empowering the citizenry, particularly where social justice is concerned. It has done so by giving them a means of expressing their political desires and concerns that cannot be completely ignored or shut off by the party-state, to the extent that that state itself wants to maintain at least the appearance of some degree of social credibility (Dowdle 2002, 84–87).

Although perhaps initially conceived of by China's leadership as a top-down exercise in social management, legal reform is now interacting with the public and the grassroots in ways that are outside of such political control. As we explore in detail in this volume, it is a process that has become markedly bottom-up—driven by complex dynamics of social participation. It survived the elite crackdown that followed the Tiananmen Square demonstrations of 1989 and it will no doubt survive the elite political paranoia that infected China in 2008. It might not come in the form of that sudden, "liberal revolution" we all have been looking for (cf. Ackerman 1992). To date, it has expressed itself more in a gentle curve of changes, one that reaches all the way back to the initial "reform and opening-up" that Deng Xiaoping brought to China in the late 1970s. It may not be as fast as we might wish and ultimately its success is certainly not at this point preordained. But as a movement, nevertheless, it seems largely, albeit glacially, irresistible, at least for the present.

D. Constitutionalism as Envisioning the State

And this suggests how we might profitably change the way we think about China's political system insofar as its relationship with constitutionalism is concerned. Constitutionalism is not a gift from the elite to the masses. It is a way of giving social meaning to the metaphor of "the state." Seen in this light, it cannot be completely controlled by the consciousness of a particular political class (such as a party or a judiciary), no matter how much they may wish to or may delude themselves into thinking that they are able to. In a country of over a billion minds, it is this distinctly *social* and *collective* aspect of constitutional meaning that really matters. And it is in constitutionalism rather than in positivist political theory, that the full developmental import of this social meaning is best perceived.

The distinctly constitutional vision of the state is clearly informed by law, but it is also informed other kinds of phenomena as well. Consider, along these lines, the different ways that the French approach the idea of the state as compared to how English or Americans do. The Anglo-American system has conceptualized the state primarily as a historical construct, and their constitutions are dedicated to ensuring that present-day government remains true to this history. To an American constitutionalist, therefore, government is something to be controlled; to be limited, constrained, and to a healthy degree, feared. The goal of such a Constitution "is not to promote efficiency but to preclude the exercise of arbitrary power," Justice Brandeis famously wrote (in dissent) in *Myers v. United States* (1926, 293). This fear of governmental power is perhaps the defining overall feature of the American constitutional system (Redish and Cisar 1991, 451).

France, by contrast, has conceptualized the state more in terms of a distinct political will. And for this reason, its Constitution is dedicated primarily to ensuring that this "will" be properly reified in governmental, and particularly administrative, behavior. In this light, government is seen as enabling the otherwise inchoate popular will that constitutes the state (Nadeau and Barlow 2005, 127–142). We might not realize it at first, but the constitutional implications of this different way of constructing the state can be profound. Their vision of the state as "enabling" in this way causes the French to prefer to work through the more democratic and administrative processes that constitute the state. This, in turn, produces a constitutionalism whose effectiveness is much less reliant on judicial power, and much more reliant on grassroots political mobilization, than that of the United States. Important constitutional disputes that in the United States would be (autocratically, in French eyes) resolved by the courts are much more likely to be ultimately resolved in France by evolutions in public opinion—as was ultimately the case, for example, with the question of whether or not to allow Muslim girls to wear religious symbols—namely headscarves—at school (Beller 2004). Whereas the first responses of a person upset with governmental behavior in the United States is often to challenge that behavior in court, the dominant response of a similarly-situated person in France would be to mobilize like-minded citizenry so as to more effectively participate in administrative and/or legislative policy-formation (Nadeau and Barlow 2005, 218; see also Henne 2003).

It is here, in the question of envisioning the new constitutional state, that we propose to begin this volume's exploration of China's constitutional potential. Note however that we are not suggesting that China has become a *mature* constitutional system. Our interest in this volume is in developmental *potential*, not developmental accomplishment. There are many who would argue that China is now not properly referred to as a "constitutional" system—for example because it lacks significant electoral democracy or significant respect for human rights. We are not here taking objection to such assertions. The question that we are interested in exploring is simply how, even without these attributes, might it be possible for a still-very-much-constitutionally-emergent China's to continue to push towards ever greater constitutional maturity?

Nor are we suggesting that China's constitutional development is essentially guaranteed. As explored in several of our chapters, it could well be that the constitutional developments we describe will be for naught. The overall dynamics of constitutionalization are ultimately too complex, too chaotic, and too spontaneous to be completely captured by human comprehension, either positively or negatively (see Dowdle 2002, 194–197). That being the case, an inquiry into potential is the best measure the human mind can equip itself with in seeking to understand the dynamics and possibilities of the "constitutional option."

II. Volume Overview

Consistent with our analysis above, the preliminary focus of this volume, that of Part 1, is on "Constitutionalism as Envisioning the State." We start with a chapter by Zhu Suli entitled "'Judicial Politics' as State-Building." This chapter recapitulates our thesis above about the conceptual symbiotic relationship between judicial power and constitutional visions of the state within the specific context of "Western" (American) critiques of China's constitution system, and particularly of the judiciary's lack of "independence in that system.

Responding to a review of his own work authored by Frank K. Upham (2005), Zhu explores how Western—or at least American—understandings about the nature of judicial independence are founded on a set of unquestioned presumptions that simply do not effectively describe China's historical vision of itself as a state. Principal among these is the idea that the state, and hence the state's courts, should exist separately and independently from political parties. He shows that not only is this inconsistent with China's own century-long concern with state modernization—a modernization which to its mind has constantly and universally been understood as having to be led, top-down, by a revolutionary party (be it the CCP or the Guomingdang (KMT))—but also that it is inconsistent with the actual experiences of the United States, in which party politics and judicial politics are in fact deeply intertwined. He argues that for the present, and unlike in the experience of Western countries, the CCP remains—for better or worse—the principal if not sole motor for modernizing contemporary China, including the modernization of China's judiciary. Although acknowledging that his claim "is controversial among lawyers and legal scholars [in China]," he posits that, "in balance, the CCP's oversight has also worked to discourage at least somewhat judicial corruption and judicial (and legal) arrogance, two by-products of the judiciary's on-going transformation."

We might note, along these lines, how the term "judicial independence" begs an unspoken prepositional object—that is, independent *from what*? We would not argue that courts should be independent from the law; or that courts should be independent from the constitutional order. Filling in this object requires us to identify the *grundnorm* of the state order, the institutional, and normative principles that are universal to "the state" itself. For largely historical reasons (namely, because the conservative founders of the American Constitution actually deeply distrusted the kind of pluralist factionalism that political parties represent), modern Western—or at least American—constitutionalism chooses not to include political parties as a constitutive normative element of the constitutional state (Wood 1993). But there is no definitional reason why this should be the case: in fact, like it or not, in many modern constitutional systems, like that of England, political parties are recognized as critical normative components of the constitutional system, as much are the courts themselves. Zhu's chapter shows how admitting that political parties do constitute key elements of the constitutional grundnorm can change significantly the normative nature of judicial independence—in that it can have a significant effect on the normative constitutional question of "independent *from what?*" In thinking about the *normative* nature of judicial independence and judicial power in China, we have to take its different vision of the constitutional state, and the party's place within that state, into account—and not *reflexively* dismiss this vision based simply on our own different visions of ourselves.

In fact, there is evidence to suggest that Chinese constitutional thinking is perhaps even more sensitive to the symbiotic relationship between constitutionalism and one's conceptual vision of the state than that which is commonly articulated in the West. It is a relationship that over a century ago was captured by the term "*fatong*," a republican derivative of the Confucian notion of "*daotong*" (Wang, 1998, 78). In chapter three, entitled "Of Constitutions and Constitutionalism: Trying to Build a New Political Order in China, 1908–1949," Xiaohong Xiao-Planes uses the lens of *fatong* to trace the early evolution of Chinese constitutionalism in Republican-period China. This period is often thought of as being constitutionally incoherent, consisting as it does of a continual succession of competing constitutional projects, many stillborn and none ultimately enjoying the authority and institutional stability commonly associated with "constitutionalism." But Xiao-Planes shows how in fact, when viewed from the lens of *fatong*, this period does indeed sport a coherent constitutional history. But it is a history, not so much of institutions and doctrines, but of searching for what the post-imperial Chinese state was all about in the absence of a defining monarch and in the presence of almost perpetual politically-existential crisis. She shows how in fact, the Republican search for a new and distinctly constitutional *fatong* displays a coherent progression of ideas about the nature of China's new, post-imperial state that culminated in the famous Tutelage Constitution of 1931. And as clearly evidenced in Zhu Suli's earlier chapter, the particular *fatong* that was ultimately articulated through that 1931 Constitution—that is, China as a dysfunctional political culture requiring "tutelage" from an enlightened revolutionary party-elite—is one that continues to significantly inform constitutional understandings of present-day China (indeed, Zhu himself traces the modern-day vision he describes back to that period).

But as Glenn Tiffert's next chapter on "Epistrophy: Chinese Constitutionalism and the 1950s" shows, the tutelage *fatong*'s "long march" into the 21st century has not been lock-step. Referencing a device (epistrophe) that is used to impart rhetorical coherence to a collection of otherwise diverse phrases (as adapted through Thelonious Monk's famous composition, *Epistrophy*, from which the chapter draws its title), Tiffert shows how as of the 1950s, underneath the inherited *fatong* of tutelage seethed a dynamic repertoire of evolving constitutional visions that worked off common themes inherited from the Republican era. And what ultimately gave meaningful coherence to this diverse repertoire of visions was not some coherent set of Rawlsian fundamental principles but a shared, ongoing, and evolving discourse, of which, as he shows, the 1954 Constitution is perhaps the prime example. We might say that, as particularly evident in the working out of the 1954 Constitution, during the 1950s the republican plainchant of "tutelage" become an increasingly polyphonic enterprise.

The importance of this underlying diversity for China's future constitutional development becomes clear in chapter five, written by Randall Peerenboom and entitled "Middle Income Blues: The East Asian Model and Implications for Constitutional Development in China." The tutelage *fatong* is not unique to Chinese constitutionalism. In fact, it is consistent with what Peerenboom calls the "East Asian" model of economic-political—and by extension constitutional—development. That model is characterized, in significant part, by a focus on promoting economic development at the expense of civil and political rights, at least during the earlier stages of the developmental process. The rationale for this particular sequencing is that at earlier stages of development, constitutional protections of civil and political rights could work to protect various forms of political behavior that can disrupt the social and political stability and responsiveness required for development. The suppression of popular political autonomy in order to promote an elite-led economic development parallels in function the tutelage phase of China's tutelage *fatong*.

Peerenboom does not endorse this developmental model. Rather, he shows how, arguendo, even if it were a workable developmental strategy, it is only enough to get the country partway along the developmental trajectory. Extrapolating from this, this could suggest that at some midway point, further development requires the adoption of a very different vision and/or role for the state, a vision in which the state is no longer a tutor directing the people on overcoming their imperfections, but a reflection of the people even in their inevitable imperfection.

This point he called "the middle income blues"—and it is the point, he argues, at which China now finds itself. (In this, he also seems to be echoing Zhu Suli, who in his chapter makes a comparable observation with regards to the CCP's recent efforts to reshape itself from a party of the ruling class into a party "of the whole people.") And if this is the case, then the polyphony that Tiffert sees lying inside the modern vision of the tutelage *fatong* becomes extremely relevant, because following Peerenboom's (and Zhu's) observations about the innate limits in the tutelage vision, the question then becomes one of "what is the next Chinese *fatong*?" Can the current system, founded as it was on a vision of the state that China may well be outgrowing, be adapted to meet the new needs of middle-income development? Can the system reproduce itself in light of these new needs? The answer depends in significant part on how much evolutionary potential there is in China's tutelage *fatong* as it is embodied in present-day constitutional discourse. And following Tiffert, the greater the diversity among the polyphonous strands of ideas that construct that *fatong*, the more likely that some of them can serve as a pivot upon which the existing constitutional system can reorient itself to its new, "post-tutelage" role.

* * *

This brings us to Part 2 of our volume, on "The Development of a Political Jurisprudence." Again, by "political jurisprudence" we do not mean here to refer to some form of juridical case law. We use "jurisprudence" as a metaphor for describing the accretional discursive synthesis of a coherent framework for making juridified sense of China's still emerging post-Mao, constitutional *fatong*. As noted above, this is a distinctly *political* jurisprudence in that the discourse being synthesized for the most part does not originate in judicial decision making. As the chapters of this Part reveal, this jurisprudence gives us a very interesting picture of China trying to make a new constitutional sense of itself.

The first chapter in Part 2 is by Tong Zhiwei and is entitled "China's Constitutional Research and Teaching: A State of the Art." It documents the reawakening of constitutional law as a course of study in Chinese law schools following the end of the Cultural Revolution. He sees this evolution as divided into three general phases. The first phase, running through the early 1980s, saw the task of constitutional law as one of liberating itself from the rigidifying grasp of the Cultural Revolution's still pervasive legal and constitutional nihilism. A second phase, which ran through 2000, was characterized by a distinctly positivist interest in codifying the structural tenants of the post-Mao, party-state. The third phase, the one China is now in, sees a shift in scholarly emphasis away from positivist structure and more onto issues of political and social citizenry, particularly those involving constitutional rights (albeit rights that are not necessarily judicially enforceable).

All in all, Tong shows us an evolving jurisprudence whose trajectory parallels the concerns suggested by Peerenboom in chapter five—for it is precisely in the development of political and social citizenry, Tong's third stage, that Peerenboom seems to suggest China's constitutional future must lie. But how should we think about the emergence of this third stage? Its resemblance to Western constitutional thought is striking. Does it represent some universal law of constitutional jurisprudence that holds that no matter what the cultural origin, constitutional systems are innately and intrinsically driven to evolve into something resembling Western-style liberalism? If so, does this mean China's older, tutelage *fatong* is really just a historical curiosity that is irrelevant to China's constitutional future?

These are questions that dominate discussions of Chinese constitutionalism today, both in and outside of China. In chapter seven, entitled "Western Constitutional Ideas and Constitutional Discourse in China, 1978–2005," Yu Xingzhong brings us into this debate, by showing the degree to which China's evolving understanding of constitutionalism has been founded on Western intellectual sources, particularly those associated with Western liberalism—for example, Ronald Dworkin, Friedrich Hayek, Benjamin Constant, and Alexis de Tocqueville. Yu argues that the significant influence of these Western thinkers is not simply an accident of history—it is in fact functionalist. At its heart, he claims, constitutionalism is a quintessentially liberal endeavor. China does not have a liberal tradition, and therefore, its development of constitutionalism has no choice but to propel itself using outside sources.

But at the same time, we also find—as explored by Ji Weidong in chapter eight on "'To Take the Law as the Public': The Diversification of Society and Legal Discourse in Contemporary China"—that other discourses also continue, even into this "third phase" as identified by Tong. These include alternative, non-liberal Western constitutional discourses, such as those of Carl Schmitt and Hans Kelsen, and more autochthonous discourses that derive from indigenous Chinese experiences (both present-day and historical). Perhaps, even more significantly, as Ji shows, these Western and Chinese, liberal and non-liberal constitutional discourses continue to interact with one another, thus perpetuating that distinctly polyphonous discourse Glenn Tiffert identified in his exploration of the drafting of the 1954 Constitution.

In this sense, China's constitutionalism moves both closer to and farther away from Western constitutionalism. It moves farther away in that the continued incorporation of indigenous Chinese experiences will inevitably push China onto its own distinctive constitutional path—as intimated by Yu Xingzhong at the end of his chapter. But as William Ewald (1994) has argued, it is precisely the national distinctiveness of its paths that characterizes so-called Western constitutionalism. As discussed above, constitutionalism is ultimately about envisioning the state. And rightly or wrongly, every polity envisions its particular "state" as a distinct phenomenon, one whose identity and character are uniquely its own. In trying to identify and define—or redefine—its own self-styled distinctiveness as a nation and as a political culture, China's constitutional emergence is in fact replicating, perhaps paradoxically, the same ultimate developmental trajectory that drove and defined the emergence of constitutionalism in Western Europe and the United States.

* * *

But the political jurisprudence of China's new, post-Mao constitutionalism is not and cannot be the exclusive product of elite intellectuals. In order to give full meaning to the constitutional state, such a jurisprudence must be a distinctly *social* construct. Its meaning cannot be controlled by a single political class or faction. At the end of the day, it must become a complex product of society as a whole. This requires us to investigate how and to what extent, in China, the rest of society might be internalizing, participating in, and ultimately shaping this emergent jurisprudence—this discursive polyphony. For it is here that lies the true force of the constitutional project: its capacity to weather the inevitable boltings and hesitations that often spring from a political elite rendered insecure by the transitions it perpetually finds itself in.

In seeking to understand this, we first need to explore how it is that this new political jurisprudence—this new *fatong*—is being transmitted to and embedding itself into everyday society. Here, as we see, the courts become relevant, because the courtroom is one of the principal fora that give the ordinary citizenry the opportunity to speak the language of constitutionalism. This suggests a different way of thinking about judicial power—the power of the judiciary to promote constitutionalism. Courts can promote constitutions, not merely through the triadic logic of neutral and principled dispute resolution, but also by embedding constitutional discourse into more everyday political culture. This is the focus of Part 3 of this volume, subtitled "Transmitting Constitutionalism: Judicial Power and the Justice System."

But why would an elite-led, modernist political *fatong* of the kind described by Zhu permit society to have access to such fora in the first place? In "Administrative Law as a Mechanism for Political Control in Contemporary China," He Xin advances an answer. Looking particularly at administrative law, Professor He argues that the state sees administrative law primarily as a means for controlling lower-level officials, albeit not the only one available to it. He shows that as Chinese society becomes increasingly complex in the wake of its ongoing transition to market capitalism, the efficacy of administrative litigation as a control mechanism grows, both absolutely and more importantly relative to available alternatives. In this way, the development of a more juridified and judicialized administrative state is in fact completely consistent with the elite-led, modernizing *fatong* articulated by Zhu at the beginning of Part 1.

But the dynamic that He Xin identifies does not get us past the transitional concerns identified by Peerenboom. As he shows, China's developmental need is not for a stronger and more effective realization of its inherited, elite-led, constitutionalism. It is for a new constitutionalism in which organic social coordination replaces political control as the defining element of the state. In this sense, the particular model of emerging judicial power identified by He Xin does not appear to contribute to this transition. Or does it?

It should not be forgotten that strategic changes in political design can often trigger a snowballing effect of unintended consequences. In this case, judicializing lower-level administrative government not only empowers the center—its intended consequence; but it also works to empower the citizenry—even perhaps as an unintended consequence.

The alternative and likely unintended constitutional consequences inherent in the judicializing processes identified by Professor He are explored in the next three chapters of this volume. The first, by Fu Hualing and entitled "Access to Justice and Constitutionalism in China," examines how government-sponsored legal-aid programs are "contribut[ing] crucially to the development of the rule of law, the empowerment of the poor, and the creation of a more robust civil society." After detailing the structure of a number of such programs, he shows how independent of any specific intention on the part of program designers, the simple fact that these centers are creating a heightened prospect of access to justice is catalyzing changed attitudes toward the role of the state and its relationship with its citizenry, both among the ordinary population and among local officials. Among ordinary citizens, it catalyzes the development of a rights consciousness that gives the language of constitutionalism direct meaning to their lives. Among local officials, he found that repeated interactions with legal-aid personnel encouraged greater comfort with norms of rule of law, and helped routinize official conformity to these norms, particularly within the courts. As described by Peerenboom in his chapter, both rights-consciousness and norms of rule of law are likely to be key components of China's necessary constitutional transition.

Administrative judicialization is also having a similar affect on the grassroots judiciary, as examined by Stéphanie Balme in her chapter eleven on "Ordinary Justice and Popular Constitutionalism in China." Investigating the relationship between judicial power and modernization at the lowest level of the rural judiciary—the Basic-Level People's Courts and the Basic-Level People's Tribunals, her chapter explores incidence of judicial activism and constitutional rights' consciousness in the context of rural justice. Like Fu Hualing, she finds that the easier it is for citizens to access courts, the stronger and more politically assertive and influential they become. But she also finds that the judges themselves are sometimes playing a critical role in this as well.

Facilitated by the basic-level rural judiciary's considerable decentralization and corresponding local autonomy, and further spurred in part by Hu Jintao's articulated concern for the special problems of rural society in China, and despite considerable hardships caused by a lack of social status and material comforts, the younger judges in these courts appear to be developing a particular professional identity in which they see themselves as agents of precisely that new modernization advanced by Peerenboom, a modernization associated with the rule of law and the protection of rights—including constitutional rights.

Finally, in "Beyond 'Judicial Power': Courts and Constitutionalism in Modern China," Michael Dowdle examines another way in which courts transmit constitutional "jurisprudence" into everyday life, by (re)presenting the state in a form that is specially amenable to popular critical reflection. Working off of the Aristotelian idea of *poiesis* (as amplified by Hannah Arendt), which posited the theatre as a particularly potent forum for catalyzing spontaneous public reflection on and reimagining of the nature of the state, Dowdle suggests that the distinctly theatrical nature of the courtroom allows it to sometimes trigger a similar effect. Perhaps the best demonstration of this in modern China is the trial of Jiang Qing (aka Madame Mao), whose distinctly theatrical elements, he argues, appeared to have triggered a widespread public reevaluation of the proper constitutional relationship between the party and the state. It was this reevaluation, he argues, that ultimately paved the way for the reemergence in post-Mao China of parliamentarianism, and through it the re-emergence of the constitutionalist *fatong*. He also argues that a similar dynamic can be seen in the litigation that is today being brought against the local state by urban workers and rural farmers. Although not particularly successful in terms of winning cases, there is considerable evidence that this litigation is promoting the development of distinctly constitutional understandings and discourses even within everyday society.

* * *

But what is everyday society doing with these new constitutional understandings and what might it tell us about China's constitutional future? In many ways, everyday society is the most important of the social locales of constitutionalism, simply because the size of that society utterly dwarfs those of the political and intellectual elite. Because of its huge size, even a barely perceptible constitutional motion within it would carry an immense momentum—a momentum that would seem well able to propel constitutional transition, albeit perhaps at a slower pace than we would like, even against the hesitations in insecure political elite. This is the focus of Part 4 of this volume, entitled "Toward a Popular Constitutionalism."

In China, the most visible bottom-up articulation of the new political jurisprudence of constitutionalism is found in the *weiquan* movement. As explored by Keith Hand in chapter thirteen, entitled "Citizens Engage the Constitution: The Sun Zhigang Incident and Constitutional Review Proposals in the People's Republic of China," the *weiquan* movement is comprised of a diverse collection of everyday lawyers, legal academics, and elite and grassroots social activists, who have begun to use the rights-based language of constitutionalism in ways both ordinary and dramatic, to insert a more 'popular' voice into China's political future. Insofar as its actual affect on policy is concerned, the reach of this movement has been so-far constrained. Yet, as Hand's chapter shows, it has by no means been negligible. As a component of constitutional discourse, this *weiquan* discourse has proven remarkably robust—a robustness that comes precisely from the social diversity that comprises the movement. And it is a discourse that the elite, although able to suppress with regards to certain issues, cannot completely silence, and cannot completely ignore.

Moreover, the political jurisprudence of ordinary society does not represent itself solely in that society's interactions with the state. As Eva Pils shows in chapter fourteen on "Rights Activism in China: The Case of Lawyer Gao Zhisheng," the discursive polyphony of post-Mao constitutionalism also sounds within and internal to that society, in the constant interactions between ordinary citizens of inevitably diverse constitutional minds. For example it sounds in an ongoing discourse she explores between pragmatic moderates seeking to reform the existing constitutional system from within and more radical activitsts, like the lawyer Gao Zhisheng who is the principal subject of her chapter, who either refuse to make the moral compromises they associate with working within the existing system and/or otherwise believe that the existing system is simply incapable of transformation.

It is in this internal discourse that the real momentum of what we are calling China's "popular constitutionalism" can be perceived. For this is a discourse that clearly takes place outside the reach of the state elite. The state may be able to silence a particular individual—as it has for the time being doing to Gao, who as of summer of 2009 is being held incommunicado by the Chinese state—but the radical alternative will always be there, even if it is only implicit. And its presence, its always implicit threat, ultimately compels the state to acknowledge and engage with at least some of the bottom-up articulations of the constitutionalism that are now constantly issuing from ordinary society.

⋆ ⋆ ⋆

None of this suggests that China's constitutional transition will ultimately be successful. The skepticism of persons like Gao Zhisheng regarding the present system's capacities to adjust to a new *fatong* merits continued and serious consideration. The volume, therefore, closes with a chapter by the historian Pierre-Étienne Will on "Virtual Constitutionalism in the Late Ming Dynasty." Will's chapter provides a useful, cautionary tale for those exploring what constitutionalism looks like in an emergent constitutional regime such as that of present-day China. It takes us back to the late Ming, which like China today, found itself in a transitional period "that…featured certain 'democratic' characteristics that might have developed, independently from Western influence, into something significant if they had not been cut short by the Manchu conquest of China in 1644." But as Will shows, they were cut short, not only by the Manchu conquest, but also by the incapacity of the imperial Ming dynastic state—the imperial *fatong*, as it were—to respond to the changes it found itself confronting. Will's chapter reminds us that the story of China's emergent and transitional constitutionalism will be one that ultimately can only be told by historians.

At the same time, however, by the time the historians arrive, in many ways it will be too late. The possibilities of human agency mean that there is always utility in trying to understand the life we're in while we're still in it. And in this regard, an investigation into the emergence and transition of constitutionalism in today's China, although it can offer little about the ultimate success of that project, can still give us a useful appreciation for its complexities, and for its potentials—both insofar as China is concerned, and insofar as the human experience of constitutionalism per se is concerned. That is ultimately the purpose of this volume.

PART 1

Constitutionalism as Envisioning the State

CHAPTER TWO

"Judicial Politics" as State-Building

ZHU SULI

1. Introduction

My book, *Sending Law to the Countryside (Song Fa Xia Xiang)* (Zhu 2000), was originally directed to a Chinese audience who I believed was too inclined to superficially import Western legal concepts or theories. But it has also captured the attention of the West as well, because it raises some hot issues regarding China's basic-level judicial system. It thereby has nourished a constructive cross-cultural dialogue.

This dialogue started with a long, critical review in the *Yale Law Journal* by Frank K. Upham (2005), a prominent Professor at the New York University School of Law. In his review, Upham criticized what he called my "uncritical acceptance of a linear version of modernization theory" (Upham 2005, 1700). I will not respond to this aspect of his critique here. Rather, I will focus on another critique of his, what he refers to as the book's "greatest flaw": namely, "the absence of politics and political power" in my book's account (Upham 1703). As he says, "aside from the small-p politics of bureaucratic infighting, power is virtually absent" from my analysis. He goes on to state:

> [A]lthough the book is a polemical attack on orthodox thinking on rule of law and the direction of Chinese legal reform…, there is little attention to the influence of the Party on the courts or, conversely, to the role of the courts in maintaining the communist regime.… It is possible that Zhu's silence is a reflection of the general lack of attention to power's role in legal scholarship everywhere, but it seems more likely that he is deliberately avoiding the subject. Whatever his reasons, the absence of politics

from the analysis is a serious shortcoming that detracts from both the academic value and the policy relevance of the work. (Upham 2005, 1703)

Such purported timidity in avoiding the dimensions of political power and politics imputes my own academic honesty, as the Chinese Communist Party (hereinafter "CCP") obviously plays a key role not only in my own research, but also in even the most day-to-day activities of the Chinese judiciary. Certainly, my analyses may need to be strengthened and further research is required. Nevertheless, written in Chinese for Chinese legal professionals and Chinese scholars, my book was never intended to address the political and ideological concerns of foreign readers.

From this point of view, Professor Upham's (and others') frustration and dissatisfaction with my book is understandable. On the other hand, however, their objections are also the products of certain kinds of analytic errors (mostly methodological) that are typical of the efforts of Western "China watchers" to understand China's constitutional system. Such errors reveal a deep ideological bias that is central not only to the West's proclaimed "moral authority" (a shaky proclamation that is evaporating in the aftermath of 9/11) but also to the Western (or at least American) notion of legal autonomy and "rule of law." The negative impact over the recent decades of these kinds of errors on Western efforts to understand China, its constitutional and legal systems, and their development, is all the more troublesome due to the reach and consequent of their influence. And this is what motivates my response.

II. Making a Distinction

At the level of everyday life, I would argue, it is very hard to identify a distinctly "party" interference in the way that Professor Upham would have me do in my study of local courts in rural China. Such efforts would only enhance ideological misinterpretations of both the CCP's and the courts' contributions to China's constitutional structure. They would not help further our understanding of the actual operation or problems of the basic courts in China.

Assertions of my alleged fear to analyze the CCP's interference in the operation of basic level courts are founded on four suppositions. The first is that there exists some pure state of reality that deserves to be called "judicial autonomy." The second is that it is possible to construct a standard or objective model of this judicial autonomy, either as a political structure or as a set of social conventions. The third is that this model can be used to show that the CCP exercises a politically-related influence. And last, that it is possible to isolate and examine the actual social effect of such influence. Rationally considered, however, these suppositions are simply unrealistic.

Both Chinese and foreign scholars—inside and outside of the legal studies field—have correctly pointed out the omnipresence of the CCP and its relatedly dominant influence throughout Chinese political society. To my understanding, although the CCP has never formally accepted the earlier republican *Guomindang* Party's (KMT's) notion of a "party-state," it has nevertheless inherited from its former political enemy the legacy of having to construct and rule a nation-state through the leadership of a single political party—a party that, as proposed early in the 20th century by Sun Yat-sen, had to be above that nation-state (Sun 1986).

In fact, the CCPs's post-1949 leadership over the nation-state has been far more extensive and effective than that of the earlier KMT. During the KMT's rule, different parts of the country were controlled by various provincial strongmen (see also Chapter Three in this volume), making any proclamation of "national unity" between 1927 and 1949 purely symbolic (Deng 1994, 299). Indeed, during this period the CCP itself represented a strong and alternative political force that was able to control substantial areas of the country with the help of its own loyal and strong army. Although the KMT included many independent and socially influential technocrats and bureaucrats, its internal incompetence caused it to remain highly dependent on the historical pattern of power-sharing cooperation with an urban gentry class. The KMT government had very little influence in rural China (Fei 1988). For this reason, the KMT was unable to consolidate its control over China, and as such was unable to implement its modernizing program (cf. Wang 1990; Zhong and Tang 1999).

In contrast, the CCP has been much more effective at constructing the People's Republic of China (PRC) into a strong and centralized, unitary state. Although China officially sports a number of other political parties, these parties all operate under the authority of the CCP. In fact, some of these other parties' leaders are themselves also CCP members—including, as I recall, former or current leaders of the China Democratic League [*Zhongguo Minzhu Tongmeng*], the China Democratic National-Construction Association [*Zhongguo Minzhu Jianguo Hui*], the China Party for Public Interest [*Zhongguo Zhi Gong Dang*], and the Taiwan Democratic Self-Government League [Taiwan *Minzhu Zizhi Tongmeng*]. It is true that since 1978, these parties have been given some space for autonomous policy formation, and the CCP has developed various formal and informal institutions for gathering and selectively adopting their policy advice. However, the overall system remains one that operates under the ultimate control of the CCP.

The majority of China's social elites, including those serving either in universities or in commercial circles, are CCP members. CCP membership even includes people who are sometimes regarded by Western observers as "political dissidents." Other social elites in China accept the political leadership of the CCP even when they themselves are not CCP members. In this sense, although the CCP has for long self-proclaimed itself to be a dictatorship specifically of China's proletarian, working classes, and although its final goal continues to be the realization of a working-class communism (CCP 2007), even long before Jiang Zemin's declaration of "the three represents (*sange daibiao*)" (which reoriented the party into a party of all the people), it ultimately had evolved into a national party that seeks to advance the fundamental interests of the Chinese people as a whole, not simply those of a particular class (see also CCP 1945; CCP 1956). And its basic goals, in this regard, are widely accepted by the Chinese people.

Because of its strict organizational structure and the influence of its political programs, the CCP's political influence is omnipresent in today's China. For this reason, distinguishing between CCP policy and governmental policy—although there are sometimes differences in terms of ideas, ideals, and conflicts of interests—is often quite difficult. For example, all of the PRC's provincial governors are CCP members who are politically subordinate to their provincial CCP Party Secretary. Party and governmental officials often rotate between party and governmental positions. Many provincial governors move on to become provincial party secretaries. Many provincial party secretaries move on to become governors of larger provinces, or move on to assume other governmental positions. This system of party-state cross-fertilization includes within its ambit every significant party and state position at the national and local levels. A similar intermingling can be found in almost all of China's social, industrial, and educational organizations.

Insofar as China's judiciary is concerned, since 1954 every president of the Supreme People's Court (SPC) has also directed the CCP's oversight of judicial operations. The presidents of lower courts have invariably occupied similar positions within their respective regional CCP organizations. Although commonly, one of the SPC's several vice president positions will be held by someone who is not a CCP member, these persons will nevertheless be carefully selected by the relevant branch of the CCP, and will be people in whom that branch has a lot of trust. Also, it is not uncommon for that person to participate in CCP meetings relevant to judicial operations.

Within such a system, it can be very difficult to distinguish whether some particular interference in judicial operations actually issues from the institution of the CCP. Not every interference with the judiciary that is formally designated as issuing from a party organization or a party official is actually in line with CCP policies. On the contrary, some of this interference pushes for outcomes that directly contravene CCP policies. Some CCP officials can and will abuse their positions within the CCP to interfere with the performance of a court so as to advance their own selfish, and often even illegal, interests. Courts and procuratorates are supposed to resist this kind of interference, according both to the law and to rules of party discipline, although it is often very hard for them to do so. It is a mistake to call such interference that operates in direct contravention of the CCP's own policies, even when it comes from persons with party affiliation, "party interference."

From within the judiciary, it becomes even more difficult to distinguish CCP "influence" from other factors affecting court decisions. A decision formally issuing from the Supreme People's Court, even from its adjudication committee—perhaps the most professionalized judicial organ within China—may simply reiterate a position previously arrived at by the Central Committee of the CCP. On the other hand, a higher court's reversal of some lower court judgment may have in fact been made autonomously, but will nevertheless be presented as the product of CCP direction in order to enhance its weight in the affected lower court. Relatedly, CCP "interference" often takes the form of generalized instructions. Sometimes, these instructions simply "interpret" particular provisions in the black-letter law. Such abstract interpretations are essentially legislative in character. And although they may implicate possible CCP interference in or usurpation of the legislative powers of the people's governments or people's congresses, they would not seem to indicate interference in the *courts* per se (which in China lack formal powers of abstract interpretation anyway). Also, such generalized instructions themselves can be subject to further "interpretation" by the court's presiding judge in the process of applying them to a particular case. In such cases, the "influence" attributed to the CCP may actually represent the judgment of an autonomous judge, disguised as an interpretation of CCP instruction.

Clearly, the party's officials and its organizations do interfere and influence the functioning of the judiciary, because of the social and political domination of the CCP. And many such interferences have been unjust and unfair, to the point of contributing to various political disasters in the history of the PRC. Yet even during the party's most radical movements, such as that of the Cultural Revolution (1966–1976), there were CCP officials and organizations—including organizations associated with the judiciary—who, within the scope of their ability and influence, reduced and even prevented some of the unfairness and injustice that stemmed from that radicalism.

Although today it is quite popular to attribute all of the problems of the PRC to the CCP, it is difficult to imagine how the current state of Chinese society and its judiciary would have been necessarily better off without the modern revolution led by the CCP. Of course, only history will have the final word on this, but the striking overall success of China's recent development forces one to acknowledge that the revolution led by the CCP has had some positive influence on China. And with that, one also has to accept that the CCP's "interference" could also, at least occasionally, have had similarly positive influences upon China's judiciary.

For example, sometimes the CCP's "interference" seeks to represent and promote a local population's particular understandings of what justice and fairness demand in the handling of a particular case. Such interference certainly does not respect the model of "separation of powers," and as such, it is often criticized by many legal scholars whose appreciation for Western practices leads them to think that the CCP should "keep quiet" with regards to cases waiting for trial. Yet, this kind of "interference" might actually be beneficial for a majority of Chinese people, who do not care about foreign experience but simply seek justice and social solidarity. From a Western constitutional perspective, such interference seems to be improper. But from a political perspective, it is hard to see why a purely "legal" control over a case is always and necessarily more morally just or reasonable than a more "political" control. Why should a technocratic and juridicalized determination always be superior to a political one? In a sense, this kind of "interference" can conceivably constitute a legitimate and beneficial exercise of the CCP's core political function of social integration and representation.

Along these lines, the CCP itself can be seen as an alternative source of Chinese constitutionalism. The CCP has long been aware that national modernization cannot be accomplished by the party's political elites alone. The task of social integration requires that the party enjoy some significant degree of voluntary support from other social forces in China. This requires, in turn, that it be able to comprehend and appreciate the different interests that underlie these different societal forces. The CCP has responded to this by adopting a certain degree of democracy *within* the party. In this sense, the party itself becomes a quasi-constitutional structure—a structure whose own internal democracy can supplement or even compete with (and through such competition improve) the more formal constitutional apparatus of the state.

III. The Problem of Reference

In fact, there exists no universal framework of reference for evaluating when "judicial independence" exists, either in China or elsewhere, or for evaluating whether and when such independence is beneficial or costly insofar as the larger constitutional order is concerned. Even where the CCP's interference is possible to identify, it is difficult to determine its actual consequences. There are a good many flaws in the PRC's judiciary. Although some of these can be attributed to the governance of the CCP, I would argue that overall, the PRC's judicial problems are much more the products of the recent, unprecedented social transformation of Chinese society. One of the reasons why I wrote *Sending Law to the Countryside* was to move us beyond our uncritical reference to simplistic Western notions of "judicial independence," so that we could more meaningfully identify and locate these problems, and thereby search for solutions more effectively.

For one thing, we might first note that all modern constitutional countries have mass-based political parties like the CCP. And although some principle of "judicial independence" is commonly acknowledged in these countries, in all these countries these political parties invariably exert significant influence over and sometimes interferences in the activities of their judiciaries.

For example, according to America's famous Supreme Court Justice Oliver Wendell Holmes, Jr., the United States Supreme Court's defining articulation of it power of "judicial review" in *Marbury v. Madison* (1803) was itself the product in significant part of the party loyalties of its Chief Justice, John Marshall. According to Holmes, Marshall saw this new power as a way to help his Federalist Party better resist the Republic-Democratic Party of then President Thomas Jefferson (Holmes 1992). Paradoxically, this new power would subsequently come to be regarded as a core component of "judicial independence" in American party politics. One may object that this is only indicative of the earlier stages of judicial evolution in the United States. But even now, such politics are still deeply embedded in American judicial functioning. For example, the American Constitution requires that federal judges be nominated by the President and confirmed by the Senate. Both of these institutions are deeply involved in party policy advancement and this clearly influences decisions regarding judicial appointments.

The American Democratic Party's successful efforts to thwart President Ronald Reagan's nomination of Judge Robert Bork in 1987 was a dramatic example of this. Bork (1990) later referred to this as an unconscionable "political seduction" of the judiciary. But isn't this simply an overstatement borne out of Judge Bork's anger? Let us imagine, instead, that the nomination had been confirmed by a Republican-dominated Senate. Would not this confirmation against the opposition of a large number of Democratic Party lawmakers, have itself been an expression of a distinctly party-driven politics? And although the politics surrounding Judge Bork's nomination were exceptionally dramatic, they were not exceptional per se.

One recent study suggests that a growing number of even noncontroversial nominations to the federal judiciary are being subject to similar kind of party-based political dynamics. It found that:

> [T]he more important the court, the greater the difficulty of having the [judicial nominee] confirmed. Although the confirmation rates have fallen and the length of the confirmation process has lengthened dramatically, the ex-post measures of judicial quality of circuit court nominees... [and] judicial independence have been decreasing over time.... The most troubling results strongly indicate that circuit court

> judges who turn out to be the most successful judges, . . . faced the most difficult confirmation battles. (Lott 2005, 443–444)

As to the cause of this, the author of the study, John Lott, speculates: "Possibly, senators of the party opposite the president only really care about preventing the best judges from being on the circuit court because they will have the most impact" (Lott 2005, 444). This implies that even in the United States, political parties themselves see judges, at least in part, as party actors.

Politics and political party interferences are evident not only with regard to the nomination and confirmation of judges, but also in the handling of particular cases. One example of this that I have already mentioned is the role that party loyalty played in the famous American Supreme Court case of *Marbury v. Madison* (1803). But many American judges, justices, and the courts they oversee evince patterns of decision making that closely track, sometimes uncomfortably so, the political platforms of the Democratic or Republican parties. Studies have found this kind of judge-party correspondence in the Warren Court (Powe 2000), the Berger Court (Maltz 2000), and the Rehnquist Court (Yarbrough 2001; Maltz 2003). The dramatic case of *Bush v. Gore* (2000) caused Americans to again remember the uncomfortably close correspondence that can run between party and court in the United States (Posner 2001; Sunstein and Epstein 2001). At the state level, in some states, the party's capacity to influence judicial decision making is further enhanced by a constant potential threat of a distinctively political—and essentially party-driven—process of judicial recall (Abraham 1998, 37–42).

Without a doubt, in China, party-based influence over the activities of the basic courts is on a different order of magnitude from that which confronts American courts. In America, the political inclinations of the judiciary may generally result from the judges' and justices' autonomous agreement with a particular party's vision of law and society. At the same time, the lifetime tenure and high salary that are generally enjoyed by American judges permit effective opposition to both government and party when the judge or justice is so inclined (Tribe 1985). In China, by contrast, judges enjoy no such protections, and party influence also comes from the party's own disciplinary oversight of judges. Chinese judges thus tend to see themselves more as civil servants than as independent professionals. They are more likely to defer to, rather than to confront, the existing political and administrative hierarchies in which they themselves are embedded. They leave the articulation of "dissenting" opinions and interpretations to legal scholars.

But what are we to make of the party's "influence" over the Chinese courts? The fact that this influence differs, either quantitatively or qualitatively, from that affecting Western judiciaries is not itself a meaningful basis for critique. In order to develop useful understanding of the problems of basic-level courts in China, and of their prospects for reform, we have to examine in detail not only the existence, degree, and process of CCP influences on judicial behavior, but also their actual social effects.

Regarding China's current, overall sociopolitical context, CCP-judiciary relations are representative of the CCP's relations with other constitutional institutions. The CPP perceives itself as, and to a great extent is, the principal driver of a necessary social transformation in China—and that includes a necessary social transformation of its judiciary. It is from this observation, and not from some abstracted notion of "judicial independence," that a study of party-judiciary relations in contemporary China should proceed.

The relationship between China's political parties and the Chinese judiciary evolved within the ongoing historical process of China's modernization. Since 1840, the most important task for China has been to transform itself: economically, from an agricultural economy into an industrial and commercial economy; politically, from a premodern, relational community into a modern nation-state; and culturally, from one dominated by extrapolations from Confucian humanities into one dominated by hard and soft scientific investigation (Suli 2004).

It is unrealistic to expect a localized, premodern agricultural society like that of China to evolve naturally and "spontaneously" in such a direction. China's recent history confirms this. On both the mainland and on Taiwan, China's effective modernization only commences with the development of an effective party leadership over the state.

As political parties, both the CCP and the KMT thus evolved under conditions and in a way that differed markedly from the political parties found in the contemporary Western world. Political parties in the West were established and operated within nation-states that had already modernized and were already effectively constituted. Both the CCP and the KMT, by contrast, have had to be much more proactive and aggressive in mobilizing China's fragmented and premodern political and social forces into a modernist national unification—and through this attain the national independence, and related capacities for social and economic development, that political parties in the West have been able to largely take for granted (see, for example, Sun 1986).

For this reason, both the CCP and the KMT were conceived of as "revolutionary" parties who opposed, not simply other political factions, but the constitutional status quo as a whole. Even after their respective overthrows were successfully completed, they had to retain their revolutionary character in order to direct the ongoing and comprehensive social revolution—that is, the economic, political, and social transformations outlined above—necessary to bring China into modernization.

This dictated that both the KMT and the CCP be elitist parties—parties capable of mobilizing and leading the masses effectively from above. Social transformation is necessarily a top-down process (Kirby 2001), because ordinary people tend to be more socially conservative than political elite. The elite nature of the CCP and KMT was reflected in their emphases on "organized democracy," "disciplined freedom," and "democratic centralism;" in the strength of their political ideologies; and their the powerful internal institutions that instilled strict party discipline (see CCP 1956; KMT 2005, Art. 3, 4, 5).

Although the KMT and CCP share a common origin as elite revolutionary parties, nevertheless there have been significant differences in their subsequent evolution that effect their relationships with their respective judiciaries. And I argue that, contrary to what most people think, these differences were determined more by the different social contexts in which these parties had to operate, and in the different social resources they had at their disposal, than by ideological differences. For a variety of reasons, the KMT inherited most of China's technocrats, professionals, and other educated elite. By contrast, it was harder for the CCP to attract such elites to join their riskier and basically more militarily-oriented adventure—although the CCP has consistently pursued a united front. The major source of membership for the CCP was poor farmers or persons from lower social and economic classes. Such persons were less open, less exposed to the outside world, and often lacked the kind of professionalized discipline and working habits that contributed to effective collective action (Mao 1975).

Lacking a significant cadre of professional and educated elite, the CCP could not transform from a revolutionary party into a governing party, because it had no population from which the necessary technocrats and professionals—such as judges, lawyers, and civil servants—could be drawn. The CCP thus continued to rely on its stronger party organization and stronger party leadership, including stricter discipline and a stronger ideological basis, to facilitate collective action in the absence of an effective administrative bureaucratization.

But this, in turn, also impeded the subsequent development of such bureaucracies. For a long time, the CCP did not feel a need for administrative bureaucratization and professionalization, either of government or of society. It remained revolutionary in character. In all aspects of governance, the CCP played the decisive role. Even after assuming control of the state, political loyalty and ideological purity remained the major criteria for selecting government employees, including judges (see, for example, Dong 2001). This began to change in the 1980s, when the CCP began to pay more attention to promoting professional training and higher education, leading to a continual increase in the number of university graduates. Relatedly, during the middle of the 1980s, the CCP also proposed a separation of party from government, but this reform was formally suspended after 1989. Nevertheless, the early 1990s saw a fundamental change in the CCP's understanding of its relationship with modern government, as evinced for example in the passage of the *Provisional Regulations for the State Civil Service* (*Guojia Gongwuyuan Zanting Tiaoli*) in 1993. Not coincidently, it was also at this time that academic criticism of appointing discharged military officers as judges started (see, for example, He 1998). This grew from the rise and growing influence within the judiciary of the first generation of trained legal professionals (whose age at the time centered around forty) since before the Cultural Revolution. It both challenged the court's established, party-centric institutional structure and led a series of judicial reform (SPC 1999a).

Today, the CCP is increasingly aware that national modernization cannot be accomplished by the party's political elites alone. The task of social integration requires the CCP to enjoy some degree of voluntary support from other social forces in China. This requires, in turn, that it learn to better comprehend and appreciate the different interests that underlie these different societal forces. And along these lines, the CCP has responded. It has promoted greater democracy *within* the party. It has adjusted its policies, relying increasingly on laws and conventional institutions of governance, such as the National People's Congress and the Supreme People's Court, rather than on revolutionary fervor. It has aggressively recruited qualified civil servants and set up bureaucracies. And finally, it has set about transforming the judiciary and improving its function. But the historical task of China's revolutionary social and political modernization cannot be accomplished all at once. The transformation of state, society, and now even the CCP itself is a process that is still going on in the PRC.

All in all, the PRC is facing many complicated problems. The task of reform is heavy and difficult, and the CCP's performance often encounters criticism from Western governments and scholars in line with their own political opinions. Some of these criticisms are justified and deserve the CCP's attention. However, we also have to acknowledge that Chinese governance under the CCP's leadership has achieved great pragmatic success. The CCP found a way to modernize the country in the absence of a preexisting modern administrative state or a modern Constitution. Today, China's inherited political and constitutional institutions may not be as effective as we would like them to be, or as they are in some other countries, but the real question is whether abolishing the CCP would make China better off and help it develop faster in the future.

Put differently, without the CCP, can China continue to develop in the way that it has? This is a difficult and emotionally charged question, one for which I have no answer. But for now, the CCP still is the most important political and developmental force for contemporary China, one for which no alternative presently exists. The CCP continues to constitute the most important component of the constitutional and governmental structure of modern China—and the core force of its modernization.

This is also true with regards to the modernization of the judiciary. Today, the CCP is still the major force mobilizing, advancing, and implementing court reforms. I do not support many of the reform measures it has promoted—some are clear mistakes (see, for example, Suli 2004). And the CCP's leadership has indeed seriously interfered with the development of a necessary quality of "judicial independence," or more particularly what we might call "judges' independence." However, I also believe that in balance, the CCP's oversight has worked to discourage, at least somewhat, judicial corruption and judicial (and legal) arrogance, two by-products of the judiciary's ongoing transformation (although such a claim is controversial, even among China's lawyers and legal scholars).

All this suggests the importance of keeping our minds open, and understanding China's judiciary in its own historical and social context. The continuing leadership and control of the CCP is simply inescapable as a historical process, and as a future dependency. For this reason alone, visions of "judicial independence" that are drawn from distinctly Western experience are not necessarily meaningful for modern China, and evaluations and judgments based upon these experiences or from their underlying ideology (an ideology that emerged in part out of the strategic consideration of Western politicians) are often likely to be of little academic or practical value for China. From the perspective of evolutionary economics, any institutional innovation that survives in competition with other social forces is a valid institution. Social development has no predetermined path or institutional model. The same is true with regards to China's judiciary.

IV. Revising the Model for Studying China

Once we understand the CCP's function of social mobilization and representation, its role in the Constitution and institutional construction of the nation-state, we must be academically vigilant regarding the relevance of the successful experiences of the West with regards to rule of law and judicial practice. Such vigilance does not imply hostility. The point is that we should not take a model that is deeply embedded in the historical, institutional, theoretical, and discursive contexts of the West, decontextualize it, and take it for granted as *the* standard of reference for China's experience. Otherwise, China's progress becomes defined solely by the standards and interests of the West.

Of course, many people who use Western judicial ideology and experiences to analyze China also make very conscientious efforts to understand

China on its own terms. But the social context and experiences they know still sometimes prevent them from placing themselves in the position of the Chinese. Their life-world limits the world of their imagination. This is not a problem unique to them, it is one common to all of us.

But there are problems that may be more particular to American scholars in their efforts to understand China. For example, during the Cold War American scholars contributed a lot to our understanding of the judiciaries and governmental structures of the former Soviet Union and Eastern Bloc countries. But, I suspect, this may also have prevented them from realizing the uniqueness of China's experience. In the Soviet Union, and in the socialist countries of Eastern Europe, the major function of the Communist Party was to control a preexisting bureaucracy, including that of judicial professionals. These American scholars therefore assume that bureaucracy and government are innately prior to the party, and that problems of governance are the result of the party imposing its control over an innately and properly autonomous latter.

This presupposition is reasonable, and possibly right, in considering the context of these particular countries. Many Red Army generals in the Soviet Union's early years were formerly military officers of the Tsar, such as the famous Marshal Mikhail Nikolaevieh Tukhachevski and the hero of the Second World War, Marshal Georgy Konstantinovich Zhukov. In order to secure the leadership and control of the Communist Party over the military, the party used political commissars to ensure the implementation of the party's policies within the Red Army. It was the same with regards to many other organizations, enterprises, and governmental agencies in the early Soviet Union, and with regard to the expansion of Soviet communism into Eastern Europe following the end of the war.

However, this presumption of the bureaucratic state innately *preceding* the party is not applicable to modern China. As we saw, in modern China, the party preceded the bureaucratic state. It is noteworthy that long before the CCP gained control of the Chinese state, CCP leaders clearly recognized the importance of this difference between their own developmental trajectory and that of the Soviet Union. In 1936, when the political commissar Yang Chengwu was appointed a commander in the People's Liberation Army (PLA), Mao Zedong explained that the PLA was different from that of the Soviet Union. He noted that in the latter, most military officers were former White Army officers. In the PLA, both military officers and political-military officers were trained by the CCP. Yang Chengwu became one of the most famous generals of the PLA, but he was not trained as a military professional (Yang 1987, 334). And his history was not unique in this regard. Similar persons could be found throughout the PLA's leadership, as well as in the leadership of other governmental and professional institutions.

This is not to say that the Chinese model of the party preceding the state is good or right as a value judgment. I am here simply making an empirical point that is of great importance not only for understanding the history of modern China, but also for developing effective and practical suggestions for China's further social, political, and judicial reform. Scholars, both abroad and in China, must be aware that such historical path dependencies channel the options available for social and legal development in China.

I expect to be criticized or even condemned by some scholars from both the left and the right—both for my almost non-differential treatment of the CCP and the KMT, as well as for my argument that the CCP represents a possible constitutional alternative for China's social transformation. This does not bother me. Such criticisms show me that I must have done and must be doing something right.

CHAPTER THREE

Of Constitutions and Constitutionalism: Trying to Build a New Political Order in China, 1908–1949

XIAOHONG XIAO-PLANES[1]

I. Introduction: Imperial Precedents

The concept of constitutional government was introduced in the 1890s in China by reform activists eager to change the imperial institutions in order to counter more forcefully the encroachments of Western and Japanese powers. The idea of a "Constitution" comprising a set of rules respected both by the ruling and the ruled, and instituting a parliament expected to reinforce the bonds between the sovereign and the people increasingly became a powerful mobilizing force among social elites and reformers within the state apparatus.

The first (and last) attempt to establish a constitutional monarchy in China dates to 1908—three years before the collapse of China's last imperial dynasty, the Qing. Subsequent regimes all engaged in the drafting of a Constitution. Jurists who had received a modern legal training usually took part in the drafting of these constitutional texts. Inspired in large part by foreign models, these constitutions were generally well formulated—they defined general principles (e.g., sovereignty, territory, population), set down the fundamental rights of citizens, and regulated the functions of the state. Some of them specified the procedures for their own revision. Beginning in the 1920s, Chinese constitutions—following the example of the Constitution of Weimar Republic (the Constitution of the German Reich, 1919)—began incorporating references to the development of the economy and education.

These constitutions had little significant impact on the actual political practice of the times. And some people have inferred from this that Chinese tradition was fundamentally incompatible with a principle of constitutional government. But to my mind, this merely reflects the difficulties of transforming thousand-year-old endogenous institutions using new and exogenous sociopolitical and cultural conceptions borrowed from Western legal thought. In fact, these periods of constitutional drafting always gave rise to fierce public debate, and this evinces that the Chinese themselves attached significant importance at least to the symbolic value of written constitutions. Contrary to common conception, the imperial Chinese state had a long juridical tradition with a well developed corpus of laws, legal theories, and practices—and this was well absorbed into the collective mindset. Social, administrative, and political agents have always paid utmost importance to the ways in which political authority was legitimated by particular works and symbols. The process of constitutional drafting in China summoned up all these experiences in a collective effort to establish a comprehensive discourse of norms and values and to adapt it to the contemporary sociopolitical context.

The Chinese word for "constitution"—"*xianfa*"—has been in use since antiquity. But originally it simply referred to a set of laws and rules relevant to the government, rather than to a fundamental law superior to all others. It was in Meiji Japan (1866–1912) that this term (pronounced *kempō* in Japanese) was first used as a translation for the Western word "constitution." The first Chinese constitutionalists then introduced this usage into China at the end of the 19th century.

But the Western idea of constitutionalism also closely parallels another important Chinese concept—that of *fatong*. The word *"fatong,"* which combines the ideas of "law (*fa*)" and "succession (*tong*)," refers to the set of rules and institutions that juridically constituted and legitimated the dynastic state. Traditionally, a *fatong* was created by the founder of a dynasty, and was then maintained by his descendants. A change in the dynasty marked its *fatong's* formal termination, even while institutional borrowings from one dynasty to another were often numerous. Although intimately associated with imperial governance, the notion of *fatong* expressed a juridico-political orthodoxy that continued to influence the spirit and the rhetoric of China's political world well into the Republican era. As we shall see in the rest of the this Chapter, China's emerging understanding of the idea of constitutionalism during the first half of the twentieth century seems very much informed by this indigenous concept of *fatong*.

II. An Aborted Attempt at Constitutional Monarchy (1908–1912)

The traditional Chinese state was represented by the person of the emperor, assisted by his administration. The last imperial regime, the Qing Dynasty of the Manchus (1644–1912), had a robust system of juridico-administrative institutions revolving around the monarch. The central government consisted of a number of distinct institutions, each overseeing a different aspect of local administration. The government defined itself as expressing the common interests of the country as a whole—and not only of those of the dynasty—and was fundamentally concerned with ensuring order, safety, and prosperity within the empire. But despite a pronounced decline in the second half of the 19th century, this thousand-year-old mandate for political centrality delimited the mental horizon of the Chinese and framed their attachment to national unity.

A. The State Reforms of the Qing

China's imperial state entered a period of decline in the 19th century. The political class, passive for a long time, eventually awoke to the new international order and the growing imperialism of industrialized nations. This caused it to begin questioning China's received model of government. After the fiasco of the xenophobic Boxer Rebellion (1899–1900) and the subsequent occupation of Beijing by European military forces, the imperial court in 1901 formulated extensive juridico-administrative, military, educational, and economic reforms called the *Xin Zheng*, or "New Policies." In the summer of 1908, the imperial empire began the process of establishing a constitutional monarchy. Projected as a nine-year program, it articulated a progressive establishment of representative institutions at provincial and local levels, culminating with the creation of a constituent national parliament, the *Guohui*. The principal intent behind this project was both to build a powerful state and to check the emergence in China of a new Han nationalism that was claiming cultural superiority over that of the minority Manchu "barbarians" then in power.

On August 27, 1908, an imperial edict called the *Xianfa Dagan*, or "General Principles of the Constitutional Government," was issued. After confirming that supreme legislative and executive power vested in the emperor, that edict planned to establish a national parliament, which was then to complete the drafting of the new constitution. This overall constitutional plan was modeled on the Japanese Meiji Constitution (the Constitution of the Empire of Japan, 1890), which itself drew from the German Constitution of 1871. The emperor continued to embody the national sovereignty, and remained the supreme arbitrator of sovereign power. But it also established an elected parliament and responsible governments and vested them with functionally autonomous with legislative and executive responsibilities.

B. Liang Qichao vs. the Tongmenghui Revolutionaries

These constitutional reforms gave significant impetus toward enlarging public participation and the body politic. According to many contemporary

Chinese commentators, the real founding father of Chinese constitutionalism was Liang Qichao (1873–1927), China's most famous political essayist of the time. To Liang, the constitutional monarchy proposed by the Qing would be sufficient to preserve political centrality and thus ensure a nation that would be outwardly strong and inwardly limited. Liang's most receptive audience was composed of provincial and local reformist officials and elites, persons who had studied in Japan, and the new political press. Through these proponents, Liang's ideas gained increasing acceptance in China.

In the 1910s, Liang was fiercely opposed by the anti-Manchu revolutionaries of the *Tongmenghui* (the "Chinese United League" or the "Chinese Revolutionary Alliance")—most of whom, like him, were living in exile in Japan. In contrast to Liang, few of these revolutionary activists paid much attention to matters of institutional design. The agenda of the *Tongmenghui,* which was founded in 1905, lay primarily in promoting the "three principles of the people"—(nationalism, democracy, and the people's welfare). But it was to the first of these principles, nationalism (*minzu*)—that is, hatred for the Manchu, that its plan of action was largely devoted. As Yves Chevrier has shown, the mental horizon of the revolutionaries was infused with Russian anarchism, fashionable at the time, with its spirit of rebellion, secret societies, and religious cults. They sought "violent struggle, feat of arms, and military heroism" and "longed for a completely equal and free society, without State or states" (Chevrier 1993, 197). Consequently, they devoted most of their energy to launching attacks against Manchu civil servants, infiltrating new armies set up in the provinces, and organizing local subversive movements with the support of secret societies.

C. The Manchu Problem

The first provincial elections, albeit with limited franchise, were organized in 1909. Four million electors participated. The reformist elites influenced by Liang entered the provincial assemblies. Despite the semi-consultative nature of these bodies, these new "representatives of the people" applied themselves with much eagerness and sense of responsibility to exercising their duties. They instigated a nation-wide mobilization in 1909–1910 for the immediate convening of a national parliament and the formation of a responsible cabinet. This mobilization resulted in a series of petitions aiming at rescuing the empire from its blindness. But the political impotence of the new, young emperor Puyi, together with increasing tax burdens, caused anti-Manchu feelings to progressively spread to all layers of Chinese society. Even former advocates of constitutional monarchy increasingly distanced themselves from the Manchu regime. To assuage these growing tensions, the Court advanced the timeline for the establishment of the constitutional system by three years.

On October 10, 1911, however, uprising broke out in Wuchang, the capital city of Hubei province. It quickly led to the secession of roughly ten provinces, mainly in the south and center of the country. On November 3, the emperor hurriedly issued a decree entitled the *Shijiu xintiao*—the "Charter in Nineteen Articles"—in which the Manchus gave up most of the prerogatives they had kept in the edict of 1908. The proposed system did bear some semblance to the British constitutional system, but the public rejected it. Even provincial constitutionalists rallied behind the rebels' camp, joining revolutionary nationalists, secret societies, and dissatisfied soldiers. Thrown into a panic, the Court called on the former leader of the powerful Beiyang Army (the "Northern Army"), Yuan Shikai, to crush the growing rebellion. But Yuan was secretly collaborating with the rebel provinces. And after these rebel provinces founded the Republic of China on January 1, 1912, Yuan Shikai quickly forced the emperor to abdicate. In return, three days later, on February 15, the new Republic's provisional assembly unanimously elected him provisional president.

Later, Liang Qichao would clearly explain that this "racial revolution" against the Manchus should merely have been a stepping stone on the way to a "political revolution" that would lead to the establishment of a powerful interventionist state, one able to take care of the socialization of the population and to bring China to its proper rank on the international scene (Liang 1986a). But carried away by their easy overturn of the imperial regime, the revolutionaries "destroyed the traditional, Confucian conception of the government without offering anything viable with which to replace it" (Escarra 1936, 129). For this reason, Yuan Shikai would soon be able to put an end to this new Republic's hastily built constitutional order.

III. The Building of a Constitutional State Proves Difficult (1912–1923)

The new Republic was conscious of the need for a vigorous central authority. For this reason, one of its first acts was to pass a new organic law that established a presidential regime, with a strong president who—it was assumed—would be someone from the original rebel provinces. Yet, faced with having to reelect Yuan Shikai to the presidency of the new Chinese republic, parliamentary leaders drafted the Provisional Constitution of the Republic of China in March 1912, which effectively deprived the President of any real power. Modeled after the constitutional system of France's Third Republic, it established a powerful legislative system that vested a now bicameral parliament with considerable authority to control legislation, policy formation, and the choice of ministers. Through this, they hoped to contain Yuan Shikai's ambitions. But the new constitutional system was incapable of resolving the incessant conflicts between the parliament, the government, and the presidency—or of remedying the resultant, chronic ministerial instability. Within two years, the unrealistic, Provisional Constitution was effectively a dead letter. Nevertheless, it would remain in force formally until 1923. In this sense, it functioned as a kind of *fatong* for the republican revolutionaries of 1911–1912, one that symbolically legitimated the new Republic's right to rule.

The new constitutional Republic's first national election, the winter elections of 1912–1913, witnessed the formation of a number of political parties and groups. The most important of these were the "Nationalist Party," founded by Song Jiaoren and which had its roots in the revolutionary *Tongmenghui* movement; and the "Progressive Party" (*Jinbudang*), which was formed out of constitutionalist adherents to the ideas of Liang Qichao. The 1912–1913 elections also marked a significant expansion of the franchise in comparison to the provincial parliamentary elections of 1909, calling some forty million men—about 10.5 percent of the population—to the polls (see Nathan 1976; Nathan 1997, 64). The more revolutionary Nationalist Party won a majority in both houses of parliament. But before he could assume office as Prime Minister, Song Jiaren was murdered on March 20, 1913—probably on Yuan Shikai's orders—and the new constitutional system fell into crisis.

A. Presidential Regime or a Responsible Government?

The new parliament immediately called for a constitutional convention, which convened on April 8, 1913. When its new draft Constitution, known as the "Tiantan Draft Constitution (*Tiantan xianfa cao'an*)"—so named because the drafting committee met at the Temple of Heaven, or *Tiantan*—was debated before the parliament from October 4 to 31, parliamentary debate again focused on the question of how much power to give the chief executive. Liang Qichao and the Progressive Party were in favor of a strong executive power with a more centralized government. Now allied to Yuan Shikai, they deemed it necessary to concentrate power in the hands of this "man of the hour" in order to stop the centrifugal political forces that had flourished since the revolution of 1911, namely the increasing power and autonomy of regional and local warlords. They also feared that the Nationalist Party, which now controlled parliament, was gaining too much power. For its part, the Nationalist Party naturally wanted a stronger parliament and a weaker central executive power.

After the parliament elected Yuan Shikai President of the Republic in October 1913, however, elements of the Nationalist Party joined forces with members of the Progressive Party. Sensing that the nascent Republic was in danger, they hastily voted to adopt the Tiantan Draft. That text represented a compromise position on the question of presidential authority: it reduced the constraints imposed on the executive without going as far as creating a real strong executive.

B. Yuan Shikai or Presidential Autocracy

But once elected, Yuan Shikai no longer needed the parliament or its new constitution. He dissolved parliament in early 1914, and suspended the provincial and local representative assemblies. He also tightened control over the central ministries and local bureaucracies, began censoring the press, and began persecuting opposition political organizations and activities. In May 1914, he replaced the still formally in-force Provisional Constitution of 1912 with a "New Constitutional Pact" (*Xinyuefa*), which established a "life presidency" with virtually omnipotent powers.

Then, in 1915, Yuan began advocating for the restoration of the monarchy. Liang Qichao reacted strongly. He underlined the fact that the actual autocratic regime that he and his political adherents had helped create was to be tolerated only for very precise and provisional purposes. A restoration of the monarchy, on the other hand, would plunge the country into political anarchy: such a monarchy would lack the strength and prestige necessary to build a strong Chinese state now that the revolution had deprived it of the quasi-mystical aura which it had during the time of the empire (Liang 1986b, 94–95). Nevertheless, Yuan crowned himself emperor on December 12, 1915, despite the reluctance of his own generals and warnings from the foreign powers that occupied various parts of China as "concessions."

Insurrections claiming the "defense of the Republic" (*huguo*) immediately broke out in several Southwestern provinces. Yuan was forced to abolished his monarchy on February 22, 1916, and he died the following June. Many other warlords took advantage of the unsettled situation to begin carving out *de facto* independent kingdoms for themselves. Most prominently, the General and a former bandit, Zhang Zuolin, assumed control over the province of Manchuria, while one of his former military officers, Chen Shufan, also a former member of the *Tongmenghui*, took over Shaanxi province. In the south, "Defense of the Republic" forces quickly began to fight each other for control of the provinces of Sichuan, Yunnan, Guangxi, and Guangdong.

C. The Deadlock of Constitutional Elaboration in 1916–1917

Following Yuan Shikai's removal from power, the Republican *fatong* again asserted its presence. Yuan's former vice president, Li Yuanhong, was made the new President in 1916. Beyond this, the Progressives and the Nationalists could only agree on the restoration of the Provisional Constitution of 1912 and the reconvening of the parliament that had been elected on April 1913. Those two parliamentary houses, whose three-year mandate had actually expired, convened on August 1, 1916. Duan Qirui, a chief of the Northern Beiyang faction, was appointed prime minister. From August 1916 to June 1917, the parliament resumed drafting a new constitution on the basis of the Provisional Constitution of 1912 and the Tiantan Draft Constitution of 1913. The debates surrounding this drafting compelled the moderate Progressive Party to establish a "Constitutional Studies Society (*Xianfa yanjiuhui*)," while the Nationalist Party (which had temporarily renamed itself the "Chinese Revolutionary Party (*Zhonghua gemingdang*)" when Yuan Shikai formally outlawed the Nationalist Party in 1913) formed its own, competing, "Constitutional Debates Society (*Xianfa shangquanhui*)." Some provincial military governors also organized themselves in associations (*dujuntuan*), which attempted to affect the national political arena by threatening to resort to violence.

Within the parliament itself, members were divided over the question of whether the Constitution should set out the powers of local and provincial government (*shengzhi*) in addition to those of the national government. Liang Qichao and the Constitutional Studies Society opposed such a development. Given the arrogance and power of many of the provincial warlords, they feared that trying to extend the reach of the Constitution into provincial government would only weaken the authority of the state. On the other hand, the more radical Constitutional Debates Society insisted that provincial powers should be codified into the Constitution. To them, the current political chaos was due to the absence of clarification of the respective powers of the center and the provinces.

After ten months of fruitless debates between the two camps, the monarchist General Zhang Xun deposed President Li, dissolved the parliament and, on July 1, 1917, attempted to reestablish China as an imperial state by restoring the last Qing emperor, Puyi, to the throne. But this "restoration" only lasted two weeks. On July 14, Prime Minister Duan Qirui was able to regain power, with the help of the Northern armies, and reestablish the Chinese Republic.

Supported by Liang Qichao, Duan then immediately called for the election of a new parliament. Sun Yat-sen, who had assumed leadership of the Nationalist Party when Song Jiaren was assassinated in 1913, launched a "Movement to Protect the Constitution (*hufa yundong*)" in Guangzhou, claiming that Duan's refusal to reconvene the 1913 parliament constituted a breach of the Provisional Constitution of 1912. Hostilities between the northern, Beiyang faction supporting Duan and Sun's southern supporters immediately broke out. Nevertheless, parliamentary elections were held in spring of 1918. But to the great dismay of Liang Qichao, these elections were heavily rigged by Duan's supporters, and they gave an overwhelming parliamentary majority to members of his "Anfu Club" and "Communication Faction (*Jiaotongxi*)"—informal groupings of technocrats and officials who Duan had placed at the head of various economic and technical organizations controlled by the state, such as railroads, telegraphs, post offices, and banks. In response, the southern provinces that supported Sun Yat-sen's Movement to Protect the Constitution refused to recognize the legitimacy of the Beiyang-controlled government, and the southern provinces supporting Sun established their own version of China's national government in Guangzhou in September 1917.

Duan's Beiyang parliament elected Xu Shinchang to the presidency (Duan being the prime minister) and began on August 1918 a new "Constitution Project" that was more or less a copy of the Tiantan Draft Constitution of 1913. But the Beiyang faction soon split into rivaling groups: the Anhui clique, headed by Duan; the Zhili clique, headed by Feng Guozhang; and a third, military-headed faction called the Fengtian clique. Parliament was suspended the following year, and from then until 1927, when Chiang Kai-shek was able to finally re-unify northern with southern China, these rival Beiyang factions continually fought for control of the government—which unlike its southern counterpart enjoyed the recognition of the Western powers and thus was able to contract for state loans overseas.

In the south, the situation was barely better. The Movement to Protect the Constitution was also dividing into rival forces. Despite the repeated attempts at negotiation, China decomposed into a myriad of large and small, generally warlord-controlled, domains.

D. The Federalist Movement and Provincial Autonomy

Sometime around 1917 or 1918, a new "federalist" movement (*Liansheng zizhi yundong*) began to emerge in China, which demanded the abolition of provincial and local military governments ("*feidu*"), the demobilization of the autonomous armies of the provinces ("*caibing*"), and the establishment of autonomous regional governments under civil control ("*zizhi*"). It was fed by new elements of an emerging civil society—intellectuals, progressive officials, a bourgeoisie, and urban middle classes—who publicized their view through telegrams, press articles, and in speeches made before provincial assemblies, public assemblies, and civil and professional associations. This movement instilled a new dynamic into China's constitutional environment, that of grassroots civic mobilization.

The movement for autonomy of the provinces came from the logic of the new urban effervescence. As a current of thought, political federalism first appeared in China in the early twentieth century. It reappeared in the early 1920s, nourished by the fact that efforts to centralize Chinese governance appeared to be fruitless. Its advocates offered to leave the question of national unity in abeyance and to found the sovereignty of the people in the establishment of "autonomous provinces (*liansheng zizhi*)," each with its own elected government operating in accordance with the province's own, autonomous Constitution. They also demanded that grassroots civic associations participate in the drafting of these provincial constitutions and in the creation of the provincial governments. These autonomous provinces would then form a federation and appoint a centralized authority of limited powers.

The federalist movement reached its climax between 1920 and 1923 and enjoyed the support of many socio-professional associations and of diverse civil and intellectual and even military figures, especially in the southern provinces. Among the federalist provinces, Hunan pushed federalist experimentation the furthest. Located in the center of China, Hunan had suffered especially hard from the military engagements between northern and southern factions. In 1920, local troops managed to drive a particularly loathed northern governor out of power. A Hunanese military leader, Zhao Hengti, then took the initiative of promoting a provincial constitutional government. This earned him the support of several influential political and intellectual figures, and of numerous civic associations. Many intellectuals participated directly in the enterprise. The provincial Constitution of Hunan was promulgated in 1921 and allegedly sanctioned by a referendum. It was also quite radical for its day: establishing, among other things, universal suffrage (including women's suffrage); a governorship, provincial assembly, and regional councils all chosen by popular vote; and an independent judiciary. The new governor and provincial assembly were elected and took office the following year.

Several other provinces followed the example of Hunan in deciding to draft their own constitutions. In March 1922, delegates from the eight principal kinds of civic associations in China—provincial chambers of commerce (*sheng xianghui*), the provincial education societies (*sheng jiaoyu hui*), the provincial agricultural societies (*sheng nong hui*), the provincial societies of industry (*sheng gonghui*), the provincial bankers associations (*sheng yinhang gonghui*), the provincial lawyers associations (*sheng lushi gonghui*), and the Press-Workers Union (*baojie lianhe hui*)—together with selected delegates from numerous provincial assemblies (*sheng yihui*) that had been reestablished around 1917–1918, organized in Shanghai a "Conference on Public Affairs (*guoshi huiyi*)," which advocated that provinces begin focusing on drafting their own provincial constitutions and establishing their own elected provincial governments. Only thereafter, the Conference concluded, should provincially-selected delegates meet to create a national constitution.

The federalist movement enjoyed support for a diversity of reasons. Many communists thought that provincial constitutionalism could benefit the mobilization of the working class. Liberal intellectuals perceived it as a means to both enlarge and rationalize the people's participation in political life. Other believed it would help limit the misdeeds of the military. Jean Chesneaux observed that while federalism represented a new and foreign constitutional notion in China, it nevertheless became "a movement of the Chinese society's traditional and conservative forces" (Chesneaux 1966, 383).

Despite its local successes, in the end, the federalist movement died because it ignored the fact that the political viability of the country depended crucially on the good will and support of the provincial military leaders. Most of these leaders only supported projects that advanced their ambitions of territorial domination. For a while, Guangdong province, with its reformist General Chen Jiangming, represented the federalist movement's best hope for spreading influence. But Sun Yat-sen had planned to turn Guangdong into a base from which to launch a military offensive against the north, and this ultimately derailed Chen's federalist inclinations (Chen 1999). At the end of the day, as Prasenjit Duara (1993) as inventively explained, the moralizing discourse of centralizing nationalism resulted in an ultimate rejection of the federalist movement and, along with it, of the associated antiestablishment tradition in Chinese politics (see also Duara 1995).

E. The Still-Born Constitution of 1923

In the north, the Zhili clique was able to assumed a somewhat stable control of the Beiyang national government in the spring of 1920. But this obviously did not resolve China's deeper institutional problems. After getting rid of Duan's chosen President, Xu Shichang, and overcoming their former allies, the Fengtian clique; the Zhili clique's leaders, Cao Kun and Wu Peifu, undertook to rally support for their authority. In May 1922 they called for the restoration of the Provisional Constitution of 1912, and for the ratification of the Tiantan Constitutional Draft of 1913. They reestablished the presidency of Li Yuanhong—who had been deposed in 1917 when the monarchical General Zhang Xun briefly restored Puyi as the Emperor of China—and reconvened the 1913 parliament that Zhang had also dissolved at that time. That parliament resumed meeting on August 1, 1922. Although public opinion was not particularly attached to this newest manifestation of the Republican *fatong*, many supported the re-convening of the 1913 parliament because they thought it could lead to the production of a Constitution that would finally unify the Chinese state. Wu Peifu, in particular, a leader of the Zhili clique popularly known as "The Confucian General," enjoyed much public respect due to his declarations in favor of a peaceful reunification of the country.

The Beiyang parliament introduced new constitutional clauses destined to clarify the respective rights and powers of both the central and the provincial governments. But the subject of provincial institutions still caused controversy. At the same time the Zhili clique's constant interference in the workings of the existing constitutional system seriously disrupted the functioning and effectiveness of that system. In June 1923, this caused President Li Yuanhong to again be removed from the presidency by a coup d'État. In seeking to become the next president, the Zhili clique's other leader, Cao Kun, openly bought the votes of a great number of members of Parliament. When he was indeed duly elected President of the Republic on October 5, 1923, public trust in that parliament collapsed. To try to win forgiveness in the wake of that scandal, the members of that parliament completed their second and third readings of the Constitution project in just six days and ratified a new Constitution of the Chinese Republic, the Constitution of 1923, on October 10. But neither parliament and its new Constitution enjoyed any support or credibility. Within a year, a new military coalition arrested President Cao Kun and again suspended parliament.

On paper, the Constitution of 1923 was significant because it enlarged the rights of citizens and designed an original blend of centralization and federalism. Some jurists see it as articulating a distinctly federal constitutional state. But it could never be effectively implemented, due to the willingness of China's other political actors and factions to do violence to political life in order to advance their own personal interests. And with the stillbirth of this most recent Republican constitutional project, the distinctively *Republican fatong* of the revolution of 1911 would fall into abeyance once and for all, to be replaced by a new *fatong* associated with the Nationalists of Sun Yat-sen.

IV. Blind Faith in the Revolutionary Party-State (1923–1947)

A. Sun Yat-Sen's Constitutional Views

All things considered, Sun Yat-sen's constitutional thinking drew from various indigenous Chinese understandings of governmental organization, Western visions of parliamentary democracy, and the Soviet vision of the revolutionary party state. His two key constitutional doctrines were "three principles of the people" ("*sanmin zhuyi*"), which he adapted from the *Tongmenghui,* and the "five constitutional powers" ("*wuquan xianfa*"). The "three principles of the people" consisted of their subsistence (*minsheng*), their sovereignty (*minquan*), and their nationalism (*minzu*). The principle of the people's subsistence described the government's responsibility to improve the people's material condition. It recalled the traditional obligation of the Confucian State to "feed the people" (*yang-min*). The principle of people's sovereignty extended further than simple electoral democracy and provided a framework for direct democracy in which the people are endowed with "rights" of revocation, initiative, and referendum, in addition to that of suffrage. The third principle, nationalism, had originally been directed by the *Tongmenghui* at removing the Manchus from power. Sun reinterpreted it as expressing a right of "self-determination" that externally directed itself against foreign imperialism and internally granted some degree of self-governing autonomy to minority ethnicities.

Sun Yat-sen also believed that in a well-organized democracy, the *quan* (sovereignty, source of power) must be distinct from exercise of governmental power, the *neng*. The *quan* belongs to the people. The *neng* belongs to the government (under the supervision of the people). In Sun Yat-sen's model, the government's *neng* consisted of five distinct kinds of constitutional powers—executive, legislative, judiciary, control power, and censorship power. Each power was to be vested in a separate institutional body, called a *yuan*. The first three of these powers appear to have derived from Montesquieu's classical theory of the separation of powers. The last two drew from traditional Chinese imperial institutions: the examination system, which controlled the selection of civil servants; and the Censorate, which supervised the behavior of public officials. Above the five *yuan* was to sit the National Assembly (*Guomin Dahui*). Its members were to be directly elected, with each representing a *xian* (the administrative districts that operate below the county level). It was primarily through their National Assembly deputies that the population would exercise the "rights" associated with the principle of popular sovereignty (*minquan*).

For Sun, however, the Chinese people were yet to reach a satisfactory level of education, or otherwise to attain sufficient political competence, to effectively exercise their sovereignty. He therefore envisioned a three-stage transition leading to the formation of a constitutional state. During the first stage, a more or less autocratic military government (*junzheng*) would have the task of unifying the country—primarily by eliminating local military leaders. Once this was achieved, a second "tutelage" stage would take place in which the people would be granted sovereignty rights over the administration of local, basic-level, and district (*xian*) government, so as to learn how to exercise these rights responsibly. The third step was that of full constitutional government, in which a final Constitution would be crafted that would extend the people's sovereignty rights so as to create an authentically democratic and constitutional national regime.

Sun rejected the Marxist notions of "class struggle" and the "dictatorship of the proletariat." But he drew much inspiration from the Soviet model of the "revolutionary party" in a one-party state, which he regarded to be a particularly effective way to achieve the first two stages of constitutional formation (see also Zhu Suli's chapter in this volume). He saw the revolutionary party as a kind of political vanguard—an institution that would be uniquely conscious of political truths and could therefore educate and guide the still unknowing masses toward a world in which equality and harmony will prevail. Sun's vision of the role of the revolutionary party in promoting China's constitutional transition would achieve the status of a blind faith within the *Guomindang's* official orthodoxy.

B. *The One Party Divided*

Sun died on March 12, 1925. In the south, his constitutional vision, particularly his vision of the constitutional role of the revolutionary party operating in a one-party state, was taken up by Chinese Nationalist party, the *Guomindang*, which in 1923 had been reorganized into a revolutionary party with the help of Soviet Komintern advisers. On July 1, 1925, while it was still just governing the Southern provinces out of Guangzhou, the *Guomindang* government promulgated its first organic law, which defined the principle of the direction of the party over the state (*yi dang zhi guo*). After its "Northern Expedition (*beifa*)", under the command of Chiang Kai-shek, reunified the country by capturing Beijing and subduing the northern, Beiyang factions in 1927, the now truly national government of the *Guomindang* promulgated a new Organic Law on October 8, 1928 announcing the end of the first, "unification" phase of Sun's constitutional program and beginning of the second, "political tutelage" phase. It also established a national government consisting of Sun's five governmental *yuan*. The Party Central Executive Committee calculated that this political tutelage phase would last for six years, during which the *Guomindang* would represent the Chinese people in the exercise of their political rights and would therefore oversee the whole of the political and constitutional apparati of the country. In order to establish the party's ideological and political supremacy new practices were introduced in public life, including the sending of political "instructors" (*zhidao*) to private, civic, and professional associations to teach the development of the proper political consciousness.

Nevertheless, political unity within the *Guomindang* was fragile. After Chiang Kai-shek assumed control of the party in October 1928, his main rival, Wang Jingwei, together with two Northern military leaders, Feng Yuxian and Yan Xishan, formed a secessionist government in Beijing in March 1929, and in autumn of 1930 promulgated the "Taiyuan Constitution." The text of that Constitution stipulated that half of the members of the legislative *Yuan* would be *directly* elected and the other half selected by the Party. It also established a national "Consultative Council" comprising of provincial and regional representatives, with limited legislative power, and conferred extensive powers to provinces and districts. But the Taiyuan Constitution would never have any practical effect. Chiang quickly defeated the secessionists, and on June 1, 1931 the *Guomindang* government promulgated its own Provisional Constitution of the Republic of China for the Period of Political Tutelage (*Zhonghua Minguo Xunzheng Shiqi Yuefa*) (the "Tutelage Constitution"), which in addition to prescribing the principles of the party's continued political tutelage, inaugurated into Chinese constitutionalism the practice of supplementing constitutional articulations of citizen's rights with counterbalancing articulations of citizen's constitutional *duties*. It also outlined, very briefly, the respective spheres of action of both central and of local governmental authorities. And it gave all rights to interpret and revise the Constitution to the *Guomindang*.

Party unity was still elusive, however. Even before the promulgation of the Tutelage Constitution of 1931, Chiang's party rival, Wang Jingwei, formed another secessionist government, this time in Guangzhou in May of 1931. But the Japanese conquest of Manchuria in 1931, and of Shanghai in 1932, mobilized public opinion throughout the country to call for the establishment of a unified constitutional government respecting civil and political liberties. The governments of Wang and Chiang reconciled underneath the banner of the provisional Tutelage Constitution, and between 1932 and 1935, Wang and Chiang shared direction of the executive *Yuan* and the military affairs committee. Sun Yat-sen's only son, Sun Fo, was put in charge of the legislative *Yuan*.

Seeking to increase his standing within the party, Sun Fo caused the legislative *Yuan* to produce and submit for public discussion a series of draft constitutions between 1933 and 1935, all seeking to bestow the legislative *Yuan* with greater power to control the executive *Yuan*. But the Party Central Executive Committee rejected these propositions. Finally, in 1936, a "Constitutional Draft of May 5th" (*Wuwu xiancao*) was produced that allowed for virtually unchecked executive power and a National Assembly (Guo*mindahui*) consisting of 1,200 elected members and *an additional* 600 members directly appointed by the *Guomindang*. The consequent elections of 1936–1937 of National Assembly delegates (*guoda daibiao*) occurred under the strict control of the *Guomindang* and local governments, the only entities authorized to nominate candidates for these elections. But with the sharp escalation of the Sino-Japanese War in summer of 1937, the *Guomindang* decided to cancel the convening of the National Assembly, thus postponing the vote for a new Constitution.

C. State Institutions and Political Parties during the Sino-Japanese War

Of course, at the same time as the *Guomindang* was unifying remnants of the Republican regime under the new banner of nationalism, the Chinese

Communist Party (*Gongchandang*) hereinafter (CCP), a rival revolutionary party also inspired by the Soviet model, had gained control of the northwest. Through the 1930s, the two rivals engaged in low-grade military conflict with one another, but the expansion of the Sino-Japanese War in 1937 caused them to form a "United Front" against the Japanese. Together, they established a new body, the "National Defense Supreme Committee (*Guofang zuigao weiyuanhui*)" on August 11, 1937 to deal with the war problems. Presided over by Chiang Kai-shek, it possessed supreme civil and military authority. In March 1938, the *Guomindang* government promulgated a new Organic Law that institutionalized the national United Front in the guise of a "People's Political Council (*Guomin canzhenhui*)," a quasi-parliamentary institution that served as the representative for the people's sovereignty until the end of the war. The law also stipulated the establishment of consultative assemblies at the provincial and local levels.

The first meeting of the People's Political Council was held in Wuhan on July 6, 1938. After that, it met in the Nationalists' new capital city. Chongqing, in Sichuan province. It was comprised of 200 delegates (*canzhenyuan*). Half of these represented China's various provinces and special regions, or Chinese living overseas. Until 1940, these delegates were all appointed by the *Guomindang* government; after 1940, those provinces and regions under governmental control were allowed to elect their own representative through "provisional assemblies," with the *Guomindang* government continuing to appoint the representatives for overseas Chinese and occupied regions. The other half of the People's Political Council delegates were selected directly by the Communist Party; by other, small political parties who also participated in the United Front; and by various cultural and economic organizations. By 1940, the total number of delegates was expanded to 240, while the number of delegates directly selected by the *Guomindang* government was reduced to sixty.[2]

Although the *Guomindang* controlled an absolute majority within the People's Political Council, Council delegates, even those from the Nationalist Party, were frequently critical of governmental policy. The Political Council had the right to put forward proposals to the government, and to examine governmental reports and arrangements, but its acts had no legal authority and the government was not compelled to respond to any of its proposals or requests. It also operated under the constant surveillance of the *Guomindang's* intelligence services. Nevertheless, the Political Council engaged in considerable activity: its debates, inquiries, motions, and proposals covered almost every field of governmental action (see Shyu 1977; see also Ch'ien 1950, 278–295).

Toward the end of 1938, the Japanese expansion in China began to subside. The *Guomindang* used this opportunity to focus on neutralizing communist expansion and increasing its hold on the urban areas under its control. It significantly restricted public liberties, which had until that time been largely unaffected by the war. In response to this, delegates to the annual meeting of the Political Council in September 1939 tabled seven motions calling for an end to the so-called tutelage period, the restoration of public liberties, and the establishment of a true constitutional regime. The Political Council also appointed a twenty-five person commission to examine the Constitutional Draft of May 5th. These actions enjoyed much popular support, and in November 1939 the *Guomindang's* Central Party Committee announced its plan to hold a special "Constituent Assembly" in the autumn of 1940. However, when that autumn arrived, it then announced that it was postponing the formation and convening of that assembly until after the end of the war.

The Communists realized that they could use the Political Council's constitutional initiative to increase their popularity. Between October and December 1939, the CCP leadership sent several directives to local party committees ordering them to actively support the Political Council's constitutional proposals. Mao Zedong delivered several speeches on the matter and published his famous "Essay on New Democracy (*Xin minzhu zhuyi lun*)" in January 1940. Beginning in 1941, the CCP, in organizing civil authority in its main territorial base (the North Shaanxi border-area), adopted a principle of universal suffrage together with a "three-thirds system" of representation (*sansanzhi*)—a system in which representation was apportioned equally between the CCP, noncommunist leftwing progressives, and noncommunist centrists (see Selden 1995, 99–143). This greatly promoted support from local elites, teachers, and students; and it made the consolidation of the CCP's power in newly controlled areas easier. It also furthered the CCP's strategy of "peaceful institutional competition" with the Nationalists, a strategy that was to greatly impress both Chinese and foreign observers, especially at the end of the war.

Outside of the *Guomindang* and the CCP, other, smaller political groups, along with many independent public figures, took advantage of the relative political easing to form the "Association of Comrades for the Construction of the Nation (*Tongyi jianguo tongzhihui*)." This organization was originally devoted simply to reducing the tensions between *Guomindang* and the CCP in order to preserve the United Front. In March 1941, it morphed into what Carsun Chang (1952) famously called a "third force (*disan fangmian*)" political organization called the China Democratic League (*Zhonguo minzhu zhengtuan tongmeng,* later simplified to *Zhonguo minzhu tongmeng*).

On September 18, 1943, Chiang Kai-shek—after renewed prodding from the Political Council—again announced his intention to organize a special constituent assembly, this time specifying that it would convene within a year after the ending of the war. In anticipation of this, a Preparatory Commission was established and placed under the patronage of the People's Political Council. However, spurred by increasing tax pressures, inflation, governmental corruption, social inequality, the compulsory draft, and the failure to effectively prosecute the war against Japan, the public was becoming increasingly discontented with the *Guomindang* government. The movement for constitutionalism expanded and intensified, resulting in a plethora of conferences and debates, and the appearance of new periodicals devoted to issues of constitutional regime. Public pressure for constitutional reform continued to mount, causing even the American government in autumn of 1944 to begin delicately suggesting to Chiang that he should take the issue of constitutional reform more seriously.

On September 15, 1944 the CCP prepared a motion calling for the creation of a coalition government that perfectly matched both the American line and Chinese public opinion. The Chinese Democratic League gave this motion its support and proposed a meeting of representatives from various parties at a general political conference. Wanting to remain in control of the situation, the government then announced that the convening of its proposed Constituent Assembly would take place on November 12, 1945.

D. The 1947 Constitution: A Failure of Political Compromise?

Japan surrendered on August 10, 1945. The CCP immediately began expanding its control over the countryside, especially in the north. Public opinion, unequivocally opposed to the idea of a civil war, forced the two parties to negotiate. In the fall of 1945, Mao Zedong and Chiang Kai-shek met in Chongqing to formulate and sign a joint "agreement in principle" to avoid a civil war. On January 10, 1946, a "Conference for Political Dialogue (*Zhengzhi xieshang huiyi*)" was convened in Chongqing. It was comprised of eight representatives from the nationalist government, seven from the CCP, nine from the Chinese Democratic League, five from the Youth Party, and nine independent persons. The Conference was intended, not only to help reconcile the *Guomindang* and the CCP, but also to design the constitutional infrastructure of the postwar state.

The Conference ended with the adoption of five resolutions, the fourth of which called for a revision of the 1936 Constitution Draft of May 5.[3] In furtherance of this, the Conference established a Constitutional Revision Committee, comprised of fifteen of its own members and ten external experts (see Chang 1952; Wang 2000). In April of 1946, the Constitutional Revision Committee produced a proposed constitution derived from an initial draft that had been written by the famous Chinese liberal intellectual, Carsun Chang (Zhang Junmai).

This constitutional proposal remained faithful to the nationalist *fatong* of Sun Yat-sen. It endorsed Sun Yat-sen's "three principles of the people," which the nationalists were anxious to keep, but added an additional, fourth principle of "direct guarantee (*zhijie baozhang*)"—which stipulated that the rights of citizens directly guaranteed in the Constitution itself could not be restricted by ordinary law—at the insistence of the other political parties represented on the Committee. The "visible" form of the political system maintained the division of governmental powers into five *yuan*. But it also expanded the powers of the legislative *Yuan*, now elected by universal suffrage, to include a true legislating power (which it did not have in the draft of 1936). The President of the Republic took on the function of supreme executive leader. The proposal also enumerated the division of powers between the central and local authorities, giving the provinces the right to elect their own governor and assemblies and to promulgate provincial and local laws on the condition that these laws remained in conformity with the Constitution and the country's national laws.

The proposed constitution proved satisfactory to both moderates and radicals. But the draft had to be approved by the leadership of both the CCP and the *Guomindang*. Unfortunately, by that time, the *Guomindang* and CCP—despite the conciliatory efforts of the Chinese Democratic League—were heading inexorably toward civil war. When the nationalist government finally convened a "National Assembly" on November 15, 1946 to formally ratify the draft Constitution, that Assembly was boycotted by both the CCP and the Chinese Democratic League. Nevertheless, the Assembly ratified the Constitution, with some minor modifications to it, on January 1, 1947. The new Constitution of the Republic in China (*Zhonghua Minguo Xianfa*) went into effect on December 25, 1947; and today it remains in effect in Chinese Taiwan.

After a tumultuous election of new delegates in November of 1947, the "First Constitutional Assembly (*Xingxian guomin dahui*)" was elected and Chiang Kai-shek became the President of the Republic on April 19, 1948 (Ch'ien 1961, 331–345). But although they were winning the elections, the *Guomindang* was gradually losing the civil war. In the second half of 1947, CCP forces were able to go on the offensive for the first time. In response, the *Guomindang*-controlled government amended the Constitution on May 10, 1948, by enacting the "Temporary Provisions Effective During the Period of Communist Rebellion (*Dongyuan kanluan shiqi linshi tiaokuan*)," which removed all constitutional constraints from the office of the Presidency. But this did not help the nationalist war effort. In 1949, Chiang Kai-shek and the *Guomindang* government were forced into exile on the island of Taiwan, bringing with them their now emasculated 1947 Constitution.

There, the Temporary Provisions gave them the power to transform the Constitution's independent constitutional structures into mere sham institutions, and in the process allowed them to establish a party-state that was even more invasive, authoritarian, and repressive than anything they had been able to establish on the mainland.

V. Conclusion: China's Once and Future Constitutionalism

During the first half of the 20th century, the Chinese adopted Western constitutionalism in order to reorganize political order and to modernize the state. After their quasi-religious form of monarchy had been discredited, constitutionalism laid the principal foundation for the state's legitimacy and power. In addition, a constitutional basis of sovereignty was recognized by international law as "a formal rule of the game in international relations between states" (Braud 1997, 37). The presence of a Constitution thus put the Chinese State on equal footing with other states. Yuan Shikai, Chiang Kai-shek, Mao Zedong, and Deng Xiaoping, all figures of absolute power, nevertheless all pledged themselves to the upholding of the constitutional rite, and in so doing subjected themselves to Western-style rules. Their purpose was to modernize the Chinese state following this model, but at a cost of an enormous distortion between the form of government that the Constitution formally articulated and the reality of Chinese politics.

By nature, constitutionalism implies a multiplicity of political players engaged in a peaceful competition for power. However, China's early constitutional experiments, those of the late imperial court and first-generation Republican revolutionaries, failed. The national entity imploded; political life became militarized; and power relations became personalized and fragmented. Due both to international pressures and the threat of civil war, reconstructing an undisputed political center became an absolute priority—justifying resort to violence and the elimination of rivals. China's constitutional journey is thus marked by a constant tension between the need to unify the nation into a coherent state and the need to peacefully regulate political competition. This would divide opinion and produce political conflict in China for over half a century.

Despite the suppressive efforts of China's many late 19th and early 20th century autocrats, an authentic public opinion had emerged at the end of the empire—articulated through the press, civic and professional associations, and through the voice of a rising intelligentsia. We saw how despite its irresolute tendencies and its contradictions, this public opinion succeeded in preventing the *Guomindang* from assuming authoritarian dimensions, at least on the mainland.

Today, although the CCP continues to formally reserve supreme political authority for itself, actual political power in China has been considerably diversified—spread among innumerable administrative agencies, regional governments, and economic and even social organizations. The purpose behind this has primarily been to improve governmental efficiency and promote economic reform. It has not been to catalyze the reemergence of a political dynamic of public opinion. Yet, because this evolution has multiplied considerably the number of players having the capacity to exercise some form of political power, it has indeed contributed to a noticeable enlargement of the political space. As we will see in other chapters in this volume, China's citizenry is again becoming aware of their rights and expressing their belief in the necessity of institutionalizing the relationships between the ruling and the ruled. Today's China is increasingly facing the same tensions as it did during the first half of the 20th century.

Notes

1. A preliminary version of this text was translated by Emilie Frenkiel.
2. In total, there were four "congresses" (*jie*) of the People's Political Council with thirteen sessions (*ci*) between 1938 and 1948.
3. The other four points included (1) details on the restructuring of the military; (2) the organization of the People's National Assembly (*guomin dahui*); (3) the composition of a coalition government; and (4) a "Program for peaceful national reconstruction (*Heping jianguo gangling*)."

CHAPTER FOUR

Epistrophy: Chinese Constitutionalism and the 1950s

Glenn D. Tiffert

I. Introduction

Imagine, for a moment, interpreting the American Constitution ignorant of *The Federalist Papers*, *Marbury v. Madison*, the New Deal, or the Warren Court. How would we comprehend English Common Law absent Coke, Blackstone, or Dicey? What if our grasp of French jurisprudence barely acknowledged the legacy of the Napoleonic Code and overlooked the political crises and constitutional innovations attending the birth of the Fifth Republic? At best, our understanding of these legal systems and the discourses that animate them would be deficient; at worst, we might misread them altogether.

The tendency in both China and abroad to treat contemporary Chinese law as discursively, even genetically, distinct from its imperial, Republican, or Maoist antecedents is therefore arresting. That many present reformers and observers of Chinese law are better versed in Jellinek, Vyshinsky, and Posner than in Shen Jiaben, Yang Zhaolong, and Zhang Youyu begs discomfiture, as does the paradox of their reluctance to take China's legal heritage seriously while simultaneously grappling with its normative and institutional legacies.

Through a glimpse into the drafting of the 1954 Constitution of the People's Republic of China (PRC), this chapter joins those who would argue for greater historicity in the study of Chinese law (see, for example, Angle and Svensson 2001; Bourgon 1998). It aims to complement the excellent tools social science has furnished for unpacking legal "modernization" by urging greater sensitivity to local and diachronic processes, especially those that borrow seemingly familiar legal concepts and institutions and then quietly refashion them into something native (Peerenboom 2007a). After all, since the shock of the First Opium War in the 1840s, China has more or less been permanently engaged in a quest for modernity; and nearly every successive generation of legal observers has borne the conceit of this phenomenon as novel, and then framed it against the favored, exogenous benchmarks of the day, only to emerge confounded that China would not submit to their designs (see, for example, Goodnow 1915; Pound 1948a; Krymov and Shafir 1959).

However, "[i]magining China's possible futures simply on the basis of its present conditions" invites misapprehension (Wong 1999, 243). It obscures the contingency in human affairs and the power of hidden, suppressed narratives to alter the course of the body politic unexpectedly. Alternatively, in contexts where sensitive ideas are expressed Aesopically, and where terms and symbols may conjure up unspoken historical associations that modify their surface meaning, our capacity to detect and interpret the semiotics of a discussion and the positional dynamics of its participants depends on familiarity at least with its background. Consider, for example, the discourse of federalism in the United States, which is encrusted with decades, if not centuries, of accumulated meaning. Finally, with respect to China, a neglect of history invites mechanistic applications of theory; for without a local, empirical dimension, there is no way to test the soundness and applicability of our theoretical tools and models, or to improve them and possibly turn them inward to reap fresh insights about our own experience.

The 1954 Constitution was a dismal failure as a body of binding rules; the twenty-one years it remained in force were the darkest and most despotic in the history of the People's Republic of China. Yet, it merits attention here because it redounds powerfully to the present in ways that belie its fate as enforceable law. Indeed, in myriad ways, the 1954 Constitution seeded China's present legal order. To begin with, it codified the institutional structure, offices, and powers of the nascent PRC state along lines that are instantly recognizable today. Its stipulations also established an acceptable framework in the PRC for speaking about democracy, rights, rule of law, political accountability, and social harmony—the very framework upon which current elaborations on those questions are based. More specifically still, the 1954 Constitution was the primary model upon which China's present Constitution, adopted in 1982, was founded. Many of the same people were involved in the drafting of both texts, and their kinship is evident. Even the present PRC doctrine of constitutional nonjusticiability originates in the 1954 Constitution (see SPC 1955; but see Wang Chenguang 1998, 18).

The 1954 Constitution bridged a century of intellectual trends and political movements, joining together several generations of jurists in an authentically Chinese discourse knit from disparate traditions. There was Shen Junru, the first president of the Supreme People's Court (SPC) of the PRC, who earned the highest *jinshi* degree in the Qing imperial examinations of 1904, studied law in Japan, was a Republican era leader of both the Shanghai Bar and the China Democratic League, and was among the "Seven Gentlemen" whose arrest by Chiang Kai-shek (Jiang Jieshi) helped to precipitate the 1936 Xi'an incident. There was Qian Duansheng, Harvard Ph.D., close friend of John Fairbank, and a leading Republican-era constitutional scholar who served as the first post-1949 dean of the Beijing University Department of Law and the founding president of what is now the China University of Politics and Law (*Zhongguo zhengfa daxue*). There was Wang Tieya, renowned scholar of international law, student of Harold Laski, a drafter of the 1990 Hong Kong Basic Law and, near the end of his life, a judge on the International Criminal Tribunal for the former Yugoslavia. And finally there were the political elites: among them, Mao Zedong, Deng Xiaoping, and Hu Yaobang, the death of whom in 1989 catalyzed the protests in Tiananmen Square.

The fascinating way in which the drafting of the 1954 Constitution brought such varied figures together illustrates a larger point—one that, although self-evident, is in practice rarely acknowledged in any meaningful detail with respect to China. That is, constitutions and constitutionalism, fundamentally expressions of ideas about the organization and functioning of a polity, respect no neat periodizations. They partake of the dynamics and often recurring political problematics in society, and are fundamentally processual in nature. Little wonder then that constitutional questions last openly debated during the 1950s drew heavily on Republican antecedents and now, fifty years later, suddenly seem salient again—questions about the rule of law, legal instrumentalism, political pluralism, restraints on autocracy, the proper balance between central and local power, the boundaries between state and party, judicial independence, and the scope and justiciability of rights, to name just a few; or that Chinese struggling to find local materials with which to build practicable, native solutions to such constitutional questions might find purchase in the pioneering work of their forebearers.

Rather than attempt a comprehensive history or textual analysis in the space available, this essay pursues the much more limited aim of demonstrating the authenticity of constitutional discourse in the early PRC and the links that bind it to China's past and future. Drawing on contemporary materials and recent Chinese scholarship, it traces the historical background, political considerations, and human inputs that underlay the formulation of the 1954 Constitution, especially the role key participants in its drafting played in nurturing and transmitting constitutionalism across the span of 20th century China. The reader should bear in mind that, as they traveled through time, constitutional norms, regardless of their points of origin, acquired new usages and meanings informed by local traditions, needs, and experiences; that is to say, they became and continue to be Chinese (Angle and Svensson 2001; Greiff 1985; Teng 2002; Fung 2006; Wong 1993). Finally, because some of the figures in the text may be unfamiliar, brief biographical notes on selected individuals appear in Appendix 4.1 for the reader's convenience. With that, let us begin.

I.

The PRC's 1954 Constitution emerged most directly out of two main texts: the 1936 Stalin Constitution of the USSR, which exemplified for the 1954 drafters distinctly "socialist" constitutional forms and doctrines, and the 1949 *Common Program of the Chinese People's Political Consultative Conference* ("Common Program"), which reflected Chinese political conditions and the Chinese Communist Party's (CCP's) own revolutionary experience on the eve of the party's ascension to power. Consistent with the pattern set by earlier Chinese constitutions, production of the 1954 text was dominated by a single political party its drafting was personally directed by Mao Zedong and the CCP's highest leaders, though some noncommunist figures also played pivotal roles in its formulation and subsequent exegeses. All of these figures were veterans of the constitutional controversies of the Republican era; and the intellectual and political currents of that time—complete with their contradictions, tensions, concerns, and priorities—inextricably shaped the enterprise.

Specifically, the Republican Constitution of 1947 schooled an entire generation in the language, rituals, syntactical conventions, normative choices, and political possibilities present in constitutionalism. It was based on the Constitutional Draft of May 5th (*Wuwu xiancao*). Originally drafted in 1936, that draft had been prepared primarily by the rival *Guomingdang* (KMT) and was strongly shaped by the political legacy of Sun Yat-sen. It sought to effectuate the transition of China from its then state of "political tutelage" (under the KMT) into a mature, democratic, constitutional order (see especially Chi'en 1961). However, for a variety of reasons, including the outbreak of war with Japan, the Constitutional Draft of May 5th was never ratified.

In the intervening years, much had changed in China. Throughout the war, Chiang's persistent efforts against the CCP aroused the patriotic indignation of many who felt that he was dissipating China's capacity to defend itself against Japan. These critics, many of them urban intellectuals who had absorbed ideas about human rights, democracy, and constitutional government from abroad, also increasingly chafed at the incompetence and growing dictatorial militarism of the KMT regime. Their views ran the ideological gamut from the Anglo-American-inspired liberalism of Chu Anping and Chen Qitian to the idiosyncratic, neo-Confucian socialism of Liang Shuming. Despite harassment, arrest, and even occasional assassination, many of them persisted in denouncing the repressive political climate, and appealed in fora such as the advisory People's Political Council and the popular and academic press for adoption of the stalled draft Constitution, rule of law, genuine multiparty democracy, and the expansion of civil and political rights (Jeans 1992; Fung 2000). Some of them remained lone voices, although others, hoping to articulate an alternative "Third Road" (*disan tiaolu*) and/or "Third Force" (*disan fangmian*) to the KMT-CCP binary, formed oppositional political groups, perhaps the most famous of which was the center-left China Democratic League whose founders included Luo Longji, Shen Junru, Shi Liang, and Zhang Bojun, all of whom played significant roles in the drafting of the 1954 Constitution and the development of the early PRC legal system.

After the victory against Japan, the Republican government convened the Conference for Political Dialogue (*Zhengzhi xieshang huiyi*) in 1946, in part to shore up its legitimacy and foster national unity. Given that the KMT and CCP had long professed commitments to constitutionalism and democracy and were now actively courting public opinion in their contest for political supremacy, this Conference, with the minor parties playing a mediating role, secured agreement on convening a National Assembly and a committee to formalize proposed revisions to the 1936 Constitutional Draft of May 5th in preparation for its adoption (see Mao 1991a; Mao 1991b). In the end, however, the outbreak of civil war further polarized politics, and the ensuing renunciation of participation by the CCP and its allies among the minor parties ensured that the resulting 1947 Constitution and its resulting government would be a mostly KMT affair. The CCP refused to recognize the legitimacy of the new Constitution and, in any case, within months, the document was itself eviscerated in April 1948 by the "Temporary Provisions Effective during the Period of Communist Rebellion (*Dongyuan kanluan shiqi linshi tiaokuan*)." These "Temporary Provisions" sharply curtailed many rights, granted the President of the Republic of China broad and unchecked "emergency" powers, and remained in effect in Taiwan until 1991.

The CCP's refusal to recognize the 1947 Constitution formalized in the legal realm what was already clear politically and militarily: that the CCP aspired not just to replace the KMT in power, but also to supersede the Republic itself. By attacking the Constitution, it essentially targeted the moral-juridical legitimacy (*fatong*) of the Republican State (see, for example, Mao 1991c). (See also chapter three in this volume, discussing the role that the notion of *fatong* has played in China's 20th century constitutional evolution.) In fact, the CCP went further still; it initially attacked the very concept of *fatong*, rooted as it was in traditional modes of political thought that the revolution aimed to supplant. In CCP usage, the term acquired a pejorative connotation, as in the common construction *wei fatong* (falsely legitimated legal authority)—contemporary CCP shorthand for the Republican legal and constitutional order (Long and Liu 2003). Although, in effect, the CCP proposed a *fatong* of its own, grounded in socialism and people's democracy, it spoke instead of building a *fazhi* (legal system), the term still most commonly in circulation, or, for a period in the 1950s, a *faquan*, which was a neologism inspired by the Russian term *pravo* that combined the dual meanings of "law" and "right" (also encapsulated in the West by the terms *jus*, *recht* and *droit*). Only recently, as the CCP has begun to reconcile itself with China's pre-1949 heritage, have PRC jurists again begun to speak approvingly of a present *fatong*.

Nevertheless, as explored earlier in this volume by Xiaohong Xiao-Planes in the context of China's Republican period constitutionalism, the concept of *fatong* remains useful because it captures the traditional and ethical dimensions of the party's quest for legitimacy and, in particular, its tacit acknowledgment that the allegiance of China's learned elite still conferred singular proof of its fitness to govern. Hence, the CCP assiduously courted intellectuals, appealing to their self-image as successors to China's imperial scholar-officials, their patriotism, and their frustrated ambitions to undertake national salvation. In savvy propaganda, it welcomed them back into politics with promises to revitalize China and to usher in an age of multiparty "New Democracy." To be sure, some of the leading advocates for constitutionalism and rule of law followed the KMT to Taiwan, but many, alienated by the experience of the preceding twenty years or held in suspicion by KMT authorities, did not (Hao 1997; Hao 2000; He 2004a; He 2004b). Through underground party cells and overt entreaties, the CCP enticed even high-ranking officials and judges of the former regime with no apparent leftist sympathies, such as the brilliant Yang Zhaolong, head of the Criminal Section of the Republican Ministry of Justice and protégé of Roscoe Pound, to stay and contribute to the building of "New China" (see Pang De [Roscoe Pound] 2005; see also Yang 2005).

In anticipation of total victory, the party convened a Preparatory Committee for a New Political Consultative Conference in June 1949. Patterned after the KMT's earlier Conference for Political Dialogue, it comprised of 134 members who had been selected from the CCP, affiliated mass organizations, minor parties, ethnic minority groups, various prominent citizens, and from among overseas Chinese (Qian 1949, 6–8). Its Standing Committee of twenty-one members was divided into working groups charged with articulating the political, legal, and institutional framework for the new regime. Zhou Enlai led the Drafting Group for what would become the "Common Program," the forerunner to the 1954 Constitution (discussed below). This Group also included numerous other top-level communist and noncommunist political figures, such as Luo Longji and Zhang Bojun. Meanwhile, Dong Biwu, the only top-level CCP leader to have had a legal education, led a group that included Luo Longji, Shen Junru, and Zhang Zhirang and that was charged with drafting what would become the "Organic Law of the Central People's Government." Together, these two complementary documents functioned as China's effective Constitution from 1949 to 1954, and they were adopted by the first plenary session of the newly constituted Chinese People's Political Consultative Conference (CPPCC) on September 29, 1949, two days before the founding of the People's Republic (Cai 2006, 11).

As the Chinese historiography puts it, the 1954 Constitution took the Common Program as its foundation and elaborated upon it (Du 2005). According to the Common Program, the PRC was to be a people's democratic dictatorship led by the working class, but uniting all democratic classes and nationalities (Article 1). It enumerated a familiar series of rights, including gender equality, and freedom of thought, speech, publication, assembly, association, correspondence, domicile, movement, religious belief, and of holding processions and demonstrations (Articles 5 and 6). With respect to economics, it took a measured, evolutionary tone, protecting private property and trade, though also announcing an intention to carry out land reform and to develop China from an agricultural economy to an industrial "state-capitalist" economy in which the state-owned sector would take the leading position, to be followed respectively by cooperatives and private (though not "bureaucratic") capital (Articles 27–38). Of particular interest for our purposes, the Common Program brought the CCP's earlier, polemical renunciation of the existing *fatong* to concrete fruition by summarily abrogating the entire "oppressive" Republican legal system, including all of its laws and regulations (Article 17). Under the Common Program, political power in the PRC was vested in the people, as exercised at various levels through their elected representatives in people's congresses and by government organs. The highest organ of state was to be the National People's Congress (NPC), and until such time as the National People's Congress could be constituted, the CPPCC would act in its stead and carry out its official functions (Articles 12–13).

Under rules adopted separately, the CPPCC fixed each of its sessions to a term of three years (Han 2004, 53). As the first session drew to a close in 1952, the PRC leadership faced a choice: maintain the status quo by convening a second session of the CPPCC, or supersede it by electing the National People's Congress described in the Common Program. According to recent Chinese scholarship, various opinions on this question were aired, but a consensus emerged to forego the NPC indefinitely. In October, 1952, Liu Shaoqi visited Moscow to attend the Soviet 19th Party Congress carrying a letter from Mao informing Stalin of this decision.

Stalin took a different view. Twice before, specifically in 1949, and again in 1950, he had personally urged Mao and Liu to promptly hold elections and adopt a Constitution. Mao had always demurred, noting that the Common Program was working well and could be amended as necessary; and that the momentous step of promulgating a Constitution should wait until the transition to socialism, when the fundamental change in class relations reflected in such a shift would necessitate it (Cai 2006, 26).

Now, with Liu once more before him, Stalin restated his position and buttressed it with several points. First, the government of the PRC had not been elected. This allowed its enemies to question its legitimacy, and to accuse it of being nothing more than a self-proclaimed, military dictatorship. Second, the country had no official Constitution. The Common Program offered little consolation here since its legitimacy and the legitimacy of all PRC laws were clouded by their origin in the equally unelected CPPCC. Third, the multiparty coalition government established by the Common Program presented a grave security risk to the CCP. Many members of the minor parties had close ties to foreign countries, especially the United States and United Kingdom, and could spy on behalf of those hostile powers. Stalin argued that the CCP could solve these problems and deny its enemies propaganda points simply by holding an election in 1954, which it would surely dominate thanks to its deep reservoir of popular support and experience with mass mobilization. Such an election would allow it to claim a genuine popular mandate and sideline its coalition partners, thereby legitimating at the ballot box a one-party state that could draft a Constitution and govern with an essentially free hand (Cai 2006, 27).

Stalin's logic evidently proved persuasive, and Mao abruptly reversed course. On December 24, 1952, the CPPCC, as one of the final acts of its first session, agreed to initiate work on an electoral law and a draft Constitution with an eye toward convening the NPC in 1953. In mid-January of that year the decision to begin work on the NPC and the new Constitution was discussed in a series of meetings chaired by Mao and Zhou Enlai and attended by leaders of the various minor parties present in the coalition government, members of the CPPCC, and of the Committee of the Central People's Government. In short order, each of these bodies established organizational entities through which the drafting process would ultimately flow. However, further progress toward a Constitution stalled for nearly one year due to a series of natural disasters, the Gao-Rao affair, and the need to hammer out an agreed ideological framework upon which constitutional drafting could proceed. The Electoral Law was completed on time and elections took place across China for people's congresses at the local, provincial, and finally national levels between 1953 and 1954.

On December 27, 1953, Mao traveled to Hangzhou for a respite from the day-to-day management of the nation. Accompanying him were two bookcases of reference materials and three of his personal secretaries: Chen Boda, Hu Qiaomu, and Tian Jiaying. Together, they constituted the Constitution Drafting Small Group ("Small Group"). By mid-January 1954, they had produced a detailed nine-month drafting plan for the Constitution, which Mao cabled back to Beijing together with the following instructions (Mao 1991d):

> [I]n order to facilitate discussion of this plan in the Politburo in mid-February, starting now I would like every Politburo member and Central

Committee member present in Beijing at once to find the time to read each of the following main reference documents:

1) the 1936 Stalin Constitution and Stalin's Report;
2) the 1918 Russian Soviet Federated Socialist Republic Constitution (read Volume One of the *Collected Materials on the Constitution and Electoral Law* edited by the Government Office);
3) the Romanian, Polish, East German, and Czechoslovakian Constitutions (read the *Collected Constitutions of the People's Democracies* published by the People's Press. The various national constitutions collected in this volume are similar with minor variations. Select the Romanian and Polish Constitutions as relatively new examples, select the German and Czechoslovakian Constitutions as relatively detailed examples with minor points of difference. If you have time, read the others);
4) the 1913 Tiantan Draft Constitution, the 1923 Cao Kun Constitution, the 1947 Chiang Kai-shek Constitution (read Volume Three of the *Collected Materials on the Constitution and Electoral Law*. These represent three models: a ministerial system, a federalist system, and a presidential dictatorship.);
5) the 1946 French Constitution (read Volume Four of the *Collected Materials on the Constitution and Electoral Law*. This represents a comparatively progressive and complete capitalist ministerial system constitution).

Please inform me of your opinions.

The drafting process hewed fairly closely to Mao's plans. His Small Group presented a preliminary draft to the Politburo for discussion on February 18, 1954. The Small Group made revisions to this draft on the basis of those discussions, and the Politburo then sent the now formalized draft to the thirty-three member Constitution Drafting Committee of the Central People's Government on March 23, 1954. From there, it was forwarded to the CPPCC and to leading cadres in provincial governments, major cities, higher military commands, and key mass organizations for comment (see *Xianfa cao'an* 1954). The Constitution Drafting Committee also met separately and jointly with seventeen CPPCC Constitution Discussion Small Groups to deliberate over the text during May and June of 1954. After further revisions, the Committee of the Central People's Government adopted the draft on June 14, 1954 and opened it up to nearly three months of public comment. Finally, on September 20, 1954 the NPC adopted the text as the official Constitution of the People's Republic of China (*Zhonghua renmin gongheguo xianfa*). Archival sources indicate that, up to the eve of adoption, every step of the process entailed multiple readings with continual feedback from diverse participants (but always overseen by the CCP), and ongoing revisions.

Advising the drafters as the text moved forward were a pair of philologists (Ye Shengyao and Lü Shuxiang) and a number of distinguished jurists (including Zhou Gengsheng, Qian Duansheng, Fei Qing, Lou Bangyan, and Wang Tieya).[1] None of these advisors were members of the CCP. The legal advisors in particular had had extremely distinguished academic careers, and were well traveled, multilingual, and conversant in the dominant trends in international legal scholarship at the time.

The record of the deliberations on the draft, once it moved out of the Politburo in March 1954, reveals lively debates over the text and countless proposals for substantive modification, many of which made their way into the final language. Importantly, the discussants made efforts to coordinate and harmonize their proposals with the parallel efforts then under way to draft related legislation, such as the Organic Law of the People's Courts, the Organic Law of the State Council, and the Criminal Procedure Law. Over several weeks in May 1954, for instance, members of the Constitution Drafting Committee met with the leaders of the CPPCC's Constitution Discussion Small Groups in joint conference. Among the party elite in attendance were Li Weihan, Tian Jiaying, and Hu Yaobang, and non-CCP luminaries such as Fei Xiaotong, Luo Longji, Shen Junru, Shi Liang, Song Qingling, Zhang Bojun, and Zhang Zhirang, virtually all of whom had actively campaigned for constitutionalism in Republican China. Every article of the draft received scrutiny (Han 2004, 131–175).

According to the archival record, in these meetings Li Weihan, Qian Duansheng, Zhang Zhirang, and Zhou Gengsheng debated the nature of the draft Constitution's grant of "judicial" authority to the courts. The original text read: "The judicial authority (*sifaquan*) of the PRC is exercised by the Supreme People's Court, local people's courts, and special people's courts established according to law." However, the conferees recommended replacing the term *sifa* with the more restrictive *shenpan* (trial or adjudication) to produce a revised text that read: "The Supreme People's Court of the PRC, local courts, and special courts created according to law exercise the official power of adjudication (*shenpan zhiquan*)." The final text of the Constitution reflects this narrower grant of authority (Article 73).

A related question arose with respect to the draft Constitution's guarantee of judicial independence. The original draft text read: "People's courts at every level exercise their *official powers* independently (*duli xingshi zhiquan*), subject only to the law." But on the grounds that the PRC was a unitary state and its courts, as institutions, were distinguished only by their delegated, functional specialization, and not by any unique, independent powers, it was suggested that this should be revised to read: "People's Courts at every level carry out *adjudication* independently (*duli jinxing shenpan*), subject only to the law." This suggestion too was taken to heart, as the final text of Article 78 of the 1954 Constitution reads: "People's Courts carry out adjudication independently, subject only to the law."

With respect to religion, the conferees also debated several questions. Under the draft Constitution, the state guaranteed to materially facilitate the enjoyment of an enumerated set of fundamental rights. Minister of Justice Shi Liang asked if freedom of religion should be included within this set and, if so, whether that would then commit the state to establish places of worship. Legal advisor Zhou Gengsheng suggested that religious freedom be excluded from the enumerated rights contained in that clause because it was best understood as a matter of individual conscience, unlike the freedom of the press or freedom of speech that, by contrast, were political in nature. Therefore, he argued, freedom of religion should be described separately, in its own article. Li Weihan and Luo Longji agreed, and the group's recommendation to the Constitution Drafting Committee reflected this position. Shao Lizi, a veteran of Sun Yat-sen's *Tongmenhui* and the pre-1925 *Guomindang*, then asked if the wording of this proposed article ensuring the right to enjoy "freedom of religious belief" should also stipulate the freedom to hold religious services. Tian Jiaying disagreed and carried the day, pointing out that if such a clause was added it would be necessary also to stipulate the freedom to proselytize *against* religion (Article 88). Notably, the current 1982 Constitution stipulates both the right of religious worship and freedom *from* religious belief (Article 36).

Similar exchanges occurred across the text, and in many cases the Constitution Drafting Committee heeded the resulting proposals for revision when it next took up the draft in late May 1954. Still more questions were raised at these meetings. Deng Xiaoping, Li Weihan, and Liu Shaoqi explored the connotations of the terms *renmin* (the people), *gongmin* (citizen), and *guomin* (nationals) as used in the draft. This discussion was particularly important because of the ideological significance attached to "the people" in Mao's 1949 essay "On the People's Democratic Dictatorship." Liu pointed out that although members of the landlord class did not fit Mao's definition of "the people," they were still citizens. Legal advisors Qian Duansheng, Fei Qing, Lou Bangyan, and Wang Tieya explained that on the basis of the opinions recently rendered by the CPPCC's Small Discussion Groups, "the people" was a social and political concept, whereas "citizen" was a legal concept, and that these two concepts had to be distinguished clearly and used appropriately in the Constitution (Han 2004, 233).

On the right of defendants to counsel, the Constitution Drafting Committee considered whether or not the proposed article should read "the accused has the right to obtain defense (*huode bianhu*)." Noting the dearth of lawyers in China, Chen Shutong did not feel comfortable stipulating a right that could not be exercised in practice and, as a result, favored the more general formulation "the accused has the right to defense (*bianhu quan*)," following Article 111 of the 1936 Stalin Constitution.[2] Deng Xiaoping, however, pointed out that defense counsel need not be a lawyer. Defendants could represent themselves, appoint a nonlawyer to represent them, or the court could appoint someone for them. The result was that "the accused has the right to obtain defense" survived (Article 76).

Even a proposed article declaring the President of the PRC, a job that was to be undoubtedly reserved for Mao, as "head of state" (*guojia de yuanshou*) fell prey to cold constitutional logic. On the recommendation of Qian Duansheng, Wang Tieya, and the other legal advisors, the Constitution Drafting Committee struck this language because it potentially conflicted with other provisions in the draft: namely, the article that defined the NPC as the highest organ of state (with the power to elect the President) and the article defining the State Council as highest administrative organ of the state.

In the end, the draft was adopted by the Committee of the Central People's Government on June 14, 1954, and, following Soviet precedent, it was opened up to three months of public comment from June 16 to September 11, 1954 (*Renmin ribao* 1954a; *Renmin ribao* 1954b). Draft Constitution Discussion Committees were formed in work units across the nation, and discussion leaders were quickly trained to direct them. The Beijing Broadcasting System aired daily explanatory discussions of the text. According to statistics reported at the time, over 1,180,420 questions, opinions, and suggested revisions were received during this period, and these were compiled, digested, categorized, and published into a sixteen-volume reference collection for the drafters entitled "Collected Opinions from the National Discussion (*Quanmin taolun yijian bianji*)." On September 8, 1954, Deng Xiaoping presided over a meeting of the Constitution Drafting Committee in Zhongnanhai to make revisions based on this public feedback. After a few minor additional changes, the NPC adopted the text on September 20, 1954, and soon enacted a host of related legislations filling out the institutional framework of the state. Originally envisioned as a transitional document that would be superseded upon the attainment of socialism, the 1954 Constitution remained officially in force for nearly twenty-one years: from September 20, 1954 to January 17, 1975.

II.

The legacy of the 1954 Constitution is manifold. It heralded a brief surge of legal construction across the PRC unmatched until the reforms of the 1980s. Then, as now, economic modernization drove much of that effort. China's march toward industrialism called for a professional corps of civil servants who were both "red and expert" to draft and apply the legislation and rules required to operate a planned, socialist economy. Law schools expanded to meet this need and to study the experience of China's allies, especially the Soviet Union. Translation and drafting projects brought Soviet and Eastern European jurisprudence to a Chinese audience, along with scores of foreign legal experts to advise on legislation, build organizational capacity, and teach law school classes. Chinese students went to Moscow for advanced legal training, and both countries exchanged fact-finding delegations to learn firsthand about the professionalized legislative organs, courts, prosecutors, legal aid offices, and public defenders contemplated under the new Constitution (Visiting Delegation 1955; Visiting Delegation 1956). These years also witnessed the founding of some of the PRC's most famous law journals, including the seminal *Faxue*, *Zhengfa Yanjiu* and *Renmin Sifa*, which explored in their pages the nature of the new rights, norms, and institutions codified by the Constitution. In these and other outlets, lawyers and academics, influenced by Soviet jurisprudence, translated the notions of rule of law and constitutionalism that had entered China during the early Republican period, and that have proved vital to its numerous constitutional movements ever since, into a discourse of "socialist legality" that promised many of the same deliverables. Examples include material produced by the China Society for Politics and Law (1954); the Ministry of Higher Education and the Ministry of Justice (1957); the Central Political-Legal Cadres School (1957); the Central Political-Legal Cadres School State Law Teaching and Research Office (1957); and the People's University Law Department (1964). The state, using its enormous capacity to mobilize people, then disseminated and popularized this language across the nation in an unprecedented constitutional education and propaganda campaign that forever altered the popular political vocabulary of China (see, for example, Xu 1955; Chen Hanbo 1954; *Xuexi xianfa ruogan wenti jieda* 1955; Jiang 1957; Liu 1954; Lou 1955; Xu 1954; Ma and Ji 1955; Wu Jialin 1954; Wu Defeng 1954; Meng 1955; Li 1956).

Tragically, the Hundred Flowers Campaign of 1956 and 1957, a period of several months during which the party encouraged citizens and especially intellectuals to openly air their opinions about its governance, marked the beginning of the end for this abortive embrace of socialist legality. Since at least 1911, Chinese law reform had foundered on instrumentalism, political expedience, and ambivalence toward due process and other restraints on absolute power. The rush of legal construction in the mid-1950s proved no different—it merely papered over the party's own particular divisions over those issues.

The Hundred Flowers Campaign unleashed a wave of pent-up criticism of the party from many levels and sectors of society. Inconveniently, some of those who had prominently participated in the drafting of the 1954 Constitution—Luo Longji, Qian Duansheng, Wang Tieya, and Zhang Bojun among them—now publicly invoked constitutional principles to take the CCP to task for regularly trampling multiparty democracy, human rights, and the rule of law. Even party stalwarts spoke out, such as senior Supreme

People's Court Justice Jia Qian, who championed judicial independence and condemned party interference in judicial cases. The party responded with the Anti-Rightist Movement of 1957, which struck the legal and intellectual communities especially hard. Lou Bangyan, Luo Longji, Qian Duansheng, Wang Tieya, Yang Zhaolong, Zhang Bojun, and countless others suffered persecution, tremendous personal loss, and in many cases arrest and long-term imprisonment. The Ministry of Justice was shuttered in 1959 and remained closed for the next twenty years. Having crushed or cowed his critics, Mao proudly declared: "The Civil Law, the Criminal Law, who remembers those texts? I participated in the drafting of the Constitution, but even I don't remember it" (Xiang 1991, 4; see also Wen 1994). Then, as proof of their contempt for legality, he and the party plunged the nation into a crescendo of increasingly arbitrary absolutism that ran from the Great Leap Forward, through the massive famine of 1960, and into the Cultural Revolution.

Following Mao's death and the fall of the Gang of Four, Deng Xiaoping steered China away from the radical leftism that had shaped its Constitutions of 1975 and 1978, and back to an evolutionary path that recalled the mid-1950s emphasis on socialist legality and modernization. Much as they had twenty-seven years before, the party's political elites again engaged constitutional specialists, Qian Duansheng among them, for guidance on how to cement this shift, restructure the state, and lay the foundations for stable economic growth. The resulting 1982 Constitution, which remains in effect today, anchored the post-Mao transformation of China and provided the space for jurists such as Chen Shouyi, Jiang Ping, Li Buyun, Qian Duansheng, Wang Tieya, and Zhang Sizhi—all of whom had either participated in the drafting of the 1954 Constitution or came of age in the brief flowering of law it spawned—to restore the legal and legislative machinery of the state; to reconstitute the legal profession and rebuild legal education; and, in time, to reopen suppressed debates on marketization, democracy, rule of law, and human rights.

The structural and normative connections between the 1954 and 1982 Constitutions are too numerous to list here, but two Chinese scholars sum up the relationship this way:

> The 1982 Constitution takes the 1954 Constitution as the basis of its formulation. From the basic structural framework established by the 1954 Constitution to the basic orientation, principles and system established by the 1954 Constitution, all were inherited and developed by the current Constitution. (Zhang and Ren 2005, 7)

Of course, this inheritance included the deep tensions that had been embedded in the 1954 Constitution as well, tensions that animate debates over legal and constitutional reform in China to this day.

All of which brings to mind the provocative identification by the historian Philip Kuhn (1999, 71) of a "persistent constitutional agenda" linking China's late imperial and modern eras. He posits that from the end of the Qianlong reign in 1790 to the present, there are three recurring problematics at the center of Chinese political life. These are (1) how to connect the enlargement of political participation in society to the absolute exercise of state power; (2) the perceived contradiction between the principle of political competition and the possibility of an impartial leadership acting in the public interest; and (3) the difficulty in reconciling the requirements of the centralized state and the interests of local communities.

One finds each of these problematics richly represented in the experience of the 1954 Constitution. Their manifestations in legal instrumentalism; in the uneasy coexistence of state and private capital; and in the tensions between party and state, political pluralism and dictatorship, and liberal conceptions of the rule of law versus more traditional Chinese articulations of the asymmetric ethical relationship between ruler and ruled, were far from novel. They are not unique to the CCP or to this particular moment in Chinese history. Analyses or prescriptions premised otherwise are bound to err. Even the language and symbols employed to negotiate these phenomena profoundly reference the past. Following Kuhn, we would do well to bear such insights in mind and, as we seek to understand the evolving normative content and boundaries of Chinese constitutionalism, pause periodically also to remember their *longue durée*. For herein lies the most significant contribution of the 1954 Constitution: political practice notwithstanding, it took a rich if problematic legacy—that of Republican constitutionalism—made it its own, and then bequeathed this endowment to later generations, secure in the knowledge that their inheritance is at once both socialist *and* Chinese.

Appendix 4.1. Biographical Notes

Dong Biwu (1886–1975) was one of the CCP's celebrated "four elders (*si lao*)." He studied law in Japan as a young man, represented the CCP in the Chinese delegation to the 1945 San Francisco Conference establishing the United Nations, and held a variety of high government posts including President of the Supreme People's Court (1954–1959) and Vice President of the PRC (1959–1975). He played an instrumental role in the legal construction initiatives of the early 1950s as Chair of the Political-Legal Committee of the Government Administration Council.

Luo Longji (1896–1965) studied at the University of Wisconsin, Madison, and the London School of Economics before obtaining a Ph.D. in Political Science from Columbia University. Prior to 1949, he taught politics and edited Tianjin's

Yishi bao, one of the four leading newspapers of the Republican period. After 1949, he served on the Government Administration Council and as Minister of Forestry (1949–1957). During the Hundred Flowers Campaign, with the support of many intellectuals, he joined Zhang Bojun in challenging the sham multiparty democracy erected by the CCP and the party's weak commitment to the Constitution and the rule of law. Accused of plotting an anti-party coup, they were named the top two national targets of the ensuing 1957 Anti-Rightist Movement.

Qian Duansheng (1900–1990) was one of the most acclaimed constitutional scholars in 20th century China. Like Luo Longji, he edited the leading Republican era newspaper, the Tianjin's *Yishi Bao*, in which he frequently also contributed on legal and political questions. He held a Ph.D. in Government from Harvard, and taught there during the 1948 academic year before being invited to serve the nascent People's Government, where he took up a position as Dean of Beijing University Law Faculty the following year. In 1952, he served as founding President of the Beijing Institute of Politics and Law (*Beijing zhengfa xueyuan*), which reorganized the law schools and political science departments formerly housed at Beijing, Qinghua, Yanjing, and Furen universities under one roof and later evolved into the current China University of Politics and Law (*Zhongguo zhengfa daxue*). Prior to 1954, he authored various studies of foreign legal and political systems, including: *The Government of France* (1934), *The Government of Germany* (1934), and *The New Soviet Constitution* (1937). With respect to China, he penned multiple articles on the Constitutional Draft of May 5th; a widely used English language introduction to *The Government and Politics of China* (1950); and cowrote the authoritative Republican era textbook *Comparative Constitutional Law* (1937). In the post-Mao era, he contributed to the drafting of the 1982 Constitution, received some of China's highest academic honors and accolades, and held numerous prestigious posts, including membership on the Standing Committee of the Sixth National People's Congress.

Shen Junru (1875–1963) obtained the highest *jinshi* degree in the imperial examination of 1904, studied law in Japan, served as Procurator-General of Sun Yat-sen's 1917 military government in Guangzhou, and was elected President of the Shanghai Bar Association in the early 1930s. Together with Zou Taofen, in 1936 he helped to organize the National Salvation Association to resist Japanese militarism, which later united with other organizations to form the oppositional China Democratic League. He was among the infamous "Seven Gentlemen" arrested and jailed for several months in 1936 and 1937 for mobilizing opposition to Chiang Kai-shek's strategy of fighting the CCP and Japanese simultaneously. The case became a *cause célèbre* in China and helped to turn many intellectuals against the KMT regime. Pressure on Chiang grew to the point that he was forced to release them "on bail" and abandon their trial. After the founding of the PRC, Shen served as the first President of the Supreme People's Court (1949–1954).

Shi Liang (1900–1985) graduated from the Shanghai Law School (*Fake Daxue*) and played a key role in the drafting and enforcement of the landmark 1950 Marriage Law while serving as PRC Minister of Justice (1949–1959). She too was a leading member of the Republican era Shanghai Bar, was among the founders of the oppositional China Democratic League, and was the only woman among the "Seven Gentlemen" jailed by Chiang Kai-shek's in 1937–1937.

Wang Tieya (1913–2003), a renowned scholar of international law, graduated from Qinghua University and pursued doctoral studies at the London School of Economics where he studied under Sir Hersch Lauterpacht and Harold Laski. He spent most of his career at Beijing University, where he chaired the Political Science Department (1946–1952), wrote the first PRC textbook on international law (1981), and pioneered the reestablishment of connections between Chinese legal education and the outside world. Among his other accomplishments, he served on the drafting committee for the Hong Kong Basic Law (1985–1990), became the first Chinese invited to lecture on international law at the Hague Academy (1990), and near the end of his life served as Judge on the International Criminal Tribunal for the former Yugoslavia.

Yang Zhaolong (1904–1979) obtained a doctorate in law from Harvard (1935) and did postdoctoral work at the University of Berlin. He wrote and taught prolifically on matters of civil, criminal, and constitutional law, and collaborated closely with his mentor and friend Roscoe Pound, who was a legal advisor to the Republican government. Yang served as a judge on the Provisional Court of the Shanghai International Settlement (1928); as a member of the Draft Constitution Committee of the Legislative Yuan (1938); and, after World War II, as chief of the Criminal Section of the Ministry of Justice and acting chief of the Supreme Court Procuratorial Office. Yang was proficient in eight languages and produced the authoritative Chinese translation of the Charter of the United Nations. In 1948, the Academy of International Law in The Hague named him one of the top fifty jurists in the world. After the founding of the PRC, he was briefly dean of his undergraduate alma mater, the most famous institution of legal education in Republican China, Dongwu (Soochow) Law School. In 1956 he was a founding editor of the seminal PRC legal journal *Faxue*. His deep associations with the KMT, and the critical spirit that estranged him from that party in the first place led to his increasing marginalization from the PRC legal community over the 1950s. After mounting sharp public criticism of the PRC legal system in 1957, he became a leading target of the Anti-Rightist Movement, and was arrested and imprisoned for twelve years. However, very recently his brilliant contributions to Chinese law and his lifelong advocacy of rule of law have been honored in a series of articles and conferences in the PRC.

Zhang Bojun (1895–1969) studied philosophy at the University of Berlin and briefly joined the CCP in 1922 under the influence of his close friend and roommate at the time, Zhu De. During the Republican era, he taught English literature, edited *China Forum (Zhonghua luntan)*, and organized a succession of political parties (including the China Democratic League) dedicated to expanding democracy in China and opposing one-party rule. After 1949, he served on the Government Administration Council and as Minister of Communications (1949–1957). During the Hundred Flowers Campaign, with the support of many intellectuals, he joined Luo Longji in challenging the sham of multiparty democracy erected by the CCP and the party's weak commitment to the Constitution and the rule of law. Accused of plotting an anti-party coup, they were named the top two national targets of the ensuing 1957 Anti-Rightist Movement. His daughter is the acclaimed and sometimes banned PRC writer Zhang Yihe.

Zhang Zhirang (1894–1978) studied law at Columbia University. During the Republican era he taught at Beijing University, was Dean of Fudan University Law School in Shanghai, edited the journal *Constitutionalism* (*Xianzheng*), and served as chief defense attorney for the "Seven Gentlemen" (see *Shen Junru* entry above). After 1949, he held a number of high level PRC governmental and legal posts, including Vice President of the Supreme People's Court (1954–1975). Interestingly, he held no party affiliation.

Zhou Gengsheng (1889–1971), sometimes referred to as the "Dean of Chinese Jurists," studied in Japan and England before obtaining a doctorate in law from the University of Paris. One of China's leading mid-century specialists in international law, he introduced the work of Hans Kelsen to China, taught at Beijing University, and was legal advisor to the Chinese delegation at the 1945 San Francisco Conference establishing the United Nations. After 1949, he was President of Wuhan University, an advisor to the Foreign Ministry, and Deputy Director of the NPC Bills Committee (*fa'an weiyuanhui*).

Notes

1. These advisors were constituted into two groups. The first group consisted of Zhou Gengsheng and Qian Duansheng, who were attached to the Politburo's Constitution Study Small Group made up of Chen Boda, Deng Xiaoping, Dong Biwu, Hu Qiaomu, Li Weihan, Peng Zhen, Tian Jiaying, and Zhang Jichun. The second group, known as the "Law Small Group (*falü xiaozu*)," consisted of Qian Duansheng, Fei Qing, Lou Bangyan, and Wang Tieya. It advised the Constitution Drafting Committee of the Central People's Government. Some of these experts also aided in the compilation and annotation of printed reference materials for the drafters (see *Renmin ribao tushu ziliao zu* 1954).
2. Article 111 of the 1936 Stalin Constitution reads in part: "the accused is guaranteed the right to be defended by Counsel."

CHAPTER FIVE

Middle Income Blues: The East Asian Model and Implications for Constitutional Development in China

RANDALL P. PEERENBOOM

1. Introduction

China has made remarkable progress in a short time in improving its constitutional and legal systems, having essentially begun from scratch in 1978 (see generally Peerenboom 2002; Chen 2004b). As rule of law and other good-governance indicators are highly correlated with wealth, China's performance is arguably best judged relative to other countries in its income class (see Peerenboom 2004a, 148). China performs better than the average country in its lower-middle income class on rule of law. China also does reasonably well on most other core indicators of good governance relative to its income level as listed in the World Bank Good Governance Indicators for 2007.[1] Few would have predicted twenty-five years ago that China's legal system would have achieved such impressive results in implementing rule of law and achieving good governance in such a short time given the size of the country and its starting conditions.

However, China's rapid progress in improving the legal system and good governance appears to be slowing, if not reversing. China's rule of law and good governance rankings were actually lower in 2007 than they were in 1998.[2] Although the lower rankings may be a statistical anomaly or due to subjective biases, there are signs of reform fatigue and diminishing returns.

China is not unusual in encountering obstacles and opposition to the implementation of rule of law and good governance at this stage of development.

Many countries are able to make some initial progress and show improvement in terms of economic growth, institutional development, and good governance given low starting points. However, once they reach the middle-income level, they get bogged down. Powerful interest groups capture the reform agenda, opposing further reforms or pushing for reforms that do not benefit the broad public (Daniels and Trebilcock 2004; Hellman, Jones, and Kaufmann 2000). Economic growth slows down or reverses and the reform momentum is dissipated. Some states settle into a stable but dysfunctional holding pattern. Others sink into chaos and become failed states.

II. Conflicts and Complexities: The Challenges for Further Constitutional Reforms

After thirty years, China is now embarking on a new—and critical—phase in the reform process. Different factors have contributed to the need for deeper reforms, and yet complicate the efforts to implement such reforms. First and foremost, economic reforms have led to a much more pluralistic society, with citizens deeply divided in their interests and normative views. The gap between rich and poor has increased dramatically since the beginning of reforms, with Gini coefficients rising from around .20 in the late 1970s to between .40 and .45 today (World Bank 2005, 72–74). The eastern region is much wealthier than the rest of the country, rural areas are poorer than cities, and laid-off workers from state-owned enterprises (SOEs) and collectives have created a pool of urban poor, most lacking education or skills to compete in the market.

Second, state organs have different interests, and support or oppose reforms based on whether they serve these interests. The procuracy, for example, seeks to expand the scope of individual case supervision and its ability to interpret laws, thus increasing its authority relative to the judiciary. The judiciary opposes such efforts, citing the need for greater independence. Government agencies are eager to expand their authority and resources by taking responsibility for issuing approvals and licensing, though less eager to provide user-friendly services to the public. Local governments seek to increase their authority relative to the central government by opposing provisions in national laws that limit their ability to establish licensing regimes or to issue regulations that restrict personal liberty.

Third, economic reforms and the government's efforts to promote rule of law and rights consciousness among citizens have led to greater demands on the constitutional and legal systems. All state actors—people's congresses, administrative agencies, the procuracy, the police—are under pressure to reform to meet the demands of a more diversified market economy and an increasingly pluralistic citizenry with greater consciousness of its rights.

People's congresses are supposed to provide a means for balancing different social interests. Administrative agencies are supposed to reduce red tape and facilitate business. The social welfare system is supposed to ensure retirees are able to collect their pensions and laid-off workers are provided unemployment benefits and job retraining. Administrative reconsideration bodies and the courts are supposed to provide mechanisms for resolving conflicts fairly and efficiently, thus providing the predictability and certainty necessary for businesses to operate and people to plan their affairs.

Meanwhile, the various mechanisms for reining in government officials are supposed to prevent abuse of power and curtail corruption and rent-seeking. In short, state organs are expected to handle matters in a just and efficient way, to be more transparent, and to allow more public input in the decision-making and supervision processes, while the establishment of rule of law is meant to provide a more rule-based method for handling society's increasing tensions, conflicts, and disputes. Unfortunately, the current mechanisms and institutions for handling these rising tensions are too weak and ineffective, as is typical in middle-income countries.

Fourth, and more specifically, the judiciary is being asked to handle many cases for which it lacks adequate competence, authority, and independence. As described by Keith Hand later in this volume controversial constitutional cases are increasingly being funneled into the courts. For example, the new propertied class is turning to the courts to protect their increasingly constitutionalized rights of property. Some social activists have sought to bring suits against local governments for forced abortions and other violations of family planning policies and regulations. A rising number of cases involve freedom of speech, assembly, and religion. In addition, many cases raise issues of social justice as those who have lost out in the course of economic reforms look to the courts for protection: what are people entitled to, given the government's goal of establishing a harmonious society (*hexie shehui*) or at least a *xiaokang* society?

Whether courts have the competence to decide such issues is a much-debated topic. There has been a global trend to funnel social and political conflicts into the courts. The results in some countries have been positive; in other cases, the result has been overreaching, ideologically driven decisions that have negative social, economic, and political consequences (see, for example, Bugaric 2001; Pangalangan 2004; Halmai and Scheppele 1997). In comparison to their counterparts in other systems, Chinese judges may be somewhat less well-positioned to handle these types of cases, due to their lower education levels and to the heavy emphasis Chinese law schools place on legal formalism.

Whether or not Chinese or other courts are competent to decide such matters, the Chinese judiciary in some cases lacks adequate authority and independence to handle these controversial issues, especially when they involve conflicts with other state organs. Funneling these divisive issues into a court system that lacks the independence and authority to handle them undermines the reputation both of the judiciary and China's constitutional system (see also the chapter by Eva Pils).

Fifth, and related, the police and procuracy are in a difficult position. They are under pressure to "strike hard" at crime and protect social order in light of the increase in crime that inevitably accompanies marketization, urbanization, and modernization. At the same time, human rights organizations, legal scholars, and the defense bar insist that criminal defendants be provided the rights granted to them under the People's Republic of China's (PRC's) laws and Constitution. As institutions, the police and procuracy have lost, and will inevitably continue to lose, power to the courts, defense bar, and the people's congresses as China moves toward a more law-based order. Accordingly, they will bear much of the blame for failing to curb crime and social unrest, while at the same time suffering diminished powers to fight the war. Not surprisingly, the police have opposed efforts to restrict the Ministry of Public Security's rule-making capacity, impose more procedural and substantive restraints on the exercise of police power, and subject police discretion to increased supervision.

Sixth, the government lacks the resources to prevent many of these conflicts from arising in the first place by throwing money at the problems. As a lower-middle income country, China is hard pressed to meet the demands for greater public spending on education, health care, social security, pollution control, and to address large regional differences in level of wealth and the rural-urban gap. It also lacks the resources to invest in institutions, including in higher salaries and better technology. Some courts in poorer western regions cannot even afford to pay judicial salaries, much less to purchase computers and other equipment. To be sure, as in any country there are debates about whether the government should be allocating so many resources to military spending, space missions, or high profile projects such as the Beijing Olympics Games of 2008, given the pressing needs in other areas.

III. The Need for Deeper Reforms

China's constitutional development is thus at a crossroads. As reforms have continued, tensions and conflicts in the political system between the ruling party and state organs, among state actors, between state and society, and among different interest groups in society have increased. At this stage, there are few if any Pareto-efficient reforms: few if any reforms that will benefit everyone. Even seemingly highly technical reforms will produce winners and losers, whether in terms of redistribution of economic resources, redistribution of power among state organs, or the strengthening of some legal actors such as the defense bar, at the expense of others, such as those members of the general public who assign a higher priority to social order.

Yet, deeper reforms are required, as is readily acknowledged by China itself (see, for example, State Council Information Office 2006). Such reforms are controversial, and hotly contested by state organs seeking to gain or avoid losing power vis-à-vis other state actors and by an increasingly diverse array of interest groups. Now that the "easy" reforms for which there has been a broad consensus have been completed, the politics of reform has become more pressing.

As the reform process in China has entered into this extremely complicated and intensely political phase, differences have surfaced over fundamental constitutional issues. For example, no longer is it sufficient to fall back on broad generalizations such as the purpose of rule of law is to facilitate economic development, provide a peaceful mechanism for resolving conflicts, promote social stability, and enhance the legitimacy of the government. Nor is it sufficient to claim that administrative law serves the dual purpose of enhancing—or balancing—government efficiency and the protection of rights; or that China needs a court system that is independent and strong, just and efficient, authoritative, and trusted by citizens. These generalizations are no doubt true; however, they do not resolve the practical issues at hand. It is not clear how these broad goals are to be translated into particular institutional reforms given the tensions between efficiency and justice; between a more independent and authoritative court and the desire of other institutions to increase their powers of supervision over the courts; and between a more open and transparent political system with a greater role for the public, and the efficiency of a reform process that has largely been led by a technocratic elite.

In these areas, further progress requires addressing such fundamental issues as: What is the role of the judiciary, administrative law regime, and the legal system more generally in a socialist rule of law state? What purposes are these institutions meant to serve? Should the reform process be top-down, bottom-up, or both? Should major decisions be made by elites, including government officials working in the system, judges, and academics? How much say should citizens have in the decision-making process?

The resolution of these issues inevitably implicates highly contentious social and political issues. However, unless these issues are addressed, legal reforms will remain at an impasse. The more limited technical reforms that have dominated the reform process to date, such as those contemplated in the Supreme People's Court's (SPC's) recently-promulgated second five-year agenda, will be at best only partially effective. The legal and constitutional systems will not be able to achieve the government's broad goals of facilitating economic development, social justice, and a harmonious society. Citizens will continue to be dissatisfied with these systems, and increasingly seek alternative means to pursue their interests and obtain justice.

To be effective, future reforms to the political-legal system must encompass at least six major aspects. First is *prevention*. Given the growing social tensions, the increasingly pluralism of society, and the inadequacy of current mechanisms for dealing with such tensions, there is a need to prevent disputes from arising in the first place. This entails addressing some of the major social cleavages, including the rural-urban income gap, the regional income gap, and the intra-urban gap between those who have benefited from economic reforms and those who have lost out.

Second, the current mechanisms for handling conflicts must be strengthened. This will require sorting out some of the institutional conflicts preventing a realignment of powers among state organs. It will require deciding what the policy should be on key issues and then translating those policies into clear laws and regulations that allow citizens to plan their lives accordingly and dispute resolution mechanisms to resolve disputes consistently based on clear legal authority. And it will require recognition of the right of citizens to challenge government acts and to lawyers to represent their clients in controversial economic, criminal, or political cases.

Third, there is a need for macro-level planning regarding which institutes will handle what type of disputes. Although there are perfectly good reasons to provide diverse mechanisms for handling certain conflicts, at present the many overlapping mechanisms for handling disputes often lead to inconsistencies, inefficiencies, and turf-battles among state organs. In the end, many disputes are funneled into the courts. Even then, the "final decisions" of the courts are subject to review and possibly reversal through various mechanisms for supervising individual cases.

Fourth, the increasing pluralism of society suggests that there will be a growing number of issues, including issues over which reasonable people may disagree. In many cases it will not be possible to reach a normative consensus. Existing procedural mechanisms must be strengthened and new ones developed to handle the increasingly diverse views in society. In particular, there needs to be greater political participation in decision-making processes, whether through public hearings, consultative committees, or participation in the nomination or elections of officials. Empirical studies have found that procedural justice, including a sense of having had a say in the outcome, is frequently more important to determining perceptions of legitimacy than the substantive outcome (Tyler 1990). This is borne out by village elections in China, which have demonstrated that people generally are more willing to compromise or accept decisions that are not in their interest when they believe they had a fair opportunity to be heard and participate in the decision-making process. This approach is also evident in the Law on Legislation, the drafting of an Administrative Procedural Law, the experiment with access to information acts, and the increasing reliance on social consultative committees.

Fifth, and as a corollary, greater attention must be paid to procedural justice in mechanisms for resolving disputes, whether through mediation, the letter and visits system, court cases, or other means. Participants must perceive the mechanisms to be fair, regardless of the outcome in the particular case. This will require addressing corruption, local protectionism, and other factors that unfairly influence the outcome. It will also increase trust in the courts.

Sixth, greater efforts should be made to explain the proper role *and the limits* of the legal system and rule of law. The legal system is not the proper forum for resolving all contentious issues. Moreover, the traditional emphasis on substantive justice—expressed through the rapidly growing reliance on letters and visits—leads to unrealistic expectations about the legal system. The unrealistic expectations undermine trust in the judiciary when the legal system then fails to resolve each and every social problem, to ensure social justice, or to provide a substantively just outcome in the eyes of all parties to a conflict.

IV. China and the "East Asian Model"

China is entering the stage of the reform process where many middle-income countries lose their way. Unfortunately, the law and development movement has yet to focus on the particular issues confronting middle-income countries and how to overcome them. One reason we know so little about how middle-income countries break into the exclusive club of wealthy states that enjoy rule of law is that few countries have succeeded in doing so in the past fifty years.

East Asian countries are the one notable regional exception. Singapore, Japan, Hong Kong, Taiwan, and South Korea all rank in the top quartile on the World Bank's rule of law index. Apart from North American and Western European countries, Australia, and Israel, the only other countries in the top quartile are Chile and French Guiana from Latin America, Slovenia from Eastern Europe, and a handful of small island states and oil-rich Arab countries.[3]

This seemingly random grouping of countries in the top quartile on the WB rule of law index have (at least) one thing in common: wealth. All of the countries in the top quartile of the rule of law index, including the East Asian countries, are high or upper-middle income countries. This is consistent with the general empirical evidence that rule of law and economic development are closely related ($r = .82$, $p < .01$), and tend to be mutually reinforcing (Chang and Calderon 2000; Rigobon and Rodrik 2005).

Why have East Asian countries been so successful? The "East Asian model" involves the sequencing of economic growth, legal reforms, democratization, and constitutionalism, with different rights being taken seriously at different times in the process (see generally Peerenboom 2007a). Admittedly, these common features are stated at a high level of abstraction. There is considerable diversity with respect to specific issues and policies. The essence of the East Asian approach has been pragmatism—which emphasizes flexibility and adaptation rather than dogmatic adherence to specific guidelines. That said, there are significant "family resemblances" (to borrow Wittengstein's phrase) or patterns among East Asian states. These similarities include:

- an emphasis on economic growth rather than civil and especially political rights during the initial stages of development, with a period of rapid economic growth occurring under authoritarian regimes;
- a pragmatic approach to economic organization, with governments following some aspects of the Washington Consensus (WC) and rejecting or modifying others; in particular, with governments adopting most of the basic macroeconomic principles of the WC for the domestic economy; rejecting or modifying the neoliberal aspects that would greatly reduce the role of the state through rapid privatization and deregulation, with the state also more active in reducing poverty and in ensuring minimal material standards to compete in a more competitive global economy; and modifying the prescribed relationship between the domestic and global economy by gradually exposing the domestic economy to international competition while offering some protection to key sectors and some support to infant industries;
- as the economy grows and wealth is generated, the government invests in human capital and in institutions, including reforms to establish a legal system that meets the basic Fullerian requirements of a procedural or thin rule of law; over time, as the legal system becomes more efficient, professionalized, and autonomous, it comes to play a greater role in the economy and society more generally; democratization, in the sense of freely contested multiple party elections for the highest level of office, is postponed until a relatively high level of wealth is attained; constitutionalism begins to emerge in the form of developing constitutional norms and the strengthening of institutions; social organizations start to emerge and "civil society" begins to develop, albeit often a civil society with a different nature and political orientation than in Western liberal democracies, and with organizations whose political agenda is subject

to limitations; citizens enjoy economic liberties, rising living standards for the vast majority, and some civil and political rights although with limitations especially on rights that involve political issues and affect the control of the regime; judicial independence remains limited, with the protection of the full range of human rights and in particular civil and political rights suffering accordingly;

- there is greater protection of civil and political rights after democratization, including rights that involve sensitive political issues, although with ongoing abuses of rights in some cases and with rights frequently given a communitarian or collectivist interpretation rather than a liberal interpretation.

This very roughly describes the developmental arc of several East Asian states, albeit with countries at various levels of economic wealth and legal system development, and with political regimes ranging from democracies to semi-democracies to socialist states. South Korea and Taiwan are previously authoritarian states that only democratized after achieving high levels of wealth and rule of law compliant legal systems. Japan fits this model as well, although it is a special case given its early rise economically and the post-War influence of the United States on legal and political institutions. Hong Kong, Singapore, and Malaysia are also wealthy, with legal systems that fair well in terms of rule of law, but which are either not democratic (Hong Kong) or are nonliberal democracies dominated by a single party (Singapore and Malaysia). Thailand, less wealthy than the others, has democratized, but has a weaker legal system and, under exiled Prime Minister Thaksin, adopted policies that emphasized growth and social order rather than civil and political liberties. China and Vietnam are at an earlier stage. They are lower-middle and low income countries respectively, effectively single party-states, that have legal systems that outperform the average in their income class but are weaker than the rest.

Admittedly, whether the postponement of democracy until higher levels of wealth and the limitations on civil and political rights are necessary for stability and development remains contested. Those who take civil and political rights and "democracy now, not later," as the metrics would deem the East Asian model a failure. While authoritarian regimes are likely to incur the wrath of Western critics, a modified East Asian Model along the lines now found in Singapore or Malaysia may be somewhat more palatable. To be sure, human rights activists, among others, would still denounce the government. However, the general public will generally be more supportive—as long as the government delivers the goods.

V. The Politics of Reform—Implications for Constitutional Development

In China, there currently appear to be three competing perspectives regarding how to respond to the increasing social tensions described above. One extreme emphasizes repression of dissent; tight limits on social organizations, and on the exercise of civil and political rights that threaten political stability; and an ideological battle to win the hearts and minds of Chinese citizens, and government officials and party members, by revamping socialism and explaining the reasonableness of the current reform agenda. Signs of this approach include the increased restrictions on the press and the Internet, the arrest of lawyers and human rights activists seeking to use law and legal channels to protect their and others' rights and interests, the closure or close monitoring of social organizations, the cancellation of academic conferences on constitutionalism and political reform, the denial of visas to foreign academics who published chapters in an edited volume that also contain chapters critical of government policies, and the extended old-school campaign to "maintain the vanguard" (*baoxian*) that has forced officials and academics to spend so much time in political meetings.

At the other end of the spectrum are those who argue that rapid and broad-ranging reforms are necessary to prevent the reform process from stalling, to meet rising demands from the citizenry, and to avoid a political crisis. Rather than tightening restrictions on civil society and the exercise of civil and political rights, they argue, the government should increasingly relax these restraints.

A third, moderate perspective acknowledges that China is confronting a variety of serious challenges to social stability, and hence that there is a need to maintain restrictions on civil and political rights. However, at the same time, it sees an equally pressing need to continue to invest in human capital, to strengthen institutions, to pay more attention to social justice and the wealth effects of economic reforms, and to gradually expand civil and political liberties—in short, to stick to the East Asian Model. Proponents of this perspective argue that although the tendency to repress dissent and limit the exercise of civil and political liberties is understandable given the rising number of demonstrations, repression alone does not provide a long term solution. It simply increases the likelihood that at some point there will be some sort of political crisis or that China will end up like other stable but dysfunctional middle-income countries.

Which perspective prevails will have significant implications for political reforms and constitutional development. At the moment, the moderate approach appears dominant. Despite a tightening in some areas, reforms have continued in other areas. The State Council's White Paper on *Building Political*

Democracy (2006) was generally reflective of this approach, with its invocation of classical ideas such as democratic centralism resting somewhat uncomfortably with calls for greater public participation and a description of new institutions such as social consultative committees (State Council Information Office 2006).

The moderate approach inevitably will give rise to criticisms from both those who think the government is being too repressive and moving too slowly on reforms, and from those who take the opposite view. Almost everyone will object to some specific policies. The Democracy White Paper's emphasis on democratic centralism seems to be an attempt to manage diverse views without allowing conflicting views or discontent to undermine political stability. Citizens are allowed to express their views on controversial issues, but only up to a point. Once the various viewpoints are debated, and the authorities reach a decision, public discussion is curtailed.

VI. Nascent Constitutionalism

At this stage, the main role of the Constitution has been to provide an initial distribution of power among state organs. The Constitution thus provides the background against which legal reforms, which frequently affect the balance of power among key state actors, are negotiated. For example, the Constitution now gives the procuracy the power to supervise the courts. In recent years, the procuracy has interpreted this power to mean that it has the authority to supervise final judicial decisions. As expected, the judiciary has argued that the procuracy's power of supervision should be eliminated, or at least limited to general oversight of the court or investigation of particular instances of judicial corruption. According to most judges, the procuracy should have no power to supervise individual cases. The courts have also come into conflict with the legislative branch over similar powers of individual case supervision, and with administrative agencies over the power of judicial review of agency decisions. For the time being, most of these conflicts can be solved only through party intervention.

But the Constitution has played a limited role in litigation to protect individual rights, for various reasons. Social activist litigation in China, as described in the chapters by Eva Pils and Keith Hand in this volume, although not unheard of, is rare because China is not a common law system where cases have precedential value; the legal profession does not enjoy a high social status; class action suits of the American variety are not possible under China's civil procedure rules; and the authorities are wary of the implications of individuals using the courts as a vehicle to pursue major social policy change. Moreover, except for one recent civil case involving the right to education, the Constitution has not been considered to be directly justiciable, and even that case did not involve enforcing the Constitution against the government (see generally Kui 2003). Courts in China also do not have the power to strike down abstract acts in administrative litigation suits; in other words, courts may not overturn a generally applicable administrative regulation or rule simply because it is inconsistent with the Constitution or higher level court decisions. Although the court may apply the higher level law in the particular case, the conflicting lower level regulation remains in place.

The absence of an effective constitutional court or review entity has further reduced the importance of the Constitution as a source of rights protection. In any case, we should not place too much faith in the establishment of a constitutional court as a way to ensure the protection of rights. Even if there were a constitutional court or similar entity, it is doubtful that the Constitution would be interpreted in a liberal way given China's prevailing statist, socialist conception of rule of law, existing threats to social order combined with support from both the ruling regime and broad public for stability, and the nonliberal orientation of the majority of Chinese citizens.

Nevertheless, the Constitution has served those inside and outside government as a source of empowerment for legal institutions and the development of constitutional norms (see generally Dowdle 2002; Cai 2005a). In particular, the Constitution has played a role in establishing broad grounds of legality, accountability, and justice that activists and reformers have then drawn on to push for reforms.

For example, as is described in more detail in Keith Hand's chapter, legal activists based their calls to eliminate Custody and Repatriation (*Shourong qiansong*) (where migrants without residence permits could be held in administrative detention centers or sent back to the countryside without a habeas corpus right to appear before a judge) in part on general constitutional principles of equality and freedom of movement. They also pointed out the faulty legal basis for this practice—national laws require that all limitations of personal freedom be based on national laws passed by the National People's Congress, whereas lower-level administrative regulations provided the only legal basis for Custody and Repatriation.

The Constitution has also provided the normative basis for a series of discrimination cases, as also detailed in Hand's chapter. In one case that combined the right to education with a discrimination claim, three students from Qingdao sued the Ministry of Education for its admissions policy that allowed Beijing residents to enter universities in Beijing with lower scores than applicants from outside Beijing (see, for example, Yu 2004b). In another case, a person infected with Hepatitis B recently prosecuted an administrative litigation suit when he was denied a post as a civil servant because of his disease. Other employment discrimination cases have challenged height, gender, and age restrictions.

Citizens have also drawn on constitutional principles to uphold privacy claims. In a much publicized case, a Shanxi couple was awarded damages after police stormed into their bedroom while they were watching an adult movie and a scuffle broke out between the husband and the police, resulting in injuries to the husband (Peerenboom 2005, 111).

To be sure, some of these cases have been dismissed on technical grounds, including lack of jurisdiction, failure to apply to the proper court, or the lack of authority to overturn the complained-of administrative act. Many of these features are typical of the more limited authority of courts in civil law systems to "make law." Nor do these cases involve political dissidents or the right to free speech. Parties who invoke the Constitution to criticize the government or call for greater democratization have been notably unsuccessful (see Peerenboom 2005, 104). Nevertheless, these cases signal an increasing willingness on the part of plaintiffs, lawyers, and courts to look to the Constitution as the basis for norms and principles that may be applied in particular cases to expand protection of the rights of individuals, subject to current doctrinal and jurisdictional limitations in the authorities of courts (see also the chapter by Stéphanie Balme in this volume).

More generally, the Constitution has provided the basis for a rule of law government in which state actors must act in accordance with law (*yifa zhiguo)* and be held accountable for their decisions. In 1999, the government signaled its commitment to a law-based order by amending the Constitution to expressly provide for a socialist *rule of law* state (*shehuizhuyi fazhi guojia*). The deepening of a constitutional norm of legality is particularly evident in administrative law, where the Administrative Litigation Law allows citizens to challenge government actions to ensure their legality (see generally Peerenboom 2002, 394).

The range of mechanisms to hold government officials and even judges accountable is increasing, although as noted their effectiveness remains limited. The Administrative Reconsideration Law allows citizens to challenge government actions on the grounds of both legality and the much wider standard of reasonableness. Administrative supervision committees play a role similar to ombudsmen in other countries. In many places, these committees have merged operationally with party disciplinary committees, enhancing their authority, even if complicating their status, in light of rule of law principles that draw a line between law and politics. People's congresses have increased legislative supervision of administrative agencies and, more controversially, of the courts. The auditing system in particular has been greatly strengthened under the leadership of Li Jianhua. Other agencies, such as the Environmental Bureau and Ministry of Labor and Social Security, have also been more aggressive in ensuring compliance with regulations.

Further, despite limitations, the media is also emerging as a significant source of government supervision, to the point where some commentators have questioned whether the Chinese media is itself becoming a "demagogue" (Liebman 2005). Citizens have effectively used the media and Internet to hold the government and even the judiciary accountable. The Sun Zhigang incident (see also Keith Hand, this volume), where a college student was beaten to death while in administrative detention, was widely discussed in the media and on the Internet. The public attention was instrumental in the government's decision to eliminate the Custody and Repatriation system, the particular form of administrative detention used to detain Sun. Similarly, the Internet was flooded with criticisms of the court for its handling of the "BMW case," where a woman from an allegedly influential family drove her car into a crowd, killing one and injuring twelve. She received a suspended sentence for negligence rather than a much harsher penalty, including perhaps the death penalty, for intentional murder (*China Daily* 2004a; Bodeen 2004). Many people believed she received lighter sentence because of her family connections. In the end, the government established a committee to review the case.

The letters and visits system provides citizens with still another channel to challenge government actions. Most governments, people's congresses, and courts have a letters and visits office to handle citizen complaints. Every year, millions of disgruntled citizens write letters to senior government leaders or make a pilgrimage to provincial capitals or Beijing to seek an audience with government officials. In 2002, the Supreme People's Court alone received 152,557 letters and visits, including 1,140 inquiries from deputies of people's congress. Some courts devote more personnel to responding to letters and petitions and supervision issues than to actually hearing civil cases (see generally Minzner 2006).

A related development has been the reliance on mass petitions signed by legal scholars, political scientists, well-known artists, and other elites in a number of high profile cases. As discussed above, legal scholars submitted a petition calling for the elimination of Custody and Repatriation after the death of Sun Zhigang. The arrests of Liu Di and Du Daobin for Internet postings also resulted in considerable public debate and in the submissions of petitions. Liu Di, better known by her Internet *nom de plume*, the Stainless Steel Rat, was a student at Beijing Normal University who was detained and then released months later for operating a popular Web site and posting satirical articles about the party, as well as articles calling for the release of Huang Qi (Pan 2003). Her detention led to two online petitions signed by over 3,000 people.

Similarly, Du Daobin was arrested for posting twenty-eight articles on the Internet, including some that opposed limitations on democracy and civil liberties in Hong Kong, and for receiving funding from foreign organizations

(*BBC News* 2004). His arrest led to a petition, signed by over one hundred writers, editors, lawyers, academics, economists, and activists, calling for a judicial interpretation to clarify the crime of subversion. After the petition, Du was convicted of inciting subversion, but his three-year sentence was commuted to four years of probation (Reporters without Borders 2004).

The use of petitions to protest government decisions and to challenge court decisions amounts to an indigenous form of litigation activism (Michelson 2006). It also seems to be an acceptable form of protest, although a recent campaign by conservative members of the party against public intellectuals, combined with the detention and harassment of several leading academic critics, suggests the limits of the government's toleration (Kahn 2004).

It is true that mass petitions that mobilize social opinion are not always successful. Although the public uproar in the BMW case led to a high level reinvestigation, the joint panel of provincial level judges and police ultimately found that the court's decision was proper. Nor are the Du and Liu cases likely to be a watershed for freedom of speech and expression on the Internet. Both were fairly marginal cases, in that Du apparently got into hot water mainly for advocating rapid democratization in Hong Kong, while Liu wrote satirical criticisms of the Chinese Communist Party (CCP) but did not expressly call for overthrow of the government or regime change.

In contrast, Luo Yongzhong was sentenced to three years' imprisonment for inciting subversion for publishing on the Internet articles calling for the overthrow of the party and criticizing the Three Represents and the government's handling of the Tiananmen incident in 1989. Similarly, He Depu was sentenced to eight years in prison for collaborating with the banned China Democracy Party, posting essays on the Internet to incite subversion, and signing an open letter calling for political reforms. According to his wife, He shouted calls for democracy and criticisms of the one-party system at his hearing. That Luo, He and others like them would benefit from petitions is unlikely (see also Peerenboom 2005, 104). The fact that legal scholars and others were willing to draft petitions for Liu and Du, but not Luo and He, suggests that they saw the former as more promising both legally and politically. Petitions are not likely to lead the authorities to change policies deemed particularly important for social stability or other objectives.

Nor are the legal and normative positions taken in petitions always so clear-cut. In the Liu Yong case, where a former delegate to the Shenyang People's Congress depicted as a Mafia boss was sentenced to death subject to a two-year suspension, public demand for the death penalty was one of the reasons the Supreme People's Court retried the case and executed Liu immediately (*Taipei Times* 2003). Indeed, there are many cases where courts have cited the anger of the public and the demand for vengeance to justify death sentences. Over 99 percent of Chinese favor the death penalty, with over 20 percent thinking there should be more executions (Hu 2002). Public opinion is therefore a double-edged sword. Although the public outcry over the Sun Zhigang incident may have played a role in ending Custody and Repatriation, the public's demand to strike hard at crime simultaneously supports a harsh penal system and administrative detentions. Many judges have complained that public uproar over cases interferes with judicial independence and undermines rule of law, either directly by putting pressure on judges to decide a certain way or indirectly by inducing political actors to take up the issue and interfere with the court.

Notwithstanding such concerns, on balance, the use of petitions and the mobilization of social pressure serve positive roles in providing a vehicle for members of society to supervise the judiciary and influence government policies.

The broad constitutional principles of rule of law and government accountability are also evident in the revamping of the administrative approval system. In recent years, the State Council has embarked on an ambitious program to overhaul the administrative review system for foreign and domestic companies alike in an effort to enhance efficiency and reduce corruption. The new approach confirms a change in policy toward greater deregulation and reliance on market forces. The Administrative Licensing Law provided further impetus for a more streamlined system and provided legal guidelines to ensure that local officials do not abuse their power. Although the reforms are in part a response to corruption and rent seeking, they also reflect the demands of citizens for fairer, more transparent, and efficient processes in setting up companies, creating mortgages, transferring technology, engaging in import and export, and conducting other commercial activities.

In addition, the China has also sought to achieve greater accountability and efficiency by enhancing transparency and increasing the channels for public participation in the rule-making, implementation, and supervision processes. The Law on Legislation opened the door for greater public participation in the lawmaking process by calling for hearings and providing for public commentary on important laws. The National People's Congress is now drafting an Administrative Procedure Law that would expand the use of hearings and create other channels and opportunities for citizen participation in administrative rule-making and decision-making processes. As is often the case, local governments have gone ahead and passed their own procedural laws. China's WTO accession agreement also requires that the public, including foreign companies, be given an opportunity to comment on commercial regulations before they become effective (but unfortunately not before they are promulgated). The National People's Congress (NPC) has also been soliciting public comment on major laws, in accordance with the Law on Legislation. In general, both the NPC and administrative agencies solicit opinions from academic experts during the law and rule-making processes.

There are currently a number of projects and experiments on public hearings—often organized in conjunction with foreign donors—that seek to address a range of issues, including when hearings should be held, how the public is to be notified, who should be able to attend and speak at such hearings (especially if the number of people wishing to attend the hearing and speak is very large), how the hearings should be conducted, and how the government should respond to inquiries or recommendations from the public.

In 2007, the State Council passed the Provisions of the People's Republic of China on the Disclosure of Government Information (*Zhengfu Xinxi Gongkai Tiaoli*). Prior to that, more than twenty provincial and municipal governments had already passed regulations on open government information (Horsley 2004). Most government agencies now also have Web sites where regulations and other information are available to the public.

The government has also experimented with citizens committees to supervise and advise on government work. Beginning in October 2003, the procuracy established citizen supervision committees in ten provinces. The system is now used by 86 percent of procuratorates nationwide. This type of committee is charged with conducting independent appraisals of cases that the procuracy placed on file for investigation, but later decided to withdraw from prosecution. According to the State Council's Building Political Democracy White Paper (2006, 110): "[Citizens supervision committees] can also participate, upon invitation, in other law-enforcement examination activities organized by the people's procuratorates regarding crimes committed by civil servants, and make suggestions and comments on violations of law and discipline discovered. By the end of 2004, a total of 18,962 people's supervisors had been selected, who had supervised the conclusion of 3,341 cases."

Citizens are also becoming more directly involved in the political process by standing for elections. Some individuals have been elected to people's congress without the backing of party or government sponsors or their employers. Sometimes, candidates run because they want to push for a particular cause, often related to protection of property interests, reflecting the emergence of a strong entrepreneurial middle class; others want to test the election laws and promote democratization.

Representatives elected to office have also begun to show a greater concern for the demands of their constituents, with some representatives emerging as populists and social activists. One congressperson received considerable attention when she took out an advertisement in the local paper soliciting opinions and requests from her constituents. Others have developed a name for themselves by advocating rule of law, democracy, and civil rights. Some are known for their advocacy on behalf of particular interest groups such as migrant workers, laid-off workers, or people whose houses have been taken by the government as part of the process of urbanization and development of city centers or industrialization in the countryside. Many of the populist legislators receive assistance from NGOs and lawyers.

More generally, the party has increased intra-party democracy and sought to enhance the quality of government officials and civil servants by requiring officials to stand for election. Some localities have experimented with election of key party members, including the party secretary. Similarly, some locales have experimented with direct elections at the town level, even though direct elections currently are as a formal matter limited to villages.

Judicial reforms have also continued, with reforms falling into three broad categories: efforts to make the adjudicative process more efficient and just; reforms aimed at enhancing the quality and professionalism of judges; and attempts to increase the authority and independence of the courts (Peerenboom 2007b).

Taken together, the various changes demonstrate an ongoing transformation in China's constitutional culture. In 2004, the Constitution was amended to provide expressly that "the state respects and safeguards human rights," indicating perhaps a greater commitment to effective realization of the rights provided by the Constitution. In any event, citizens and reform-minded insiders alike are taking advantage of the political space created by the government's invocation of rule of law, constitutionalism, and human rights to force the government to make good on these lofty goals. Although the legitimacy of the government is primarily dependent on continued economic growth, complemented by appeals to a rising nationalism, it also depends, to some extent, on the government's ability to carry through on its promises to establish rule of law, abide by the Constitution, and enhance citizen participation in government.

To be sure, the government has moved cautiously on political reforms, as other successful Asian states did. Clearly, the government does not want to lose control. The direct election of representatives to people's congresses is still limited to the lowest level of rural governance. The courts lack adequate authority and independence to handle politically sensitive cases fairly. Despite improvements, many governmental institutions remain weak.

At present, however, the biggest limit on constitutionalism and constitutional reform is arguably that there are wide disputes at a fundamental normative level over the type of society China should be. The differences between statist socialists, soft authoritarians, communitarians, and liberals preclude the type of supermajorities needed to legitimate major constitutional reforms. Although the Constitution has been amended three times since 1982, these changes have either been minor or served to provide a greater role to market forces and the private economy—an area where there is already a sufficiently dominant view among the various groups to legitimize these changes. To the extent that a dominant view exists on civil and political issues, the resulting amendments would probably produce a nonliberal state rather than a liberal democracy, at least if the process is determined by majoritarian preferences rather than a narrow group of elites.

VII. Conclusion

Efforts to establish a socialist rule of law state have resulted in major changes affecting virtually all aspects of the legal-political system in China. Reforms have led to significant changes to party-state relations and state-society; to major governing institutions including the people's congresses, the procuracy, the police and the legal profession; as well as to the administrative law regime and the judiciary.

Nevertheless, the success of other Asian countries that followed the East Asian Model, and the failure of many other countries elsewhere in the world to maintain the reform momentum, suggest that unless Chinese leaders are able to continue to marshal the political will needed to push ahead with bold and progressive reforms, the reform progress will stall. China may very well become another one of the many middle-income countries with a dysfunctional legal and political system, or perhaps even slide backward and become one of the all too familiar examples of failed state that once showed great promise.

However, if it continues to push ahead with reforms, to invest in human capital, to strengthen institutions, and to attend to the negative effects of economic reforms on those left behind by the market, it may manage to achieve results similar to those achieved by other East Asian countries. If so, constitutional development will continue, as evident in the deepening of constitutional norms, the strengthening of institutions, and the slow but steady expansion of civil and political liberties, albeit still subject to limitations when the exercise of such rights threatens social or political stability. Democratization in the sense of national elections would be postponed until a higher level of development, although when that would occur is hard to predict, and it is not inevitable. In any event, a democratic China need not be a liberal democratic China. Constitutionalism can take many forms, including ones with greater toleration for nonliberal, communitarian, or collectivist approaches to rights issues.

Notes

1. Data comes from the World Bank website. See Governance Matters 2008: Worldwide Governance Indicators, 1996–2007. http://info.worldbank.org/governance/wgi/sc_chart.asp.
2. Data comes from the World Bank website. See Governance Matters 2008: Worldwide Governance Indicators, 1996–2007. http://info.worldbank.org/governance/wgi/sc_chart.asp.
3. These include Antigua and Barbuda, Barbados, the Bahamas, Bermuda, the Cayman Islands, Malta, Martinique, Mauritius, Puerto Rico, and Samoa, in addition to Oman, Qatar, Bahrain, Kuwait, and the United Arab Emirates. Several of the island states rely heavily on tourism and the provision of financial services to companies looking for tax havens for economic development. Most have populations between 50,000 and 500,000.

PART 2

The Development of a Political Jurisprudence

CHAPTER SIX

China's Constitutional Research and Teaching: A State of the Art

TONG ZHIWEI

I. Introduction

A country's level of legal education and research usually correlates with the development of its legal system. The modernization of academic constitutional research in China during the post-Mao era confirms this. Since the late 1970s, China has experienced some of the fastest economic growth and social progress in its history. This has worked to improve and develop its legal system. Since the onset of Deng Xiaoping's open-door policy, investigations into constitutional issues in China have become pervasive, reflecting the new demands of this economic revolution. Yet, the understanding of constitutional law in China has been and largely still is constrained by modern China's post-1949 experiences. In this chapter, I explore the development of constitutional law in China from the late 1970s, when Deng first initiated his open-door policy, to the present.

II. Constitutional Education and Research in China Since the Late 1970s

As it is well known in China, the modern notion of constitutionalism was born in the West. Constitutional law gradually developed into an independent jurisprudence with the evolution of modern Western constitutions. Before the Opium War, some Western missionaries, such as K. F. A. Gutzlaff, sought to introduce Western constitutional philosophy to China. After the Opium War, several prominent Chinese scholars and political actors, such as Lin Zexu and Wei Yuan, also began promoting Western constitutional systems and concepts, thus establishing the foundations for China's modern constitutionalism (He 2004c). Nevertheless, because the legal doctrines of constitutional government remained underdeveloped during the late Qing dynasty and Republican era, constitutional consciousness in China remained weak.

Before 1949, courses in constitutional law, when taught at all, were part of the political science curriculum rather than the law curriculum. Examining primarily the constitutions and constitutional systems of European countries and the United States, those courses tended to ignore China's own constitutional reality. The main efforts of constitutional scholars during this period focused on translating works by foreign scholars, explaining Sun Yat-sen's "five powers" constitutional system and comparing China's domestic constitutional practices with those of the West. China's various pre-1949 constitutions and draft constitutions were discussed primarily to highlight and criticize China's lack of constitutional development.

During the early years of the People's Republic of China, constitutional education and research operated in accordance with the Soviet model. The lack of adaptation to the Chinese context, either in terms of content or terminology, is striking (Zhang Qingfu 1989, 79). The Soviet jurist Andrey Vyshinsky, in particular, had a great influence both on China's Constitution and on its constitutional thinking. His formal definition of law, for example, shaped the legal culture of an entire generation in China. In 1938, Vyshinsky had argued that: "laws are comprehensive rules of conduct, enacted by the state or an authorized regime, reflecting the will of the ruling class, and carried out by the state's coercive power in order to protect, consolidate, and develop the social relationships and social order that are suitable and favorable to the ruling class." Vyshinsky's particular notion of an "iron law" had been abandoned by the Soviet Union in the late 1950s, however, it remained a dominant understanding in China for decades. Today, Vyshinsky's definition of law continues to cast a shadow over the understanding and teaching of constitutional law in China (Dong 1989).

Modern China adopted its first Constitution in 1954 (see also Tiffert, this volume). However, that constitution's impact on actual political practice in China was slight. By 1966, it was considered *effectively* null and void, and courses in constitutional law disappeared from the Chinese curriculum.

Constitutional education and research in China was only restored, and then very timidly, in 1977–1978. In the late 1970s, local universities again began to enroll students for undergraduate and graduate law programs. Courses in constitutional law were resurrected as part of the legal curriculum. From 1977, law departments (*falu xi*) and law faculties were reopened or otherwise established at Beijing University (*Beida*), Jilin University, Hubei Financial

College, and in other places. In all, these programs enrolled 223 undergraduate students for that year. In 1978, a number of other universities, including People's University (*Renda*) and the Southwest University of Politics and Law, also reopened or established law departments, and the total number of law students rose to 729. Additional law schools were later opened at places such as the Northwest University of Politics and Law, the East China University of Politics and Law, and the Zhongnan University of Politics and Law. By 1980, fourteen universities had opened legal studies programs, enrolling 2,828 students (Zhou 1990, 157).

With this, a new chapter was opened in Chinese constitutional law education. The academic environment in general, and the legal academic environment in particular, became increasingly less hostile to constitutional legal studies. Interactions among legal experts about constitutional law increased. In 1985, the establishment of the China Law Society, a national academic body with numerous local branches at the provincial level, further helped catalyze these interactions. All in all, over the last thirty years, constitutional education in China has developed rapidly in many different areas. Yet, major crucial problems remain.

III. Constitutional Education in China Today

Today, Chinese constitutional law is one of the fourteen core courses of the undergraduate legal curriculum, as established by the Ministry of Education. Yet, mainland universities only provide one semester of constitutional law and the number of class periods scheduled per week is minimal compared to other courses.

Originally, the foundational course in constitutional law in the undergraduate legal curriculum was divided into two parts. The first part consisted of an analysis of Western constitutions. The second part consisted of an analysis of China's Constitution and constitutional history. Later, such courses focused increasingly on China's Constitution, often neglecting the comparative perspective. Today, undergraduate constitutional law studies include the following topics: introduction to the basic principles of the Constitution; the development of the Constitution and the character of the state; the political organization of the state; the structure of the state; and the basic rights and obligations of the citizens.

In the main, China's constitutional legal education focuses on the fundamental principles of the political and legal systems, and not so much on civil rights (see below). This latter part usually accounts for only 10 percent of our textbook space and teaching syllabus. The main reasons for this is found in the Soviet heritage that continues to inform the discipline and in the fact that

China does not have a system of judicial review per se, and thus does not yet have a significant legal corpus of constitutional law cases. With regards to the teaching of civil rights, this latter situation leads to an embarrassing result. Because one cannot find a significant civil rights jurisprudence in Chinese law, this key aspect of the constitutional law syllabus derives almost exclusively from foreign cases. These cases are drawn primarily from American constitutional jurisprudence. However, some are also drawn from the constitutional jurisprudence of, in decreasing order of relevance, Germany, France, and Japan.

Unfortunately, Chinese students are often not keen to study constitutional law. Consistent with current teaching methods in China, teacher-student interactions are still primarily hierarchical and traditional, and thus do not encourage much openness of thought on the part of the students. Students tend to equate constitutional studies with political indoctrination, or otherwise regard constitutional principles as a set of theoretical dogmas disconnected from the real life. All this makes it difficult to instill something resembling a "constitutional consciousness" in the students.

Over the past thirty years, many teaching materials on China's constitutional law have been published. From 1980 to 1999, seventy books or major constitutional education materials were published in China. However, the quality of constitutional law course books in China is often not satisfactory. Law faculties in China like to publish their own constitutional law textbooks, edited by their own faculty, in order to enhance their academic reputation. But these textbooks are sometimes of low academic quality, and occasionally contain serious errors. This also results in a lot of redundancy and waste in the effort and resources devoted to the discipline, and it prevents the development of a more concentrated and authoritative corpus of teaching materials, one that could be more easily updated and could facilitate the pedagogical and conceptual development of the discipline.

Beginning in 1978, Beijing University, People's University, the Law Institute of the Chinese Academy of Social Sciences, and Jilin University also began recruiting students to graduate programs in the field of constitutional law. The enrollment of constitutional law graduate students has since expanded, from around a dozen per year in the early 1980s to almost 300 per year in 2000. Beginning in 1984, the Law Institute of the Chinese Academy of Social Sciences also opened a doctoral program in constitutional law. The other leading law faculties mentioned above quickly followed suit. By 2001, seven educational or research institutions in China had established Ph.D. programs in constitutional law. This number grew to sixteen in 2006.

Today, graduate programs in constitutional law have become increasingly standardized throughout the country. Common examples of courses offered in these programs include "The Chinese Constitution," "Constitutional

Problems," "Foreign Constitutions" and, less frequently, "Comparative Constitutional Law." In addition, these programs will often offer additional thematic seminars on topics such as the people's congress system, constitutional supervision, the party system, local legislation, and the protection of basic civil rights. In Ph.D. programs, the courses are generally more theoretical and the teaching method focuses more on self-learning. Students in these programs will also usually take two or three courses in subjects outside the program's core public law curriculum. Ph.D. dissertations in constitutional law have also made significant progress since the mid-1990s, but their overall level remains below what might be hoped for some thirty years after the rebirth of constitutional legal studies in China.

IV. Constitutional Consciousness and Education

A country's Constitution is closely related to its people's daily life. Therefore, the Constitution should contribute to the social development of the country and enjoy stability and legitimacy. Since the end of the Cultural Revolution, the history of constitutional law in China is a history of scholars who have tried to positively influence China's social development by means of constitutionalism.

The history of constitutional development in post-1978 China can be divided into three phases. The first phase, what we might call the "early phase," ran from 1978 to 1982. The main focus of this phase was to identify the new tasks of the state, which was then moving away from an ideology of class struggle and planned economic activity. Since the founding of New China, its Constitutions have always had a strong ideological flavor, one especially associated with the extreme left. Therefore, the major accomplishment of this early phase was to liberate constitutional studies from these rigidifying influences.

The second phase ran from 1982 to approximately 2000. During this period, constitutional scholars devoted themselves to refining and implementing the new institutional framework established by the 1982 Constitution. They focused primarily on articulating the basic tenets of the party-state system, and on proposing draft amendments and supplemental provisions to the Constitution. This was followed by a third phase, from 2000 to the present, which is characterized by constitutional scholars devoting increasing attention to issues surrounding the constitutional provision and protection of fundamental civil and political rights. Since the 1970s, comparatively, little published research has been devoted to fundamental, civil, and human rights. Between 1982 and 1999, articles on constitutional law published nationwide totaled around 2,900, of which only 350 were related to civil and human rights issues. Only 12 percent (32 of 226) of the academic monographs published during this period in the area of constitutional law focused on civil and human rights, and most of these were released after 1990 (Han and Hu 2004, 957–959).

Constitutional pedagogy in China continues to be underdeveloped. Since the 1970s, constitutional research has traditionally aimed primarily at explaining the text of the Constitution and making doctrinal interpolations from these texts. Very few academic investigations engaged in argumentation or focused on the actual experience of the Constitution. The situation was certainly the product in part of the fact that constitutional practice in China at the time was underdeveloped. However, it also reflects the fact that constitutional thinking in China is still in its infancy. Even today, China still does not have an academic journal devoted to constitutional law: articles on constitutional law are published in general legal journal.

However, since 2000 a significant number of more mature studies in the field of constitutional law have been published. Notable among these include *Constitutional Collections*, edited by Zhang Qingfu (2001); *Public Law*, edited by Xia Yong (1999); *The Study of Public Law*, edited by Hu Jianmiao (2002); *Comments on Constitutional Government and the Rule of Administrative Law*, edited by the People's University Constitutional and Administrative Law Research Center (2004–2007); and *Report of the Development of Constitutional and Administrative Law in China* (published by People's University Press in 2005). These publications have played an important role in the development of constitutional studies in China, and have greatly promoted students' understandings of the usefulness of the Constitution.

Since the end of the 1970s, constitutional scholars in China have contributed not only to the development of China's legal pedagogy, but also to the actual social and legal development of the constitutional system. At least ten constitutional law scholars worked for the Secretariat of the Constitutional Revision Committee as members or consultants during the drafting of the 1982 Constitution. During the drafting of subsequent amendments to that Constitution, the Chinese government has paid ever greater attention to the opinions of constitutional scholars, providing an increasing diversity of channels for them to express their views. In the mid-1980s, several prominent constitutional law scholars were appointed by the Standing Committee of the National People's Congress to the Basic Law Drafting Committee for the Hong Kong Special Administrative Region and the Macao Special Administrative Region. Numerous constitutional scholars have also participated in the drafting of constitutionally relevant laws such as the Electoral Law, the Organic Law of Local Government, and the Law on Legislation. Between August 2003 and December 2005, among the ten legal experts appointed as assistant directors or deputy directors of the then seven (now nine) special standing committees of the National People's Congress (NPC), two were scholars of constitutional law.

V. Some Continuing Problems

Notwithstanding its rapid development, constitutional practice in China does not yet provide the full resources necessary for advanced constitutional study. For example, although China's Constitution articulates the foundations of a kind of constitutional review system (Li 2002), there are no actual cases of constitutional review. Even today, we do not have a constitutional jurisprudence in the real sense of the term. This may help explain a particular shortcoming in our Constitutional law scholarship. Constitutional training focuses almost exclusively on abstract and theoretical teachings. It does not use practice to inform theory. For its part, constitutional scholarship generally is forced to operate along one of the following routes: either to ignore altogether China's most pressing constitutional issues; to explore these issues through the use of abstract doctrine and hypothetical cases; or to look at similar issues as they arise in foreign countries. Such choices limit the scholar's potential impact on China's constitutional development. Compared to other areas of law, the content of China's constitutional education therefore is abstract and empty.

Compared with the past, the status of constitutional study in China's legal curriculum has not improved significantly. As mentioned already, constitutional law is one of the fourteen compulsory courses in the undergraduates' legal curriculum. It should therefore hold the same status as criminal law, civil law, or economic law. However, in practice, constitutional law does not occupy a significant portion of the undergraduate law curriculum in many Chinese law faculties. The civil law curriculum, for example, generally includes numerous courses, each of which runs for a semester. Cumulatively, such courses account for some 288 course periods in the undergraduate law curriculum. By contrast, the constitutional law curriculum generally only accounts for fifty-two course periods. Constitutional law makes even less a contribution to the graduate legal curriculum. According to the "Guidelines for Professional Training Programs Leading to a Master of Law Degree" promulgated by the Ministry of Education, courses in constitutional law need only be "elective and recommended" for such programs.

In line with the above, constitutional knowledge among many legal scholars remains weak. A number of legal experts and jurists, including a few constitutional scholars, lack knowledge and consciousness of the Constitution. The recent discussions over the draft Property Law (*Zhonghua Renmin Gongheguo Wuquan Fa*) (2007) reflect the practical inadequacies of China's constitutional education over the past thirty years.

Within academic circles, many people's understanding of constitutionalism and constitutional law in China is detached from China's reality. Although continuous efforts have been made to advance our discipline, we must acknowledge that although much of constitutional theorizing in China can be highly sophisticated, little actually reflects and influences the realities of

Chinese society. Western constitutional theories have become the dominant references for most constitutional scholarship in China. Unwilling to face the reality of China's present constitutional system, Chinese scholars of constitutional law turn a blind eye to China's current constitutional framework.

For example, a number of Chinese scholars working in the realm of constitutional jurisprudence, when they lecture on the protection of citizen's rights, tend to assume that the courts enjoy or should enjoy the same role in China's constitutional system as their American counterparts do in the American constitutional system. More particularly, they assume that the development of a constitutional jurisprudence should extend primarily from judicial interpretations of the Constitution by the Supreme People's Court (SPC), and that China must therefore build a judicial framework in which the Supreme People's Court is given the principal right to interpret the Constitution. Relatedly, they also advance cause-lawyering as a primary means for the social development of constitutional rights. Their idea is to use the courts in China to complete a "revolution" of state power, by changing the judicial system and placing these courts at the core of a particular program of political activism.

I consider this idea unreasonable, both detached from China's basic conditions, and contrary to basic legal principles. It may be reasonable and even legitimate for judges in China to advocate for such power. However, it is less understandable why constitutional scholars would advance such positions. After all, this kind of judicial interpretation and application of the Constitution would provoke a wide range of important issues, as it is closely related to the state's political organization. It would affect the status and authority of the NPC and its Standing Committee, as well as the relationship between the NPC and other central organs, including the SPC. Such a development would require a complete reorganization of our whole political system.

By ignoring this, the Chinese constitutional scholars who advocate judicial interpretation and application of the Constitution ignore the actual historical and cultural processes of constitutional development. The way they comprehend China's constitutional problems is shaped by their understanding of an idealized constitutional system, such as that of the United States or that of Germany. They do not question whether or how such systems are relevant to China's situation. They simply import alien institutions into China's constitutional system in an ahistorical way.

Indeed, efforts to try to transplant the American model of judicial review into China's constitutional system have sometimes had adverse effects in practice. Many legal experts now think that whenever a basic civil right is violated in China, the first if not the only response should be a lawsuit. In fact, the primary means of applying the Constitution in civil law systems is through legislation. Courts in such systems usually apply the Constitution only indirectly, via reference to such enabling legislation. Only in common law countries and

Japan do the regular courts have the authority to *directly* interpret and apply the Constitution to individual cases. This is why in China, efforts to resolve constitutional controversies through courts, which may have played some minor role in stimulating people's constitutional consciousness, have often failed (but see the chapter by Michael Dowdle in this volume).

The only way to effectively implement and develop China's emerging constitutional culture is to take account of China's unique legal culture and legal traditions as they are reflected in the provisions of the Constitution. In our current system, reviewing for constitutionality can only feasibly be done through *informal* procedures. As Keith Hand's chapter in this volume shows, the Sun Zhigang case illustrates this perfectly: when the Guangzhou municipal government's treatment of this young man under the Custody and Repatriation system aroused public anger and claims of unconstitutionality, the State Council moved to abolish that system by working internally and informally with the NPC Standing Committee. Scholars have pointed out that a sort of *sub rosa* mediation system exists underneath the framework of our Constitution (Deng 2003). Such coordination is thus more appropriate to the current system than review and revocation by the NPC or the SPC acting by itself.

In China, scholars are increasingly confusing the distinction between "illegality" and "unconstitutionality." Unconstitutionality usually refers to the acts of *public authorities* that violate the principles, the rules, or the spirit of the written Constitution. However, scholars have begun conflating and confusing unconstitutionality with simple illegality. For example, some constitutional scholars have begun to label as "unconstitutional" acts performed by powerful economic, cultural, scientific, or technical organizations unconnected with the state. Although research into the legality of the behavior of such powerful organizations is very important, one must acknowledge that, at the present time, the biggest threat to the development and implementation of constitutionalism and constitutional rights in China still stems from the behavior of public and quasi-public bodies. By expanding the realm of the "unconstitutional" to encompass the behavior of private as well as public actors, these scholars make it even more difficult to find solutions for the problems of constitutional implementation in China. They also deflect public attention away from the true cause of the Constitution's limited effectiveness in China.

Another striking aspect of constitutional scholarship in China is the lack of a common constitutional culture and set of values amidst constitutional experts. In a "normal" constitutional state, I believe that constitutional scholars share common values and understandings about the object of their research and agree on the academic concepts that contribute to the modernization of the state. However in China, our constitutional scholars share no consensus about our basic constitutional values, and engage in endless academic debate on such issues.

At the same time, however, many Chinese scholars are also unwilling to express their own views and opinions. Constitutional scholars in China must often operate in patronage networks organized around their particular institutions and particular "big men" within those institutions. Under such conditions, it is often difficult for a scholar to experiment with his or her own ideas, particularly when they diverge from those of his or her network patron. In fact, the publication of new ideas by an unknown scholar can easily be seen as a threat to the patronage ordering of his or her network, and can severely limit the younger scholar's opportunities for professional advancement.

Because there is no strictly scientific criterion for scholarship in the area of jurisprudence, a problem of low research quality is also obvious. Many scholarly studies are simply redundant. For example, between 1994 and 2006 the China Journal Net lists more than 331 articles under the headings or keywords: "review of constitutionality."

VI. The Road Ahead: New Tendencies in the Development of China's Constitutional Education and Research

The last few years have seen some new and positive developments in Chinese constitutional jurisprudence. These include better teaching materials; the development of more interdisciplinary constitutional research; and a growing interest in human rights cases and issues.

Since the year 2000, teaching materials for courses on constitutional law in China have become more systematic and professional. Under the old teaching system, textbooks on China's Constitution focused primarily on the reproduction of relevant texts and documents. Newer teaching materials have emphasized the internal logic of the constitutional system, and reflect a growing concern for a more scientific development of the discipline. Both *Researching Constitutional Law,* by Han Dayuan, Lin Laifan, and Zheng Xianjun (2004) and *Constitutional Law Studies*, edited by Professor Mo Jihong (2004), are examples of more theoretical discussions on the Constitution and constitutionalism that try to shed light on the need for innovation within the discipline. Chinese teaching materials and research output have also begun to make greater use of the case-based research methodology (see, for example, Han and Mo 2005).

Constitutional legal training at the graduate level also seems to have stabilized.

New areas and forms of constitutional research have also emerged. Most significant among these is research that combines constitutional law with other branches of law. An example of this can be seen in the debates that surrounded the recent drafting of China's new Property Law (2007), which merged constitutional theory with questions of economic organization and of the nature and legal consequences of corruption. Another example is found in the work of a growing number of scholars looking at the relationship between the Constitution, the Criminal Procedure Law, and the rights of criminal defendants.

And lastly, a key recent development in constitutional education in China is the growing interest in the protection of human rights. Prior to 2004, constitutional textbooks in China focused primarily on analyses of state power. Analyses relating to civil rights, for example, accounted for only around nine percent of the materials found in the first edition of *The Chinese Constitution,* edited by Professor Xu Chongde (1996). By contrast, they account for almost 20 percent of the materials found in the second edition of that book, published in 2004 (Xu 2004). Similarly, during the 1980s, on average only ten papers per year were published on this subject. By the 1990s, this average had grown to around twenty papers per year. And in 2006, there were 113 papers published on this issue.

This sudden increase in academic attention has been due in part to the emergence of key social problems relating to the municipal expropriation and demolition of urban housing and the corresponding scope of citizens' property rights protections. The successful modernization of China's major cities, including the building of new public facilities, has required the demolition of many old houses, and the public expropriation of the property of millions of people throughout the country. In many of these cases, citizens are aware that the government and powerful developers worked together to deny basic protections for property rights to the affected households. In 2007, constitutional scholars in China began a wide-ranging study to try to integrate constitutional theory and legal and political practice in exploring ways to address the social and constitutional problems caused by this kind of appropriation.

This increased attention to constitutional rights can also be seen in the analyses and discussions that surrounded the recent "Pengshui poetry case" (see Guo 2006). During the autumn of 2006, a cadre in Pengshui County of Chongqing Municipality was charged with slander and libel for having sent a sarcastic political poem to his colleagues via a mobile text message. Detained for five weeks by the public security bureau before being released on bail, the civil servant was finally compensated and pronounced innocent. The incident captured the attention of the entire country (see also *Nanfang Dushi Bao* 2006). The local population, in particular, was even further incensed when they became aware that the local party secretary, who prompted the illegal arrest because he was offended by the satire, had nevertheless been promoted to deputy director of an important bureau in the municipality.

Some constitutional scholars even desire to become constitutional practitioners and promote values through constitutional litigation. Professor Zhou Wei, author of *Fundamental Constitutional Rights* (2006), has been a leading exemplar of this development. As detailed further in the chapter by Keith Hand, he has brought many suits to court in order to try to protect constitutional rights of citizens by the direct enforcement of our Constitution's principles, particularly regarding issues of discrimination. His involvement has had considerable impact in promoting people's concerns about the fundamental unfairness of many kinds of common discriminatory practices.

Note

Translated from Chinese by Lin Gui and Stéphanie Balme.

CHAPTER SEVEN

Western Constitutional Ideas and Constitutional Discourse in China, 1978–2005

Yu Xingzhong

I. Introduction

Since its inception in 1949, the People's Republic of China (PRC) has enacted four constitutions, and a quasi Constitution called the Common Program of the Chinese People's Political Consultative Conference (1949). These constitutions have served the government well in legitimizing its domination and in promoting its political programs. But due to the lack of effective enforcing mechanisms, they had almost no direct relevance to the daily life of the Chinese people.

Since 1999, however, the Constitution seems to have been animated by some magic touch. Judges began to invoke constitutional provisions to justify court decisions on civil matters; ordinary citizens began trying to use the Constitution to curb unlawful government annexation of private properties; government officials also began arguing for greater respect for the Constitution in order to promote social stability.

This sudden rise of constitutional consciousness is the outcome of diverse forces in China's political and social arena. These forces each have had their own agenda for promoting the Constitution. For instance, some government officials want to use the Constitution to strengthen official party ideology; some judges want to use the Constitution to expand the sphere of influence of the judiciary; some scholars see constitutionalism as a way of modernizing and pursuing better governance; and some individuals use the Constitution as a means to fight against injustice.

Many of these political-economic factors have been explored in depth. But one factor needs to be more fully explored—that is, the influence of Western constitutional theories on Chinese constitutional scholarship in the reform era. This includes both American constitutional thought and, to a lesser extent, continental European constitutional thought as well.

This chapter attempts to look at this factor by examining how Western constitutional theories have been introduced into China by various scholars and how they have actually influenced Chinese constitutional mentality since 1978. It begins with a brief discussion of the nature of Chinese constitutional discourse. It then analyses several areas of China's emerging constitutional thinking in which Western scholars have played a significant role. The chapter concludes by pointing out some of the limitations of current Western constitutional theories as they are understood and utilized in China.

II. Chinese Constitutional Thinking in Transition

A four-thousand year history of rewarding the good and punishing the evil has naturally fostered a strict and powerful legal tradition in China (see Bodde and Morris 1967; Chu 1961; Zhang 1986). In their competition for position of authoritative ideology in Chinese history, Confucians, Taoists, Moists, and Legalists respectively praised or devalued the idea of governing by law, resulting in a cluster of vague ideas and statements about law that were to become eternal sources of disputes and misunderstandings for Chinese as well as foreign scholars (Alford 1986; see, e.g., Unger 1976). These ideas and statements, however, never went beyond the theme of whether it is wise to use law, and if it is, how law should be used, to reward or punish (see Liang 1987).

Thus, despite its long legal tradition, China did not have much to offer to the world constitutionally speaking. It is often claimed that the Chinese word for "constitution," "*xianfa*," was imported from Japan (as many modern terms were). The word "*xian*" did in fact exist in classical Chinese—it meant "law, order, or edicts" and had some normative implications. But it did not mean "constitution" in modern sense, in the sense of the laying out of government structure and the protection of individual rights. There is a chapter in one of *The Classics,* the *Shu Jing* (*The Classic of History*), which describes something resembling a Constitution. The chapter is called "*Hong Fan* (The Great Plan)," and it contains an exposition of nine categories of government affairs. It was, however, not well-known or followed by any ruler in the course of dynastic politics. There was also very little discussion, if any, in *The Classics* about individual rights. And the idea of using an authoritative legal document to lay out the structure of government never emerged.

Modern constitutional discourse in China began in the 1830s when China was witnessing earth-shaking changes in its traditions. But the first Constitution in China did not appear until more than seventy years later (see Xie 2004, 2–4; see also the chapter by Xiaohong Xiao-Planes earlier in this volume). Subsequent traumatic events—such as wars with foreign powers, civil wars, upheavals and revolutions—gave this discourse an uneven history. It began as a hope for a powerful modern state, but was cut short by a series of revolutions, and then resumed after the communist revolution of 1949 with a somewhat reconfigured political ideology (see the chapter by Glenn Tiffert in this volume). Following the founding of the PRC in 1949, China's constitutional discourse has gone from focusing on Marxist ideology in the early 1950s; to promoting indigenous constitutional ideas during the Cultural Revolution; to encouraging a more liberal appeal in promoting economic reform in the opening-up era.

Entering the 21st century, constitutional discourse in China is witnessing unprecedented prosperity and diversity (see, for example, Han 2006; see also Tong Zhiwei, this volume). From 1978 to 1988, China's legal reform focused primarily on criminal law and criminal procedure, as the tasks facing legal reformers were mainly related to establishing and maintaining social and political order during the reform and opening-up period. Beginning in 1985, China began focusing on reforming its economic institutions. With the deepening of these economic reforms, there appeared a great need for legal rules concerning business transactions and investments. A large number of laws regulating civil law relations were made to meet these new needs.

But since 1998, in order to address changed circumstances and respond to foreign and domestic calls for rule of law and greater protection of human rights, China has directed its attention increasingly to better administration and better protection of individual rights, thus opening a new page in the history of its legal reform. In 1998, at the 15th Congress of the Chinese Communist Party (CCP), the CCP leadership promised to establish the country as a "a socialist country with the rule of law." The government has made enormous efforts to promote law and legal institutions: including sending people abroad to study; running cooperative training programs with Western countries; and supporting research projects on constitutionalism, human rights, and public law. Frequently heard now is that the rule of law means the rule of the Constitution. In 2003 Xiao Yang, then President of the Supreme People's Court (SPC), said that the authority of the Constitution must be upheld (Xiao 2003). Hu Jintao, the President of the PRC and the General Secretary of the CCP, has also made speeches demanding that government officials act within the Constitution (see Hu 2003). All in all, the Chinese government has appeared very supportive of fostering constitutional consciousness in Chinese society.

The unprecedented rise of constitutional consciousness in China has been a natural outcome of this process. It has been a rise in which PRC constitutional scholars have played a very significant role. There has been a proliferation of books, articles, conferences, and websites on constitutional law and constitutionalism in China. Academic discourse on issues such as the rule of law, the supremacy of the Constitution, fundamental constitutional principles, constitutional protection of human rights, constitutional supervision, right to education, equality, nondiscrimination, and various other rights have contributed to this rise of constitutional consciousness. The status, prestige, and influence of constitutional law scholars also has risen accordingly. The argument that the rule of law means the rule of Constitution especially has put the Constitution at the forefront of legal reforms. In 2003, for example, constitutional law scholars in China appealed to the National People's Congress Standing Committee for constitutional review of Custody and Repatriation regulations following the Sun Zhigang incident (see chapter by Keith Hand in this volume). More recently, academic constitutional discourse has compelled the National People's Congress (NPC) to revise the draft Property Law (*Zhonghua Renmin Gongheguo Wuquan Fa*) (2007).

In all these discussions and debates, Chinese constitutional scholars have conscientiously looked to American and continental European constitutional ideals for inspiration. It is no exaggeration to say that Chinese constitutional discourse has been significantly "Westernized."

III. Western Influences on Constitutional Discourse in China

As described above, notions of constitutionalism deriving from the West entered China more than one hundred years ago, but did not really meet with full acceptance until the end of the 20th century. Today, many well-known works by Western constitutional scholars have been translated into Chinese. These include Bruce Ackerman's *We the People* (1991); Ronald Dworkin's *Taking Rights Seriously* (1977) and *Law's Empire* (1986); Friedrich Hayek's *The Constitution of Liberty* (1960) and works by Cass Sunstein and Richard Posner (American influence has been especially predominant in Chinese constitutional discourse). All of these are foundational references for Chinese postgraduate students working in areas of legal theory and constitutional law.

While translating and introducing Western books and articles, Chinese constitutional scholars have also incorporated into their own writings the ideas and principles of these liberal constitutionalists. One good example of this is found in the work of Professor Li Buyun of the Law Institute of the Chinese Academy of Social Science. As an advisor to the ad hoc Constitutional

Revision Working Group, Li has lectured to the top leaders in China on constitutional issues. During the early 1990s, Li spent a considerable period of time at Columbia Law School, exchanging ideas with Louis Henkin, Andrew Nathan, Randle Edwards, and other American scholars. These discussions formed the basis of a series of influential articles he later wrote on the fundamental concepts and principles of constitutionalism—articles that advocated including principles of human rights, rule of law, democracy, and constitutional freedoms into Chinese constitutionalism.

For example, in an influential article entitled "An Outline for Implementing the Strategy of Governing the Country in Accordance with Law," Li (1999) argued that the Chinese vision of rule of law is marked by ten major characteristics. These include a comprehensive legal system, sovereignty of the people, protection of human rights, checks and balance on power, equality before law, supremacy of law, administration according to law, judicial independence, due process, and obedience to law by the party, most of which are obviously liberal values. In another much-read article entitled "Several Theoretical Issues in Constitutional Studies," Li (2002) wrote: "there are two core issues in constitutionalism: one is to constrain state power and regulate its limits and procedure. The other is to provide for the rights of the citizens." In both these articles, Li's arguments are obviously following mainstream American constitutional thought.

All in all, there is now a large literature in China discussing major liberal constitutional notions and how they might contribute to constitutional theories in China. Particularly prominent among these are the notions of rule of law, of individual rights, of judicial review, of limited government, and of the nature of a democratic civil society. As we explore below, all of these discussions have drawn heavily from the work of Western scholars.

A. Albert Venn Dicey, Friedrich Hayek, and Chinese Discourse on the Rule of Law

Since Aristotle, many Western thinkers, such as Grotius, Spinoza, Hobbes, Locke, Rousseau, and Montesquieu, have contributed to the notion of the rule of law. The most thorough and explicit explanation of the concept, however, was given by the British constitutional scholar, Albert Venn Dicey. According to Dicey (1981, 110), "rule of law" means first of all that "the absolute supremacy or predominance of regular law as opposed to the influence of arbitrary power, or even of wide discretionary authority on the part of government." Second, it also means "the equal subjection of all classes to the ordinary law of the land administered by the ordinary law courts... which excludes the idea of any exemption of officials or others from the duty of obedience to the law which governs other citizens or from the jurisdiction of the ordinary tribunals" (Dicey 1981, 120). Building on Dicey's formula, Friedrich Hayek (1944, 54) provided an even clearer formulation of rule of law, maintaining that "[s]tripped of all technicalities this means that the government in all its actions is bound by rules fixed and announced beforehand—rules which make it possible to foresee with fair certainty how the authority will use its coercive powers in given circumstances, and to plan one's individual affairs on the basis of this knowledge."

The particular notions of "rule of law" advanced by Dicey and Hayek have significantly influenced Chinese constitutional discourse. In the 1980s, Chinese governmental officials, scholars, and the general populace showed great interest in the idea of "rule of law." The government and many legal scholars saw it as a strategy for governing the country; commoners began to use it to seek justice in protecting their own rights. Slogans like "rule the country in accordance with law," "managing water resources in accordance with law," and "managing forestation in accordance with law" could be seen everywhere in China. In newspapers, magazines, and scholarly works, there appeared a large number of articles about "rule of law" and "running the country in accordance with the law." Suddenly, rule of law became quite fashionable—if not obsessively so.

Of course, interest in rule of law was not then new for the Chinese. Ever since the late Qing reforms of the 19th century, the Chinese have been trying to understand the meaning of and uses of "rule of law" (see Wang 2002). But the Chinese interest in rule of law that began in the 1980s was different from this earlier pursuit. The late Qing reformers were skeptical about rule of law, or they only had a rough idea as to its meaning. They were not certain whether rule of law could be used to change China, to emancipate the Chinese people, or to make China into a strong country. They were not certain whether it was worth pursuing.

By contrast, since the late 1980s Chinese interest in rule of law has proceeded with unquestioned certainty regarding its virtues. The Chinese regard the concept of rule of law, however vaguely defined, as an absolute good, and as the only possible way for China and the Chinese people to enjoy modern, workable government. At the beginning of the 21st century, it seems to be China's only option for fulfilling its ambition of modernization. Despite disagreement over the concept of the rule of law, it is now seen by Chinese scholars and government officials as the highest ideal for what is described as China's ongoing "transitional period."

At the same time, the introduction of classical liberalism and modern legal philosophies over the last two decades has also considerably reshaped Chinese scholars' understanding of law and legal institutions in the West, and provided new theoretical lenses for them to evaluate the existing legal system of China.

In the aftermath of the Cultural Revolution, which is often associated with "rule of man," the idea of the rule of law, as advocated by Western liberal scholars became all the more attractive, and was wholeheartedly embraced by Chinese scholars. There was a proliferation in the literature on rule of law and related issues in Chinese magazines, periodicals, and books (see generally Chen 1999–2000).

Hayek, in particular, is one of the most frequently referenced theorists in this literature. Professor Deng Zhenglai of Jilin University, for example, has devoted most of the last twenty years studying Hayek. His ideas on Hayek have greatly influenced young Chinese political and legal scholars. Deng has translated most of Hayek's writings into Chinese, of which Hayek's *The Constitution of Liberty* (1960) has become particularly widely read by Chinese scholars and students. Deng also wrote extensively and systematically on Hayek's theories of society and law. In two articles published in 2002, Deng went to great lengths to discuss what he called Hayek's "theory of the Common-Law state with rule of law, based on spontaneous ordering and an evolutionary dynamic of law," arguing authoritatively that Hayek's theories on rule of law present a model of rule of law that is distinct from that of the continental law tradition that China is pursuing. What is implied in this argument is that state-sponsored continental legal transplantations may not have been as effective as has been thought, and there is thus need to look at Anglo-American traditions of rule of law as well (see Deng 2004, 245–367).

B. Ronald Dworkin and the Emergence of "Rights Talk" in China

Perhaps the most obvious sign of Western, and particularly American, influence on Chinese constitutional discourse can be seen in the growing Chinese acceptance of "rights talk." Ancient China did not have a concept of rights. Again, as was the case with constitutionalism, rights talk or rights theories entered China only in late 19th century, when China began to be more actively engaged with foreign cultures. Classical Western theories on natural and individual rights first became popular among the new Chinese intellectuals of the early 20th century, but they were soon replaced by theories of legal positivism that arose in the West as a reaction against classical, natural-rights theories.

After the founding of the PRC, a Marxist conception of rights took center stage. Marxism saw rights as correlative to duties, and as class oriented, with collective rights being much more significant than individual rights. Even where it recognized constitutional rights, Marxism argued that such rights were overshadowed by the interests of the state and the collective.

This is in sharp contrast with the liberal conception of right that see fundamental, individual rights as somewhat absolute "trumps" over more collective interests. Most famously, Ronald Dworkin has argued that there should be some institution serving as a check and balance on the majoritarian legislature to guarantee that in the pursuit of the majority will, the legislature does not violate the basic rights of individuals. In Dworkin's words, fundamental rights should take precedent over even the most democratic of processes when those processes threaten such rights (Dworkin 1977, 184–205).

Since the reform era, "rights" has become a buzzword for Chinese legal scholars, lawyers, and government officials. This, of course, was not achieved in one stretch. There were doubts and debates over whether China should adopt arguments made by Western rights advocates that the science of law is the science of rights. Some, like Zhang Wenxian, believed that legal studies should focus on rights (see Zhang 2002). Others like Zhang Hengshan, argue that legal science is the science of duties (see Zhang 1989). Eventually, the rights argument triumphed—not only in the academic world but also in the political world. After a decade-long debate, the protection of fundamental, individual rights has now been written into the PRC Constitution.

Dworkin is the most important intellectual resource in this rights talk movement.[1] Many of his books—including *Taking Rights Seriously* (1977) and *A Matter of Principle* (1986)—have been translated, by and large accurately, into Chinese. Articles discussing his theories of law and theories of rights have appeared in Chinese legal periodicals since the late 1970s. There has been an enormous amount of literature in Chinese devoted to the study of his legal and constitutional thought. Dworkin's name has become so popular that even scholars outside the legal world know about him. The first translation of *Taking Rights Seriously* was a best seller in China. In 2002, when he was invited by the Qinghua Law School to visit China, he was treated like a deity. A seminar organized by an academic bookstore in Beijing was attended by over one hundred selected intellectuals (see *Gongfa Pinglun* 2002).

Dworkin's theories of rights and law have influenced several generations of Chinese constitutional scholars. *Taking Rights Seriously* was first introduced to China by Pan Handian, a senior scholar and translator, who translated some excerpts from that book in 1980. In 1981 Professor Shen Zongling's book, *Contemporary Western Legal Philosophies*, devoted a chapter to Dworkin's natural law theory. Later on, scholars like Zhang Wenxian (1987) have offered more detailed and updated studies of Dworkin's notion of law as integrity and interpretation.

By 2005, rights-based arguments had become firmly implanted in Chinese soil. Younger generations of Chinese legal scholars now talk about rights as if they were homegrown truths. Government officials are also able to refer and appeal to rights in their policy debates.[2] There is no doubt that such rights talk—and in particular Dworkin's thinking about rights—has exerted tremendous and lasting influence on Chinese legal and constitutional thinking.

C. *Marbury v. Madison* and the Judicialization of the Constitution

In China, there has recently emerged a kind of constitutional "judicial activism" that is also a reflection of American influence on Chinese constitutional discourse. In China's political system, the constitutional position of the judiciary has traditionally been very weak. In particular, the power to supervise the enforcement of the Constitution has traditionally and formally vested in the hands of the NPC, not those of the courts. The NPC is the supreme organ of the state power. It has the power to legislate and to supervise the work of the executive, judicial, and procuratorial organs. The SPC, by contrast, is appointed by the NPC and works under its formal supervision. To many, it would seem to be somewhat "impudent" for the SPC to review and sit in judgment of the constitutionality of laws passed by its constitutional superior.

In fact, prior to 1999, there was not a single instance of constitutional review by the PRC judiciary. There were not even any provision for such review. And the courts accepted this arrangement. In 1955, the SPC declared the use of constitutional provisions in criminal adjudication inappropriate (see SPC 1955). In 1986, the SPC again made it clear that the Constitution should not be cited in adjudicating cases (see SPC 1986). As a result, many of the fundamental rights (and duties) specified in the Chinese Constitution remain true only on paper.

Since 1999, however, Chinese courts have become more willing to implicate constitutional norms into their decision making (see also Balme, this volume). One particularly dramatic case of this was the *Qi Yuling* case. In that case, the SPC, in defiance of its previous constraints, adopted a proactive attitude that expanded the scope of its interpretative jurisdiction to include the PRC Constitution's guarantee of a "right to education."[3] This has been labeled the "first constitutional case" in the history of the PRC. It caused heated debate over the so-called "judicialization" of the Constitution.

The *Qi Yuling* case was actually a civil case involving the defendant's misappropriation of the plaintiff's name. Having passed the provincial entrance examination for specialized vocational schools, the plaintiff, Qi Yuling, was admitted to Jining Commercial School in Shandong Province. Yet the admission letter for Qi was picked up by her classmate, Chen Xiaoqi, who then enrolled in the Jining School under Qi's name. Upon graduation, Chen then took a job under Qi's name and worked for ten years before her false identity was discovered by Qi Yuling herself. Qi then brought a lawsuit in the Intermediate People's Court of Zaozhuang in Shandong province, claiming misappropriation of her identity (the civil version of identity theft) and violation of her right to an education. The trial court awarded her RMB 35,000 for Chen's misappropriation of her name, but declined to provide remedy for the violation of her right to education, saying that she had waived that right by subsequent actions.

Qi Yuling then appealed that decision to the High People's Court of Shandong Province, arguing that her subsequent actions could not be construed as waiving her civil-law right to education. Because of the complexities of the case, the High Court filed an inquiry to the SPC seeking direction as to the right to education question. In a surprise reply, the SPC (2001) directed to the High Court that the plaintiff's "right to education" was a *constitutional* right under Article 46 of the PRC Constitution, and that as a constitutional right it could not be waived.

This was the first time that a Chinese court had ever cited a constitutional provision in issuing a judicial interpretation. Not surprisingly, it generated a good deal of political and legal controversy. Some saw this as China's first case of judicial review, and believed that the SPC, in expressly citing to Qi Yuling's constitutional rights in this case, has opened a new chapter in PRC constitutional development. On the other hand, many critics argued that the SPC was wrong to cite a constitutional provision in this case—first, because that case is clearly a civil law case, to which the General Principles of Civil Law rather than the Constitution were applicable; and second, because the Constitution itself was not justiciable.

In the midst of this debate, an article by an SPC Judge—Huang Songyou, one of the drafters of the SPC interpretation—publicly defended that interpretation by comparing it to the famous American case of *Marbury v. Madison* (1803), which established judicial review as a part of the American Constitution. Huang noted how in that case, the Supreme Court of the United States pioneered the practice of judicializing of the Constitution by declaring that legislation that contradicts the Constitution can be annulled by the courts. In doing so, they made constitutional interpretation an ordinary part of the judicial process. He argued that *Marbury* has become an international trend, and that China, with the deepening of its ongoing reforms, also needs to begin referencing constitutional provisions in order to more effectively uphold the law (Huang 2001).[4]

D. *Benjamin Constant and the Nature of Popular Sovereignty*

While Anglo-American influence has been particularly dominant in contemporary Chinese constitutional discourse, continental European influence, especially French influence, is also present. In the early part of the twentieth century, French constitutional thinkers were more inflential in China than Anglo-American thinkers: Rousseau, Montesquieu, Voltaire, Dedroit, to name just a few, had very significant and lasting influence on both intellectuals and revolutionaries in China. In the present era, however, for some reason French thinkers seem to be less influential than their Anglo-American counterparts. Nevertheless, Foucault, Bourdieu, and Derrida are part of the compulsory reading list for the students of philosophy and cultural criticism, while two other French thinkers, Benjamin Constant and Alexis de Tocqueville, seem to be enjoying a growing popularity among political scientists and constitutional scholars in China.

Benjamin Constant's influence comes from his critique of Jean-Jacques Rousseau's notion of "popular sovereignty." Rousseau had argued that the sovereignty of the state stems from the *collective* general will, and that as such it is both unlimited and superior to individual will. This vision has reigned over official Chinese political mentality for almost a century. In critiquing Rousseau, many scholars rejected his "popular" basis of sovereignty due to certain totalitarian features. Constant, on the other hand, was much more nuanced in his critique. For Constant, the principle of popular sovereignty is beyond debate. But he also argued that such sovereignty must in essence be constrained by the independent needs and existence of the individual.

Like Rousseau, the current political culture of China sees China's popular sovereignty as inviolable and unlimited. Constant's argument thus provides a subtle reminder that the sovereignty of the state over its individual citizens may not be as total as Chinese politicians are wont to assume. For constitutional scholars in China, Constant is thus appealing because he viewed political power as a necessary evil that must be limited.[5] His arguments are used to advance the idea that government's power can be limited by constitutional principles, by institutional arrangements that check and balance power, and by external factors such as the independent rights of individuals.

In China, Constant's arguments win him followers, particularly among those who are keen on constitutional reform. Professor Li Qiang of Beijing University, for example, is among those who are most enthusiastic about Constant's ideas. He believes that Constant figures very significantly in the history of the development of liberty. He argued in a preface he wrote to the Chinese translation of Constant's most famous political writings on liberty and constitutionalism that even though Constant could not be said to be good at speculative thinking, he had the sensitivity of a man of letters and the pragmatism of a statesman. He also pointed out that Constant's political ideas, especially ideas on totalitarianism and liberty, are extremely profound and had lasting impact on ideas of liberalism that emerged later (see Li 1999).

E. Alexis de Tocqueville and Democratic Development

Another French thinker who has attracted many followers in China is Alexis de Tocqueville.[6] The Chinese translation of his *Democracy in America* appeared in 1988 and is constantly quoted by Chinese political scientists and legal scholars (see Tuokewei'er [Alexis de Tocqueville] 1988). Tocqueville is an important intellectual source for China's further democratic reform. For example, Mao Shoulong, a constitutional scholar in the People's University of China, has argued that *Democracy in America* presents great opportunities for Chinese readers to understand patterns of democratic development, both in mature democracies and in developing democracies as well (see Mao [undated]). Mao argued that although China is not an ideal democracy, democracy is developing there. It is simply that China's democratic revolution is still ongoing. For this reason, China must draw on the experience of democratic revolutions in other countries of the world.

Tocqueville's ideas on centralized power in a democratic society, on the "tyranny of majority," and on the merits of civil society have been widely accepted and quoted by Chinese scholars. One scholar, Gong Qun (2005), has argued that the principle of majoritian decisionmaking leads to rule by majority, and that the rule by majority often results in a dictatorship of the majority. Chen Binghui (2004b) has argued that Tocqueville's concept of tyranny of the majority has become a common topic in contemporary theories of democracy. As he sees it, many scholars have come to reject democracy based on their misinterpretation of that concept, but in fact Tocqueville was not opposed to democracy—his argument is that one must adhere to democratic principles of government decisionmaking while at the same time preventing the emergence of a "tyranny of the majority." Tocqueville is also regarded as one of the first persons to recognize the role of civil society in promoting freedom and democracy. His argument that a relatively independent and pluralistic civil society is an indispensable component of a constitutional government's capacity to restrain political power has been carefully studied in China (see, for example, Chen 2004d).

IV. Asian Values, Chinese Characteristics and the Limitations of the Influence of Western Constitutional Theories

But the current Western influence on Chinese constitutional discourse is limited by a tension between universalism and cultural relativism. On one hand, liberal constitutionalism is often portrayed as a universal paradigm upon which China is expected to build its constitutional and legal framework, design its constitutional enforcement mechanisms, and implement its substantive principles. On the other hand, there is a constant urge in China demanding "Chinese-ness" in whatever the Chinese are engaged in doing. Any "constitutionalism with Chinese characteristics" or "Chinese constitutionalism" will have to struggle with this tension, and whatever hybrid form of constitutionalism that is able to emerge out of this tension will take time to appear.

Since the latter half of the 20th century, constitutional studies in many Asian countries have become conscious of the special constitutional identities of their respective cultures. There is also some discussion about a "pan-Asian" version of constitutionalism. So far, however, no systematic theory of constitutional law that could be adequately called "Asian constitutionalism" has emerged. Despite Lawrence W. Beer's effort to articulate a constitutionalism practiced in Asian countries that might be different from the liberal constitutionalism embraced by the United States and other Western democracies, the notion of an "Asian constitutionalism" has not gone beyond the application of liberal constitutionalism to Asian historical and cultural backgrounds.

The idea of a (pan-)Asian constitutionalism thus remains a vague consciousness among a few, mainly Asian, constitutional scholars. Han Dayuan, an enthusiastic advocator for Asian constitutionalism in China, argues that Asian constitutionalism is defined by a conspicuous intellectual trend that moves away from "Western Centrism" in constitutional thinking and captures the distinctive theories and practices of constitutionalism in Asian countries. Yet he also acknowledges that the main values that Asian constitutionalism embraces—such as rule of law, democracy, and protection of citizens' rights—are drawn from liberal constitutionalism. If there is anything distinct about Asian constitutionalism, perhaps it lies in the constitutional emphasis its advocates attach to the role that economic development, state building, and community values play in the constitutional framework. But these roles can also be seen simply as complements to liberal constitutionalism, which would make Asian constitutionalism merely a variant of liberal constitutionalism, rather than a brand new version of constitutionalism.

In the Chinese context, the idea of an Asian constitutionalism is more like a close cousin to Western constitutionalism—related to the household, but living in a different house. One major conviction of many Chinese reformers is that China can keep its unique national and cultural identity intact in the process of modernization. The government has long been pressing for a socialist system and a socialist market economy with "Chinese characteristics." This goal has even been incorporated into the Chinese Constitution and its laws. But the question of what, exactly, these "Chinese characteristics" are is yet to be worked out. If anything significantly different from liberal constitutionalism eventually appears, it will not be called "Asian constitutionalism," at least in China, but "constitutionalism with Chinese characteristics," because of China's obsession with Chinese-ness and indifference to the larger concept of "Asia," which often reminds the Chinese of the bad experience of Japanese invasion in the 1930s and 1940s.

V. Conclusion

The introduction of Western constitutional theories into Chinese political and legal culture has obviously affected the way that Chinese constitutional scholars and reform-minded officials have thought about China's future constitutional development. Anglo-American influence already has brought about significant changes in Chinese constitutional law. Continental influence is also obvious, but its practical impact is yet to be as keenly felt. The impact of Western constitutional theories, however, is still limited. The concern with Chinese-ness, a lack of effective enforcement mechanisms, and the interest of the party and the state, all work to reduce the effectiveness of these theories.

Notes

1. A Chinese-character Google search of Dworkin's name (*Dewojin*) retrieved over 42,900 items on May 26, 2007.
2. A Chinese-character Google search of the term "rights" (*quanli*) retrieved over 75 million items on May 26, 2007.
3. Article 46 of the PRC Constitution provides: "[c]itizens of the People's Republic of China have the duty as well as the right to receive education. The state promotes the all-around moral, intellectual and physical development of children and young people."
4. In December 2008, the Supreme People's Court (2008) formally annulled its *Qi Yuling* Interpretation (the court's final judgement for Qi Yuling, however, was not affected).
5. A Chinese-character Google search of Constant's name (*Gongsidang*) retrieved over 17,200 items on May 26, 2007.
6. A Chinese-character Google search of Tocqueville's name (*Tuokewei'er*) retrieved over 388,000 items on May 26, 2007.

CHAPTER EIGHT

"To Take the Law as the Public": The Diversification of Society and Legal Discourse in Contemporary China

JI WEIDONG

I. Introduction: The Diversification of Social Life 1979–2005

According to a Durkheimian perspective of sociology, traditional China was a segmented society. In order to maintain the coherence of the country as a whole, it was therefore necessary to define a single set of dominant values and reify these values in the state's unified bureaucratic organization. However, often, symbolic interactions that were founded on webs of meaning and personal ties played a much more important role than bureaucratic organization in China's social ordering. This resulted in another kind of "organic solidarity"—one based on sustained relationships and mutual help shaped by long-term networking.

In the 20th century, China's Communist Party (CCP) disintegrated this traditional network society, replacing Confucianism with Communism, and strengthening the state's centralized bureaucratic organization. Under the constitutional regime set out in 1954 (see also the chapter by Glenn Tiffert earlier in this volume), the first twenty-five years of Modern China—from 1954 to 1978—could be considered the period of the "organization man," as exemplified in the idealized figure of the selfless soldier, Lei Feng.

The post–Cultural Revolution period, by contrast, has been a time of liberalizing and diversifying national values. It has become the time of Cui Jian—China's first rock star, who with his wild singing has inspired many young

Chinese to dance simply for their own personal joy. Market-friendly economic reforms have diversified society; ideological consensuses have broken down; and traditional ethics and trust relationships based on community, as well as visions of paternalistic tender heartedness and public order fostered by a unified socialist state power, are progressively becoming a part of the past.

Therefore, it is necessary for today's China to quickly build a new consensus for public affairs. This may require that more focus be given to issues of the juridical framework, in order to reconstruct the public sphere. It may mean that one of the core ideas of traditional Chinese legalism—that of "taking law as the public (*yifa weigong*)," in the words of Chen Liang in the Song Dynasty—is enjoying a revival. It may also mean the beginnings of a dialogue between China and the West about the nature of constitutionalism and modern rule of law.

II. The Significance of Legal and Constitutional Discourse in the Emergence of the Three Public Spheres

Presently, three kind of public spheres are taking shape in China. One is a "local" sphere of public opinion that is emerging in the rural areas, and which is comprised of the so-called "popular feelings" networks and village committee elections. Another is found in China's emerging cyberspace. The third, what Philip Huang calls "the third realm," is manifested principally in the courts of law, through which individuals are able to enter into a dialogue with the state.

A. The Local Sphere

The emerging local sphere of legal and constitutional discourse consists of three components. The first is found in the "Charters of Self-Government" that serve as "mini-constitutional conventions (*xiao xianfa*)" with regards to local level politics. The second is found in the "Village Pacts" that establish the political behavioral norms for villagers. The third is found in the specific regulations that establish the administrative behavioral norms of the village committees.

The emergence of a local public sphere in rural society was greatly catalyzed in 1998 when the State Council and the CCP jointly issued a circular promoting transparency and democracy in rural village management (State Council General Office 1998). This circular required that the three components of the local sphere be worked out in light of the public will, and through a process of equal participation, repeated discussions, and voluntary agreement by the people (see Zhang 1999). Charters of Self-government must be vetted and approved by the villagers at Village Assembly meetings. These meetings are also often attended by one or more officials from the township level. Village Pacts and local administrative regulations must also be discussed at Village Assembly meetings.

Public discussions regarding justice or fairness play an important role in the implementation of these conventions, pacts, and regulations. For example, the production responsibilities concerning collectively owned land that are prescribed in a village pact may be changed in response to objections subsequently raised during a meeting of the Village Assembly. In fact, all Charters of Village Self-government state that one of the duties of both Village Assembly representatives and Village Committee members is to listen and respond to precisely this kind of objection. Particularly when many villagers begin to feel that the present pattern of contracted-land distribution has become unfair, the Village Committee is supposed to respond and adjust the relevant contractual relations (cf. Li and O'Brien 1996).

Historically in China, rural public discussion had traditionally been framed by customary rules passed on from generation to generation. Since the 1980s, however, the basic features of public opinion in the rural area have evolved so as to promote free communication among the people and between the people and local government. Overall, the nature of this communication is harmonious rather than antagonistic. Villager-government interaction is not structured as a zero-sum game but as a positive-sum game (see also Ji 2004a).

According to the Organic Law of Village Committees, the Village Assembly—which is comprised either of all the members of the village who are at least eighteen years of age, or of representatives drawn from each village household—is the supreme decision-making organ of the village. It is supposed to approve all major village decisions by vote taken in meetings in which there is a quorum of at least half of all adult villagers, or at least two-thirds of the household representatives (Article 17). The Village Assembly is generally convened by the Village Committee; however, it can also be convened by petition of ten percent or more of the adult population of the village (Article 18). In addition to discussing possible changes to the Charter of Self-Government, the Village Pact, and local administrative regulations, the Village Assembly is also to deliberate on the annual report of the Village Committee as well as issue annual appraisals of the 200-250 Village Committee members (Article 18). The Village Assembly may also interrogate the Village Committee whenever necessary (Article 22). The Village Assembly must meet a minimum of once per year.

In some villages, Village Assemblies are even given the powers to veto decisions by the Village Committee that were made without public discussion. Although this idea is wonderful in theory, it still has a long way to go before becoming a standard and effective component of villager-Village Committee relations.

This emerging local public sphere has spawned many different and original forms of public communication within and between local communities. For example, one township in Henan Province has designed a public feedback system it calls "The Echo Wall." The Echo Wall is a public board on which any villager from within the township may post signed or anonymous opinions, suggestions, or criticism relating to village governance, to which the relevant Village Committee must post an open reply within five days.

In fact, most villages in China have set up similar "Open Village Affairs Boards (*cunwu gongkai lan*)," together with "Supervisory Suggestion Boxes (*jiandu jianyi xiang*)." It has been reported that this "One Board, One Box" system could play an important role in making public affairs better known to the public, as well as in the formation of an atmosphere in which all villagers participate in the discussion, determination, and management of village affairs. In addition, many villages and towns have instituted a "popular feelings talk network"—a kind of multichannel realm for open dialogue and public communication. All in all, although this practice of rural self-government was originally the product of state design, we can find it becoming more and more spontaneous in its various operations and structures.

One of the principal limitations currently affecting this sphere is that its public discussions are generally limited to a particular population within the local community. Most Village Pacts exclude "outsiders"—including those who live in a village without residence permits (*hukou*) registered in that village—from Village meetings (see also the chapter by Stéphanie Balme later in this volume). However, they still nevertheless impose fees and responsibilities on these outsiders (Ji 2004a, 266).

B. *The Digital Marketplace of Public Opinion*

At the same time, a new aspect of the public sphere is emerging in the area of information technology and the Internet. Although the Internet has also begun to permeate rural life, its impact is most felt in urban areas. According to incomplete statistics, the registered population of Internet users in China exceeded one hundred million people in 2005. Given that many other users have not necessarily registered for their own Internet accounts, but share accounts that have been registered for by others, the population of Chinese netizens may be much more.

At the present stage, the public sphere of cyberspace has been opening in two directions. One can be characterized as an "information commons" that is composed of a large number of websites, academic net-forums, and message boards in which Netizens post opinions concerning public topics. Given governmental regulations controlling Internet access, however, the communicative activities in this aspect of public cyberspace is somewhat restricted at present.

The other direction in which this new cyber sphere is emerging is in the area of "e-government." This includes "China Electronic Governance" experiments in Shenzhen City of Guangdong Province, Qingdao City of Shandong Province, and Mianyang City of Sichuan Province; the introduction of the "National Internet Tax-paying System"; and "e-court" projects overseen by the Supreme People's Court (SPC) that seek to "virtualize" court administration (see also Ji 2001).

C. The Third Realm and the "Judicial Mass Line"

A third component of China's emerging public sphere is found in the courts. The demands of rule of law have helped generate a kind of public discursive reflection on the nature and legality of public decision-making and dispute resolution in China (see also the chapter by Michael Dowdle later in this volume). Insofar as the courts are concerned, this reflection has resulted in the emergence of a "judicial mass line," in which the activities of the courts are increasingly exposed to public supervision. This judicial mass line is manifested in a number of ways. For example, some criminal convictions have been justified in court opinions by reference to mass opinion and emotional rhetoric—by noting, for example, that the case "has incurred the greatest popular indignation," or that "the feelings of the masses run high and are filled with indignation." In a sense, courts are using such offenders and lawbreakers as "negative teachers."

It is also manifested in an increasing use of live telecasts of trials; court questionnaires; and the growing use of court observers. Among many legal academics, however, there is growing anxiety about the development of this "judicial mass line." They see an innate conflict between this development and notions of judicial independence, between the procedural demands of justice and the expressive demands of direct democracy. They fear that the courts' supposedly scientific evaluation of both evidence and the law could be distorted by the sensationalized journalistic reporting of high-profile cases. Strengthening public supervision of the courts, without providing real rights of expression, could merely result in the establishment of a "pseudo" public opinion that is really being manipulated by state power.

III. Discourse Changes and Western Impact

The current contestation between rule of man and rule of law actually began in the late 1970s. In 1985, the catchphrase "rule under law" became a part of official discourse, and replaced the traditional legalist proposition "rule by law." The Chinese government began to talk officially in terms of "rule of law" in 1996, and later decided to build China into a kind of socialist rechtsstaat by 2010 (see He 2005).

A. Theoretical Development in Law and Politics

A general survey of the theoretical developments underlying "rule of law" in China during the last twenty-five years reveals four broad trends (see also Deng 2006). The first was called "Legal System Engineering." It combined Roscoe Pound's sociological jurisprudence with system theory, cybernetics, and information theory. This was very popular in the 1980s, and the first national symposium on "Legal System Engineering" was held in 1985. "Legal System Engineering" consisted of two aspects. One was the objectification of legal concepts and the idea of law as a science. The other sought the development of a unified vision for governmental social control, one that integrated traditional conceptions of good governance with the idea of "socialist legality."

The second trend was the "right-centered approach." Professors Zhang Wenxian and Zheng Chengliang of the Jilin University Department of Law, together with other young scholars, argued that shifting China's approach to legal reform from a "duty-centered" approach to a "right-centered" approach would better accommodate the needs of modernization. This "right-centered approach" exerted a tremendous influence upon legal thought and practice in China in the late 1980s.

The third trend involved the indigenization of legal studies. This trend was led by Zhu Suli, who used it to counteract the universalist assumptions about "law" that have tended to dominate Chinese thinking about legal reform. Zhu's work advocated using folk law and China's legal history as valid and distinctive sources of law and legal tradition in China. He saw social order and its legitimacy as deriving primarily from local meanings, with significant incommensurability existing between different institutional designs.

A fourth trend is seen in judicial reform, which became prominent in the late 1990s. This involves creating a more independent judiciary and strengthening powers of administrative litigation. One important result of this trend is the "Building the Legal State" program adopted in 2004.

B. The Selective Reception of Western Legal Theories

Western legal theories have been selectively received in China. Among these theories, we can distinguish four classes, based on whether their ends are idealist or pragmatic, and on whether their means are gradualist or immediate. (Compare with Eva Pils' comparison of consequentialism and deontologicalism in Chinese rights-defense philosophy later in this volume.) An example of an idealist and gradualist theory would be Friedrich Hayek's theory of law and freedom, which advances an ideal of economic libertarianism that is to be realized through a gradualist developmental process of "spontaneous ordering." Friedrich Savigny's historical jurisprudence would be an example of a theory that is gradualist but pragmatic, since he saw law as arising out of the pragmatic reality of social tradition rather than some ideal of economic libertarianism or social justice. Carl Schmitt's "political decisionism," which advocates the attainment of national strength through the imposition of a sovereign will, is ideal and immediate. Hans Kelsen, who focused on the possibilities and limits of positivist legal drafting and development, is immediate but pragmatic.

Among these perspectives, Hayek's theory on "spontaneous order" and Schmitt's view of "political decisionism" are the most popular among younger Chinese scholars. They also provide a useful lens for exploring some of the problems found in public discourse concerning rule of law in China today.

1. *Spontaneous Order, Indigenous Norm, and Cultural Conservatism*

Hayek's theory of the symbiosis between freedom and law was introduced into China in the late 1980s, and it exerted great influence in the late 1990s. His works have been translated and thoroughly analyzed by Professor Deng Zhenglai, an interesting liberal scholar known as the first self-employed research worker in China. The basic feature of Deng's portrait of Hayek is that he locates the foundation of Hayek's theory in a particular view of "cultural evolution" that extrapolates a "law of freedom" from learned customary rules. As Deng puts it:

> I think that it is "cultural evolution," the system of social norms that comes into being based on evolutionary, rational knowledge, that runs through the whole construction of Hayek's theory on rule of law.... Hayek's theoretical system itself is completely based on a view of "cultural evolution." (Deng 2002, 83)

Deng's view made it comparatively easy to introduce Hayek's theory into China, and it encouraged Zhu Suli's efforts to indigenize legal theory in China as well. But Qin Hui, a famous liberal intellectual and historian in China, noticed a hidden problematic in the relationship between Hayek and cultural conservatism. Qin (1999, 119) has said that "through reading Hayek's works we understand that freedom should be asked for. But the real issue for us is how to get that freedom." In this way, he exposed a paradox that links freedom and coercion, spontaneous order and planned social change: Without political struggle (and the attendant coercive aspect that that "struggle" implies), how can any type of legal order become a law of freedom? In fact, freedom has to have its basis in a kind of non-freedom, otherwise the law of freedom will itself be unsustainable.

2. *The Incomplete Link between Political Decisionism and Popular Opinion*

Another rule of law paradox involves the relationship between routine order and states of exception, and between formal justice and substantive justice. In China, this paradox is especially evident in the dilemma between law-abiding and law-changing. Carl Schmitt's theory about the relationship between politics, juridical order, and the national will strikes a sympathetic chord in many Chinese people. In particular, his theory on politics and public law has been aggressively explored by Professor Liu Xiaofeng (2002, 30):

> [At the time Schmitt was writing], Germany was in a state of exception (a severe disturbance of both international and domestic politics). Only those people who disregarded this political reality could naïvely believe that the state could be fully maintained merely through the legitimacy of the legal order, without any attendant substantive and autocratic power. What Schmitt challenged was just this kind of naïve liberalism, which believed that the legitimacy of legal order was itself enough to keep the institutions functioning. A politically mature liberalism, by contrast, should extend its recognition of civil society to a recognition of the political dictatorship of a sovereign state.

Some more radical Chinese legal scholars have constructed out of Schmitt's ideas a critique of liberal democracy. For example, Professor Liu Feng (2002, 384–385) has claimed that:

> The ideology of liberalism equates the ruler with the ruled, for example, in order to fly the banner of "by the people, of the people, and for the people." However, this is only an illusion, because the so-called "people" have become synonymous with particular interest groups. What made Schmitt uneasy with the mass politics of representative democracy was that the people's sovereignty was being replaced by competition between social groups and the ideologies of radical parties.... In light of this situation, Schmitt exposed the morbid state and logic of liberalism [i.e., of representative democracy] with a keen eye. However, there is a problem with his thought on sovereignty: it is how to guarantee decisionalism without degenerating into an unlimited autocracy.

At the level of international relations, however, and especially insofar as clashes between state interests and individual liberties at this level are concerned, some jurists and public intellectuals have begun changing their viewpoint so as to side with the demands of state interests. For example, Dr. Jiang Shigong, a gifted young scholar of jurisprudence who drafted the *Manifesto of the Community of Jurists* several years ago (Jiang 2002), made some comments in 2004 on the "Color Revolution" in Eastern Europe that surprised many. He said:

> We will never regard the Constitution as only a legal document. Why? Because the Constitution cannot guarantee itself. The Constitution must

> be ensured by a political power beyond the law. In fact, this problem is precisely the focal point in the debates between Schmitt and [Hans] Kelsen.... As Schmitt said, the major issue of politics is to distinguish between ourselves and the enemy. The problem is not one of "freedom" but one of conquering that enemy. This is the essence of politics, the essence that liberals always dare not face.... Only in the critical moments of seizing state power or of life-or-death struggle can we really understand why Schmitt detests the endless dialogue of political romanticists. (Jiang 2004.)

It is understandable why some scholars in China might be deeply worried about imbalances between competing social interests and values causing social order to fall to pieces. In such situations, turning to political power as a means for resolving such crises is the traditional Chinese way. What is new here is the combining of this historical tradition with Schmitt's particular theories of law and politics.

IV. Legal Discourse in China: Some Representative Thinkers

What are the different ways that Chinese scholars are thinking about rule of law? Prior to the "Neo-Enlightenment" of the 1980s, Chinese notions of law and legalism were dominated by Soviet-style theories of the need for state dominance. Originally, Chinese scholars sought to supplant this Soviet vision with some vision of "natural law." However, such transcendentalism had a hard time taking root in China due to China's strong tradition of secular rationalism. In any event, this Neo-Enlightenment was halted by the Tiananmen Square Demonstrations in 1989. The 1990s saw the rise of more conservative explorations of Chinese legalism, such as those focusing on national culture and what we termed above "legal indigenization." It was against this background that Soviet legal theory has enjoyed somewhat of a revival in the guise of Schmitt's political decisionism, as well as in the emergence of of the "New Left" and in an embrace of critical legal studies.

Today, we can distinguish some basic dimensions to Chinese legal discourse. We might start by identifying the four basic elements of a social system: political power (the government); economic interests (the market); cultural traditions (ethics); and the liberties of the subjects who are interacting with the social system. Inherent in these dimensions are different motives for the development of law. The first motive is found in utilitarian calculations of political power and economic rationality. The second is found in the ethics of cultural tradition and local knowledge. And a third is found in the need to guarantee universal freedoms of human rights and social justice.

Spanning any two of these motives are the particular perspectives of important Chinese legal scholars. Some scholars, for example, combine political utilitarianism with the local ethical order. Zhu Suli would be a representative of this perspective. Others, like Liang Zhiping, see a linkage between the local ethical order and universal justice. On the other hand, there are also people who are exploring the relationship between state power and human rights, in order to push forward a top-down political reform. Xia Yong is a good example of this approach. Recently, a variant of this approach had emerged that seeks to integrate the different perspectives and values of the above groups by focusing on improving and rationalizing various procedures associated with the delivery of justice. This is the "neo-proceduralist perspective," which has been advocated by people such as myself and He Weifang.

A. Zhu Suli and the Relationship between Law, Power, and Local Knowledge

As noted above, Zhu Suli is one of the major proponents of a vision that seeks to explain law as a relationship between state power and local ethics. Zhu's theories are based on a particular vision of "local knowledge" as informed by the ideas of Hayek. In discussing the relationship between legal development and spontaneous order, for example, he has argued:

> The modern rule of law as an institution cannot be built up by "legal transformation" or by transplanting. It must be built from the indigenous resources of China. The reasons for this are found in the locality of knowledge and in limited rationality. (Suli 1996, 17)

Zhu considers modern rule of law to be simply a particular form of social ordering. Relatedly, he sees local and other "private" forms of social orderings as particular variants of rule of law. In this aspect, he argues that it is possible to say that in China, the demand for rule of law is simply a demand for order:

> Under this meaning, I think that the order inside a local society is the product of long-term and stable rules just like state law—except that the modern state is able to maintain its social order through its monopoly on violence. Therefore in this meaning, we can say that this kind of local social ordering is also a kind of legalization. (Suli 1999, 155)

At first glance, this particular vision might seem very different from the Schmittian hypothesis of the unity of the total state. But in fact, both are founded on a conception of the "leader state," in which the rule-of-law "rechtstaat" is always to be conditioned by and subordinated to the ideology of the state. In his other articles, Zhu actually criticizes the "rule of law" of Friedrich Hayek and Max Weber, and even sometimes praises "rule of man" (see, for example, Suli 1998b; Suli 1998a).

B. Liang Zhiping: Local Knowledge as Universal Justice

Liang Zhiping also sees an important role for local knowledge in China's legal development. But this was not always the case. In the 1980s, for example, he wrote:

> The destiny of legal reform rests on the outcome of cultural construction. Legal problems are ultimately cultural problems. Therefore, we should not simply focus on purely legal reform and practice, but pay more attention to the cultural structure and cultural order as a whole.... The old order of the ancient civilization has already withered away. The more important thing is that we have the possibility to build up a new civilization. And this is exactly our hope. (Liang 1991, 343–344)

Later, however, he rethought his position on the legal modernization process. In 1997, he pointed out:

> If we break away from the dichotomy of tradition and modernity, and abandon the practice of observing and criticizing with an arrogant attitude the ideas, behavior and life-style of the peasantry, then we must admit that formal law, although often regarded as progressive, is not necessarily rational. Relatively speaking, the normative knowledge of the peasantry is not necessarily less advanced or more irrational [simply] because of its traditional characteristics. (Liang 1997, 465)

In many ways, Liang's ideas resemble those of Zhu. But they differ in one key aspect: Zhu sees local knowledge in more utilitarian terms, as important sources of local social order. Liang, by contrast, ascribes local knowledge with much more universal and ethical importance. To him, such knowledge is relevant, not only to understanding the dynamics of social control, but also to understanding the nature of justice itself.

C. Xia Yong: From State Legitimacy to the Art of Governance

Like Liang, Xia Yong's viewpoints have also changed over the years, from focusing on value systems and social meanings to focusing more on technical problems and juridical functionality. In the early 1990s, Xia bravely explored the relationship between guaranteeing human rights and the legitimacy of state law. He argued that:

> Human rights as a legal principle means that the goal of state law and governmental activities should include recognizing, safeguarding and realizing the basic rights of the people; it should not present an obstacle to or infringement upon the people's rights, otherwise no state legitimacy will be left. . . . It is never justified to deprive people of their human rights. (Xia Yong 1992, 171)

Later, however, he began to see rule of law more as an art of governance. But he argues that it has also come to be regarded as the symbol of a modern and civilized state, and it is through this role, as an important tactic in the construction of a strong state, that rule of law should guide institutional reform in modern China. In other words, rule of law appears to give expression to an important *essence* of modern political systems. Together with other civilization indexes, such as democracy and liberty, it represents a conduit for receiving Western modernism and thus for becoming a member of the community of modern civilizations (Xia Yong 2005).

V. The Rise of Neo-Proceduralism

Xia's interpretative turn may have been intended to harmonize the differences in outlooks and values found in technocratic, formalist, pragmatic, and rationalist visions of rule of law. This is also the concern that underlies Chinese neo-proceduralism, which focuses on the procedural side of the legal order. Neo-proceduralism sees a link between legitimacy and good process. It therefore addresses itself to issues such as the problem of procedural instrumentalism (see also Ji 2006; Ji 2002; Ji 1993). In this sense, neo-proceduralism resonates with the work of Hayek, Schmitt, and even Savigny.

He Weifang is a strong proponent of neo-proceduralism in China. It has been a key aspect of his efforts, both as an academic and as a lawyer and social activist, to promote judicial reform. In 1997, he wrote:

> Viewed from a perspective of constructing rule of law, the court must be the leading organ of dispute resolution, and its judicial activities must have a strong impact upon a diversified society. This impact surely involves judicial power autonomously negotiating with the other social forces. Strengthening the court's position in these negotiations will not guarantee that the court will actively seek a goal of justice. However,

> without this kind of power, it is simply not possible for the judicial system to get the support and resources necessary to adjust social relations effectively, and to develop law and jurisprudence through judicial activity and legal reasoning. (He 1997, 122–123)

He also pays much attention to the importance of legal professionalism. He has for this reason criticized the way that many grassroots judges are selected in China:

> Maybe this practice [of selecting judges from laymen] can promote the popularization of the judicial system and can restrain the tendency of the judiciary to cut itself off from the masses. However, it also has the following negative effect—namely, that the judiciary is not comprised of a coherent body of professionals. It is exactly the opposite: judges cannot fully understand each other, and have different understandings of the substantive law and procedural rules. As a result, there is an inevitable fragmentation [of the judiciary] that weakens the power of the legal profession and hampers the development of legal order. (He 2002, 184)

The courts have been stressing the need for "judicial efficiency" since 1988. At first, this was motivated primarily by a desire to lighten the fiscal burdens that litigation imposed upon the state, and to help clear the growing backlog of cases that were waiting to appear before the courts. For example, in order to lighten the courts' burden of securing evidence, China adopted an adversarial model of litigation in which responsibility for securing evidence was shifted to the parties. The drive to promote judicial efficiency was originally regarded as simply a minor tweaking of the existing system. However, it quickly grew into much more than that, as the reform movement increasingly embraced not only concerns of efficiency but also popular demands for greater fair play and procedural justice. A growing professionalization of both the bar and the judiciary further catalyzed this development. For this reason, even after the backlog of cases had been cleared up, the significance of procedure continued to grow in Chinese socio-legal discourse.

Here I would like to address the most important aspects by which Chinese legal theorists have integrated the conception of procedural justice into more traditional concerns for judicial reform. To a great extent, social ordering in China in founded on a personal guarantee responsibility system (*chenbao zerenzhi*). This involves developing chains of personal relations that help guarantee socially-appropriate performances of contractual or legal obligations. This kind of mechanism also underlies much of the performance of the state's public law obligations. But modern law seems to be incompatible with this system, as its institutional design places much greater emphasis on a depersonalized "freedom of choice" with regards to one's personal responsibilities. This modern kind of legal order is legitimated by the notion of "procedural" due process. Therefore, the idea of procedural justice and the idea of personal responsibility seem mutually exclusive. Paradoxically however, as Chinese society and its social values have diversified, both these two approaches to social ordering have shown themselves to be essential components of judicial reform. In fact, their relationship is complementary rather than antagonistic.

Let me give two examples here. The first involves the development of the "trial-flow tracer system." The other involves the development of what is called the "objective court management system" (see generally Ji 2004b).

The Chinese people have long complained about the opacity of the judicial decision-making process. The trial-flow tracer system is intended to increase the transparency of adjudication and of conformity to procedural due process. According to the "Five-Year Program for Judicial Reform" announced by the SPC in October 1999, the trial-flow tracer system will put into place a system for tracking court cases through each stage of the adjudication process. This will improve the fairness as well as efficiency of adjudication. After this is implemented, the SPC then wants to develop a "Grand Registry (*Da Lian*)" to further improve the tracer system. This will extend that system to include case acceptance or rejection decisions made by Court Registrar's offices. All in all, such a system would help better guarantee procedural due process and restrict the discretionary power of the judge by increasing the visibility and accountability of judicial decision-making at each stage of the adjudicatory process.

Case tracing would work as follows: Suppose a litigant submits a complaint. Normally, the Court Registrar will then assign a venue and term of session to the case. After assigning judges to the case, the Registrar will then turn over the litigation documents, together with an execution tracking card, to the assigned judges. At the same time, he or she will also input general information about the case into an electronic database (an "e-filing"). The judges now responsible for the case must also immediately put into that database each decision and each development that occurs during the adjudicative process. The court's supervisory department will then track and oversee the whole course of trial, checking and evaluating the performance of the judges (i.e., "e-monitoring") in real time, as the adjudication is ongoing.

With the trial-flow tracer system in place, it will then be possible to set up a set of quality indices for objectively measuring and evaluating adjudicative performance. This is the proposed "objective court management system." Such indices would include those focusing on compliance with court rules and procedures, the efficiency of trial management, efficiency in the finding of fact, accuracy in the application of laws and sentencing, and so on.

With these developments, judicial reform in China could now enter a new stage. A key feature of this new stage involves the changing relationship between the people's congresses and the people's courts, or more generally between legislative power and judicial power. This involves the development of new, outside checks on the judicial system, that further supplement the judiciary's own internal checking mechanisms, such as those described above. The most important of these outside checks is the system called "*gean jiandu* (individual case supervision)."

Individual case supervision came to prominence around 1998, and was the product of a desire to subject judicial activity to greater democratic scrutiny. It involves having the people's courts, when they try a major or important case, or a case that has significant impact upon the local society, invite deputies from the local people's congress to witness the trial. It also gives the local people's congresses and their standing committees authority to recommend retrial in those cases in which they have found particularly egregious procedural or legal errors. While controversial, even within China, this individual case supervision system is not without merits. In contrast to the a separation of powers system, in China the legislative power—deriving as it does directly from the people—is given higher constitutional authority that sits above that of any other constitutional body. By making the people's courts at the various levels more politically and constitutionally accountable to their corresponding people's congresses, individual case supervision helps reify this fundamental principle of China's constitutional structure.

Nevertheless, the introduction of this new system does significantly threaten the constitutional principle of judicial independence. The SPC has therefore opposed the encroachments this new system represents. For example, in a judicial interpretation made on August 13, 2001 as part of the *Qi Yuling* case (see also Yu Xingzhong's chapter earlier in this volume), the SPC sought to establish for the courts a power of judicial review, that is, a power to interpret and apply the Constitution to particular cases—what is called "*xianfa sifahua* (taking the Constitution as adjudicative norm)" (SPC 2001). Prior to that interpretation, the power to "interpret" the Constitution has largely been regarded as a power belonging to the National People's Congress alone, not to the judiciary. Although the SPC (2008) subsequently disavowed its *Qi Yuling* interpretation in December 2008, the larger ongoing competition between *gean jiandu* and *xianfa sifahua*, or between the principles of "legislative supremacy" and "judiciary independence," in China's constitutional system, remains strong.

VI. Conclusion

Can China realize the goal of building up a socialist rule of law? Here I would like to conclude with a few general and optimistic remarks on the future of China's juridical order. Once judicial power goes so far as to lead to the introduction of judicial review, the relationship between the legislative power and the judicial power will have to be reorganized. With the qualitative leap in judicial interpretation that occurred in the *Qi Yuling* case, China's judicial reform has already begun to shake-up the political system, which as we saw above regards the National People's Congress as enjoying supreme constitutional authority.

As the Chinese people begin to explore constitutional litigation and public law litigation, they must confront the basic concern about how to keep the balance between judicial constitutional review and popular sovereignty. No matter what kind of institutional model China adopts, judicial constitutional review itself will surely lead to an increase in judicial power and legal professionalism. This will promote the "polyarchy" of China's constitutional system. It may lead to greater democratic control over adjudication, in order to avoid the threat of a "judicial oligarchy." But in any event, in China, from now on, judicial reform, whichever way it goes, will implicate political reform.

In my opinion, China is in the process of de-ideologicalizing of its judicial system, by slowly recognizing that in judicial cases, juridically proper procedures are more important than politically desired results. This means that "socialism" in China will eventually have to cast aside the "ism" and leave only the "social" there. To a certain extent, this suggests the establishment of a kind of "social rechtsstaat." To achieve this goal, two basic developments are necessary. The first is that of a judicial constitutional-review system. The other is a set of procedures for ensuring the competence and accountability of political power, even in states of emergency or exception. Once judicial reform in China goes deep enough to effect the establishment of judicial constitutional review, the relationship between the legislative power and the judicial power will have to be reorganized, and political reform will have to follow. And for once, even extraordinary politics can be subject to legal channeling, as the people will be able to reject any kind of extralegal power. Of course, such reforms cannot be fulfilled automatically. Social pressures are indispensable for inducing legal introspection into governmental decision-making (see also the chapter by Fu Hualing later in this volume). As to this aspect, we find that taxpayers and the rightful owners of farmland are becoming critical pressure groups for China's ongoing "constitutional revolution."

PART 3

Transmitting Constitutionalism: Judicial Power and the Justice System

CHAPTER NINE

Administrative Law as a Mechanism for Political Control in Contemporary China

He Xin

I. Introduction

No one would dispute that one of the key characteristics of administrative law in contemporary China is the dominance of administrative power. Compared to the rights of affected private parties, administrative power is staggeringly formidable; compared to more legally developed countries, the scope of administrative litigation leaves much of administrative behavior unchecked. It is widely held that China's administrative law has been, at best, a rather limited instrument in guarding the rights of citizens.

However, we should not overlook an important development that has occurred since the mid to late 1990s: the state has made substantial efforts in strengthening administrative law, and administrative procedure in particular. It has promulgated numerous new laws in this area—including the Administrative Reconsideration Law (ARL), the National Compensation Law (NCL), the Administrative Licensing Law (ALL), and the Administrative Penalty Law (APL). In its promotion of "administration in accordance with law (*yi fa zhi-zheng*)," the State Council has also issued at least two monumental directives: the "Decision to Comprehensively Implement Administration in Accordance with the Law" in November 1999 (State Council 1999) and the "Outline for Comprehensively Implementing Further Administration in Accordance with the Law" in March of 2004 (State Council 2004a). Unlike the half-hearted "rule by law" slogans that appeared in the 1980s, the strengthening effort of the 1990s was not symbolic but institutional. Not only are administrative procedures clearly and sometimes meticulously detailed in relevant law and directives, but also relevant institutions and personnel have been put in place to help ensure that these procedures are in fact carried out. As of now, almost every administrative regulating entity has established a specialized administrative reconsideration office, usually headed by one of its higher-ranked officials. There is little doubt that the state has taken this effort seriously.

This development is somewhat puzzling, however: why has the state been willing to tie its own hands with these new administrative procedures? This development is especially baffling because China has little tradition of administrative law; and its ruling Communist Party (CCP) has explicitly rejected as incompatible with China's soil the Western idea of "checks and balances" that administrative law is supposed to embody.

To date, there have been two major theories as to why administrative law has developed, but both are inadequate in answering the question posed above. The first theory is that of "power control," which emphasizes administrative law's role in restraining otherwise unruly administrative power (see Hung 2004). The second and more influential theory is that of "balancing"—which is often prefixed with "modern"—which maintains that administrative power must be subject to certain restraints, and that private interests must be protected so to achieve some degree of balance (see Luo 1997).

For advocates of these theories, explaining away the recent development of administrative law is, perhaps, an easy job: they simply argue that the development is a result of their theories persuading the state to restrain administrative power. But in fact, they offer little hard evidence as to the link between the persuasive force of their respective theories and the actual motives of those officials working to promote administrative law in China. They do not explain why the state, which enjoys significant benefits from unchecked administrative discretion, would be willing to forego these benefits to buy into these theories. Why did these theories get an easy sell in this case, but not in other circumstances where advocates have invariably complained about the state's continued, "conservative" stubbornness? Why, in terms of timing, did a meaningful "administration in accordance with law" not occur until the late 1990s? In other words, why at this moment and in this particular regulatory space, have these efforts convinced the stubborn "conservatives" to make compromises here, but not elsewhere?

By putting China's administrative law into greater political and social perspective, this chapter offers an alternative explanation to the recent development of administrative law in China. China's legal system has not evolved in a vacuum; it is a part of politics. More specifically, China's administrative law is not simply an application of modern legal principles such as "administrative fairness," "due process," "balancing," or "power control." It is also a mechanism for the state to restrain the power of lower-level governments and to discipline their deviant behavior, ultimately achieving the goal of *political* control. Since it is a kind of control that is exercised through laws and legal institutions, it might be called "juridical control."

Juridical control is only one of many different kinds of political control mechanisms, however. The extent to which administrative law or juridical control is developed or used would largely depend on whether it, as a particular form of political control, is effective and convenient compared to other forms of political control. When the primary goals of the state are to rapidly achieve economic development and promptly implement new policy, administrative law will be slighted, due to its cumbersome procedures and potential interference with the execution of administrative power. Its development would be further circumscribed if there were other political control mechanisms, such as the petitioning (*xinfang*), that the state could use to effectively oversee lower-level government. By contrast, when social conflicts mount and the state switches its administrative focus from one exclusively on economic development to one that pays greater attention to harmonious society-building, administrative law becomes more desirable, both because of its relatively fairer process and its cheaper oversight cost. Its desirability would be further enhanced because other mechanisms would become less effective in light of the changing interaction between upper and lower level government. In this situation, the state will gradually strengthen the development of administrative law.

Note also that "political control" is fundamentally different from "power control" (see Guo and Song 1997). "Power control" refers to the direct and universal restraint of state power; whereas "political control" primarily refers to how one component of the state, that of upper-level government, works to control another component of the state, that of lower-level government, to make sure that lower-level government indeed pursues the goals of upper-level government. Further, "power control" primarily focuses on the relationship between administrative power and affected private parties, whereas "political control" is more concerned with the relationship between public parties, namely upper-and lower-level governments. Finally, "power control" sees administrative law simply as a means for restraining state power. "Political control" is more nuanced, and recognizes that administrative law can in fact be used to empower the state under certain specific socioeconomic conditions.

This chapter argues that the recent development of administrative law in China has much to do with the changing socioeconomic conditions of the late 1990s. Enlarged income gaps between the rich and the poor, mounting social conflicts between the haves and the have-nots, and deepening confluences between officialdom and business, all contributed to this change. All have caused administrative law to become more effective as a political control mechanism. It is the changing demand of political control under these changing socioeconomic conditions, rather than the tenuous pressure allegedly brought by the need for "power control" or "balancing," that seems the most likely midwife for the birth of "administration in accordance with law."

This focus on political control sheds important light on the underlying institutional logic and the actual operation of China's emerging administrative law, which in turn will help us better perceive its possible developmental trajectories. Furthermore, it also helps us think about the possibility of a distinctly Chinese version of constitutionalism, one which is able to circumscribe administrative governance in spite of the fact that the idea of checks and balances remains alien.

In the next section, this chapter will introduce the background of political control in contemporary China. Working from the principal-agent model of microeconomics, it analyzes the various political control mechanisms and explores how political control has historically been achieved between upper- and lower-level governments. It will also show that administrative law could be regarded as one of several forms of political control—and indeed, a seemingly not very effective one—used by higher-level government in China. Section III then provides a case study demonstrating this in the context of urban housing demolition. It shows that compared to other approaches, the perspective of political control can provide unique insight in explaining and understanding the development of administrative law during the 1990s. Section IV examines the historical development of administrative litigation in China. It shows how as long as other mechanisms remained effective, administrative power has generally sought to prevent judicial interference in administrative behavior. Section V explores how political and economic changes in the 1990s have effected the development of administrative law. The chapter concludes with some implications of all this for thinking about a distinctly Chinese constitutionalism.

II. The Background and Mechanisms of Political Control in Contemporary China

Before the late 1970s reforms, it is well-known that political intervention in social and economic activities was omnipresent in China. This relationship between the state and society has been accurately characterized by Zou Tang (1994) as a special type of totalitarianism: one in which political entities were able to freely penetrate into and control any field, class, or economic activity at any time. With the commencement of these reforms, however, the state, in order to develop its economy, had to give up this totalitarian model because it stifled desirable economic development, particularly at the grassroots level. The state instead began using legal rules and legalistic forms of policymaking to "regulate" (as opposed to dictate) socioeconomic activities (Shue 1988).

An important component of these economic reforms involved encouraging local governments at various levels to develop their local economies. As a result, local economic performance has since become a vital criterion for evaluating and promoting local officials. Under this institutional arrangement, many local governments, to achieve better economic performance, have eagerly provided local enterprises with capital, raw materials, human resources, scarce information, tax holidays, and administrative convenience. In this regard, local government has become an integral part of local enterprise—a developmental model that has been accurately described by Jean Oi (1992) as the "corporatization of local governments." While the actual functioning of local governmental entities across the country was far from uniform, it is fair to say that on the whole, local government has generally played an indispensable role in economic development during the reform period—and that China's political system in general should be regarded as "developmental" in nature (Baum and Shevchenko 1999).

The changes triggered by these reforms affected the dynamics of how upper-level governments controlled their subordinate governmental entities. Upper-level governments no longer enjoyed the largely seamless command-and-control possibilities of the totalitarian model. In fact, upper-level governments found they had little say over the direction of local economic activities, other than through the appointment of lower-level officials.

The state as a whole thus faced a dilemma regarding how to both effectively control lower-level governments and achieve economic development—a dilemma that could be vividly illustrated in a principal-agent model. Because lower-level officials are appointed, promoted, reprimanded, and removed by upper-level governments, the lower-level governments should, at least in theory, follow the instruction of the upper-level governments. In this sense, lower-level government would largely seem to be regarded as an agent of upper-level government, one whose goals are supposed to be the same as those of its upper-level principal. But in practice, lower-level government invariably has its own preferences, and will frequently slight or even ignore the goals of upper-level government in pursuit of its own goals.

As many studies have shown, such inconsistency in local and central preferences is quite conspicuous in China. Most critically for our purposes, while lower-level governments tend to agree with the central government that economic development is important, they often do not share the central government's counterbalancing concern with promoting social harmony. They will frequently sacrifice this aspect of central-level preference in pursuit of their own, much more narrow concern for economic development at whatever social cost.

To address this kind of discrepancy, upper-level governments must develop various mechanisms to oversee lower-level governments and discipline their deviant behavior. The remainder of this section will examine the features and functions of these various oversight mechanisms.

The first and perhaps the most commonly seen oversight mechanism is what is sometimes called the "police patrol," through which upper-level government continually monitors how lower-level government follow instruction from the above. Examples of this mechanism include routine inspections and financial audits (see Jiang 1993). While this mechanism may have some chilling effect on lower-level frolics, it is relatively easy for lower-level governments to get around. For one thing, there always exists information asymmetry between upper-level and lower-level governments with regards to lower-level governmental conditions, needs, and behavior. As a result, it is rather difficult for upper-level officials to obtain accurate information regarding lower-level conformity with their preferences. Relatedly, lower governmental entities significantly outnumber upper-level governmental entities. An upper-level government thus often lacks the energy and resources necessary to monitor, much less to discipline, all the subordinate governmental entities inside its jurisdiction. For these reasons, it is quite easy for lower-level governments to cope with or even dodge investigation from the above.

The second commonly seen control mechanism is that of "fire alarms"—namely the media and various citizen petitioning systems. Both media reports and citizen complaints can reveal problems of lower-level government behavior that upper-level government can then target with direct investigation and discipline. This reduces the cost of upper-level monitoring and inspection, by ameliorating the information asymmetry situation of disadvantaged upper-level governments (Cai 2004).

This mechanism also has its drawbacks, however. It can be easily sabotaged by lower-level governmental countermeasures, such as by lower-level governments threatening and repressing the media and potential petitioners. The effectiveness of the media and of petitioning is made even more vulnerable by their funding and structure. The media, for example, is basically owned and thus controlled by the local governments in which they are located. While they often reveal some minor problems of these governments, they generally lack the resources and political independence to disclose significant scandals. As for petitioning, upper-level governments must still discern whether or not a petitioner's complaint is authentic, and the costs of this threaten to become overwhelming given the huge number of petitions it receives. Although petitioning decreases the cost of obtaining information, it increases the cost of discerning information—and whether it places the upper-level governments in a better position than before is a complicated question to answer. Due to the lack of resources, upper-level governments often find that they have to ask the very lower-level government who is the target of some complaint to itself conduct investigation into that complaint (and bear the costs of that investigation). When this happens, the end result is more likely to be that the petitioners face reprisals from the complained-of lower-level officials, while the problem remains unaddressed. The chance of getting a petitioned-of complaint investigated and resolved seems more or less the same as that of winning a lottery.

Along these lines, administrative law can be seen to be a third type of political control mechanisms—it restrains the power and disciplines the deviant behavior of lower-level government by exposing deviant local administrative behavior through litigation in court. Administrative procedure requires local administrative entities to open their decision-making process, and in turn allows upper-level governments to *indirectly* oversee local-level governments. In contrast to the direct command-and-control forms of political control discussed above, in this mechanism it is the private parties who are affected by the behavior of lower-level governments, rather than the upper-level governments themselves, who are the direct oversight entities. This change from direct to indirect oversight has important implications, which in some context make administrative law more desirable for upper-level governments. First, administrative law ameliorates the informational disadvantages of upper-level governments. Administrative procedure and litigation give private interests a much better opportunity to make their complaints heard, which makes it more difficult for a lower-level government to cover up deviant behavior. Second, administrative law and litigation also allows upper-level governments to transfer oversight costs to the affected private parties (McCubbins, Noll, and Weingast 1987).

On the other hand, however, administrative procedure also lengthens the administrative decision-making process, which impedes policy implementation. In tying the hands of administrative power in this way, administrative procedure decreases administrative flexibility and increases administrative costs associated with rapid regulatory responsiveness.

Administrative litigation evinces the same general characteristics as a mechanism of political control. But unlike administrative procedure, in administrative litigation the more direct oversight comes from the judiciary rather than the citizen complainants. Although in China, the judiciary is widely regarded as less powerful than the administrative system, it still enjoys a certain degree of independence from local governmental actors. Local administrative actors often have ways to exert influence on the judiciary, but they find it very difficult to have full control over it.

From this perspective, administrative law is only one of several oversight mechanisms. Moreover, due to the degree with which it interferes with administrative flexibility, administrative law seems unlikely to be the most important control mechanism in the state's toolkit. Although the other two mechanisms—police patrols and fire alarms—also have their shortcomings, because they basically conduct their oversight from inside the administrative system, they do not threaten to as drastically impede state regulatory responsiveness. They are hence naturally favored by a "developmental" government, one that invariably regards rapid and efficient implementation of administrative policy as a top priority. It is true that the defects of these mechanisms have led to numerous undesirable consequences, including "wherever there is a policy from the above, there is a counter strategy from the below" (He 2004). But so long as the CCP enjoys more or less total control over all levels of China's political situation, the state always has capacity to directly address these negative consequences.

For instance, when the local regulatory situation in one industry deteriorates, the state can freeze the regulatory environment via short-term but urgent administrative directives. The state can also intensify the frequency of police patrols investigation into the regulators, for example by deploying more investigation teams to the problematic area, which will surely alleviate the problem at least temporarily. After the regulatory situation has returned to normal, the state can restore local administrative discretion. That is another reason why the state has little incentive to overhaul the system. As a more long-term cure, the state can improve the overall quality of administration by improving existing central-level monitoring processes and/or securing more qualified personnel. An example of this can be found in recent state efforts to strengthen petitioning systems (which as we saw are a kind of fire alarm mechanism) in order to maintain their effectiveness under the new political and economic conditions (*Liaowang dongfang zhoukan* 2003).

Because of the availabilities and general effectiveness of other mechanisms, the state seems to have little incentive to develop administrative law as an alternative control mechanism. From this standpoint, administrative litigation, an institution outside the administrative system, would seem to be even less desirable to the state than administrative procedure. This is because administrative litigation would not only affect internal administrative efficiency, but also place more checks on the whole administrative system. As the experience of many other countries shows, a developmental country under the control of a single political party long in power usually lacks incentive to adopt administrative litigation as a control mechanism, and rarely opens up its administrative decision-making process to legalistic rigidities (see also Ramseyer 1994).

III. Urban Housing Demolition: A Case Study

This section will use urban housing demolition as a case study to illustrate how the perspective of political control can enhance understanding of the functioning of China's administration by showing why administrative procedure and administrative litigation have been underused in this sector, and what the prospect for their development is. There are many reasons for choosing this issue as a case study: it has become a hot spot of social conflict; it greatly impacts municipal revenues—a large portion of which derive from real estate development; and it, in turn, has been strongly affected by the changing socioeconomic conditions associated with reform. This sector, therefore, constitutes an ideal aperture for exploring the changing landscape of political control and the development of administrative law.

Urban housing demolition has been closely connected with the development of an urban real estate market. During the early stages of economic reforms, all urban real estate was owned by the municipal government. Economic reform greatly increased China's urban population, and this created an enormous market for the development of residential and commercial real estate. Both the central government and local urban governments found a shared goal in developing this urban real estate market: both believed that this development would stimulate local and national economic growth.

But such development often required the demolition of existing buildings, and the relocation of their residents. The residents often vigorously resisted such relocations. Against this backdrop, the State Council issued the 2001 Urban Housing Demolition Administrative Provisions (*Chengshi fangwu chaiqian guanli tiaoli* 2001) (hereinafter "Demolition Provisions"), which require developers to negotiate a "demolition agreement" with affected residents that details the compensation to be given to these residents. But the Demolition Provisions further provide that the developer can apply for a "forced demolition" when the residents do not accept a developer's compensation proposal that has been approved by municipal authorities. While the Demolition Provisions allow residents to challenge a municipally approved compensation proposal in court, Article 17 stipulates that the courts cannot stop or suspend a forced demolition that has been approved by the municipality. Thus, the Demolition Provisions give urban governments virtually complete control over the demolition process: the demolition license is issued by the local government, the level of compensation can be mandated by that government, and forced demolition can also be mandated by that governments.

Although on the surface urban governments play a neutral role in the demolition compensation agreement—which by definition is a "civil (*mingshi*)" agreement between two parties with equal legal status—in fact they invariably stand behind the developer. The developer and the owners are not on an equal footing in the negotiation regarding the demolition compensation—putting it more radically, we may say that the owners are held at gun point in such a negotiation. Even if the owners and the developer eventually reach an agreement, it is often an agreement that is not based on mutual consensus, but on duress.

This is because the growth and privatization of the real estate market encourages collusions between local governments and real estate developers. Local governments receive much revenue from the sale of municipal lands—much of which is occupied by urban housing—to developers. Of course, no one would purchase such land for redevelopment unless they had assurance that they could in fact clear the land of its existing structures.[1] Moreover, the less it costs to clear the land, the more the land can sell for. Thus, urban governments have significant interest in helping developers clear occupied land as quickly and cheaply as possible.

This confluence of local officialdom and real estate businesses impose grave hardships on many of the urban dwellers whose homes are being demolished. But the Demolition Provisions, as demonstrated, can do little to help these people—indeed, these Provisions effectively prevent them from being able to save their homes or otherwise get reasonable compensation.

The scope of judicial review that is provided by these Provisions is very limited. The Demolition Provisions allow residents to initiate an administrative lawsuit regarding the compensation proposal approved by the municipal authorities. However, it does not allow them to challenge the more fundamental issue of forced demolition. Governmental authorities have a green light with regards to this matter once the relevant licenses have been issued. The residents do not have any opportunity to challenge or contest the awarding of demolition licenses. Under relevant legal provisions, they are not considered "affected parties" eligible to bring suit until after the licenses are issued. But assuming the licenses were issued according to proper administrative procedure, they cannot contest them *ex post* because Article 5 of the Administrative Litigation Law (*Zhonghua Renmin Gongheguo Xingzheng Susong Fa* 1989) (hereinafter ALL) clearly stipulates that administrative litigation covers only the legality of concrete administrative behavior.

Even with regards to reviewing compensation, the courts' hands are largely tied. In an interview with the author in August of 2004, an official in charge of housing demolition in the Beijing Bureau of Land and Housing Administration said that by the time such cases get to the courts, "the rice has already been cooked"—that is, that the building at issue has often already been demolished.[2] A court seeking to step in at this late stage would only find itself ignored and, if it presses the issue, politically embarrassed. That is why many local courts refuse to take such cases. Indeed, the Supreme People's Court (SPC), after some hesitation, recently issued a decision that makes it easier for local courts to refuse to hear compensation cases (SPC 2005).

No wonder the Demolition Provisions are referred to as "vicious" by many urban residents. Consequently, many residents threatened with demolition of their homes have adopted alternative, more socially disruptive methods for challenging these decisions—methods such as sit-ins, demonstrations, traffic-blocking, petitioning, or even self-immolations.

As the infringements on urban dwellers become increasingly outrageous, sooner or later social stability is threatened. Since this affects the interests of upper-level governments, it causes them to try to enhance their political control over runaway local governments. For example, against the mounting social conflict caused by urban housing demolition, the general office of the State Council issued a directive in June 2004 entitled "Notice Regarding Constraining the Management of Urban Housing Demolition" (State Council 2004b) that forbade "savage" demolition. This Notice directed that, with the exception of a few projects of major and significant implications, all demolition projects had to be immediately suspended. Governments at other levels also issued similar directives to ease social tension.

But since upper-level governments have no viable institutions that allow them to systematically and efficiently process these housing demolition disputes, they are unable to resolve the problems of numerous city dwellers. Local governments have been very resistant in implementing these directives, since they threaten the local governments' own interests in promoting the real restate business, from which local officials can often take a bite. To make sure that the directives are implemented, upper-level governments have to initiate further "enforcement campaigns." These campaigns usually include mobilizing various resources, setting up leadership groups, seconding personnel from other governmental branches, and demanding the full cooperation of lower-level officials. In part because the directives and the campaigns increase the risks to those officials who dare not to toe the line, this kind of enforcement can be quite effective, especially in the short term (State Council 2004b, Art. 6). But the effect is hard to sustain over the long run because the campaigns themselves involve a huge resource costs. These campaigns are very much like a political gust—they are strong, but do not last long. When the gust is over, local officials and businessmen will once again collaborate with each other, maximizing their mutual interests and obstructing information channels between above and below (see, for example, He 2003).

Since urban housing demolition causes serious social conflict, it has drawn a lot of attention from China's legal academy. Some maintain that the Demolition Provisions contravene higher ranked laws such as the Constitution or the Law on Legislation (see Fei 2004; Lu [undated]). Some complain how the administrative licenses issued prior to the demolition license are not judicially accountable (Xu 2004). Others assert that the Provision's rules on compensation negotiation are not detailed enough, so that the principle of "fair compensation" remains a blank slogan without corresponding procedural guarantees (see Lu [undated]); or that the current situation derives from inadequate civil protection of property rights (Ceng 2005). All argue that to solve the problem, either relevant provisions have to be amended, or relevant governmental authorities have to be held responsible, or greater due process in the demolition process has to be introduced, or the Property Law, which was then still in the drafting process, has to be expanded to more explicitly protect urban property rights to residential land.

If any of the above proposals are adopted and implemented, the urban housing demolition situation would undoubtedly be improved. But for lawyers who are concerned with the real world, this is definitely a big "if." None of these proposals or concerns are so earth-shattering as to likely escape the awareness of State Council regulators. There are reasons why the system stays the way it is. As long as these reason still exists, it seems very unlikely that the State Council will discard the existing system.

From this perspective, to improve the situation needs at least two preconditions. First, that developing the real estate business is no longer one of the top priorities of local urban governments, or that local economic performance ceases to be an important evaluation and promotion criterion. Second, that upper-level governments realize that administrative procedure and administrative litigation are more effective under the changing socioeconomic conditions. But as for now, these preconditions are not sufficiently met. However, as we shall explore more fully in the next section of this chapter, as social conflict becomes more and more serious and the current political control mechanisms become increasingly ineffective, upper-level governments, and the central government in particular, could find an administrative law solution more and more appealing. In this way, the perspective of political control helps understand the issues, problems, and development of urban housing demolition regulation.

IV. The Fight over the Scope of Administrative Litigation

This section will focus on how the administrative system and the judicial system have contested the scope of administrative litigation. It illustrates that as long as alternative control mechanisms are available, the state does not need to, nor is it necessarily willing to, adopt administrative litigation as a device for overseeing lower-level administrative entities. This unwillingness largely derives from the potential for interference that administrative litigation holds for the responsive implementation of administrative policy. In fact, in comparison with the potential interference of the media, petitioning, or administrative procedure, that of administrative litigation is the most significant. Not surprisingly, administrative power would rather resort to these other mechanisms of control in order to preserve administrative discretion.

This point will be further illustrated by the historical account that follows. In the drafting of the ALL, the scope of administrative litigation review was a very controversial issue. The main argument for a narrower scope of review was that the judicial system should neither unduly affect the implementation of administrative policy nor reduce administrative efficiency (see Jiang 1993, 41). The legislators generally agreed that administrative litigation should not prevent administrative entities from effectively and efficiently administering and regulating society (Wang 1989). The force of this argument is seen in the fact that, in comparison with counterparts in other countries, the scope of administrative litigation in China is rather narrow.

Even despite this, the administrative system still viewed the ALL as a potential threat. Only two months after the ALL became effective, the State Council issued its Administrative Reconsideration Rules (*Xingzheng Fuyi Tiaoli* 1989) (ARR), an administrative regulation which would apply to the whole administrative system across the country. A particularly eye-catching feature of the ARR was that the scope of administrative reconsideration was almost tailor-made to that of the ALL—the regulation was obviously a self-defense measure to protect the administrative system (A Ji 2002). The overall effect of the ARR was to preempt possible administrative litigation actions, and only such actions, by assigning initial responsibility for handling such disputes to the administration itself. To structure the scope of administrative reconsideration in this way certainly was to guarantee a least-restrained administrative power.

As the fight over the scope of administrative litigation evolved, the SPC, through its judicial interpretative power, subsequently promulgated the "Opinion on Several Questions Related to the Implementing the People's Republic of China Administrative Litigation Law" (*Guanyu guanche zhixing "zhonghua renmin gongheguo xingzheng susongfa" ruogan wenti de yijian* 1991). This Opinion clearly expanded the scope of administrative litigation—for example, by making justiciable the concrete behavior of some entities that are only ambiguously "administrative" (see Art. 2).

Under the current constitutional framework, the administrative system was not able to subvert this judicial opinion. However, it was able to figure out ways to reduce the possibility of being interfered with by the judicial system. First, it modified the ARR in 1994, and then had it upgraded to a formal law—resulting in 1999 in the Administrative Reconsideration Law (*Zhonghua Renmin Gongheguo Xingzheng Fuyi Fa* 1999) (hereinafter "ARL"). It is true that administrative reconsideration procedure operates parallel to that of administrative litigation, and that choosing reconsideration, in most situations, does not deprive the party of a subsequent right to litigate. However in reality, through the establishment of the ARR and the ARL, the administrative system has largely transformed reconsideration procedure into an effective filter for administrative litigation. This is because a considerable amount of potential administrative litigants would prefer the lesser costs and greater convenience of reconsideration, and as a result, it significantly reduces the likelihood that administrative entities would be directly challenged in court. For the administrative system, the reconsideration procedure serves as an important institution overseeing lower-level administrative entities, indirectly reducing the potential interference from the judicial system.

The fight over the scope of administrative litigation is not limited to administrative reconsideration. Initially, the Administrative Licensing Law (*Zhonghua Renmin Gongheguo Xingzheng Xuke Fa* 2004) seemed to expand the scope of administrative litigation by making reviewable numerous kinds of licensing behavior that had previously not been reviewable. Some experienced judges expected administrative litigation to dramatically increase for this reason. To their surprise, such increase did not occur. This is because local administrations set up internal licensing institutions in response to the ALL that again effectively usurped demand for potential litigation.[3]

But what is the impact of these filter institutions on the effectiveness of the administrative litigation system? One indicator is the disproportionately high success rate for plaintiffs in China's administrative litigation. Of the 51,370 administrative cases heard in 1995, plaintiffs prevailed in around 15 percent (*Zhongguo Falu Nianjian 1997*, 48). On the top of that, another 23 percent of plaintiffs agreed to withdraw their lawsuit on the condition that the administrative entities would either modify or rescind their original administrative behavior (*Zhongguo Falu Nianjian 1997*, 48). In total, roughly 40 percent of plaintiffs were able to use administrative litigation to successfully intervene in administrative behavior—much higher than their counterparts in the United States (12 percent), Taiwan (12 percent), and Japan (4–8 percent) (Peerenboom 2002).

This abnormally high success rate has several implications. First, China's judicial system is not a rubber stamp: the fear of the administrative system that the judicial system will interfere in its regulatory efforts is not groundless. But on the other hand, one should not therefore jump to a conclusion that China in fact has an independent and competent judicial system. A good deal of evidence suggests, on the contrary, that the judiciary is rather weak and incompetent (see, for example, Hung 2004). But relatedly, it might also suggest that persons aggravated by administrative malfeasance will not file administrative lawsuits unless the administrative behavior is so outrageous that they can be relatively assured of a sympathetic court. This suggests that the administrative system, through procedures such as administrative reconsideration and the like, has indeed been effective in preventing a large amount of administrative disputes from reaching the courts, albeit in significant part by rectifying the inappropriate behavior of their subordinate entities (A Ji 2002).

V. The Impact of Changing Socioeconomic Conditions on the Development of Administrative Law

The above analysis demonstrates that as long as the state can maintain political control via other mechanisms, it lacks incentive to develop administrative law. In other words, whether the state further develops administrative law depends on the effectiveness of alternative oversight mechanisms. The more effective these alternative mechanisms are, the less likely the state will turn to administrative law.

But the effectiveness of all these mechanisms is not static; it can change with changes in socioeconomic conditions. Some previously effective mechanisms may become ineffective under new conditions and vice versa. Based on this analytical framework, this section explores the questions raised at the beginning of this chapter: why did the state start to strengthen administrative procedure in the late 1990s, but not before? And why did this strengthening focus on administrative procedure rather than administrative litigation?

From the beginning of the reform to the mid-1990s, alternative political control mechanisms—police patrols and fire alarms—had been largely effective. Over this period, the state had effectuated some degree of retreat from the totalitarian control of society. However the principal goals of both upper-and lower-level governments were concerned primarily with economic development. Under these circumstances, problems of information asymmetry were not serious, and thus did not significantly impact the effectiveness of police patrols and fire alarms as control mechanisms.

Since the mid-1990s, however, a series of changes occurred in China's socioeconomic landscape that have significantly altered dynamics of political control. The first is the local corporatist arrangements, discussed above, that developed between local officialdom and businesses. The confluence has aggravated information asymmetry between upper-and lower-governments—"clogging China's two-track politics" (He 2004). Under this form of corporatism, local officials have become, not merely the agents of upper-level government, but also the agents of local businesses. At the initial stage of reform, this emerging confluence between local government and local business was not necessarily detrimental to upper-level political control.

After the mid-1990s, however, it began aggravating the interests of other social classes, which in turn began to cause social upheavals, which have concerned upper-level governmental entities much more than lower-level governmental entities (see, for example, Wang 2006). Local governments thus whitewash incidents of social unrest, by obstructing central investigations, censoring local media, and disrupting petitioning—in short by interrupting the channels by which upper-level governments gather information. From the standpoint of upper-level governments, their political control, still relying on these alternative mechanisms, has encountered growing difficulties. Under this new situation, police patrols and fire alarms mechanisms have become much less effective at maintaining upper-level political control.

Another socioeconomic change that has impacted the regulatory effectiveness of police patrols and fire alarms is that economic reform has gradually evolved from a "win-win" situation into an increasingly zero-sum game (Hu, Wang, and Zhou 2003). A telling example of this can be found in comparing land reforms of the 1980s with the reform of state-owned enterprises (SOEs) in the 1990s. The land reforms—namely the implementation of the household responsibility system—significantly increased the economic development of rural areas, benefiting almost everyone in rural society. But the reform of SOEs has had a more zero-sum result: workers lose, through massive layoffs; while management wins, through sell-offs and/or higher profitability. Across society more generally, privately owned and foreign-invested economic sectors have developed rapidly. While at the same time, the income gap between management and blue-collar workers has noticeably enlarged: the Gini Coefficient of China has now become one of the highest in the world (Li 2004).

Under such circumstances, central authorities must reflect on the consequences of focusing solely on economic development, and start building institutions that are conducive to social justice rather than to economic growth. Indeed, since China's economic development has already achieved huge success, especially in the coastal areas, the need to develop the economy at all costs has become less pressing. The top priority of the central government has shifted from pure economic development to harmonious society building.

Under these new conditions, the utility of police patrols and of fire alarms as mechanisms for political control becomes less effective, and control of administrative procedure becomes increasingly viable. As mentioned above, the reason why control of administrative procedure was not favored by administrative power earlier was because it unnecessarily complicated the rapid implementation of developmental policy. But under the current situation, the original drawback of administrative procedure becomes much less pronounced, because as discussed above, China's outstanding developmental successes make the rapid implementation of new developmental policy much less necessary.

On the other hand, as we have seen, regulation of administrative procedure can effectively reduce the oversight cost of upper-level governments and ease social conflict, since under such mechanisms, affected private parties and the media replace upper-level governments as the direct monitor of the decision-making processes of lower-level governments, as happened recently with regards to the Yuanmingyuan Administration Office's proposed project for water conservation in the Yuanmingyuan pond (see *People's Daily Online* 2005). In many ways, such parties are in a better position to monitor lower-level governments than higher-level governments. Since private parties and the media are all based at the same locality as the local governments, they are better able to gain accurate information about local conditions. Unlike upper-level governments, these parties cannot be easily blindfolded by lower-level governments. Moreover, the affected private parties have a strong incentive to make their voices heard, because their own interests are at stake. They will surely try to figure out the real situation while the sent-down inspectors of upper-level governments would simply get drunk in welcome banquets set up by lower-level officials. Although lower-level governments might still figure out counterstrategies in administrative procedure, these strategies will often involve changes in behavior that are nevertheless favorable to the interests of upper-level governments (see also Spence 1999).

For similar reasons, these changes in socioeconomic conditions also make administrative litigation more salient as a means of political control. But from the standpoint of administrative power, administrative litigation is not as desirable as administrative procedure, for two reasons. First, although both can be time-consuming, lengthy, and even cumbersome, these "negative" characteristics are more obvious in administrative litigation than in administrative procedure. Second, administrative litigation involves interference from outside the administrative system, which threatens to be less sensitive to issues of administrative efficiency and regulatory responsiveness. It could also be more likely to expose administrative scandals that are especially damaging to the reputation of the whole of China's administrative apparatus.

VI. Conclusions and Implications

By looking at China's administrative law from the perspective of political control, this chapter offers an interpretation of its evolution during the reform period. By examining the characteristics of various political control mechanisms in relationship to particular socioeconomic conditions, this chapter suggests that during the initial period of reform, the state's need to efficiently and flexibly implement its developmental policies explains in large measure the underdevelopment of administrative law. As the need for rapid and efficient implementation diminishes, and as the traditional political control mechanisms become less effective, administrative law can become more prominent. In a way, the state's pursuit of development also partially explains (and even justifies) the dominance of administrative power and the conspicuous power imbalance between administrative entities and affected private parties.

In explaining why China's administrative law has functioned in this particular way, this chapter agrees somewhat with the claim that the underdevelopment of administrative law is due partly to the fact that the leadership has not paid much attention to it. However, the chapter does not attribute this inattention simply to the leadership's historical errors or hostile ideology or rejection of separation of powers. Instead, it points that there are functional reason why the leadership has paid so little attention to administration law and why it seems to be paying more attention to it now.

The chapter thus casts doubt upon a popular but barely corroborated explanation for the currently backward state of administrative law in China—the so-called lack of legal consciousness among China's citizens. When Westernized legal scholars and reformers encounter difficulty in China, they seem all too ready to blame the ignorance of the general Chinese public and the formidable conservativism of its political leadership. What should really be blamed, however, is their own failure to realize the underlying needs and logics of China's evolving regulatory environments. A change of approach is therefore imperative for understanding the dynamics underlying the development of administrative law in China.

This chapter also offers an optimistic but cautious view of the future trajectory of China's administrative law, juridical control more broadly, and a possibly emergent constitutionalism. Although it agrees that the development of administrative law will inevitably be limited in countries with only one ruling party (Ramseyer 1994), it also suggests that a rule of law, or more precisely, rule by law, can be established in China (see Peerenboom 2002). This possibility exists not because rule of law is universally constructive and necessary to economic development, as alleged by some advocates of the simplified version of the law-and-development movement. Instead, it is because China has developed such a need in its particular, local political and economic context (see also the chapter by Fu Hualing later in this volume). The possible establishment of rule of law comes simply from a plain fact that it is becoming a more effective means of political control. It is becoming more useful as a way for the quasi-authoritarian regime to rein-in its subordinates. It can help the state achieve some goals that cannot be achieved by other traditional political control mechanisms.

As this movement toward rule of law has become increasingly entrenched on an institutional level, it is possible that China may be constructing a particular kind of constitutionalism—one in which the role of judicial power is limited, but in which administrative power is constrained through countervailing administrative constraints on administrative procedure. Under such a Constitution, administrative power will remain formidable, but it will nevertheless face constitutional controls that are significant, albeit controls that are internal rather than external.

In this sense, my prediction is cautious: the development of administrative law, or ultimately, of a kind of constitutionalism, depends significantly on the development of particular political and economic conditions within the country. These conditions are neither inevitable nor inevitably permanent. For this reason, the process and development of juridical control and constitutionalism can always threaten to become stagnant or be reversed.

This perspective, in a sense, opens a new window into studying the evolution of the regulatory regime of China. Different from more static analyses of China's administrative law, this perspective allows us to appreciate the actual dynamics that underlie its development. It pulls "politics" back into the vocabulary, reviewing an idea that had long been abandoned and has even become repulsive to some—that "law is a mechanism that the state uses to maintain its political control." This is the reality; and it is that way for a reason. Only through a solid understanding of the logic that underlies this reality can one put forward meaningful and feasible suggestions for reform.

Along these lines, this perspective suggests some new questions that might improve our studies into China's administrative law. How has the dynamic between lower-and upper-level officials actually been affected by the development of administrative law? To what extent can the principal-agent model be applied horizontally to relations between the courts and their respective Communist Party committees? How does political control operate in different administrative areas, such as environmental protection, intellectual property protection, industry and commerce administration, and foreign direct investment? How is political control evolving in these areas in line with new socioeconomic conditions? How do these different arenas of control affect one another? How will administrative litigation and judicial review develop and how will this process affect various administrative behaviors? Here this chapter comes to an end, but one hopes that it is also the start of such investigations.

Notes

1. A former mayor of Shanghai admitted that thanks to the developmental model, the reconstruction of Shanghai's inner city only took ten years, which would have taken a hundred years otherwise. As of 2000, the lease of land-use right in Shanghai has attracted at least 100 billion RMB (Ren 2003).
2. Interview with an official in charge of housing demolition in the Beijing Bureau of Land and Housing Administration, August 2004.
3. Telephone interview with a judge in a basic-level court in Guangzhou, Guangdong province, on July 30, 2005.

CHAPTER TEN

Access to Justice and Constitutionalism in China

FU HUALING

I. Introduction

A neglected aspect in the study of post-Mao Chinese legal and constitutional reform is the importance and potential of social intermediaries, the legal professions in particular, in developing China's emerging rights-based constitutional systems. Scholars and commentators have conducted extensive studies on the supply-side of the legal system (see, for example, He Xin's contribution to this volume), including the expansion of new legal norms and the growth and entrenchment of legal institutions (see, for example, Chen 2004a; Peerenboom 2002), but for the most part few have taken the demand-side of this system seriously. Only recently have researchers started to pay attention to the issues relating to the role of rights consciousness in legal development and the processes through which the legal profession might facilitate such rights consciousness and rights practices (see, for example, Gallagher 2006; Michelson 2008; see generally Diamant, Lubman, and O'Brien 2005).

Support groups in civil society, such as NGOs, have played an indispensable role in the successful development of civil rights. As Charles Epp has shown, rights-based disputes do not arrive in courts "as if by magic." Even with a rights-friendly court and a rights-friendly culture, aggrieved individuals still need to claim, argue, and develop their rights in courts. This mobilization process, according to Epp, "depends on resources, and resources for rights litigation depend on a support structure of rights-advocacy lawyers, rights-advocacy organizations, and sources of financing." The failure or success of a rights revolution in a country depends principally on the availability of a preexisting vibrant support structure (Epp 1998, 18).

This chapter examines the contribution of one particular type of institution in the support structure for China's rights-based legal development: legal aid centers at the county level. Relying on interviews of legal aid managers and lawyers,[1] and site visits in five legal aid centers in Yunnan Province and the Inner Mongolia Autonomous Region in the second half of 2005,[2] this chapter analyzes the *potential* role of legal aid in providing access to justice, developing the rule of law, and empowering rural communities, highlighting the positive development of legal aid in rural China. The author's conclusion is that legal aid is having a genuine impact, both at the individual level and at wider levels, on some of the immense array of social justice problems facing China at its current stage of social and economic development. Legal aid is, in one sense, a "drop in the ocean," but it could nevertheless work in building a foundation for a growing rule of law and constitutionalism.

II. Structure and Function of Legal Aid in China

Like reforms in other sectors of the legal system, the creation and development of legal aid followed a "from scandal-to-reform" pattern. In the early 1990s, a lack of access to justice on the part of the poor led to a series of widely reported, horrific tragedies which caught the attention of decision makers. Those tragedies and scandals demonstrated to many the necessity of legal aid. Under the leadership of Xiao Yang, then Minister of Justice, China started to develop its legal aid system in 1994 (Zhang and Gong 1998). In less than ten years, China had established a functioning legal aid system. By 2005, this included 3,129 legal aid centers (up from 1,235 in 1999); 11,377 legal aid staff members (up from 3,920 in 1999), among which some 7,429 were qualified lawyers; and funding of over 280 million RMB (up from less than 30 million RMB in 1999). In 2005, the legal aid system handled 253,665 cases (including criminal, civil, and administrative cases) (*Zhongguo Falu Nianjian* 2000; *Zhongguo Falu Nianjian* 2006).

There is now also a legislative framework for legal aid in China (see also Choate 2000). The State Council enacted the first national Legal Aid Regulation (*Falu Yuanzhu Tiaoli*) (LAR) in July 2003. This Regulation articulates the general principles of legal aid in China, the scope of legal aid, and application procedures. According to the LAR, legal aid is a government responsibility. The Ministry of Justice (MoJ) and its lower-level counterparts—the provincial Departments of Justice (DoJs) and county-level Bureaus of Justice (BoJs)—must establish legal aid centers to provide legal aid services within their respective jurisdictions. Each legal aid center is to have a salaried staff with legal training to screen legal aid applications and make final decisions as to whether legal aid will be provided. Legal aid centers can decide either to have legal aid cases handled by their salaried staff or to refer cases to private practitioners for handling. The LAR allows for both means-testing and merits-testing for selecting cases.

A county BoJ does not merely administer the legal aid system. It also provides a variety of other legal services, including mediation and legal consultation. However, the division of labor between legal aid and these other legal services is not clearly delineated. As a matter of practice, legal aid centers also assume some responsibility for these other services, even though these functions are not clearly set out in the LAR. Legal aid directors acknowledge that their time and resources are equally divided between litigation and other legal services.

Since the MoJ initiated legal aid services in China in the mid-1990s, it has encountered many obstacles. Given that legal aid largely relies on local human resources and financial support, the first of these involved enlisting local political support. In the beginning, many local political and party officials had never heard of legal aid and had no concept of its purpose. They saw law simply as an instrument of governmental control, not as a vehicle for public empowerment (see also the chapter by He Xin earlier in this volume). The second obstacle was the huge social demand for these scarce legal resources. According to internationally adopted standards, by the end of 2005 there were some 120 million to 130 million Chinese living below the poverty line (*China Daily* online edition 2006a). At best, the over 250,000 legal aid cases handled in that year met only one-third of the actual legal needs of the very poor.[3] Central and local governments have been unable to provide sufficient financial support to legal aid centers. This problem is particularly acute in the western region of the country because of the poor economic performance of that area.

There is also a lack of qualified legal aid lawyers, managers, and policy makers. As of 2002, China officially had about 110,000 licensed lawyers (*People's Daily* (online edition) 2002). However, these lawyers tend to cluster in large cities and are rarely present in rural communities. For example, according to a report issued by China's National People's Congress, 206 counties in China do not have any resident lawyers at all. There are only approximately 24,000 lawyers practicing in China's twelve western provinces and autonomous regions, with each lawyer serving an average of approximately 20,000 people. Even then, most of these lawyers work in the cities, whereas the population—particularly the impoverished population—of the region remains overwhelmingly rural.

A. Contracting Out

At the county level, legal aid lawyers handle most legal aid cases. However, legal aid centers are allowed to refer cases to private legal practitioners (referred to as "social lawyers"). One of the unique characteristics of China's legal aid system is its ability to impose legal aid duties on private legal practitioners (with only a small subsidy or even no remuneration at all). In 2004, social lawyers handled more than half of the legal aid cases in China.[4] This is because the MoJ is also the regulatory body for China's legal profession, with the power to issue, renew and revoke practitioners' licenses. Under the LAR, a competent BoJ may suspend the license of a law firm under its jurisdiction for a period of between one to three months if the firm refuses to undertake a certain number of legal aid cases; and it may also suspend the practice certificates of lawyers who refuse to accept or otherwise terminate legal aid assignments without proper justification. Until recently, the imposition of these mandatory legal aid responsibilities has not been seriously debated in China, although many lawyers—especially elite commercial lawyers—have complained about it (see also Luban 1988; Ellmann 1990). There seems to be a number of reasons to support the imposition of this kind of public service on private attorneys. Politically, China's socialist vision of the legal profession demands lawyers and, for that matter, judges, to be responsive to the need of the people and socially responsible, at least ideologically. This is a worthy tradition that the Bar should honor. And in any event, it is not possible at present for the organized Bar to resist such demands.

There is also a moral duty on the part of the Chinese Bar to provide public legal services in the current economic environment. Although the Bar does not have a monopoly in the legal services market, it is the most dominant and most protected player in that market—supported in significant part by an artificially low admission rate as maintained by the government, and preferential tax rates. Mandatory public service can be seen as a public compensation for the economic benefits that the Bar receives from these special protections of its profession (Fu 2007).

Finally, the requirement of provision of public legal services does not present an undue burden on private practitioners. Chinese law is not very technical and lawyers are mostly general practitioners. Most lawyers in China are thus capable of handling most kind of litigation. In addition, the mandates of public services are flexible. To meet a public service obligation, lawyers and their firms have the options of donating money in lieu of donating their time. It has indeed become a common practice for large firms to exercise such buy-out options by hiring other lawyers to meet the firm's public service obligations.

The number of legal aid cases that a lawyer is required to handle varies from one location to another, depending on the number of lawyers available, local needs, and the capacity of the legal aid centers. Generally, it ranges from one to three cases per year. Rural lawyers tend to work more closely with legal aid offices, and take on more legal aid cases. They have also developed more innovative ways of providing legal aid, including handling cases referred by the legal aid center at a discounted fee, a practice that is not recognized by the MoJ.

B. Legal Aid and Mediation

The purpose of legal aid is not merely to seek court-based solutions. In addition to juridical remedies, legal aid in China also attempts to provide justice in the broad sense, as anything that gives practical and lasting support for a client's legal rights and interests. Under this broader vision of justice, litigation is frequently seen as a last resort. And mediation—although not a compulsory step before litigation—is often first pursued whenever possible.

Legal aid centers often go to great lengths to persuade the parties involved to reach a settlement through mediation. Politically, mediation is a more viable solution in cases challenging a powerful or resourceful opponent; economically, settlement through mediation avoids court fees and other expenses of litigation; and socially, a settlement agreement reached through mediation can be easier to enforce. Mediation also helps the parties more easily restore their relationship once their particular dispute is resolved.

Legal aid lawyers stress the importance of mediation particularly in two types of cases. The first are cases in which parties have a long-term relationship that is likely to continue. A good example of this are cases relating to the support of aging parents. There are a surprisingly high number of cases in which adult children intentionally neglect their aging parents, especially in impoverished areas. Overall, 16 percent of civil legal aid cases in China in 2004 related to the maintenance of parents, spouses, and children,[5] particularly the maintenance of aging parents. And this percentage was likely much higher in relatively impoverished rural communities.

According to legal aid directors in Yunnan and Inner Mongolia, for each such case that is litigated, about six such cases are mediated outside the court. Legal aid lawyers strongly encourage the parties in such cases to reach an agreement. Even where the dispute has entered the judicial process, the legal aid lawyer and the court will work to encourage the parties to reach a settlement. Legal aid lawyers explain that they are reluctant to litigate these cases because while it is easy to win such cases on behalf of the aging parents, such victories are really only of limited value to those clients. Court-ordered maintenance is normally limited to periodic provisions of cash. With the passing of time and waning of the attention of the legal system; the parents will likely sooner or later encounter increasing difficulties in collecting payment. Abandonment will again occur, often in more aggravated form. In rural China, there is no other caretaker for the elderly except their families, so rebuilding the family bond is really often the only hope for the parents. However, a court decision cannot order the children to love and to care for their parents; it cannot order a son to take a sick mother to hospital; or visit her on special occasions. This is a moral responsibility that can only be instilled through nonformal legal means, such as mediation.

The other type of cases that legal aid lawyers prefer to settle rather than to litigate are cases in which the respondent is a politically influential person or organization. In these circumstances, legal aid tends to rely on litigation only as a last resort. The reason is simple and straightforward: where a respondent is influential and powerful, the court may not be able to adjudicate the dispute independently and fairly. Even where a favorable court order is awarded to the plaintiff, it may be of limited value because there are many ways in which a powerful defendent can substantially dilute or frustrate the enforcement of a judgment (by bribing judges, for instance). On relative terms, Chinese courts perform better in disputes between ordinary and relatively equal parties than in disputes involving one party that is politically powerful (Fu 2003).

In difficult cases with great disparities of power between the parties, such as cases involving government departments, legal aid generally sees a mediated settlement as being in the best interests of the weaker client. This is not to say that legal aid is not willing to confront the government. Legal aid staff conceded that although their institution is relatively weak in comparison to many other government institutions, legal aid lawyers are ready to initiate court action as a last resort, once all efforts to settle have failed.

The fact that legal aid is a government function enhances the status of legal aid centers and increases the effectiveness of mediation. According to legal aid lawyers, as a functioning unit of the BoJ, a legal aid center can enhance the bargaining power of their client and put additional pressure on the other side to settle. In mediating a dispute, a legal aid center can mobilize political and social support for their client. Facing difficult cases and wayward parties who refused to settle, legal aid centers in both Yunnan and Inner Mongolia have on occasion secured the intervention of the Chinese Communist Party (CCP) and/or local governmental officials; been able to use the media to shame opposing parties into settling; and been able to compel employers to put additional pressures on the opposing parties to settle amicably. Mediation conducted by a legal aid center thus offers alternative useful strategies for assisting the client, even though mediation is often much more time consuming.

III. Legal Aid and the Development of Legal Justice in China

A. Legal Aid Provides Access to Justice

Legal developments in rural China over the past decade have paradoxically restricted access to justice by peasants in a number of ways. First, the number of branch court offices in the townships has been substantially reduced. The basic-level courts had started to create branch offices in rural townships in the early 1980s, in response to the increasing legal needs in the countryside. Around 14,000 such branches were established, and by 1998, China had 17,411 branch courts with 75,553 judges and support members, reaching the initial objective of setting up one branch court for every three townships. Due to various political, economic, and legal reasons, however, the judiciary started to restructure the branch courts in the late 1990s reversing the trend of extending the judiciary further into rural society (Fu 2004). Some branch offices were merged, while others were closed and judges returned to the county courts (Shao 2001). It is estimated that the branch courts that remain operational have been reduced by a half or two-thirds.

Second, riding on the tide of judicial professionalism and the newly found commitment to adversarial proceedings in civil litigation, basic-level county courts place the burden of proof and of gathering evidence squarely on the plaintiffs. However, due to lack of lawyers, most civil litigants in rural county courts go unrepresented. In an inquisitorial system, unrepresented litigants (who very often do not have any legal knowledge) could receive assistance from the courts' judges in preparing their pleadings. In this way, the reform of civil procedure has further prevented financially disadvantaged litigants from gaining access to justice.

Without legal aid, cases involving the poor would be ignored by the state and be invisible to the public. They would be left unresolved or resolved with tragic results. For example, in cases relating to the support and maintenance of aging parents, of which more will be said below, the assistance of legal aid centers in impoverished areas has stimulated important changes in local norms and practices. The recent surge in such cases in many rural courts correlates strongly to the expansion of legal aid services in these areas (see, for example, Zhou [undated]).

In civil litigation, legal aid assistance enhances access to justice in a number of ways. First, it assists in the filing of the case and in collecting evidence; it can also induce the courts to reduce, waive, or delay payment of court fees; finally, it can assist with making submissions in trials and in the enforcement of judgments.

Collecting evidence is a difficult task. The capacity of legal aid recipients to gather evidence is limited, and it is the duty of legal aid staff to work with their clients to produce a case that is acceptable to the court. Enforcement of civil judgment also presents a serious problem in China. As is well documented, Chinese courts, due to a number of reasons, often cannot effectively enforce their decisions. Because of their position as BoJ officials, legal aid lawyers can help overcome such enforcement problems.

The most difficult task for the legal aid representative is to persuade the courts to waive court fees, and legal aid centers have had only limited success in achieving this goal. County courts are extremely reluctant to waive court fees even where the legal aid cases qualify for waiver under the court's own criteria. Despite repeated instructions from the Supreme People's Court (SPC) and the MoJ in the 1990s calling for the reduction, waiver, or delay of payment of court fees in legal aid cases, local courts, which are dependent on court fees for their basic operations, in general are at most only willing to allow a limited delay in payment.

The courts often use a number of strategies to collect fee payments at different stages of the litigation process. For example, a court may refuse to accept a case without payment, or it may refuse to hear the case after its acceptance; or it may refuse to hand out its decision without first being paid, even if the judgment is in favor of the client (in which case, the court fee would formally be the responsibility of the losing party).

Finally, we might also note that provincial-level legal aid centers rarely handle legal aid cases directly. They mainly serve as policy and administrative centers and refer cases to social lawyers after a verification process. The MoJ has insisted that provincial-level legal aid centers in particular focus on policy issues and not be involved in individual case-handling.

B. *Legal Aid Promotes the Rule of Law*

The development of rule of law depends not only on sound institutions but also on the mobilization of those institutions. Assisted by legal aid centers, hundreds of thousands of poor and otherwise powerless aggrieved individuals are using the courts and mobilizing the law. Through this process, they contribute to the establishment of rule of law in China.

Collectively, their cases build up pressure that changes institutional behaviors and norms. Ordinary people, and their disputes and claims on matters related to their daily life, have often played a practical and meaningful role in pressuring the government. The elderly demanding their pension payments; neglected parents demanding maintenance; injured workers and patients demanding compensation; and in general, aggrieved people asserting their rights; all comprise a leading force in making government more responsive and responsible. Law reform in China is an initiative of the central government, but more importantly it is also a result of pressures from Chinese society.

Legal aid contributes to rule of law first by bringing more disputes into the legal framework, thus making law a dominant force for normative and institutional order. By proactively identifying rural disputes and bringing them up for a legal solution in the courts, legal aid lawyers have initiated a process that has the potential for widening the social and political reach of the law, and for strengthening the influence of legal decision-making in rural society.

This is not to argue that every social problem benefits from a distinctly legal solution. In a society with strong communities and a robust civil society, most grievances are settled through self help, unassisted negotiations, or are mediated by a third party within the immediate community. Only a small percentage of disputes percolate into the legal system for a court-based remedy. In China, depending on the nature of the dispute and the relations between the parties concerned, there are various fora in rural communities for the effective settlement of disputes—including village-based mediation, administrative mediation organized by the township government, or mediation initiated by the legal aid lawyers. However, the coexistence of such extrajudicial fora does not necessarily mean law and court-based remedies are irrelevant. On the contrary, in China, as elsewhere, the law and the courts system continue to provide important guidance and references for these other dispute-resolution mechanisms (sGalanter 1983). The common thread that permeates both adjudication and these other forms of dispute resolution is the mobilization of legal norms under.

Aggrieved individuals seek assistance of a third party only when self help fails to address their grievances effectively. However, there are disagreements on what type of third-party assistance aggrieved individuals in rural China prefer to pursue. The dominant view is that peasants prefer to seek "justice from above"—that is justice provided by authorities from their local communities. But Ethan Michelson has challenged this "justice from above" view and argued convincingly that, considering the totality of the grievances and disputes that arise in rural society, what he called "justice from below" is more effective, and indeed aggrieved peasants prefer to have their disputes resolved locally, often informally or administratively (Michelson 2007).

There is merit to Michelson's critique of justice from above. Justice from below is effective and desirable especially for the everyday, comparatively trivial, disputes that commonly arise among peasants. The path to "justice from above" can be chaotic and the results are frequently disappointing—the Letters and Visits (*xingfang*) system only very rarely succeeds in providing remedies for individual grievances (Minzner 2006). Finally, given the high litigation costs and other barriers to accessing courts, it is often impractical for poor peasants to have their cases solved by these courts.

Some see a distubing, "neo-Machiavellian" aspect to legal aid in China as well. It is commonly asserted that legal aid entrenches CCP rule by strengthening its policy control over the countryside (Wang 2005; see also the chapter by He Xin earlier in this volume). Legal aid also can act as a safety valve that calms angry parties who might otherwise be more active in resisting a systemically oppressive political regime. When the poor are given "effective" access to justice (as defined by the state), they develop what some argue to be a misplaced trust in existing political institutions and practices (see also the chapter by Eva Pils later in this volume).

Legal aid thus buttresses the legitimacy of the government instead of challenging it. As one county-legal aid center director succinctly put it, when facing a public rally by a group of aggrieved individuals, the relevant authority's immediate reaction used to be to use the police to detain the organizers and disperse the crowd. Now, it is to use the legal aid center to negotiate with the organizers and participants to resolve the dispute through legal means. In one county, the legal aid center is intentionally located in front of the

CCP/government compound in order to prevent complainants from reaching other CCP and government offices.

Nevertheless, despite Michelson's critique, the importance of access to justice-from-above should not be underestimated. When the stakes are high in a particular case, one naturally wants to move up to the next tier in the dispute pagoda and look for a more formal and institutionalized solution. The courts, as the most specialized institutions for dispute resolution, are able to provide specific solutions when other, more local and informal, forms of dispute resolution fail. Although courts in China often fail to fulfill this specialist function satisfactorily (studies of Chinese courts reveal high dissatisfaction rates, see, e.g., Gallagher 2006), the courts remain in this regard a resourceful institution with great potential.

Law is as innately an instrument of social action as it is of political control. As Mary Gallagher has recently pointed out: "Laws are significant because they shape the expectation of citizens. They are written guarantees, and even when, or especially when, they go unfulfilled, they have important consequences for social action" (Gallagher 2005; see also Fu and Cullen 2008; Dowdle, this volume). It is true that many legal rights in China are especially vague, but they are vague in part because they are not used. Legal aid stimulates the use of such rights and, in the process, makes them more powerful. The Chinese court system, as limited as it is, is still an important forum for the development of norms of justice. By giving citizens an opportunity to articulate and vindicate their legal rights with a formal authority that is not provided to them by other dispute resolution channels, legal aid allows the law and its rights to assert their authority and radiate their effect in society.

The importance of legal aid can also be seen in its litigation results. In the vast majority of legal-aid civil cases, the client wins. Nationally, among the 61,744 legal-aid civil cases that went to trial in 2004 (which accounted for 73 percent of all legal-aid cases that year) clients won in 90 percent of the cases. And in 2003, the success rate for legal-aid civil litigation was 89 percent. Among legal-aid administrative-law cases, 85 percent went to trial, and clients prevailed in 75 percent of the cases going to trial. It is indeed rare, according to legal aid directors, for them to lose a case in court (Ministry of Justice Legal Aid Center, 2005). The faith of the thousands of citizens seeking access to the courts through legal aid is therefore warranted.

C. Legal Aid Empowers Communities by Facilitating Networking, Outreaching, and Rights Consciousness

1. Networking

Legal aid improves networking between rural communities and larger society. The Chinese political and legal systems are characterized by compartmentalization. Governmental, quasi-governmental, and nongovernmental organizations are divided and separated vertically and horizontally. Horizontally, the political and legal sphere is divided into many regulatory systems, with more competition than cooperation among these system. The police, the court, and the MoJ largely operate without concern for the needs or demands of the other. Vertically, a lower level institution is accountable both to the local CCP Committee and government, and to its superior institution at the next higher level. For example, a county court may refuse to honor an intra-governmental agreement reached between the SPC and MoJ on waiving or reducing court fees for a legal aid case, until that agreement is transformed into a "red-letterhead" document (*hongtou wenjian*) issued by the local Committee of the CCP. It is difficult to perceive, much less penetrate, the bureaucratic walls that separate institutions on the same and on different levels. However, legal aid is now well placed to challenge these interdepartmental barriers.

Legal aid institutions in China are developing close working relationships with other legal institutions. This is possible largely because legal aid centers in China are governmental departments mandated to play a leading role in securing the support and cooperation of other relevant institutions through joint conferences, consultation/coordination meetings, and joint issuance of policy documents. In one prefecture in Yunnan, for example, the DoJ, when facing difficulties with other legal institutions, would sometime seek assistance from the officials in charge of the legal aid system for that prefecture. Because of his seniority, this official was able to call a meeting among all these institutions to discuss the matter and produce mutually workable result.

A smooth working relationship with the courts is particularly important for the establishment of an effective local legal aid system. At the initial stage of its development, a legal aid system must rely on referrals from courts for its intake. Referrals from courts not only increase the number of legal-aid cases, but also symbolize the court's recognition of the importance of legal aid. Judicial referral is a mutually beneficial process. Facing ever increasing litigation rate, the courts are eager to refer unrepresented and unprepared cases to legal aid centers so that these cases are in good order when and if they eventually do come to the court. For the legal aid centers, a court referral symbolizes that the court has considered the case and will take it seriously if it goes back to the court.

Second, because legal aid lawyers enjoy the status of public officials, and because they are "repeat players" in the court system (Galanter 1974), legal aid lawyers are generally received and treated with significant respect by the courts. In many tangible and intangible ways, judges treat the government's legal-aid lawyers more politely and seriously than other lawyers. With the assistance of the BoJ, for example, these lawyers often have better access to court files—a right that all Chinese lawyers have in theory but which is often restricted in practice. As such, legal aid compensates for a structural deficiency of China's legal profession.

A legal aid center also works closely with other quasi-government offices and grassroots organizations, in particular those of the All-China Women's Federation, the All-China Federation of Trade Unions (ACFTU), and the Association for Disabled Persons—organizations whose members often make up a significance portion of that center's legal aid recipients. From the very beginning of legal aid development, the MoJ sought cooperation with those representative organizations. Together, they issued joint instructions on requiring legal aid centers to provide priority service to these particularly vulnerable social groups. In addition to passively receiving referrals from those organizations, legal aid centers have occasionally utilized the political and financial resources of these quasi-governmental organizations in handling cases. For example, one legal aid center sought the assistance of a local branch of the ACFTU to pressure a construction company to make overdue salary payments to a group of migrant construction workers; another invited representatives of the Association of Disabled Persons to attend mediation sessions in a personal injury cases and to bringing pressure on a township government that was reluctant to compensate a peasant who lost one of her arms while working for that government.

Legal aid could do much more in soliciting support from those organizations. In principle, these organizations are the official representatives of these vulnerable groups in Chinese society, and thus have a duty to offer more assistance when referring their cases for legal aid. However, it seems that the cooperation between legal aid centers and those organizations is largely driven by government policy. It is not actively offered by the social organizations themselves. Even the MoJ criticizes the legal aid centers' relationship with those organizations as "formalistic" and "superficial." This is due in part to the fact that all these representative organizations have their own legal-aid like departments that have also been working actively for the interests of their constituents both at the policy level and the level of individual cases. They often regard the expansion of legal aid under the MoJ as an intrusion into their autonomy.

Thus, while networking and multi-institutional approaches are important as a general matter for legal aid in China, the details of how legal aid centers can work with these other organizations have been contentious. The ongoing debate has been whether China should have a plurality of legal aid systems dispersed among different organizations, or a single legal aid system under the central control of the MoJ. Social organizations naturally prefer to maintain their own independent legal aid services. For example, many local branches of the All-China Women's Federation want to be able to receive, screen, and litigate cases relating to women's rights issues independently of any involvement by local legal aid centers. So far, the MoJ has successfully lobbied against this kind of legal aid pluralism however, and is establishing a monopoly over the provision of legal aid services. The MoJ is cynical about other organizations' requests for independence, seeing them as little more than veiled attempts to gain access to China's meager legal aid funding.[6]

To further institutionalize the working relationships between the legal aid centers and social organizations, the MoJ is in the process of establishing representative offices in these organizations. The purpose of these representative offices is to provide easier access to the legal aid system, so that when aggrieved individuals visit these social organizations, they can simultaneously contact the local legal aid center, thus expediting the referral process. Under proposed rules, social organizations would be responsible for setting up, staffing, administering and (most importantly from the MoJ's perspective) financing their own specialized legal aid offices. For their part, the MoJ's legal aid centers would be responsible for policy development and case-quality control.

Legal aid also helps connect rural communities with higher political environments. One important effect of legal aid is that rural communities no longer remain closed societies that are sealed off from state law. Legal aid creates a network that links the primary, indigenous, and semiautonomous social ordering of rural communities with the higher levels of state law (compare Galanter 1983).

2. *Reaching Out*

At the township level, the principal office in charge of dispute resolution is the Justice Station (JS) headed by a Justice Assistant (JA). The principal responsibilities of a JA are to organize and guide mediation work in rural villages; to train the mediators of those villages; and to mediate difficult disputes that village mediators fail to resolve. By the end of 2005, China had 41,143 JSs with 99,800 staff members (*Fazhi Wang* 2006).

A JA performs different functions depending on his or her working relationship with the county legal aid center. These include referring cases to the county legal aid center after verifying the client's eligibility; helping the legal aid center in collecting and preparing evidence for litigation; assisting legal aid lawyers in conducting mediation; supervising the enforcement of mediation agreements and court decisions; and even directly representing legal aid clients in county court.

Further incorporation of the JAs into the legal aid system would promote a more robust rural dispute resolution network founded on law. The township JAs, through litigation and by interacting with judges, have become an increasingly integral part of the legal aid system. In cases involving the maintenance of aging parents, for example, the county legal aid center is responsible in individual cases for getting payment agreements through mediation or litigation, while the JA is responsible for ensuring that the adult children honor that agreement. Prepared by this kind of training and fortified through work experience, JAs become increasingly competent and confident in providing supervision and guidance for mediation at the village level, and in handling disputes. Because of the JA's pivotal role in dispute resolution at the township level, his or her more active involvement in legal aid services—especially in court proceedings—could produce a ripple effect that reshapes the role that law and rights play in resolving disputes in rural townships.

3. *Legal Aid and Rights Consciousness*

Legal aid in rural China has also promoted rights consciousness and empowerment. Since the early 1980s, the government has been actively promoting the concept of rule of law. It has enacted a series of laws that, on their face, create important legal rights for citizens and limit the power of government authorities. The BoJs, as part of national campaigns, conduct periodic legal publicity and education campaigns, aiming at promoting rule of law values and the enhancement of rights consciousness among the general public. These campaigns have been successful in popularizing legal knowledge and increasing popular awareness of rights.

All this has created political and legal opportunities for ordinary citizens to assert their rights in fora provided by law (see generally O'Brien and Li 2006). Such education campaigns have not addressed the more institutionalized problems these people are facing, however. Peasants, for example, now know their rights, and become more agitated than before when their rights are violated. However, the available dispute resolution institutions do not match the increasing expectation and demand. Access to law is meaningless without access to professional support.

Here, too, the impact of legal aid is particularly profound in rural China. For many years, the Chinese government has generally ignored the peasant population except when collecting fees, levies and taxes; and enforcing the one child policy. The level of poverty in certain rural communities is indeed staggering. Critical legal needs in the countryside have long gone unrecognized and unaddressed: such as aging parents requiring maintenance; and injured workers and victims of road traffic accidents or medical malpractice requiring legitimate compensation. These individual tragedies and misfortunes are not particularly visible, but they provide concrete evidence to local populations of the social inequality in Chinese society. They provide vivid illustrations of the continuing injustices and unfairness suffered by much of the rural population.

Increasingly, however, there are free, helpful, and distinctly legal remedies for the long ignored and suppressed peasants. Such unprecedented generosity has had tremendous psychological impact both on legal aid recipients and on their communities. In addition to practical legal advice and other forms of legal assistance, legal aid gives clients confidence and fortitude in seeking to challenge and overcome local injustices. Their very visible mediation and litigation of hundreds of ordinary cases leads many other vulnerable individuals not only to develop but also to act upon a growing sense of legal rights and justice. They thus help instill an important sense of self-respect and empowerment, particularly among the vulnerable and disadvantaged. Rational and reflective peasants learn to mobilize the law to their own advantage, while at the same time learning its limits as well (see also Gallagher 2006).

In fact, the vast majority of legal cases in China are not socially significant, and administrative cases, in particular, continue to remain a very tiny percentage of the cases in Chinese courts. Although legal aid centers should not shy away from difficult and controversial cases, they should not seek to achieve the goal of pursuing high profile cases by deliberately sacrificing attention to the everyday cases of ordinary people. Routine grievances, like those involving personal injury, traffic accidents, or family disputes, carry their own significance, both for the parties involved and for society at large. Through such cases, the activities of legal aid services create a centrifugal dynamic that has a wider impact than simply on the individual case or the individual person. A legal aid case not only represents a decision, it also disseminates information that there are procedures and institutions for aggrieved individuals to voice their claims and seek remedies. Former legal aid clients are themselves among the best promoters of legal aid, and more importantly, of more general increased access to rights-based justice (see also Gallagher 2006).

All in all, the ultimate test for legal aid is not whether an individual case is won or lost. It is whether the process of legal mobilization has empowered the disadvantaged in society. The legal aid process should be treated as an educational process, an awareness process, a capacity-building process, an organizing process and an empowerment process.

Legal aid in China raises awareness of issues relating to broad social policy. Particularly in the West, it is often forgotten that even in China, there is a common ground between the state and the rights-bearing individual: legal aid can support and enhance their mutual interests (see also the chapter by He Xin in this volume). Legal aid has grown over the past decade largely because of this identification of interests. The state now increasingly prioritizes the protection of the rights and interests of many weak groups in society, be it the rights and interests of aged parents in receiving desperately needed support from their children, or the rights and interests of the injured and their families in receiving compensation from those who injured them. Particularly at present, and particularly in rural areas, the combination of law and legal aid offers both the state and the individual an important means for realizing these shared interests.

IV. Conclusion

Access to justice is as fundamental an interest for the poor as it is for anyone else. China's authoritarian government once relied on police powers and other administrative methods in settling or otherwise repressing disputes. Now, it is providing its poor critical resources that allow them to seek rights-based remedies in the courts. China's three-decade long process of legal reform has produced a sophisticated set of supporting laws and legal institutions, even while the associated social and economic transition has brought about a surge in social conflicts. There is still a huge gap between the world in which disputes take place and the world in which disputes are resolved. Poverty, geographic distance between courts and rural communities, and the increasing bureaucratic fragmentation of political culture continue to crucially limit access to justice.

However, legal aid in China is closing the gap between these two worlds and is playing an instrumental role in improving such access. A legal system is functional only when it is mobilized by ordinary individuals. Ultimately, the driving force for law reform comes from grassroots demands for such reforms. Through mediating and litigating hundreds of thousands of cases each year, legal aid contributes crucially to the development of rule of law, the empowerment of the poor, and the creation of a more robust civil society.

Notes

1. Interviewees included two officials from the Ministry of Justice (MoJ) Center for Legal Aid, five legal aid lawyers at provincial legal aid centers, and six legal aid directors at county legal aid centers. Interviewees also include numerous legal aid recipients.
2. The legal aid centers the author visited are better off in terms of financial support, quality of management, and internal organization. They are thus not representative of legal aid centers in China.
3. Statistics provided by lawyers in the MoJ Center for Legal Aid.
4. Statistics provided by lawyers in the MoJ Center for Legal Aid.
5. Statistics provided by lawyers in the MoJ Center for Legal Aid.
6. Other justifications offered by MoJ for their monopoly include (1) that social organizations are not really social at all, but are as much a part of the government as the MoJ, and thus there is no need to create a parallel system of government legal aid services; (2) that social organizations, while performing an important role in protecting the rights of their members, lack the legal expertise and qualified personnel necessary to handle legal aid cases; and (3) that legal aid funding is limited and such limited resources should be centralized and allocated rationally for more effective use.

CHAPTER ELEVEN

Ordinary Justice and Popular Constitutionalism in China

STÉPHANIE BALME

The judge, even when he is free, is still not wholly free.

He is not a knight-errant roaming at will in pursuit of his own ideal of beauty or of goodness. A judge is to draw his inspiration from consecrated principles. Wide enough in all conscience is the field of discretion that remains."

Benjamin Cardozo (1921, 141)

I. Introduction

For fifteen years, between 1889 and 1904, Judge Paul Magnaud, the politically and socially liberal president of the Tribunal of the First Instance in Château-Thierry (a well-known commune located in the French Champagne region), pursued a campaign against traditional jurisprudence. Famously nicknamed "*le bon juge* [the good judge]" by the academician Anatole France in 1900, his opinions and decisions leaned in favor of the weaker party. He acquitted theft defendants who pleaded hunger as a defense for stealing bread or begging (see the *Menard* Case and the *Chiabrando* case). He imposed liability without fault in automobile accident cases. And he granted divorce by mutual consent (not recognized by legislation in France until 1975) (see also Gény 1954). Never in the past had judicial activism appeared in such a dramatic way in France, and his decisions became the subject of violent controversies both within the judiciary and within the court of public opinion.

In May 2003, Li Huijuan, a judge on the Luoyang Intermediary People's Court in Henan Province, in a case involving a seed contract, found a local price regulation in conflict with the national seed law, and declared that local regulation "spontaneously invalid." In China, judges do not have the power to declare a local regulation facially invalid on the grounds that it contradicts the Constitution or higher-level legislation, and in October of that year, the provincial High Court not only overturned her judgment, but also requested that the Intermediate court fire her. As with Judge Magnaud, her decision sparked much discussion and criticism in China, both in the media and among Chinese scholars (Yardley 2005; see also Balme 2005).

Of course, Judge Li, like Judge Magnaud, is an outlier. But this is changing. This chapter addresses the emergence of judicial activism and constitutional rights consciousness in the context of rural justice in contemporary China—that is, that of the Basic-Level People's Courts (*Jiceng renmin fayuan*) and Basic-Level People's Tribunals (*Jiceng renmin fating*). Looking at land-rights issues (*tudi quan*), and in particular at so-called married-out women cases (*waijia nu* or *chujia nu*), it explores why, and under what circumstances, some local judges on these courts and tribunals are increasingly willing to engage in a practice of *weiquan*, or "protecting the rights of people."

This chapter will first show that although courts do not enjoy formal power of constitutional review in China, a kind of popular constitutionalism is nevertheless emerging within the rural judiciary. This constitutional judicialization has been aided by the Chinese Communist Party's (CCP's) new focus on "harmonious society," which has effectuated a partial transfer of authority and responsibility to the judicial sphere by emphasizing the role judicial dispute resolution plays in promoting social stability. It argues that, surprisingly, local judicial activism is being catalyzed by the low status and prestige enjoyed by local judges within Chinese society. This lack of status and prestige has provoked a crisis in the professional identity of an increasingly professionalized rural judiciary. And paradoxically, the local judiciary's embrace of a judicialized popular constitutionalism is one way in which it seeks to promote its professional identity. Finally, we shall also see how judicial mediation has emerged as the predominant vehicle for this kind of judicial activism. This is because the structure of that mediation makes it especially conducive to judicial deployment of constitutionalist language. All this goes against the common wisdom that states that traditional and rural Chinese culture is incompatible with modern constitutionalism.

II. Ordinary Justice in Rural China

Between 2005 and 2008, I conducted fieldwork on numerous basic-level courts and tribunals in Shaanxi and Gansu provinces, as well as on some in

Shanghai. This chapter focuses on one Basic-Level People's Court, and its three Basic-Level People's Tribunals (which I will designate as "Tribunal A," "Tribunal B," and "Tribunal C"), in Shaanxi province. In the process of conducting this fieldwork, I observed numerous mediations and trials involving civil, administrative, and criminal cases. I also met with local judges associations and participated in judicial training programs. And I have interviewed hundreds of judges.

Shaanxi is a beautiful rural province located in the very heart of China. It is the home of the internationally known writer Jia Pingwa. Thirteen dynasties founded their capitols in this province. It was here that China's "Han" identity and civilization initially emerged; it was here that the concept of a unified and centralized Chinese nation was born. Shaanxi was also a very important locale during China's Maoist period: it was in its second largest city, Yan'an, that the CCP was headquartered after the Long March in 1937, and where it remained until 1947.

Today, the province has developed a strong culture of unified power, as well as a strong consciousness of the political and social role of civil servants. Shaanxi is an important experimental site for Hu Jintao's "new socialist countryside" program (World Bank 2006), which calls for "building the countryside into areas characterized by enhanced production, well-off living standards, healthy rural culture, neat and clean villages, and democratic management" (CCP and State Council 2006; see also Chen 2007). Under the auspices of this program, the central government has promoted the development of more effective and professional legal services in rural areas (*Xinhua News Agency* 2006), particularly in order to placate growing social anger over local land-use decisions. The prevalence of new slogans like "bringing judges closer to the citizens (*faguan weimin*)" and "justice for the people (*sifa weimin*)" shows how local and ordinary judges are intended to play a key role in the implementation of this program.

III. A Bottom-Up Judicialization

In China, the basic-level courts and tribunals officially occupy the lowest tier of a four-tiered judicial system (actually five-tiered if we include Basic-Level People's Tribunals as a separate tier beneath the basic-level courts system, see below). There is at least one Basic-Level People's Court for each county-level administrative entity in China. According to Article 20 of the *Organic Law of the People's Courts* (*Zhonghua Renmin Gongheguo Renmin Faguan Zuzhi Fa* 1979), basic-level courts have original jurisdiction over all civil and criminal cases arising in their county except when the law provides otherwise. Article 13 of the *Administrative Litigation Law* (*Zhonghua Renmin Gongheguo Zhengzhi

Susong Fa 1989) also gives them first-instance jurisdiction over administrative litigation suits as well.

People's Tribunals are subdivisions of basic-level courts. They are most generally located in remote rural areas. There are approximately 3,000 basic level courts and 12,000 basic-level tribunals in China. Until recently, in addition to adjudicating minor cases, they were also responsible for carrying out other political and societal functions, such as supervising the one-child policy, disseminating CCP propaganda, and gathering people to perform collective tasks.

Together, these basic-level courts and tribunals adjudicate around 80 percent of the cases brought before China's courts. The study of these courts and tribunals therefore is very relevant for understanding the deep transformations affecting China's judiciary, as well as for understanding how ordinary people conceptualize law, state power and their own rights.

In Shaanxi, a basic-level court is comprised of between thirty-five and sixty judges, and has a staff of around 200 to 250. A tribunal is composed of a President, one Vice-President, one or two judges, and is staffed by one or two clerks. Nominated by local people's congresses, tribunal judges are paid by local governments. Traditionally, a tribunal's budget came in part from its litigation fees (of which it was allowed to retain some fixed percentage), as well as from money allocated to it by provincial-level authorities. Reforms in 2009, however, have sought to centralize local courts' budgets (Balme 2009). In 2006, the system for managing litigation fees was reformed, so that tribunal budgets were no longer tied to their collection of litigation fees. In late 2006, the State Council issued the Measures on the Payment of Litigation Fees (*Susong Feiyong Jiaona Banfa* 2006) (effective April 1, 2007), which mandated a drastic reduction in litigation fees in order to reduce China's notorious "peasant burdens." This has had a direct and immediate negative impact on the budgets of rural courts and tribunals, and for many of them has severely diminished their capacity to deliver local justice. Interestingly, according to interviews, neither the Supreme People's Court (SPC) nor the Ministry of Justice were consulted by the State Council before issuing this order.

In the courts I observed, all the tribunal presidents were university graduates, except for one. Not all were formally trained in law, however. But of those who were not, all had received intensive legal training, either on general matters or on important legal texts such as the 2007 Property Law or the newly amended Lawyers Law.

IV. Rights-Based Judicialization

Between fifty and sixty percent of the cases handled by these courts involve family disputes, domestic violence, traffic accidents, labor contract law issues, and minor criminal offences. A further twenty-five to thirty percent involve land disputes. The figures from one basic-level court located in a suburb of a large city in Shaanxi show it issuing an average of 2,400 judicial decisions each year since the year 2000, with an average annual caseload growth of between three to five percent. Within this, there is a growing judicialization of matters related to rights issues. According to one local judge, the number of cases related to the "defense of rights (*weiquan*)" has been increasing at a rate of around 15 percent per year. This is part of China's larger *weiquan* movement, which—while not formalized—consists of a growing, loosely organized collection of lawyers and social activists who, alone or sometimes in collaboration with the media, use the institutions of the law to defend and advance their and others' of fundamental legal and/or constitutional rights (see generally Pils, this volume; see also Hand, this volume).

An example of this right-based judicialization is found in the Shaanxi courts' increasing willingness to handle legal disputes involving "married-out" women (*chujia nu*)—women who marry husbands outside their birth village, leave that village to live with their husband, and whose village of legal residence thereby becomes ambiguous due to lack of administrative clarity and often conflicting village practices and traditions. As explored in a detailed study by He Xin (2007), these disputes generally revolve around the rights of married-out women to compensation, dividends, and relevant benefits relating to the sale of collectively-owned land in their home or resident village. Most real property in a rural village is collectively-held by the members of that village. When a village government requisitions some of the village's collectively-held land in order to make it more suitable for sale or transfer to private entities, it is required to compensate the village's legally-defined members. Such compensation is frequently denied to married-out women, however, often in violation of these women's legal rights as village members. This may be due to a number of factors. The first is a cultural background of centuries of discrimination against property ownership by women in rural China. A more obvious cause for this exclusion, however, is purely economic: the total amount of land requisition compensation is fixed, so reducing the number of people included in the pot—such as by refusing to include married-out women—will increase the share received by the remaining members.

In his research, He Xin examined how several courts in Guangzhou handled cases involving married-out women. He found that these courts routinely refused to accept such cases. He concluded that this refusal actually represented an *extension* of judicial power. The courts "pushed away [these] disputes to the [local] governments" while at the same time retaining authority to "review the governments' decisions [in the handling of these cases] in administrative litigation." In so doing, he writes, "the courts largely avoid[ed] the

Table 11.1 Number of *"married-out-women"* cases handled by the People's Tribunals of a rural asic-level court in the western region of Shaanxi

	2001	*2002*	*2003*	*2004*	*2005*	*2006*	*2007 (From January to June)*
People's Tribunal A	20	25	21	19	24	11	57
People's Tribunal B	—	18	24	22	18	17	21
People's Tribunal C	—	23	19	21	42	28	18
Total	20	66	64	62	84	56	96

legal barriers and the difficulty in judgment enforcement, but retain[ed] an advantageous position in [their] power relationship with the governments" (He 2007, 207).

In contrast to He Xin's observations in Guangzhou, however, Shaanxi courts appear to have been much more willing to accept married-out women cases. As shown in Table 11.1, local courts in the western part of Shaanxi have been routinely accepting such cases for years. Interviews with and reports by local court officials reveal that Shaanxi courts began accepting these kinds of cases following a 1999 interpretation of the new Land Administration Law promulgated by the Shaanxi High (Provincial) Court. As one basic-level judge reported in an interview, "although statistics by the Shaanxi High People's Court on cases of income distribution in collective economic organizations (i.e., villages) only started coming out in January 2006, I know that our court began to accept these cases in 1999 as tort cases." Moreover, between 2005 and 2008, a majority of the women who brought these cases actually won their suit, according to interviews. Courts have consistently held that excluding married-out women from compensation for appropriation of collectively-owned land violates both these women's rights to property and basic principles of gender equality. (This does not imply that the judgments are effectively enforced, however.) In the subsequent sections to this chapter, I explore why the Shaanxi courts have been more aggressive in accepting and resolving these kinds of cases.

V. A Political Decision

In Shaanxi, the courts' decision to accept married-out-women cases was the culmination of a long political battle that not only pitted government against judiciary but also the judiciary against itself. Interviews revealed that conflicts of interests between the SPC on the one hand and several provincial High Courts on the other played themselves out in their differing interpretions the law. In mostly rural Shaanxi, provincial governmental evaluations of the local situation meshed with a political desire on the part of the central government to promote social stability by protecting collective land from unfair appropriation.

With regards to resolving the problems of married-out women, four key legal issues had to be addressed before these cases could be routinely brought before the Shaanxi courts. First, both married-out women and Village Committees needed to be recognized as equal subjects before the law. Along these lines, on July 9, 2001, a written reply by the Research Department of the Supreme People's Court, issued under its own name, to a query by the Guangdong High Court on "the question of whether People's Courts shall accept disputes over the distribution of income by rural collective economic organizations" announced that "disputes over income distribution between a rural collective economic organization and its members are regarded as disputes among equal subjects" (Supreme People's Court Research Office, 2001a).

Second, such complaints had to be brought into the courts. In the 2001 Reply discussed immediately above, the Supreme People's Court Research Office also held that as long as a complaint is in compliance with Article 108 of the Civil Litigation Law (*Minshi Susong Fa* 1991), "[c]ourts shall accept cases of married-out women involving land compensation fees disputes." Another reply by the Supreme People's Court Research Office issued to the Shaanxi Provincial High Court on December 31, 2001 confirmed that land compensation fees and resettlement subsidies were indeed justiciable (Supreme People's Court Research Office, 2001b).

In 2002, however, the Civil Tribunal of the Supreme People's Court published under its own name a ruling that conflicted with the Research Office's two earlier replies asserting that courts should *not* accept such cases. This interpretative conflict was resolved on July 29, 2005, when the SPC confirmed the Research Office position by issuing under its own name an "Interpretation Regarding Applicable Legal Issues for Hearing Cases about Rural Land Contracting Disputes." This interpretation stated in relevant part that:

> Any ... infringement upon a woman's rights and interests as a member of a collective economic organization based upon her unmarried, married, divorced or widowed status; or infringement upon the equal rights and interests as members of a collective economic organization of a husband or a child who as moved to a wife's residence after marriage, shall be arbitrated by the government at the township level. Injured parties also can apply to the arbitration agency in charge of land contract arbitration, or bring the case to a People's Court. And the People's Court should accept such cases. (SPC 2006)

A third issue that impeded the bringing of married-out-women cases before the courts was that of determining who exactly should be entitled to receive compensation for rural land requisition. Along these lines, the SPC's afore-mentioned Interpretation stipulated that:

> [A] rural collective economic organization, Village Assembly, or Village Group Assembly may decide, *in accordance with the democratic discussion procedures as provided for by the law*, to distribute land compensation that has been received by the collective economic organization. If anyone meeting the qualifications for being a member of the collective economic organization when the land requisition plan was decided requests his or her share, that request shall be granted unless otherwise provided for by [local regulation]. (SPC 2006) (emphasis added)

That same Interpretation also stated that rights to compensation for requisition of collectively-held land vested in "all persons meeting the membership qualifications of that collective economic organization." But there is no national legislation defining the criteria for being a member of a collective economic organization. Therefore, such determinations have generally been left to local, "democratic procedures," as per the SPC's Interpretation.

Local Village Committees are often reluctant to recognize village membership in married-out women that were born in the village but subsequently have moved to their husband's village, because they consider such women as "belonging" to their husband's village (therefore the expression of "married-out" women). But on the other hand, the Village Committees of a married-out woman's new village of residence also tend to regard such women as not being members of their village as well. Local regulations and customs frequently try to resolve this conundrum by equating village membership with village residency permits, i.e., *hukou*. But there are numerous problems with this approach. First, a married-out woman is under no legal obligation to transfer her *hukou* to her new village of residence. At the same time, the process of transferring *hukou* requires the approval of the authorities of the village being transferred to. Such authorities are often reluctant to accommodate such transfers, in some cases precisely in order to limit the number of potential land compensation beneficiaries. And there is no legal remedy available when a village government fails to approve a request to transfer a *hukou*. Therefore, most of the judges I interviewed regarded as "unreasonable" and "non-implementable" requirements that demanded *hukou* in the collective.

The other way in which village membership is most commonly defined is through long-standing residency in the village (even when the formal *hukou* vests in some other locale, as would often be the case for example with persons who initially left their village to attend university or vocational school, or to join the armed forces). But this definition brings with it its own set of problems. In their search for jobs and income, many rural peasants are forced to leave their home villages for long periods of time without gaining residence any place else. In such circumstances, these peasants are still intimately tied to their village of origin, even though they have resided outside that village for significant periods of time.

Beyond this, proving a permanent or regular residency can be very difficult. Village governance focuses primarily on families and households, rather than on individuals. For this reason, it is often difficult to prove (or disprove) a particular individual's actual residency within the village. In addition, no legal criteria currently exists to define what constitutes residency. As noted above, in the case of married-out women whose *hukou* is still registered in their village of origin, but who live with their husband in a different village, there is a real social question as to which of these two villages is their legal residence.

In light of such concerns, the Shaanxi judges I interviewed reported that they usually simply consider whether the claimed membership has been recognized through some action of the village or its Committee. Obviously, those holding local *hukou* would automatically be regarded as members of the collective. But for those whose *hukou* has not been transferred to the place of the village, the judge would consider whether they have consistently fulfilled their legal obligations to the village, or whether they or the Village Committee are the ones principally responsible for their *hukou* remaining in their village of origin.

A fourth and related issue that impeded the bringing of married-out women cases before the courts involves the question of village governmental autonomy. The Organic Law of Village Committees (*Zhongguo Renmin Gongheguo Cunmin weiyuanhui Zuzhi Fa* 1998) clearly gives villages autonomy to administer their own affairs. Article 1 of that Law states that "this Law is formulated in accordance with the relevant provisions of the Constitution of the People's Republic of China with a view to ensuring self-government by the villagers in the countryside, who will administer their own affairs in accordance with the law." Article 2 states that "[t]he Village Committee shall manage the public affairs and public welfare services of the village, mediate disputes among the villagers, help maintain public order, convey the villagers' opinions and demands, and make suggestions to the people's government."

Local judges in Shaanxi often expressed concern both about the principle of village self-government and about the local village government's use of this self-government (Kelliher 1997; An 2007). From the local court's perspective, how should a village government's power be regulated? Courts must guarantee the legitimate rights of village self-government but at the same time protect the rights of individuals when they are infringed upon by this self-government. The principle of village self-government, combined with the current lack of uniform implementing regulations, allows each village to formulate its membership criteria based on what it believes is right or fair, or simply on what it believes is in its own best interests. But village membership also represents one of the primary social safety nets for rural peasants. In cases, such as those involving married-out women, that span multiple villages with multiple regulatory schemes, each looking out for its own interests, the very real needs of the individuals concerned are often left vulnerable and unprotected.

VI. Empirical Examples of Judicial Activism in Married-Out Women Cases in Shaanxi

Nevertheless, my investigations suggest that Tribunal judges in Shaanxi can take a very activist stance in favor of the land-rights claims of married-out women. As one judge explained:

> Regarding married-out-women cases, we judges can completely rely on our own [Shaanxi] law for protecting their rights. As I have said, if the traditions and superstitions of our country are biased against women, the law itself is very clear on the principle of legal equality between men and women. Therefore, whenever someone is discriminated against because of gender; our courts possess all the legal authority necessary to fulfill the spirit of our national law.

Along these lines, Tribunal judges frequently cite from the Law on the Protection of Women's Rights and Interests (*Zhonghua Renmin Gongheguo Funu Quanyi Baozhang Fa* 1994). As one Tribunal judge expressed during the mediation of a dispute involving land-rights of married-out women (discussed in our third case study below):

> I personally think that there are plenty of laws and regulations that can guarantee the land-contract rights of married-out-women. Among the laws we usually quote are articles from chapter five of the Law on the Protection of Women's Rights and Interests, which is entitled

> "Rights and Interests Relating to Property." Article 30 states that "the state shall guarantee that women enjoy equal rights with men to property." Article 32 [states that] "Women shall enjoy equal rights with men in the contracted management of rural land; in the distribution of the proceeds of collective economic organizations; in the receipt of land requisition and occupation compensations; and in the allocation of house sites." Article 33 [states that]: "No organization or individual may infringe upon a woman's rights and interests in a rural collective economic organization on the ground that she is not married, is married, is divorced, or has lost her spouse."

Judges frequently also draw support from Article 6 of the Law on Land Contract in Rural Areas (*Zhonghua Renmin Gongheguo Nongcun Tudi Chengbao Fa* 2002), which states:

> In undertaking land contracts in rural areas, women shall enjoy equal rights with men. The legitimate rights and interests of women shall be protected in contract. No organization or individual may deprive them of the rights to land contractual management to which they are entitled, or infringe upon such right.

They also draw from Article 105 of the General Principles of the Civil Law (*Zhonghua Renmin Gongheguo Minfa Tongze* 1986), which commands that "[w]omen shall enjoy equal civil rights with men."

Beyond this, however, Tribunal judges also draw support from what the judge above referred to as the "spirit" of the law. Like the "good judge" Paul Magnaud of the French Third Republic, the more activist of the local judges in Shaanxi seem to be asking themselves how would an honest person or a good cadre behave in the circumstances before them. And they render their decisions accordingly, by equating the demands of such good behavior with "the spirit of the law." It is through this reference to a legal "spirit" that is related to but transcends the boundaries of formal legal text that popular constitutionalism begins to manifest itself in local jurisprudence.

In this way, Tribunal judges can evoke constitutional values in their decision making without directly citing constitutional text. I therefore argue that what these judges call the "spirit of the law" actually refers to a particular form of what the Introduction to this volume termed "popular constitutionalism"—a form of constitutionalism that is found not so much in formal texts and documents, but in individual sentiments of justice. As we see in the cases described below, for Tribunal judges, this activist, constitutional "spirit" is closely associated with an emerging consciousness of judicial professionalism.

Case 1: A Married-Out Widow Sues Her Native Village for Compensation for Appropriated Land before a People's Tribunal in June 2006 in Western Shaanxi.

A married-out widow and her son came before a Tribunal in western Shaanxi to sue the Village Committee of her native village for refusing to compensate her and her son for land that had been requisitioned by the village to build a highway because she had transferred her *hukou* to her husband's village upon marriage. (After her husband's death, the Village Committee of her husband's village also refused to recognize her continued membership in that village, based in part on a traditional belief that a married-out woman continued to "belong" to her native village.)

The mediation, which lasted several weeks, was conducted by a Tribunal consisting of two judges drawn from the basic-level court of the county. Its hearings were conducted in the presence of two-thirds of the defendant Village Committee (that of the plaintiff's native village). Mediation meetings were often tense, and the head of the Village Committee often refused to participate. The senior judge on the Tribunal, who was also the President of the county's basic-level court, even questioned whether the court should have accepted the case.

Nevertheless, the plaintiff ultimately prevailed, due to the activism of the tribunal's junior judge. That judge was able to require that the Village Committee affirmatively prove that the plaintiff had in fact actually departed from her native village. As noted above, since village governance and record-keeping focuses on households rather than on individuals, such a proof often can be very difficult for a Village Committee to muster.

The junior judge also excluded from the Tribunal hearings accusations regarding the plaintiff's moral character. Some on the Village Committee had sought to accuse the plaintiff of having an affair with another man during her marriage. The junior judge convinced the Tribunal that it had no legal authority to deprive a person of his or her rights simply because he or she had behaved in morally reprehensible ways.

In advancing these claims, the junior judge's presentation of the nature of the case was particularly forceful. He portrayed this case as ultimately being due to the "corruptly-minded" head of the village. He assailed the Village Committee for electing such a Village Head, and urged the villagers themselves to think more deeply about the people they would choose as their representatives. His orations skillfully referred, not only to legal texts and tropes, but also to the political language that the CCP had used to promote the development of Village Committees during the 1980s, and in particular the special role the Village Committees were supposed to play in increasing the accountability of local leaders and implementing "socialist democracy."

Case 2: A Married-Out Woman Sues Her Husband's Village for Compensation for Appropriated Land before a People's Tribunal in December 2006 in Western Shaanxi.

A married-out woman had been granted usage rights over a parcel of village collective land by the Village Committee of her new husband's village while she was still in the process of transferring her *hukou* to that village. These land-use rights were subsequently taken away from her in a latter redistribution by the Village Committee, and the head of that Committee began also impeding her efforts to complete the transfer of her *hukou*. This was probably because her husband's former wife, herself a married-out woman, unexpectedly continued to register her *hukou* in that village, and thus had to be included in the village's land redistributions. Excluding the husband's present wife from the new redistribution scheme allowed the village to maintain the size of the other villagers' distribution share. (This hypothesis is supported by a claim the woman made during the Tribunal hearing at which she said that the head of Village Committee had exerted pressure on her to drop the suit by offering to help her complete the transfer of her *hukou* if she dropped her claim to village land during the present redistribution.)

A People's Tribunal was asked to mediate the dispute. In interviews conducted during the mediation, both the judges of the mediating Tribunal expressed outrage at how the village authorities "clearly relied on a deliberately incomplete vision of the law." Nevertheless, it was also clear that the Tribunal's senior judge did not want to become involved in the local affairs of the village. He questioned whether the Tribunal had jurisdiction over this situation. Specifically, he questioned whether the Tribunal had the authority to compel the village head to complete the woman's hukou transfer, and whether it had authority to compel the Village Committee to include the woman in the village's land-redistribution scheme.

Nevertheless, the Tribunal ultimately ruled in favor of the married-out woman, finding that:

> The plaintiff has been deprived of her legal right to transfer her *hukou*. Her not having a *hukou* [in her husband's village] was caused by the illegal behavior of the Village Committee. Therefore, the rights of the plaintiff have been infringed. The plaintiff has become a permanent resident of the village through marriage. This, being an independent source of rights, entitles her to enjoy these rights. Since the plaintiff is [legally in the village], and the marriage between her and her husband is also legal, then the reasons given by the Village Committee [for excluding her from the redistribution scheme] are not acceptable.

The Tribunal's ruling was again due in significant part to the aggressive activism of the tribunal's two junior judges (both of whom were women). The junior judges were particularly upset by the fact that the Village Committee members, including the village head, never showed up during mediations. (During one of these meetings, a clerk had to be sent to roundup at least one representative of the Village Committee so that the mediation could commence.) The younger judges also challenged the professionalism of the senior judge for his reluctance to take charge of the mediation.

By the end of the mediation, the Tribunal's negative attitude toward the village leaders, both on the part of the junior judges and on the part of the senior judge, had catalyzed their empathy for the plaintiff. The insult to their professional standing that they perceived in the dismissive attitude of the Village Committee and its head provoked a distinctly "activist" willingness to deliver justice according to law and fairness. Not only did the Tribunal find in favor of the plaintiff, but it also went beyond the four corners of the dispute to rule that *the ex-wife* also continued to have a right to a share in the village's redistribution scheme, since her *hukou* remained registered in that village and she continued to reside there as an individual household.

Case 3: A Collective Action Challenging a Village's Compensation Distribution Scheme before a People's Tribunal in June 2007 in Western Shaanxi

The third case involved twenty-one families from the same village who collectively sued their Village Committee over its scheme for distributing compensation for the requisition of collectively-held land. Five of these families included women who had been excluded from the distribution scheme due to having "married-out" to husbands residing in other villages. During interviews, these women stated that they had sued the Village Committee "on behalf of themselves and all other similarly situated wives in the district." Their purpose was not only to secure a judicial remedy and obtain compensation, but also to denounce a wrong they believed had been done against them and others living in similar circumstances.

Again, the married-out women won their case. As with the second case study discussed above, the Tribunal evinced a distinctly activist aggressiveness that appears to have been triggered by the noncooperative and dismissive attitude of the Village Committee. Not only did the Committee often refuse to send representatives to the Tribunal hearing, but also when they did attend, they treated both the Tribunal judges and the "barefoot lawyer" who represented the plaintiffs (herself a member of the village) with open contempt. Indeed, Committee representatives openly denigrated the Tribunal judge, accusing them of being "corrupt civil servants" and "enemies of the people." The junior judges on the Tribunal (both of whom again were women) were particularly infuriated by this behavior, and began to openly favor the plaintiffs—sometimes giving them advice (and otherwise conversing with them) in the corridor before or after mediation sessions.

VII. Social Status and Professionalization

Local judges hold a fragile political position in the contemporary Chinese State: they are expected to be both defenders of the state against the people and defenders of the people against the state. Paradoxically, although judges as a class appear to be more sensitive to the people's misery than other civil servants, surveys also reveal that the ordinary population has the least respect for judges in comparison to that they hold for other civil servants (see also Liu 2003). This is not all that surprising. As the anthropologist Marcel Henaff (2002) has shown, conspicuous wealth contributes essentially to the development of legitimacy, professionalism, and social recognition within a profession. But a rural judge's income and living conditions are not much different from those of the upper-average rural peasant. In Shaanxi for example, between 2005 and 2008, local judges' salaries ranged between 900 and 1,300 RMB per month, with additional compensation for housing and family expenses that could amount to an additional 250 RMB per month. By comparison, in 2005 the average salary of a state-owned-enterprise worker in Shaanxi was 1,268 RMB per month. Judges working in People's Tribunals typically live, at least part time, in state-owned dormitories located at their work place—also much like the ordinary blue-collar worker of a state-owned enterprise.

As a result, China's rural grassroots judiciary lacks the social capital necessary to achieve the higher social status of a "profession" (compare with Piant 2006). Rural, basic-level judges are often called "basket judges" (*lanzi faguan*) or "generalist judges" (*zonghexing faguan*), derogatory terms that refer to the fact that they have to preside over a full spectrum of legal issues, rather than being able to specialize in particular kinds of cases (e.g., civil, criminal, or economic) as do the judges in more prestigious urban courts. The professionalized character of Tribunal judging is often even less pronounced. As Zhao Xiaoli (2002) explains: "[Tribunal judges] spend most of their time investigating evidence, collecting testimonies, and preparing case files, rather than on developing legal reasoning and legal argument. A qualified [Tribunal] judge is one who knows how to prepare the case files correctly."

In addition, villagers often regard People's Tribunals simply as inert conduits for sanctioning state violence. In the eyes of many villagers, the People's Tribunal and the local police station are simply two sides of the same coin.

They do not associate these tribunals with independent notions of justice or fairness.

In interviews, rural basic-level judges constantly expressed frustrations with their low social (and economic) status. As I observed, during trials and mediations both local officials and ordinary residents often treated these judges with disdain, if not out-and-out contempt. As described above, village heads frequently refused to attend tribunal mediations. It was not rare to see local residents sitting and talking informally on the judges' bench prior to the judge's arrival for a hearing, or to see judges having to shout down the courtroom for quiet and respect in the process of these hearings.

Administrative decentralization within the judicial system also impedes the development of a professional identity within the basic-level rural judiciary. The dependence of these judges on local authorities for their salaries and housing prevents them from building horizontal solidarities across jurisdictions and vertical solidarities with upper-level judges. Under such conditions, collective mobilization by rural judges to advance their status and working conditions would appear to be almost impossible.

Relatedly, there is distinct lack of ritual and gravitas in rural court proceedings, and this too contributes to the lack of social authority and credibility faced by rural judges. The present system for grass-roots rural judging was set up in the 1980s, and was designed after the "Ma Xiwu" system that the CCP developed in the 1940s. Ma Xiwu was a CCP cadre who invented a system of dispatching itinerant tribunals to try cases in the locality in which they arose. In today's rural China, the word most commonly used to refer to the local judge is still *shenpanyuan*, meaning "adjudicator," rather than the more formally *faguan*, or "judge"—a usage that was introduced by Ma Xiwu's original system. Under the Ma Xiwu system, judges could issue judgments anywhere and anytime, both inside and outside the courtroom. Not only did this facilitate informal judicial decision making, but it also allowed for many instances of judicial injustice. In the 1950s, rural tribunals and courts were expected to function as "knife handles (*daobazi*)," to be used as "weapons of the proletarian dictatorship." Staffed primarily by judges drawn from the military and dressed in military-like garb, these courts functioned primarily as tools of party-state repression and control. The judicial informalities characteristic of this system worked to kill any popular conception of judging as a distinct "profession" among the rural population.

This political legacy of this history continues to affect rural courtrooms today. Article 33 of the new Code of Judicial Ethics, for example, establishes a distinctive civilian dress code for judges (see also Grimheden 2004). But rural judges often only wear their official dress on special occasions. And when they do wear offical dress in court, rural plaintiffs and defendants often find it difficult to differentiate the judge from the procurator, and sometimes even from representative counsel, as all will often similarly dress in black, Western-styled clothing. There are no established procedures for introducing a judge to the courtroom, or for announcing his or her exit. In presiding over a courtroom, rural judges rarely use a gavel (which is new to them).

Nevertheless, as we saw above, the rural judiciary *is* becoming professionalized. Indeed, information collected from the most-recently published judicial yearbook of Shaanxi (dated 1997!) shows a clear development of this judicial professionalization. In 1990, only 29.4 percent of the judicial staff working in Shaanxi had received associates or bachelor degrees; by 1996, 85 percent of these staff had received such degrees. Moreover, as of 1996, 24 percent of the judicial staff who had earlier been appointed without higher-education degrees had gone on to receive intensive legal training at local university law schools or via special programs run by the judiciary itself. (On the other hand, the already high ratio of male to female judges is increasing, despite the fact that newly-appointed women judges tend to be relatively better trained than their male counterparts, as evinced by their greater likelihood of holding a higher-education degrees, and their higher average scores on the National Judicial Examination.)

The case studies discussed above show, paradoxically, how as rural judges become increasingly conscious of and dissatisfied with their lack of professional status, they become more inclined to activism. They see such activism as a means of promoting their professional status. This was true even with regards to judges who had been reared under the earlier, more socialist legal culture—indeed, such judges appeared even more inclined to activism, because they had not been so socialized to the figure of the neutral judge, a very recent conceptual development in China (see Zhu, this volume). To them, judicial professionalism lies in a particular empathy with weaker parties and a particular sensitivity toward abuses of the rights of these parties (see also Fu, this volume). The more judges became professionally active, the more they tended to sympathize with disadvantaged defendants and plaintiffs (such as married-out women) whom they perceive as victims of injustice and discrimination.

VIII. Tribunals vs. Trials as Vehicles for Rural Popular Constitutionalism

Interestingly, it is the rural People's Tribunal, rather than the rural courtroom, that may represent the most effective vehicle for the further development of a jurisprudence of popular constitutionalism in today's China. This is because hearing processes in formal courts tend to be very bureaucratic (another holdover from the 1950s). Evidence and testimony are often simply read out directly from written documents by the parties during the proceedings.

Spontaneous expression is often nonexistent. Participants are expressly discouraged from making emotive appeals. At one divorce trial that I witnessed, when a plaintiff started appealing in tears to the importance of the "constitutional principle of men and women being equal before the law," she was immediately silenced by the main judge and reprimanded for her lack of "self control," and for the legal "irrelevance" of her plea.

Such rigidity and formality make it very difficult to appeal to fundamental constitutional rights in the courtroom. The Constitution is formally nonjusticiable, and thus foreign to these more juridified styles of legal expression and discourse. Indeed, judges who cite the Constitution or other nonjusticiable legal sources in their opinions will often find such citations expunged from the official reports of those cases by their courts' Adjudication Committees, and may find themselves disciplined as well (as happened to Judge Li in the Seeds case discussed at the opening of this chapter).

Tribunal mediations, for the most part, do not suffer from such constraints however. Tribunal procedures—being reserved for "minor" disputes—are not overseen by an Adjudication Committee. They are much less formal. Judges and parties frequently engage in spontaneous, vigorous, and dramatic debate. My own observations suggest that more than a third of each mediation process is devoted to exploring the personal backgrounds and experiences of the people involved. Although Tribunal judges will still often ask particularly emotional plaintiffs to "control their nerves," tears, expressions of anger, and other kinds of emotive appeals are generally much more acceptable in Tribunals than they are in formal litigation of the courts.

Tribunal-based mediation is also a particularly popular form of adjudication among basic-level rural judges. The fact that such mediations are not subject to oversight by the court's Adjudication Committee allows Tribunal judges to personalize their decisions and thus promote their professionalized independence in a way they cannot do during trials. These judges also have more leeway in conducting Tribunal hearings. There is much less demand on the part of the judicial administration for quick judgments that are easily enforcemented. For these reasons, activist rural judges find Tribunal mediation to be a particularly effective way for delivering a distinctly constitutionalized justice, and constitutional principles are an increasingly common *de facto* referent in rural Tribunal mediation.

Beyond this, China's central judicial administration is now seeking to increase the jurisdiction of People's Tribunals to include minor administrative cases and disputes involving rural property expropriations. Both kinds of cases are likely to further increase the capacity of Tribunal mediation to further catalyze a jurisprudence of popular constitutionalism.

IX. Conclusion

To date, judicial activism in China has yet to achieve the drama of Judge Paul Magnaud in Chateau-Thierry. But rural judges are increasingly asserting themselves against blatant political and social unfairness. Such evolutions trace the slow transformation of the Chinese judiciary from a purely administrative agent into an agent of social justice. Among a growing number of local rural judges in China, judicial activism is both the cause and the consequentce of the central government's emphasis on improving the societal and political role and status of the judiciary. The slogan "protecting rights is the improvement of justice (*weiquan shi sifa de jinbu*)" expresses the trajectory of this evolution quite eloquently.

In this way, the Chinese judiciary is following the global trend in the expansion of judicial power (see Tate and Vallinder 1995). This study confirms the observations of legal sociologists such as Herbert Jacob that the easier it is for citizens to access courts and tribunals, the stronger and more influential these courts and tribunals become (Jacob et al. 1996, 243). But there is also a downside to this increased access. This is the increasing workload of courts; and the increasing institutional pressures that come from assuming greater responsibility for resolving key societal problems without necessarily enjoying the powers or the means required to carry out this responsibility. In China, local justice has generally not been given the institutional capacity necessary to address effectively the growing challenge of maintaining and promoting social stability that has recently been thrust upon it.

But China's popular constitutional judicialization is not solely, or even primarily, a top-down process. As the chapter by Keith Hand in his volume so convincingly shows, it can also be the product of a civil society that is becoming increasingly aware of its status as rights-bearing citizens and increasingly assertive when the state fails to acknowledge or protect their rights from political, social, or economic oppression. Combined with my own findings of the growth of a popular constitutionalism among the rural judiciary, this suggests strongly that, contrary to common assumptions, China's rural, basic-level courts and tribunals are playing a key role in the development of constitutionalism and rights consciousness in rural China. And building constitutionalism in the countryside will prove crucial for building constitutionalism in China as a whole.

CHAPTER TWELVE

Beyond "Judicial Power": Courts and Constitutionalism in Modern China

MICHAEL W. DOWDLE

I. Introduction: China's "Constitutional Option"

Since the turn of the new century, there has been an explosion of popular constitutional discourse in China. However, the courts seem curiously absent from this emergence. Standard constitutional thought, at least as it comes out of the Anglo-American world, tends to view neutral and independent courts—and in particular "judicial review"—as the centerpiece of a functional constitutional system. Is China a case of "constitutionalism without courts?" (cf Dowdle 2002). Or does the apparent lack of judicial presence in this new discourse render this discourse developmentally meaningless, a mere anomaly in a larger trajectory that is fatally stalled? (see Pei 2006).

In this chapter, I argue that in fact, courts have been playing a significant role in China's emerging constitutionalism—albeit a role that is different from that which dominates the attention of most Anglo-European scholars. I will call this role one of "constitutional *poiesis*," in reflection of its close semblance to Aristotle's articulation of the role that tragic drama played in the constitutional development of Athens in Ancient Greece. And it is a role, I assert, that does indeed generate lasting and positive developments in China's constitutional environment.

My argument proceeds in two sections. In the next section, I fashion that alternative model of judicial constitutional contribution that I am calling "constitutional *poiesis*." Under this model, courts can contribute to constitutional development not simply by resolving constitutional disputes in a neutral and independent manner, but also by compelling the citizenry to reimagine the meaning of the constitutional state. Then, in Section III, I apply this new model to present-day China, and show how a dynamic of court-triggered constitutional *poiesis* is clearly in play there, and how it is affecting significant changes in China's larger constitutional environment.

II. Rethinking Judicial Power

It was noted in the first chapter to this volume that the standard model of "judicial power" is not in fact well suited to examinations of developing constitutional systems. The model of judicial power presumes the presence of strong, independent, and neutral courts, whose decisions will be authoritative throughout the political community. But emerging constitutional systems are unlikely to possess such juridical institutions. Does this mean, as suggested by Bruce Ackerman (1992), that courts have little role to play in such scenarios? Here, I propose that they do have a role to play, albeit one that is quite different from that described by the model of judicial power.

A. Constitutional Poiesis: Courts and Representation

I start by noting that insofar as some kinds of cases are concerned, courts are not really neutral, third-party resolvers of disputes. As germinally defined by John Marshall in *Marbury v. Madison* (1803), the courts are ultimately simply agents of the state's bidding, a bidding that is expressed in the form of "law"—an always somewhat amorphous set of commands whose common element is that they are all said to emanate from the state rather than from some other source of social authority (see also Sager 1990, 898–899). In other words, the courts actually can be seen as intrinsically "representing" the state, and in cases where the state is also a party (such as criminal cases), the particular nature of the court's status and neutrality can be ambiguous, even in the most mature constitutional systems (Shapiro 1981, 26-28; cf. *Kress v. France* 2001). And it is precisely in this resultant ambiguity that the source of their alternative contributions to constitutional development can be found.

In saying that the courts "represent" the state, I do not mean "represent" in the agency sense of the term. "The state," in this sense, is ultimately a metaphor (see also Skinner 1989). The courts' "representation" thus requires not simply fidelity to some actual third-party, it ultimately requires that courts effectively reproduce the metaphorical entity they are being seen as representing. In this sense, a court's particular "representation" of the state, at least insofar as criminal and other public law cases are concerned, recalls that political-cognitive dynamic that Aristotle famously termed *poiesis*.

Poiesis, the classical Greek term for "production," refers to the process by which an artist in particular "reproduces" reality. What is distinctive about this form of reproduction is that it is not simply replicating the thing being reproduced. Such production, according to Aristotle (1968), ultimately requires imagination, and not simply mimicry, because its ultimate manifestation has to take place inside the head and imagination of the viewer.

Aristotle himself associated *poiesis* primarily with the theatre—particularly with classical Greek tragedy. He argued that because theatrical drama appeals to experience rather than to theoretical extrapolation, it is able to reproduce reality in a way that triggers public reflection on the implications nature and possibilities of that being reproduced.

The similarities between theatre and trial are fairly obvious, both in social consequent and in technique. A trial, like the classic Greek tragedy, revolves around an event—the crime or malfeasance—that encourages imagining about the nature of social (including political) relationships (as are in the courtroom expressed in terms of fault, duty, responsibility, etc). Of course, trials make pronounced use of theatrical elements. The trial revolves around a highly scripted "plot"—the dramatic interactions between the opposing presentations of defendant and plaintiff—that serves to explore a particular theme—what the common law calls the "cause of action" and "theory of the case." All of this is framed and contextualized by dramatic deployments of spectacle—the distinctive dress and accoutrements of the judge, the swearing in, the bailiffs' calls, the responsorial of examination, cross-examination, and objection. Even the layout of the courtroom—historically designed as it was specifically to accommodate public viewing of a trial—resembles that of a theatre. Indeed, a constitutionalist who equates courts simply with some rationalized form or pattern of decision making may well be missing the forest through the trees. As explored by Michael Asimow in particular, there is good reason to suspect that insofar as general society is concerned, the social-constitutional legitimacy of the courts depends at least as much on their particular theatricality as on the empirical utility of their formal institutional procedures (Asimow 2005).

B. *Of the "Constitutional," the "Democratic," and the "Theatrical"*

In order to better understand how courts might contribute to constitutional development in this manner, we might also explore the symbiotic relationship between *poietic* theatre and democracy. This is, of course, the principal context through which Aristotle developed his understanding of *poiesis*. In the 20th century, this linkage was also famously explored by Hannah Arendt, who characterized theatre as "political art par excellence." "Only there," she wrote," is the political sphere of human life transposed into art." (1998, 188)

Both Aristotle and Arendt argued that it was through the theatrical presentation of historical tragedies that classical Greek communities began thinking about and debating the nature of their shared history, and through it the nature of their identity. This idea is further elaborated by Paul Kottman, drawing from earlier work by Charles Segal:

> In Euripides' play [*Hippolytus*], as Segal argues convincingly, the performance of "rituals of lamentation" can be regarded as characterizing and reflecting an emerging polis that is "conscious" of itself as a community and cognizant of the theatre as an artifice through which that community is both represented and constituted.... What Segal wants to underscore is the fact that tragedy represents an important moment in the formation of the polis's own self-awareness, an awareness that only emerged through the work of tragic representation. Ritual commemoration or suffering, he argues, was imitated in order to "reflect on the ways in which Greek society represents itself through collective expressions as myth, rituals, festivals." (Kottman 2003, 91)

Similarly, Jean-Pierre Vernant has argued that the origins of classical Greek democracy might be found precisely in this newly self-aware polis "turn[ing] itself into a theatre" (Vernant 1992, 36).

The heart of this perceived symbiosis between theatre and democratic identity is said to lie precisely in the particular phenomenon of "representation" that we explored above in the context of the courts. Again, to quote from Kottman:

> With the birth of tragedy the community of spectators begins to find itself in, and in fact to constitute itself through, the work of a shared self-representation.
>
> Of course, this self-representation is more than a mere self-reflection. For the Greeks, according to Jean-Pierre Vernant, tragedy did not simply offer an uncritical mirror of the polis; rather tragedy was the putting-into-question of the polis itself. That is to say, tragedy "depicted the city rent and divided against itself" in at least two senses: first, insofar as the tragedies themselves—in both form and content—presented the polis undergoing various crises, and second, insofar as the dramatic representation itself could be seen as taking on a life of its own, quite apart from the lives of the spectators. (Kottman 2003, 92)

Aristotle famously referred to this particular form of representation as *mimemata*. Two aspects of this mimematic form of representation deserve particular mention insofar as our own investigation into the poietic function of the courts is concerned. First, the representation is distinctly "pre-philosophical," in Hannah Arendt's terminology. By "imitate[ing] man in his relation to others" (Arendt 1998, 188), as contrasted to simply didactically explicating a particular sequence of cause and events, theatre is able to appeal directly to experience without the *a priori* intermediation of, and resultant filtering by, existing narrative understandings (compare also Berger and Luckmann 1966). This pre-philosophical character is essential for freeing the imagined from the actual—for generating "man-made dreams produced for those who are awake," in Plato's (1961, 266C) evocative description. Another key aspect of mimematic representation is the psychological factor of "distance." The political self-reflection that theatre provokes is in the form of a "cool" reflection. This "coolness" allows the polity to reflect on itself, its rents, and crises from a psychological distance that avoids triggering conflicting passions and recriminations that might otherwise threaten to tear it apart. In theatre, distance is effectuated by the device of artifice, the artificial and overtly fictive traditions and practices that characterize theatrical presentation (see also Kottman 2003).

This explication of the symbiotic linkage between the experience of theatre and the development of democracy finds strong parallels in the particular ways that courts archetypically operate. Like the tragedy, a criminal or public-law trial revolves around an event of crisis, a conflict that represents a possible "rent" in the polis itself (see also Braithwaite 2006). The representation of this conflict is distinctly "pre-theoretical," portrayed—as we saw above—via the choreographed interaction among distinctive characters engaged in distinctive forms of relationships (e.g., judges directing lawyers; lawyers questioning witnesses; plaintiffs (or prosecutors) contesting defendants) compared rather than through a single, didactic narrative. The trial's *mimenata* is produced using a highly artificial medium, most particularly the artificial language of the courtroom (see Bentley 1964, 87), which for better or worse prevents the representation from devolving into a endless cycle of passions and recriminations, a cycle that might otherwise destroy the observer's coherence of *reflective* consciousness (Nussbaum 1996).

And the direction of this reflection, the imaginations it produces, can often escape efforts of *a priori*, philosophical, or ideological filtering. Hence, the "cool" self-reflection triggered by the trial can take on a "life of its own," to use Kottman's phrase, through which political imagining and reimagining develop in very unexpected ways, as we shall see in the case of China.

III. The Courts and Constitutional *Poiesis* in China

This model of constitutional *poiesis* suggests an alternative research strategy for examining the Chinese judiciary and its role in China's constitutional evolution. It is a strategy that focuses on how the courts might contribute to larger social reimaginings about and understandings of the character of the Chinese state—in other words, its constitution. In exploring for such contributions, we would approach the court as a kind of forum, not simply as a third-party decision maker or dispute resolver. We would not conflate courts simply with judges. Rather, we would recognize that important contributions to Chinese constitutional understanding can come from elsewhere in the courtroom—including the parties and even the audience. We would also recognize that the public constitutional imaginings that emerge from courts can often be very different from those that the judge or the state intended to project.

A. The Trial of Jiang Qing (aka "Madame Mao")

Consider along these lines the infamous show trial of Jiang Qing—aka "Madame Mao," the wife of Mao Zedong. Traditional constitutional analyses dismiss the possible constitutional import of this trial, I suspect, because they presume that since it did not feature an independent judge or an independent decision-making process, it could not make significant contribution to constitutional system. Our discussion of constitutional *poiesis*, on the other hand, suggests that this presumption can be fallacious.

The trial involved Jiang Qing's role in the Cultural Revolution.[1] Beginning in the middle 1960s, China experienced a particularly traumatic experiment in social reengineering called the Cultural Revolution. The Cultural Revolution sought to "modernize" Chinese society by destroying all entrenched political power structures, save for those at the very top of the state. The theory was that China's lower-level power structures had developed their own, innately conservative interests, and that these interests were impeding the state's ability to radically refashion Chinese society into that pure communism that was China's true teleological destiny. Once such power structures were destroyed, it was thought, the state would be free to realize its communist perfection.

Of course, it didn't work that way. The destruction of lower-level power structures resulted in anarchy. The power vacuums created when these structures were destroyed were quickly filled by competing petty demagogues leading their own political mobs. Class tensions that had been suppressed by the Chinese state reasserted themselves. Instead of triggering social transformation, the Cultural Revolution devolved into an endless spiral of often violent and even sadistic vendettas, retributions, and assertions of petty tyranny. Many of China's top leaders were victimized during this anarchy. Some, like President Liu Shaoqi, were imprisoned. Others, like Deng Xiaoping, were forced to live away from their families in remote rural communities and work as laborers on farms or in factories. China's more educated citizens were often humiliated and brutalized by being publicly beaten, whipped, denounced or threatened. Deng Xiaoping's own son was paralyzed from the waist down when a revolutionary mob threw him from a second-story window because of his father's position.

The figurehead for the Cultural Revolution was Mao Zedong. Since 1949, Mao had been China's most visible and influential political figure. He was the formal leader of China's Communist Party, which in turn was the ultimate political authority in the Chinese state. He also enjoyed tremendous social prestige, having been officially and widely credited (at least in the People's Republic of China (PRC)) with leading China's liberation from both Japanese and capitalist oppression. Mao had retreated from politics in the early 1960s (still retaining his formal titles), but returned to active politics a couple of years later because, he said, he was dissatisfied with the direction of China's political evolution. It was he who formally launched and gave name to the "Cultural Revolution" at the Eleventh Plenum of the Eighth Chinese Communist Party (CCP) Central Committee in August 1966. It was also he who gave the Cultural Revolution its popular force and legitimacy.

Mao died in September of 1976, and with his passing, the Cultural Revolution lost its motive force. Two months later, thirty of Mao's closest advisors during the Cultural Revolution were arrested and charged with various crimes relating to that movement (see *Beijing Review* 1980c). Of these, four—Jiang Qing, Zhang Chungqiao, Wang Hongwen, and Yao Wenyuan—were assigned principal responsibility for the Revolution's excesses. Charged variously with treason and plotting against the state, they were dubbed "the Gang of Four" by China's state-controlled media, who also conducted an intensive media campaign portraying them as the real villains behind the Cultural Revolution. A year later, in August 1977, Mao's personally designated successor, Hua Guofeng announced the formal end of the Cultural Revolution at the 11th Party Congress of the CCP.

Four years after their arrest, the individual members of the Gang of Four were tried in a series of highly publicized trials. These trials marked the first time these defendants had been seen in public since their arrest and subsequent public vilification. The trials were televised, broadcast over the radio, and extensively reported in the press. The intent in so publicizing these trials is generally said to have been twofold. First, the new party leadership intended to use these trials to establish an official history of the Cultural Revolution. The tragedy of the Cultural Revolution posed a problem for the new party leadership—that Revolution had been proposed and sponsored by the same political figure that the party-state claimed gave it its special authority to govern, Mao Zedong. Moreover, Mao had legitimated the Cultural Revolution by appealing the same set of ideological principles and vocabulary that the party-state had used and continued to use in asserting its own legitimacy. And the apparati most symbolically associated with the party-state—primarily state media and propaganda organs—consistently publicly endorsed this movement.

The party leadership therefore needed a way to distance the party-state (which gave them their own claims to political legitimacy) from the calamity of the Cultural Revolution. Through its trials of the Gang of Four, it sought to publicly establish that the Cultural Revolution was not really a product of the party-state, but that it was really the product of bad individuals who were seeking to take over, and thus opposed, the state. In this way, the new party leadership could both disassociate themselves and the party from the Cultural Revolution and preserve their legitimating identity as those who would continue to lead China to that socialist destiny that Mao had earlier identified.

The party leadership also sought to use these trials to demonstrate the return of "law" as a source of state authority. The Cultural Revolution was marked by an express rejection of law. Law was portrayed as one of the principal ways through which established local power structures impeded China's communist transformation. With the ending and discrediting of the Cultural Revolution, the new leadership wanted to further distance itself from that past by showing how law would henceforth become a critical tool in the construction of China's social transformation. And consistent with this, the legal formalities of the trial were scrupulously observed, which as we shall see was a key factor in catalyzing the trial's particular, unforeseen, and certainly unintended *poietic* effect.

The trials of the Gang of Four are thus an archetypical example of what we are calling "constitutional *poiesis*." The party was using the court as a kind of theatre through which it could re-present and re-produce its relationship with "the state" before the Chinese "polity." It was using the trial to provoke a particular reimagining of what the (party-)state really was—and in particular that it was something different from that which had been produced by the Gang of Four. Consistent with the dynamics of this *poiesis*, the theatrical elements of the trials were particularly pronounced. The courtrooms resembled a large theatre, in which the principal actors—the prosecutors, defendants, and witnesses—narrated their presentations in a distinctively framed space. The judges wore distinctive uniforms that both distinguished them from the ordinary citizenry and associated them particularly with the state (*Beijing Review* 1980a). Trial procedures and formalities were scrupulously observed. The separate roles of judge, prosecutor, and attorney were clearly defined and rigorously conformed to. The judges and prosecutors treated the defendant with the formalized dignity and respect that was her appropriate due in a trial environment. The discourse of the trial, like that of trials everywhere, was declamatory. Defendants, witnesses, and prosecutors argued and expressed themselves through oration rather than through true interstitial discussion—resulting in that distinctive, responsorial choreography that gives trials everywhere both their drama and their artifice (see *Beijing Review* 1980b; *Beijing Review* 1980c; *Beijing Review* 1980d).

Of course, the outcome of these trials, including their sentencing, had been determined long before the trials themselves were held. The judges and prosecutors, the orations and declamations, were indeed simply for "show." However, we earlier intimated that constitutional *poiesis* can operate according to its own logic, a logic that can easily cause it to escape even the most determined efforts of elites to channel it by controlling the decisional outcomes of the courts themselves. And this is indeed what happened in the most dramatic of the Gang of Four trials, that of Mao's widow, Jiang Qing.

Jiang Qing was probably the most publicly reviled of the "Gang of Four." Popularly referred to as the "white-boned demon" after a well-known character in classical Chinese fiction, she had been appointed Deputy Director of the Cultural Revolution in 1966. A former movie actress who married Mao in 1939, she served as the Cultural Revolution's "cultural commissar." Many felt that Jiang had been particularly ruthless in using her newfound political power to settle, often viciously, old scores and perceived slights. Beyond this, Jiang's promiscuous past and her relationship with Mao, which many saw as a seduction, also added a salacious aspect to her trial. Indeed, some of her more famous vendettas during the Cultural Revolution had an aspect of sexual vindictiveness to them—such as her persecution of Fan Jin, the woman who had married Jiang's second husband after Jiang herself had separated from him in 1931; or her persecution of Mao's former wives and their children.

The more melodramatic and personal character of Jiang's trial was highlighted by the particular charges brought against her. In contrast to the rest of the Gang of Four, Jiang was not charged with conspiring against the state. Instead, the charges focused on her presonal, spiteful persecution of people who, for whatever reason, she felt threatened by. This meant that the trial itself would focus more sensationally on Jiang's personal life and relationships. All this helped ensure that Madame Mao's trial would be a particularly interesting theatre indeed.

But also in contrast to the other Gang of Four defendants, Jiang—defending herself—chose to confront the prosecution precisely on the constitutional issue that the party leadership had hoped the proceedings would establish by default. She neither denied nor apologized for her leading role in the Cultural Revolution, or for persecuting those who offended her. Rather, she asserted that she operated precisely as an agent of the party-state. She noted how the Cultural Revolution had been announced by Mao and approved by the party itself; how it had been overseen by Mao, and through him by the CCP; and how both it and she had always remained subject and subordinated to his and the party's ultimate authority. She claimed that she did not do anything that she was not authorized to do. She also remained unrepentant. She argued that the Cultural Revolution was justified, that it was consistent with the party-state's own responsibilities in leading Chinese society out of its oppressed past. She claimed that it was the present government that was the true usurper, in that it, not her, had abandoned the ideals that gave the party-state its authority and legitimacy.

Of course, as noted above, the formal outcome of the trial was never in doubt—Jiang was found guilty and sentenced to death with possibility of reprieve after two years of "good behavior" (her sentence was indeed reprieved to life imprisonment; and in 1991, she committed suicide while in prison). But if the party leadership could script the court's decision, it could not script the actions of the defendant. In asserting her claims, the former actress showed that she was indeed a master of the theatrical. She knew the court's script, and knew when and how to deviate from it to maximum effect. Perversely, having been freed from having to worry about the actual outcome of the case, Jiang was able to focus her energies on gaining control of the trial's drama and what we are arguing to be its *poietic* dynamics. Her efforts in this regard have been well described by Richard Thwaites, then in China as resident correspondent for the Australian Broadcasting Corporation:

> Tonight, Jiang Qing is to make her final appearance. . . . Jiang Qing has fought her trial with scorn. She has abused the prosecutors and questioned their authority. She has shouted down weeping witnesses as they accused her, with palpable hatred, of cruel persecutions going back to rivalries of youth. She has maintained that she has committed neither crimes nor errors, but simply acted in accordance with policies of the Party Central Committee, and authorised by Chairman Mao himself. Earlier television excerpts from the trial have shown her dragged from the court, shouting and struggling, after refusing to keep silence.
>
> There is silence now in the watching families as the cameras show Jiang Qing led to the dock in handcuffs. She is identified as Prisoner Jiang Qing, and given her last opportunity to speak. Jiang Qing knows she is speaking to all China, and she repeats her assertions that it is she, not the alleged victims, who is persecuted. All those writers and party hacks deserved what they got in the Cultural Revolution, they were all bourgeois criminals. The family mutter in amazement as the ageing actress pulls a manuscript from her jacket pocket, and begins to declaim a poem she says has taken her a year to write—a poem accusing the current regime of betraying the Chinese revolution, and of destroying its true heroes, the activists of the Cultural Revolution.
>
> The court tolerates her poem impassively. Jiang Qing asks them how they can lay charges of counter-revolution against her, the wife of Chairman Mao for thirty-eight years, without accusing the

> Chairman of the same offences. The prosecutor replies that while Mao may be responsible for not seeing through her counter-revolutionary plotting, he is not responsible for the offences themselves. The family show no reaction to this. Jiang Qing's role as a scapegoat must be a tacit one.
>
> The prosecutor is asking for the death sentence on Jiang Qing, for conspiring to split the nation in civil war and to undermine the authority of the Communist Party. Jiang Qing shouts from the dock: "I wish I had many heads for you to chop off, one at a time, so that I might be a martyr many times over for the revolutionary ideals of Chairman Mao and the Cultural Revolution." These stirring lines, familiar in the scripts of revolutionary propaganda movies, and here it is for real, with Jiang Qing playing her final scenes. (Thwaites 1986)

As noted above, the party leadership had intended that the trials absolve the party-state from complicity in the Cultural Revolution. However, at the end of the day, it was Jiang's vision—a vision that saw the Cultural Revolution as a natural and logical resultant of the way that the party-state framed its own legitimacy—that would resonate with the country. After Jiang's trial, it was clear that the party-state would have to accept some degree of responsibility for the excesses of the Cultural Revolution (Terrill 1999, 344).

So, what does all this have to do with China's constitutional option? In reconstructing the party-state in the aftermath of the Cultural Revolution, Deng Xiaoping appears to have had little interest in creating a constitutional structure (Tanner 1994, 73–75; Dowdle 2004). He continued the old tradition of ruling through the CCP, while using the constitutional apparatus simply as a bureaucratic repository in which he marginalized political opponents while still allowing them to save some degree of political face. But one such opponent, Peng Zhen, was not so willing to go gently into that good night. Peng, formerly head of the Beijing branch of the CCP, was assigned leadership over the National People's Congress (NPC), a traditionally rubber-stamp parliament with no real say over state policy matters. Two years after Jiang's trial, Peng began to use an argument strikingly similar to that advanced by Jiang in her trial defense, in advocating for the strengthening of the NPC and the larger constitutional system vis-à-vis the party itself.

Like Jiang, Peng claimed that the Cultural Revolution had been the result, not of bad people, but of the then nature of the party-state system itself—a system in which an innately insular party apparatus was able to completely and comprehensively assume the identity of the state per se. The only way to guard against a return of such runaway political extremism, he reasoned, was to introduce into the entity of "the state" other political structures—constitutional structures—that, because they were institutionally outside the party, could open up the state to a wider diversity of understandings and sensitivities than could be provided by the party alone (Peng 1990a; Peng 1990b). And as Peng made these arguments, the NPC—and through it the larger constitutional structure—indeed began gaining some degree of autonomous authority. Today, many constitutional scholars, particularly those associated with the NPC itself, credit Peng with catalyzing the emergence in China of a still vague but clearly identifiable "constitutionalism" operating distinctly from the CCP (see, for example, Jiang 2002a; Dowdle 1997, 22–23).

Did that particular *poiesis* that Jiang Qing was able to trigger in her trial contribute to the effectiveness of Peng's argument? We probably will never know. However, we *do* know that Jiang's *poiesis* was effective insofar as the general polity was concerned; that it triggered precisely that popular reenvisioning of the relationship between the party and the state that the state itself had hoped to avoid. The fact that that reenvisioning also resonated very closely with the vision that Peng would successfully begin to advance some two years later, suggests that a hypothesis of such a causal linkage deserves some degree of respect.

B. "Micro-Poiesis": Courts and "Citizenization" in Shanghai Labor Litigation

The Jiang Qing trial is an example of the phenomenon of constitutional *poiesis* in the context of what we might call "notable cases"—cases that for some reason or other capture the attention of the national populace. This is, obviously, where such *poiesis* would seem most likely to be visible. As described above, the single trial analogizes very readily to a theatrical drama, and in this context the metaphoric linkages between constitutional *poiesis* and theatrical *poiesis* are most readily apparent. The notable case also represents a singular event, with a distinctive story. Such tags make it easy to connect this event to subsequent constitutional trajectories.

However, we should not confuse lack of visibility with lack of existence. There is good reason to suspect that constitutional *poiesis* can also operate on a much lower, much more opaque, and diffuse, but equally effectuous and significant, level—that is, through the interaction of many small-scale cases that incrementally coalesce into new constitutional imaginations. We might call this particular variant of constitutional *poiesis*, "micro-poiesis."

Consider, for example, the recent emergence of a growing constitutional discourse in China on "*gongminhua*"—that following David Kelly we might translate as "citizenization" (Kelly 2006). Broadly put, citizenization refers to the way in which individuals become autonomous, constitutive members of the political community. Like what we are calling constitutional *poiesis*, citizenization essentially involves a reimagining of the state—substituting a modernist notion of citizenship for an older, premodern vision of state-individual relationship, that of being a "subject" (Kelly 2006, 187). Under the older vision, the subject's relationship with the state is ultimately a paternalistic one. She might benefit, perhaps significantly, from the state's benevolence, but ultimately, that benevolence is the product of a political will over which she herself has no authority or input. The modern vision of citizenship, by contrast, sees the individual not simply as a passive recipient of state authority (and hopefully benevolence), but as one who actively contributes to that authority, by virtue of her autonomous participation in political society.

The dynamic of citizenization thus requires a reconceptualization of the state, from a paternalistic, protecting entity that exists independent of the subject to a creature of the subject's own making and responsibility. This particular aspect of citizenization had been amplified in a recent article by Yu Jianrong (2004a), a sociologist at the Chinese Academy of Social Sciences, on patterns of rural grassroots resistance. Looking at recent evolutions in rural agrarian efforts to resist injustices in and abuses by local government, Yu sees that resistance as having evolved from a strategy that he, following Kevin O'Brien and Li Lianjiang (2006), calls "resistance through law *(yi(1)fa kangzheng)*" into a strategy of what he calls "resistance in accordance with the law *(yi(3)fa kangzheng)*." "Resistance through law" refers to a strategy in which resisters use central laws and policy dictates to delegitimate local governmental actions. Such resisters use the law as a weapon, as a higher source of authority that is distinct from themselves but nevertheless operates in their interests. By contrast, "resistance in accordance with the law" refers to a strategy in which resisters use the law, not as the basis for directly delegitimating political behavior, but as a basis for justifying the terms and forms of their own autonomous rights of resistantce. Here, the law became a shield rather than a weapon. It is not being used to compel the state simply to do as the state itself commands, but as a tool for compelling the state to address to the resisters' own, autonomous understandings of what justice demands (Yu 2004a, 50). Of course, these understandings may indeed resonate in the formal law. However, not necessarily.

Thus, what distinguishes resistance in accordance with the law from resistance by law is that the former allows the resister to justify her resistance by appealing, not simply to the state's benevolence, but to her own capacities as a thinking and experiencing member of the political arena. Seen in this light, the evolution in rural resistance from "resistance through law" to "resistance in accordance with law" is clearly a form of "citizenization" as we have described it above. When resisting through law, the authority that the resister asserts in justifying her demands is that of the state, rather than her own. She thus ultimately remains wholly dependent on the state's autonomous benevolence. This replicates the paternalistic vision of the state we associated with the notion of "subject." By contrast, resistance in accordance with the law asserts that she herself has autonomous capacities to understand, evaluate and contribute to state policy—state "behavior," to continue our metaphor—independent of whatever the particular legal articulations that formalize this "behavior" say. And when that resister does assert her independent sources of authority in this way, she is becoming one who is not simply subject to the state's authority, but who is autonomously able to authoritatively reimagine, and hence is able to personally constitute, that authority (see also O'Brien 2002).

Mary Gallagher (2006) has found a very similar transformative dynamic at work in the industrial labor community, another area in which the discourse of citizenization is particularly prominent (although she frames this transformation in different terms). Examining what she calls the "legal consciousness" of industrial workers who use the courts to challenge management handling of labor disputes, she, too, finds in these communities a transformation of people's understanding of the state. This transition is from what we might call legal idealism—a legal consciousness that idealizes the legal protections offered by a benevolent, but ultimately paternalistic state—to a different form of legal consciousness that she terms "informed disenchantment"—a more realistic, cynical vision of the ability of the law per se to completely encompass the state's defining responsibilities.

Paradoxically, however, she also notes how this new and cynical consciousness of informed disenchantment actually ends up empowering the resister:

> The focus that informed disenchantment brings to the "contradictory and contingent nature of legal consciousness" also helps us make sense of the large differences between attitudes and behavior exhibited by the plaintiffs in this study. While plaintiffs' attitudes and evaluations of the legal system were almost always uniformly negative and critical after the dispute had ended, they were surprisingly resilient when it came to actual and expected future behavior. The vast majority of the plaintiffs pledged that they would sue again for a similar problem; indeed, a small but not insignificant number of disputants had already moved on from their first dispute to other legal battles. A sense of disenchantment did not lead to despondency or resignation; plaintiffs put more emphasis on the educative aspects of legal mobilization, vowing to return to the law again, better prepared and less naïve, and also prepared to transmit their lessons to friends, relatives, and coworkers with similar grievances. (Gallagher 2006, 786)

The transformation from legal idealism to "informed disenchantment" tracks the transformation of subject into citizen that we explored above. Like the "resisters *by* law" in Yu's analysis, the typical legal aid plaintiff in Gallagher's account initially sees herself as a subject of the state, a beneficiary of the paternal state's autonomous desire to protect her through its laws. Experience with the litigatory process transforms this vision in two ways. First, it makes her "disenchanted," because she now realizes that the state cannot in fact provide such protections without her participation. However, it also makes her "informed"—we might even say "empowered," as Gallagher herself says—because she also realizes that she herself can take responsibility for and contribute to those protections that she used to see as being purely the state's prerogative.

The process of informed disenchantment thus involves the same kind of reimagining of the state—from being a paternalist protector to being in some ways a creature of one's own autonomy—that we saw being invoked by the idea of citizenization. In the words of one of Gallagher's interviewees:

> I didn't know a single thing about the labor law [before the litigation]. During Mao's time, everything was handled for us, like children. I used to think that only bad people file suit, now I know everything... arbitration, first appeal, second appeal.... I am so angry and frustrated. I didn't use to be like this. My poor parents at home. They are over 80 years old!! I'll do anything to help these kinds of cases. (Gallagher 2006, 808)

Gallagher also notes how through the experience of litigation, "[p]laintiffs also gained... the ability to know when they are being fairly treated, when they are being coerced or deliberately intimidated, and when the process is thwarted by corruption and close connections between officials and employer" (Gallagher 2006, 801); how they were "better able to evaluate the ability of different institutions to issue fair decisions" (Gallagher 2006, 802); and how they "develop[ed] an approach to the media and winning over public opinion as part of a broader strategy to influence their court cases. Winning the battle outside of the courtroom becomes part and parcel of an overall successful strategy to win a case" (Gallagher 2006, 802). Issues such as what constitutes public fairness, public coercion, and corruption, and the relationship between state authority and public opinion are inseparable from the question of what the state is. To question such issues, to learn new ways of thinking about these issues, is synonymous with reimagining the state itself.

Gallagher's study is particularly useful for our purposes, not simply because she elaborates another aspect to this larger, reimaginative constitutional movement of citizenization, but because she also examines specifically how everyday litigation in everyday courts are contributing to this movement:

> Through the process of legal mobilization [i.e., litigation], plaintiffs also learned about how legal institutions interact with and can be affected

> by other institutions, including the media and the petitioning offices of government bureaus. Plaintiffs were better able to evaluate the ability of different institutions to issue fair decisions.... [They] also developed an approach to the media and winning over public opinion as part of a broader strategy to influence their court cases. Winning the battle outside of the courtroom became part and parcel of an overall successful strategy to win a case. (Gallagher 2006, 802)

We might say that the court gives litigants a more "direct" experience interacting with the state (through its laws). And this seems to be causing these litigants to rethink the nature of the state and its laws, and of their own relationship with that state.

Moreover, Gallagher also finds that the empowering aspect of "informed disenchantment" is not related to the actual decision in the case—it is not dependent, in other words, on the dynamics of judicial independence and/or judicial neutrality that dominate our more traditional understandings of the courts' contributions to rule of law. Indeed, the very concept of "informed disenfranchisement" means that an unfair judge and a nonindependent court contribute as much if not more to this catalytic reimagining as a fair judge or an independent court:

> A healthy sense of cynicism and disappointment with the law was common among the plaintiffs as they went through the legal process and discovered it to be more complicated than they expected and more advantageous to employers with their wealth of legal experience, their ability to hire skilled lawyers, and their importance as employers and investors in the local economy. The vast majority of plaintiffs reported, however, that they would sue again if they encountered another employment dispute, and for many this extended to other types of disputes as well. Eighty percent of all plaintiffs reported that they would sue again if they encountered another employment dispute. This tendency was not significantly affected by the outcome of the case—those who lost were almost as likely to want to sue again as those who won (88 percent versus 100 percent). (Gallagher 2006, 804)

Again, this seems to track very closely our own discussion, in which we saw the driving force behind constitutional *poiesis* to lie in the intrinsically *mimematic* representational character of the court at trial, and in the direct and spontaneous vision it gives of the character of the state, rather than in the decision of the judge.

In sum, Gallagher seems to be describing a process that is in fact a form of what we are calling constitutional *poiesis*—a process in which interaction with the court at trial triggers a reimagining of the nature of the state and its relationship with oneself, which in China often takes a particular form of citizenization she calls "informed disenchantment." The principal difference is that the reimagining documented by Gallagher is not the product of a single trial that captures public imagination. It is the product of a large number of trials, each of which is itself insignificant insofar as the public is concerned, but which nevertheless cumulatively spark collective and spontaneous reflection regarding the nature of the state and its responsibilities.

But how does it do this? How do insignificant trials nevertheless catalyze a collective, public reflection? Gallagher's account suggests at least one way that the individuated experiences of non-notable trials can nevertheless coalesce into "collective" reflection. In the case of industrial dispute litigation in Shanghai, the collective aspect of this reflection is generated by "social networks" of similarly situated, disaffected workers.

> Legal mobilization through legal aid can mitigate plaintiffs' feelings of isolation and embarrassment by providing a social network and a fixed space through which plaintiffs can interact with each other, student volunteers, and legal aid staff. Many plaintiffs reported hearing about a new strategy or a relevant regulation while waiting in line at the legal aid center. Some workers find that their cases are similar, form a relationship, and help each other with their suits. Others realize by listening to the complaints and problems of those around them that their own grievance is part of a broader systematic trend.... A young worker was struck at how serious the problems were of the older people crowded around him. "I thought if [the director of the center] can help these people, then surely he should be able to win my case." (Gallagher 2006, 805–806)

It remains to be seen, however just how prevalent the dynamic of or potential for micro-poiesis is in the Chinese courts. Yu Jianrong's claim that the rural peasantry is moving away from strategies of "resistance by law" to strategies of "resistance according to law" could suggest a dynamic inapposite to that described by Gallagher: a dynamic in which exposure to an ineffectual court system is indeed causing the citizenry to abandon that system in favor of other fora (see also the chapters by Keith Hand and Eva Pils later in this volume). Does this mean that Gallagher's court-philic disenchantment represents the past and Yu's court-phobic disenchantment represents the future? Or can we explain these very different responses by urban workers and rural peasants to their similarly "disenchanted" experiences with China's courts as nevertheless both being products of the same constitutional trajectory?

Our above description of constitutional *poiesis* suggests that it well could be the latter. We need to recall that constitutional *poiesis* is not an inevitable product of simply calling something a "court of law." As we have seen, it is the product of a particular set of ritualized and abstracted formalities that are frequently associated with courts: formalities in language, formalities in procedure, formalities in roles, even formalities in architecture and dress. A number of studies have found that rural courts in China tend to operate with pronounced informality (see, for example, Zhu 2000; see also Balme, this volume). They do not adhere to the stylized trial choreography that we normally associate with court proceedings—the distinctive speech patterns, typecast roles, and distinctive vocabulary. If this is the case, then it would suggest that rural courts would in fact not be as effective in catalyzing constitutional *poiesis*. Their lack of formality prevents them from effectively "reproducing" the state in a way that allows for reflection and reimagination. In this sense, both Yu and Gallagher might be consistent with a larger trajectory of constitutional *poiesis* in China.

IV. Conclusion: An Appeal for Greater Understanding

The traditional constitutionalist paradigm of the courts—courts as independent and neutral resolvers of constitutional disputes—has unfortunately blinded us to other ways that courts can contribute to a polity's Constitution development. Investigations into the Chinese judiciary invariably focus on the quality of the judge, the quality of the decision, and/or the courts' formal institutional positioning within China's larger political and constitutional architecture.

However, this presents a very impoverished view of the courts, and of constitutionalism. Constitutionalism is not simply the product of elite intentions. It is the product of a society's own understanding about itself. And crucial to this social understanding are the attitudes, expectations, and imaginations of the everyday citizenry. Of course, individually, these attitudes, expectations, and imaginations appear insignificant, particularly in comparison with those of politicians, judges, and maybe even law professors. But there is good reason to suspect that small as they might be individually, collectively, they are in fact much more significant, and more powerful.

This suggests a number of shifts in our analytic focus, in looking at the courts' possible contributions to constitutionalism, particularly in emergent constitutional systems like that of China.

First, we need to start paying attention to the actual arguments that are being advanced by the parties in litigation. Investigations into everyday Chinese courts rarely if ever treat such argument seriously. And yet, as we have seen above, a party's argument can actually often have more lasting constitutional impact than the court decision. We need to take their symbols seriously, including the resurgent Maoist and Marxist symbology that many of us, at least in the Anglo-American world, often find personally objectionable.

Along these lines, we need to approach these arguments and their symbology through what Donald Davidson (1973) has famously termed a "principle of charity"—a principle that assumes that the speaker might actually be trying honestly to tell us something useful and important (see also Dowdle 2002, 76–86). Thus, if a plaintiff is seen to appeal to Maoism, Marxism, or even to the virtues of the Communist Party, for example, we should not automatically assume that she is simply supporting, perhaps out of ignorance or corruption, the return of a cruel dictatorship that uses violence and terror as a means for obliterating all interests other than its own (see, for example, Link 2005; compare with Lee 2007). We also need to consider the possibility that she is subtly seeking to challenge whether China's post-Mao evolutions are really producing a vision of the state that she finds appealing.

Finally, we also need investigate whether and how these arguments and constitutional symbols diffuse through the larger polity. In what kind of courts and what kind of disputes are they more likely to appear? How are they being interpreted and reinterpreted? Are they diffusing beyond the courtroom walls? How? Who is watching the case (or these cases) and listening to these arguments? Who is talking about the case? What are they saying about it?

It is hoped that this composite examination of the studies by Kelly, Yu, and Gallagher has at least suggested the kinds of constitutional insights these questions can generate, and by extension what is lost when they are ignored. However, unless and until we start taking the ordinary Chinese plaintiff, and through her the everyday citizenry she represents, seriously—as thinking, rational beings capable of generating their own constitutional force and authority through collective deployment of their own, autonomous constitutional imaginations—our conclusions say more about us than they do about the Chinese.

Note

1. Unless otherwise noted, information in this section regarding the trial of Jiang Qing comes from Terrill 1999, 333–347.

PART 4

Toward a Popular Constitutionalism

CHAPTER THIRTEEN

Citizens Engage the Constitution: The Sun Zhigang Incident and Constitutional Review Proposals in the People's Republic of China

KEITH J. HAND

I. Introduction

Shortly after assuming leadership of the Chinese Communist Party (CCP) in the fall of 2002, Hu Jintao proclaimed that China's "broad masses" should view the Constitution as a "legal weapon for safeguarding citizen rights" (*Zhongguo xinwen wang* 2002). In recent years, citizen activists have tested the limits of this rhetoric by advancing constitutional claims in different legal fora. Some of these efforts have focused on the people's courts (see Pils, this volume). But as noted throughout this volume, neither the government nor the courts recognize the Constitution as being justiciable (see, e.g., Supreme People's Court 2008). Other citizens have focused on an alternative legal mechanism that the government *has* explicitly recognized as a legitimate forum for constitutional complaints: the constitutional review procedure established under Article 90(2) of China's Law on Legislation (*Zhonghua Renmin Gongheguo Lifa Fa* 2000). This provision grants Chinese citizens the right to propose (*jianyi*) that the National People's Congress Standing Committee (NPCSC) review administrative regulations and local laws that they deem to be inconsistent with national law or the Constitution. (This citizen proposal right should be contrasted with the right granted to state organs such as the State Council, the Supreme People's Procuratorate, and provincial people congresses in

Article 90(1) of the same law to demand (*yaoqiu*) NPCSC review of such legal conflicts.) Subsequent National People's Congress (NPC) procedures clarified that the scope of review also includes Supreme People's Court judicial interpretations (*Xinjing bao* 2005).

Since 2003, a growing number of citizens have taken advantage of this mechanism to advance constitutional claims. The defining event in these efforts took place in the spring of that year, when legal reformers leveraged public outrage over the death of a young man named Sun Zhigang in police custody and filed a proposal with the NPCSC challenging a form of administrative detention called "custody and repatriation" (C&R). This citizen challenge generated widespread discussion of constitutional enforcement and inspired numerous subsequent constitutional claims. Whereas only a few proposals had been filed under Article 90 prior to the Sun Zhigang incident, citizens have since sent the NPCSC at least thirty-six requests for constitutional and legislative review on topics ranging from re-education through labor and Internet content rules to employment discrimination and injury compensation standards.[1]

This chapter examines the constitutional dynamics of the Sun Zhigang incident and subsequent foci for constitutional review proposals. An examination of these citizen proposals suggests that although the review mechanism articulated by the Law on Legislation has numerous deficiencies as a legal process, citizen constitutional claims are promoting China's legal and constitutional development in several respects. First, when there is a degree of policy flexibility on the part of the leadership on legal and policy reform issues, a carefully crafted constitutional review proposal can help focus public attention on an issue and push authorities to move related reforms forward. Second, by filing proposals and thereby occupying the limited space for constitutional review that the leadership has created, reformers can exert pressure on the party and government to make this existing space meaningful in practice and thereby establish a foothold for expanding the scope of constitutional review in the future.

II. The Sun Zhigang Incident

A. The Detention and Death of Sun Zhigang[2]

In mid-March 2003, a twenty-seven-year-old Hubei man named Sun Zhigang was stopped by police outside an Internet café on the outskirts of Guangzhou. Although Sun was in Guangzhou legally, he had not yet obtained a temporary residence permit and was not carrying his identification card. As a result, he was detained on the suspicion that he was an illegal migrant, held overnight, and transferred to a Guangzhou C&R center the next day.

Under China's residence registration (*hukou*) system, the Chinese government has tightly controlled internal migration between urban and rural areas for decades (Congressional-Executive Commission on China 2005). C&R was a controversial form of administrative detention closely connected to these controls. The 1982 Measures on Custody and Repatriation of Vagrants and Beggars in Cities (*Chengshi liulang qitao renyuan shourong qiansong banfa* 1982) (the "C&R Measures") gave civil affairs and public security bureaus virtually unchecked power to detain beggars and vagrants in urban areas and to repatriate them forcibly to their place of registered residence. Although these measures were designed in part to provide relief and shelter to indigent persons, in practice, public security officials used them to manage the flow of migrant workers and rural undesirables into China's urban centers (Yun 2003; Yan 2003). Chinese commentators and international human rights organizations had long criticized pervasive corruption, extortion, and abuse in the C&R system (see, for example, *21 Shiji Jingji Baodao* 2003; Chen 2003a; Human Rights in China 1999).

Several days after Sun's detention, employees of a medical clinic affiliated with the C&R center announced that Sun had died suddenly of heart problems. However, Sun's body showed signs of abuse, and an autopsy performed nearly a month later found that he had died of injuries caused by blunt trauma. On April 25, after an exhaustive investigation, the Guangzhou newspaper *Southern Metropolitan Daily* published a detailed report on Sun's death. This report and an accompanying editorial cited local Guangzhou regulations to demonstrate that Sun should not have been detained in the C&R center and suggested that Sun had died as a result of being beaten in custody (*Nanfang dushibao* 2003a; *Nanfang dushibao* 2003b).

The report on Sun's death immediately inflamed public opinion. Although party authorities in Guangdong banned local media reports on the case, national media outlets picked up the story, which soon became a fixture in daily headlines (Liebman 2005; see also Hand 2006, 122–123). The case captured the attention of Chinese society, and waves of protest filled online chat rooms. Commentary on the case included not only statements of outrage over Sun's death and demands for punishment, but also broader complaints about the C&R system and the pervasive abuses of that system by law enforcement personnel (Hand 2006, 123).

This public response created extreme pressure on authorities to investigate Sun's death. By mid-May, government officials acknowledged that Sun had been wrongfully detained and announced that they had arrested thirteen suspects: eight patients at the C&R center's clinic, who were charged with beating Sun; and five employees of the clinic, who were accused of inciting the beating (*Xinhuanet* 2003b). In early June, the trial of these twelve defendants opened in the Guangzhou Intermediate People's Court. According to published accounts of the courtroom testimony, clinic guards were angered that Sun had screamed for help and ordered eight detainees to beat him as punishment. Within days, twelve of the defendants were convicted and given sentences ranging from three years' imprisonment to death. In two separate trials, an additional six public security officers were convicted of dereliction of duty and sentenced to prison terms ranging from two to three years (*Zhongguo lüshi wang* 2003b; *Xinhua News Agency* 2003a).

B. Constitutional Arguments Raised in Reaction to Sun's Death

Chinese legal reformers viewed the controversy over Sun Zhigang's death as an opportunity both to challenge the C&R system and to establish a precedent for constitutional review in China. In May 2003, three young legal scholars named Xu Zhiyong, Teng Biao, and Yu Jiang submitted a formal proposal to the NPCSC under Article 90(2) of the Law on Legislation (Yu et al. 2003) (the "Review Proposal"). The Review Proposal challenged the legality and constitutionality of the C&R Measures. Under the People's Republic of China (PRC) Constitution and the Law on Legislation, it is the NPCSC, rather than China's judiciary, that has the power to invalidate laws and regulations that conflict with the Constitution. In practice, the NPCSC has not actively exercised this power (Lin 2005; Teng 2004a). Legal scholars hoped that by filing the Review Proposal, they would breathe life into the NPCSC's constitutional review mechanism. "This is not aimed just at the Sun Zhigang case," said Xu Zhiyong. "We are concerned about the system itself. A mechanism for reviewing violations of the Constitution should be established and initiated in order to root out abuses and innovate continually" (Cui 2003). Scholars expressed strong support for the Review Proposal and concluded that its filing was as significant as the Sun Zhigang case itself (see, for example, *Jingji guancha* 2003; see also Wang 2004, 159).

The Review Proposal was written in the form of a legal brief and relied on legalistic arguments to challenge the C&R Measures. The first argument was that the Measures violated the allocation of lawmaking powers set out in Articles 8 and 9 of the Law on Legislation, a core component of China's constitutional architecture. Article 8 of that Law provides that "[t]he following affairs shall only be governed by statute: . . . (5) coercive measures (*qiangzhi cuoshi*) and penalties (*chufa*) involving the deprivation of the political rights or personal freedom of citizens." Article 9 provides that the NPC or the NPCSC may authorize the State Council to formulate administrative regulations on the matters listed in Article 8 "except for matters concerning criminal offences and their punishment, coercive measures and punishments involving the deprivation of the political rights or personal freedom of citizens, and the judicial system." The C&R Measures (Arts. 5, 6) and related implementing rules—including the "Detailed Implementing Rules for the Measures on Custody and Repatriation of Vagrants and Beggars in Cities (Temporary)" (*Chengshi liulang qitao renyuan shourong yisong banfa shishi xize (shixing)* 1982), passed by the State Council in 1982, and also subordinate rules issued by lower-level government entities—contained provisions that were clearly "coercive" under the Law and Legislation (cf. Zhang 2005), and thus constituted clear violations of that law (see *Renmin Wang* 2003; Yan 2003).

The second argument was that the C&R Measures violated Article 37 of the PRC Constitution. This Article provides that "[t]he freedom of the citizens of the PRC is inviolable. No citizen may be arrested except with the approval or by a decision of a people's procuratorate or by a decision of a people's court, and arrests must only be made by a public security organ. *Unlawful* deprivation or restriction of citizens' personal freedom by detention or other means is prohibited, and unlawful search of the person of citizens is prohibited [emphasis added]." This argument had two variants. Some commentators concluded that the Measures technically violated Article 37 because the C&R Measures were "unlawful" under the Law on Legislation. Others argued that C&R was by its nature a constitutionally impermissible violation of citizens' "personal freedom" (compare Tong 2003, Yan 2003; with Guo 2004).[3] The drafters of the Review Proposal did not specify which interpretation they were relying on.

The Review Proposal received significant attention in the Chinese media. The drafters, recognizing that their proposal would have little impact if it were not publicized, had coordinated with national media and carefully timed the submission of the document to maximize media coverage (Teng 2004b). On May 16, the *China Youth Daily* published a supportive article on the Review Proposal, noting the arguments and motivations of the scholars and hailing their decision to make use of the Law on Legislation to propose review of the C&R Measures. Media across China reprinted the *China Youth Daily* story and published other articles on the Review Proposal (Cui 2003; Teng 2004b). On May 22, a different group of five prominent legal scholars submitted a second petition to the NPCSC calling for an investigation into the C&R system, an act that helped to maintain public focus on the incident (see He et al. 2003). By late May, the NPCSC publicly acknowledged receipt of the Review Proposal and indicated that it was considering the document (Nie 2003).

In early June, after the trial and conviction of Sun's alleged attackers, authorities moved to address the broader concerns that the incident raised. On June 18, official media reported that the State Council, at an executive meeting chaired by Premier Wen Jiabao, had approved a new regulation to replace the C&R Measures. This regulation, entitled "Measures on the Administration of Aid to Indigent Vagrants and Beggars" (*Chengshi shenghuo wuzhuo de liulang qitao renyuan jiuzhu guanli banfa* 2003) ("Aid Measures"), directed civil affairs bureaus to establish *voluntary* aid stations to "provide aid to indigent vagrants and beggars and safeguard their basic subsistence rights and interests." It also prohibited forced commitments and repatriations (see also *Xinhua News Agency* 2003c). Chinese commentators reacted to the repeal of C&R Measures with euphoria, declaring that the day would be "entered into the history books" and that "this milestone will always remind us to cherish and strive for every right to which our citizens are entitled and to promote political civilization, the rule of law, and social progress in China." (Xiao 2003; see also Zi 2003)

Although expressing vindication and a sense of empowerment with the State Council's decision, however, some observers noted with disappointment that the State Council's voluntary reform of the C&R system had sidelined the groundbreaking process of constitutional scrutiny by the NPCSC. By unilaterally repealing the C&R Measures, the State Council had eliminated the need for NPCSC review and, therefore, the possibility of a constitutional precedent. Some Chinese scholars noted that the failure of the NPCSC to exercise its review powers made the Sun Zhigang incident less significant for rule of law development in China than it otherwise would have been. Others expressed concern that this would bring an end to citizens efforts to initiate NPCSC review (see, for example, Leu 2003; Tong 2003; Teng 2003a).

As the government implemented the Aid Measures and instituted a series of additional law enforcement reforms related in part to anger over the Sun Zhigang case (Congressional-Executive Commission on China 2004, 24–25), it also adopted countermeasures to bring closure to the incident. In late July 2003, authorities moved to reassert control over public discourse by banning further reporting on Sun Zhigang, suppressing a similar review proposal challenging China's re-education through labor system (see below), temporarily restricting public discussion of constitutional reform in the media and in academic conferences, and closing several Internet web sites that had been major forums for discussing Sun Zhigang's death (Pomfret 2003; Teng 2003b). These actions demonstrated the state's ability and determination to maintain control over the constitutional discourse that Sun Zhigang's death had helped set in motion.

C. Sociopolitical Factors Contributing to the Decision to Repeal the C&R Measures

In the Sun Zhigang incident, a confluence of external sociopolitical circumstances created conditions favorable to a positive reform outcome. These included a leadership transition, a political crisis generated by the outbreak of Severe Acute Respiratory Syndrome (SARS), political concern with the ramifications of a more formal and drawn out NPCSC review of the C&R Measures, and the adoption of effective advocacy strategies by legal intellectuals pushing reforms.

1. Leadership Need for Constitutional Legitimacy

The Sun Zhigang incident took place against the backdrop of a politically tense leadership transition in China and the upheaval of the SARS crisis. In late 2002 and early 2003, Hu Jintao succeeded Jiang Zemin as the leader of the party and the state. An ally, Wen Jiabao, replaced Zhu Rongji as Premier of the State Council, China's highest administrative organ. However, Jiang retained the post of Chairman of the Central Military Commission and placed his allies in a majority of the positions on an expanded CCP Politburo Standing Committee. These events left Hu's status and authority relative to Jiang unsettled and generated speculation that the two leaders were engaged in a power struggle (Fewsmith 2003b; Miller 2003a). As they assumed their new posts, Hu and Wen emphasized reform themes of governing for the people, stressed greater government transparency and openness, and took steps to promote understanding and implementation of the PRC Constitution in an effort to bolster their popular support (Fewsmith 2003b; Miller 2003b).

The SARS crisis in early 2003 brought these new leadership dynamics into sharp relief. For weeks, Chinese officials fearful of the economic and political repercussions of the outbreak maintained that the disease was under control. In April 2003, however, the central government was forced to acknowledge that the number of SARS cases had not been accurately reported to the public. This admission created a legitimacy crisis, but also gave Hu and Wen an opportunity to reinforce themes of openness that they had been trying to project, demonstrate their leadership, and contrast themselves with Jiang (who had come across as aloof on the SARS issue) (Fewsmith 2003b). The temporary emphasis on openness and combating SARS provided citizens with space in which to advance their challenge to C&R. The decision to repeal the C&R Measures provided Hu and Wen with another opportunity to reinforce their constitutional credentials and rebuild government legitimacy in the wake of the SARS debacle. There was already some flexibility on reforming C&R. According to Chinese sources, the government had been considering reform of the C&R system for a number of years, and a State Council General Office (2003) directive issued in early 2003 indicates that senior officials were aware of abuses in the system (see also Zhao and Shen 2003; *Xinhua News Agency* 2003d). In March, Huang Jingjun, a member of the Chinese People's Political Consultative Conference, submitted a proposal calling for a firmer legal basis for the C&R system and rectification of C&R abuses (*Xinhuanet* 2003a). By responding to the citizen call to address an injustice and repeal C&R, Hu and Wen were able to extract significant propaganda value on an issue that did not really threaten fundamental state or party interests, and thereby strengthen their position in the leadership transition.

2. The Review Proposal Created the Prospect of a Constitutional Precedent that the Government was Anxious to Avoid

The Review Proposal created a potential institutional conflict between the NPC and the State Council. Although the NPC is the paramount legislative organ in China and the NPCSC in theory has the power to annul State Council regulations that conflict with the Constitution and national law, the NPCSC has not exercised this power in practice (Teng 2003a). The Review Proposal put the NPCSC in a politically awkward position of possibly overturning a State Council regulation. Rather than engage in a formal, extended constitutional process that could undermine the State Council's authority in the public's eyes, the NPCSC and the State Council conducted behind-the-scenes consultations to find a solution that could address the underlying social concern without calling into question the State Council's authority. The reasonable solution, other than taking the politically risky step of ignoring the Review Proposal, was for the State Council simply to repeal the C&R Measures (Teng 2003a; Wang 2004, 115, 165; Tong 2003).

In addition, an NPCSC decision to cancel the C&R Measures would have created a precedent that could potentially have threatened other administrative measures. "Re-education through labor" (RTL), another form of administrative detention created by administrative regulation rather than by national law, is vulnerable to the same legal arguments reformers made against the C&R Measures in the Review Proposal. Unlike C&R, however, RTL is much more central to the operation of China's public security system. According to constitutional law scholar Tong Zhiwei, the government was concerned that a review decision by the NPCSC in the context of C&R would encourage citizens to launch challenges to RTL and other rules that Chinese authorities depend on more heavily than C&R (Tong 2004). Such concern was evident in official media coverage of the State Council's decision to repeal C&R Measures, which avoided discussion of the constitutional infirmities of the regulation (*Xinhua News Agency* 2003c; Teng 2003b). By repealing the C&R Measures itself, the State Council avoided such a precedent.

3. Legal Intellectuals Worked Effectively within the System by Casting Their Calls for Reform as Consistent with the Leadership's Stated Emphasis on Constitutional Supremacy

As noted above, Hu Jintao placed strong emphasis on the supremacy of the PRC Constitution in late 2002 and early 2003. In addition to casting the Constitution as a weapon to be used in safeguarding rights, Hu noted that government deficiencies had lead to a failure to observe law in some cases and stressed that the NPC and its Standing Committee should "shoulder the duty to supervise the implementation of the cardinal law in practice, and *firmly rectify acts that violate the Constitution*" (emphasis added) (*Zhongguo xinwen wang* 2002). This and other rhetoric opened the door to spirited discussion of constitutionalism in China in the first half of 2003 (see also *Zhongguo lüshiwang* 2003a).

Reformers challenging the C&R system used these rhetorical themes to their advantage.

The authors of the Review Proposal intentionally relied on a very technical, legal argument, rather than emotional appeals, to avoid politicizing their challenge to the C&R Measures. The Proposal does not even mention the Sun Zhigang case. As Teng Biao (2003b) noted, "[i]t was not an appeal, but an exercise of citizen proposal rights granted by the Constitution and the Law on Legislation. It was not a protest, but citizens carrying out the practice of law within the cracks in the system."

This approach allowed them to cast their effort as consistent with leadership objectives. By invoking the citizen proposal mechanism clearly provided for in the Law on Legislation and making a rational and technical argument that the regulations were unlawful (rather than challenging the legitimacy of the regime as a whole), the three scholars could claim to be using the law as a weapon to protect citizen rights and calling on the NPCSC to exercise its constitutional supervision function, just as Hu Jintao had instructed. This effort received favorable coverage in the Chinese media. One party publication explicitly endorsed the approach of these scholars, praising them for "taking the path of citizen proposals to participate in politics" and for playing a crucial role in "solving problems within the constitutional framework" by "guiding society to use rational, legal methods through which to express indignation" (Cao 2003; see also Cai 2005a).

The legal reformers active in the Sun Zhigang incident calculated that by working within the system and relying on technical legal challenges, they were more likely to achieve a positive result and avoid a political backlash. "I have respect for those who raised human rights issues in the past," said Xu Zhiyong. "But now we hope to work in a constructive way within the space afforded by the legal system. Concrete but gradual change—that is what most Chinese people want" (Eckholm 2003; see also *Renmin wang* 2003). As these and other comments suggest, the drafters of the Review Proposal hoped to achieve modest but meaningful reform that they could build on in the future.

The efforts of these legal scholars were critical to the reform outcome in the Sun Zhigang incident. Legal reformers could not have achieved their goals in the absence of aggressive media reporting on the Sun Zhigang incident and the tide of public opinion it produced. However, without the directed efforts of these legal scholars, the government may have been able to assuage public anger by quickly punishing those responsible for Sun's death or implementing superficial reforms to C&R. The constitutional review proposal provided legitimacy and power to the voices of average citizens and channeled public outrage over Sun Zhigang's death into a defined, well-grounded constitutional challenge to C&R that could be cast as an effort to advance stated leadership goals.

D. Constitutional Impacts of the Sun Zhigang Incident

The Sun Zhigang incident not only led to the repeal of C&R, but also had broader influence on China's constitutional development by establishing a precedent for the acceptance of constitutional review proposals, promoting constitutional consciousness, and empowering citizen activists.

1. Impact on the Development of Constitutional Review

The drafters of the Review Proposal hoped that by publicly exercising their right to call on the NPCSC to annul the C&R Measures, they would create a precedent for NPCSC review. They did not achieve this goal. Despite the fact that the NPCSC failed to act, however, the Sun Zhigang incident had a significant impact on constitutional development in China. From a long-term perspective, the incident clarified the right of citizens to submit proposals to the NPCSC, accelerated the creation of embryonic institutions and procedures within the NPCSC to review such proposals, and raised public consciousness of the Constitution and constitutional review.

The fact that the Review Proposal was filed and formally accepted by the NPCSC was a step forward for China's constitutional development. Although the Review Proposal was not the first citizen proposal filed under Article 90(2) of the Law on Legislation (see, for example, Shang 2000), it was the most prominent and well-publicized. NPCSC officials not only publicly acknowledged that they were considering the Review Proposal, but also emphasized the importance of constitutional review and the NPCSC's review function (Nie 2003). China's state-run legal press encouraged citizens to use the Constitution to protect their rights and the following year, NPC officials again publicly confirmed that citizens could exercise the proposal right (see Du 2003; *Xinhuanet* 2004). Such statements placed an official stamp on the efforts of scholars to exercise an important legal right and legitimized arguments that the NPCSC should carry out its supervisory role in practice. By clarifying the citizen proposal right under the Law on Legislation, the Review Proposal opened the door for the filing and acceptance of future review proposals.

The Sun Zhigang incident, and the surge of public interest in the Constitution that it generated, also appear to have accelerated NPCSC efforts to develop constitutional review procedures. When the Review Proposal was filed, numerous legal experts criticized the NPCSC because it had no procedures for handling and replying to such citizen proposals (see, for example, *Jingji guancha* 2003; Deng 2003). At the time, an NPCSC official acknowledged this problem and expressed confidence that the Sun Zhigang incident and related discussion would push China's rule of law process forward (Nie 2003). In June 2004, the NPCSC announced that it had established a new administrative office to review legislative conflicts and related citizen proposals and make recommendations on addressing them (*Xinjing bao* 2004). The *China Daily* tied this reform to the Sun Zhigang case and characterized it as a response to "mounting public demand that [the NPC] rectify its constitutional oversight" (*China Daily* 2004b). In December 2005, the NPCSC took a further step, issuing two circulars that set out detailed procedures for handling proposals for NPCSC review of administrative regulations and judicial interpretations. Press articles on the procedures were reprinted on the NPC and *Guangming Daily* Web sites, and connected this reform to the Sun Zhigang incident as well, calling on readers to remember "Sun Zhigang's epitaph" (*Xinjing bao* 2005b; see also Lan 2005; *Xinjing bao* 2005a).

It would be premature to conclude that the reforms described above represent the emergence of an institutionalized and independent legal process for constitutional review. In fact, the limited nature of the reforms suggest that they may be part of a leadership effort to demonstrate progress on the issue of constitutional review while staving off demands for more robust constitutional enforcement mechanisms and maintaining tight control over constitutional claims. Nevertheless, they represent small but nevertheless significant advances. The NPC has now legitimized the citizen proposal right in practice and has publicized the fact that it has adopted detailed procedures to handle such proposals. The establishment of the review mechanism and the official recognition that it can and should be used opens up expanded space for future citizen constitutional claims. References to Sun Zhigang in discussions of these reforms demonstrate that the incident was a factor in pushing the reforms forward.

2. *Constitutional Consciousness and Citizen Empowerment*

The Sun Zhigang incident also intensified public discussion of constitutionalism and added a new dimension to this discourse by focusing attention on the issue of constitutional review. Interviews with the drafters of the Review Proposal indicate that even these three highly educated legal scholars were initially unaware that the Law on Legislation gave them a right to submit constitutional review proposals and only "discovered" it with excitement after several weeks of discussion and research on the Sun Zhigang case (*Nanfang zhoumo* 2003b). In reports on the Review Proposal, mainstream Chinese media explained the proposal right and stressed that the mechanism was a tool that not only legal experts, but also ordinary citizens, should use (see, for example, *Nanfang dushibao* 2003c; Cui 2003; *Jingji guancha* 2003). Such reports undoubtedly exposed many citizens to the concept of constitutional review for the first time. Reformers viewed this contribution as critical, noting that only citizen pressure and real-life precedents could activate China's dormant constitutional review procedures (Teng 2004a). This discussion had a profound impact on constitutional awareness in China. Even the *Guangming Daily*, a party publication, opined that "the supreme authority of the Constitution is carved into the hearts of every citizen at the moment," and that the Sun Zhigang case was "an opportunity for an intellectual movement to actively protect the Constitution that is gradually rising in Chinese society" (Cao 2003; see also Deng 2003).

This awareness, and the partial reform victory in the Sun Zhigang incident, generated a sense of citizen empowerment. Although the strategy of using incidents or individual cases to promote broader legal reform was not new (see Liebman 1999, 271–272, 278–279), legal reformers in the Sun Zhigang incident applied this strategy in a more aggressive and public manner, drawing on constitutional arguments and leveraging a surge of public opinion to challenge a flawed national regulation. While in the absence of an NPCSC decision or official acknowledgement, there was no way to prove that the Review Proposal itself triggered the repeal of the C&R Measures, the State Council's decision nevertheless offered what many interpreted to be a dramatic illustration of the effectiveness of citizen action.

Chinese citizens exhibited not only hope and exhilaration at this outcome, but also a new sense of confidence and purpose. In the wake of the Sun Zhigang incident, reformers refined and publicized strategies for bottom-up constitutional activism, including "rights defense" (*weiquan*) actions and impact litigation (*yingxiangxing susong*) (see, for example, Wang 2003; Teng 2003b; Teng 2005; Ji and Wang 2005; *Radio Free Asia* 2006j). More importantly, as noted in Section I, a cadre of rights defenders, public interest lawyers, and average citizens have continued to advance new constitutional arguments in subsequent proposals for NPCSC review, and in litigation. (Several of these will be discussed in Section III.) Chinese scholars and lawyers have cited the Sun Zhigang incident as a catalyst for this new wave of constitutional activism (Cai 2005a).

III. Citizen Constitutional Challenges Subsequent to the Sun Zhigang Incident

This section presents four examples of citizen proposals for NPCSC constitutional review that were developed and submitted subsequent to the Sun Zhigang incident. These examples illustrate a range of constitutional challenges and official responses, and highlight the conditions under which constitutional appeals may be effective tools for promoting specific legal and policy reforms. They also demonstrate that lawyers are filing such appeals with broader, constitutional development goals in mind, similar to the scholars in the Sun Zhigang incident. In the first two examples, citizens advanced constitutional arguments in the pursuit of reform goals that were unrealistic in the existing political environment or raised sensitive political issues. The immediate impacts of these proposals appear to have been limited or nonexistent. The second two examples, both involving constitutional challenges to discriminatory rules or practices, demonstrate that a positive reform dynamic similar to that in the Sun Zhigang incident has been created in some subsequent cases. As these examples suggest, when media coverage focuses public attention on an injustice or issue of broad concern and there is a degree of government policy flexibility, constitutional appeals may be helpful in promoting specific legal and policy reforms.

A. *Challenges to Re-education through Labor*

Immediately after the repeal of the C&R Measures in 2003, reformers launched a challenge against China's re-education–through-labor (RTL) system. Under China's RTL system, public security bureaus have the power to send citizens, without trial, to "re-education through labor" camps for terms of up to three years, with the possibility of a one year extension, for a variety of illegal acts. RTL, like C&R, was established by administrative regulation and was vulnerable to the same constitutional arguments that were made against C&R in the Review Proposal (see Hung 2003). However, in this case the government refused to repeal the system under challenge. The RTL challenge highlights the importance of leadership flexibility and illustrates the limits of party and government responsiveness to citizen constitutional review proposals.

In June 2003, a Beijing scholar named Hu Xingdou attempted to build on the success of the Sun Zhigang incident by filing the first of two proposals with the NPCSC challenging the legality of RTL. His first proposal, submitted only days after the State Council announced the repeal of the C&R Measures, was a short, technical document that drew on the Constitution and Law on Legislation and replicated the legal arguments made against C&R in the Review Proposal (Hu 2003a). Hu noted in online comments (Hu 2003b) that the proposal was an effort to breathe life into a constitutional review process that had been left "stillborn" after the State Council voluntarily repealed the C&R Measures. He characterized his proposal as a "second wave" effort to establish constitutional review and expressed hope that there would be third and fourth waves. In July 2003, Chinese media reported on the torture death of an RTL inmate named Zhang Bin under circumstances that resembled those of Sun Zhigang's death (*Ming Pao* 2003a). Seeking to build upon this, Hu several months later filed a second, significantly longer proposal challenging RTL (Hu 2003c). This proposal repeated the legal arguments of the first, but added emotional descriptions of RTL abuses, a more detailed constitutional analysis, and appeals to China's leaders to recognize that it was in their political interest to abolish the system.

Although Chinese media reported on the death of Zhang Bin, the level of such reporting did not approach that in the Sun Zhigang incident. According to official reports, senior leaders issued firm and timely instructions in response to the Zhang Bin case, and authorities imposed harsh sentences on the alleged perpetrators of that incident. In late 2003 and in 2004, official media also emphasized government efforts to humanize RTL centers (see, for example, Guo 2003; see generally Congressional-Executive Commission on China 2004, 17). At the same time, authorities reportedly barred the Chinese media from covering Hu's constitutional review proposals and warned Hu not to publicize his efforts (*Ming Pao* 2003b).

Unlike in the case of C&R, the leadership was not flexible on the issue of repealing RTL, which it continues to rely upon as an important mechanism of social control (Ma 2003; see also Peerenboom 2004b). This lack of flexibility, in turn, probably resulted in government efforts to limit media coverage and preempt public pressure for systemic reform. At least from a short-term perspective, Hu's constitutional review proposal was a failure: it neither resulted in the repeal of RTL nor established a constitutional review precedent. The case demonstrates that constitutional arguments may not be sufficient to catalyze reforms when other factors, such as a government predisposition for reform and intense media coverage, are not in place.

From a long-term perspective, however, constitutional challenges to RTL may have contributed to pressure for a reevaluation of the system. Although RTL remains in force, the government is now considering a national "Law on Correcting Unlawful Acts" to provide a statutory, rather than simply administrative, basis for the RTL system. The drafting of this national law, an effort that directly addresses at least one of the arguments in Hu's constitutional review proposals, has opened the door to discussion of modest reforms to the system. These possible reforms include reducing the maximum RTL sentence from three years to eighteen months, allowing RTL suspects to hire a defense lawyer, and providing for formal RTL hearings and appeals (Congressional-Executive Commission on China 2005, 28). In February 2006, *Xinhua* published a commentary on RTL acknowledging that the system lacks a legal basis and that current RTL procedures fail to uphold the basic demands of fairness, openness, and justice as demanded by the Constitution (Lin 2006). Although Chinese leaders ignored calls to repeal RTL in 2003, they seem to feel the need to respond to the argument that RTL lacks a proper legal basis by both founding the system on stronger legal legitimacy, and making modest changes that address some basic complaints about it. This long-term response is one indication of the importance the leadership places on maintaining the appearance of legality and illustrates the related role that citizen constitutional appeals may play in promoting modest reforms.

B. The Aegean Sea Group Constitutional Review Proposal on China's Internet News Management Regulations

In a second example, this one from early 2006, citizens used the constitutional review mechanism as a forum for political protest, challenging administrative regulations on Internet news content. This case suggests that politicized constitutional challenges to core regime interests have limited potential as vehicles for generating public discussion and movement on specific reforms.

In March 2006, after the Zhejiang Press and Publication Administration closed down a number of Web sites shortly before the annual meeting of the NPC Plenary Session, a consortium of independent Web site operators calling themselves the "Aegean Sea Incident Constitutional Review Application Delegation" filed a constitutional review proposal with the NPCSC challenging the Provisions on the Administration of Internet News Information Services (*Hulianwang xinwen xinxi fuwu guanli guiding* 2005) (the "Provisions") (see generally *Congressional-Executive Commission on China Virtual Academy* 2006b). The Provisions, issued by the State Council Administration Office and the Ministry of Information Industry in the fall of 2005, empower local press and publication bureaus to close any "Internet news information service" established without the authorization of the State Council Information Office. They also require such services to have 10 million yuan in registered capital in order to receive authorization. The authors of the proposal argued that the Provisions violate the rights to freedom of speech and the press enshrined in Article 35 of the Constitution. They also argued that the rule violates the PRC Administrative Licensing Law, which states that industrial licenses may only be established by national statute (passed by the NPC or the NPCSC) or by administrative regulation promulgated by the State Council. The Provisions, by contrast, were jointly promulgated by a State Council sub-bureau and an agency rather than the State Council itself. Finally, they also asserted that the violation of a public law such as the Administrative Licensing Law is a *de facto* violation of the Constitution (see *Congressional-Executive Commission on China Virtual Academy* 2006c).

Similar to the RTL proposal, the Aegean Sea proposal directly challenged a core control mechanism of the Chinese party-state—in this case, legal controls over news and information. Moreover, the Aegean Sea proposal was much more "politicized" than the others discussed in this chapter. Like the other proposals, it presented distinct constitutional arguments and was addressed to the NPCSC office charged with reviewing legislative inconsistencies. But while reformers in other cases have been careful to cast their proposals as efforts to advance stated government and party interests, the Aegean Sea proposal was clearly framed as a protest against regime power. The title of the proposal, which was published as an open letter, read like a political call to arms: "Demand for Thorough Repeal of the 'Provisions on the Administration of Internet News Information Services'—Netizens of the World Sign On!" The authors further declared that once the number of signatories on the proposal reached 10,000, if the NPCSC had not conducted a review and announced its decision, they would apply to a "model constitutional court" composed of Chinese scholars and "authoritative persons" for review.[4]

Unlike the more technical and politically cautious proposals discussed elsewhere in this chapter, the Aegean Sea proposal failed to catalyze any reform movement and may even have contributed to a political backlash. It was not covered in the domestic state-run media (although it was reported and discussed in foreign media and on dissident and rights-defense Web sites). Moreover, in October 2006, the founder and editor of the Aegean Sea Web Site, a vocal and experienced dissident named Zhang Jianhong, was arrested and charged with subversion (*Congressional-Executive Commission on China Virtual Academy* 2006d). The NPCSC never responded to the proposal, and, as of August 2007, the Provisions remained in place unamended.

C. The Hepatitis B Discrimination Cases

In 2003, two legal cases and corresponding efforts to challenge pervasive official discrimination in public employment against carriers of the Hepatitis B virus ("HBV") presented reformers with an opportunity to press for legal and constitutional reforms similar to that in the Sun Zhigang case. Legal reformers took advantage of public attention on the issue and pursued constitutional challenges against HBV discrimination both by filing litigation in the courts and by sending a constitutional review proposal to the NPCSC. Their efforts arguably contributed to pressures for systemic legal reforms to address the issue of HBV discrimination and established antidiscrimination principles that could be used to challenge other forms of discrimination in the future. Moreover, their discussion of constitutional principles in these legal forums maintained public focus on the issue of constitutional review after the Sun Zhigang incident. Indeed, some Hepatitis B activists drew explicit parallels between their cause and the Sun Zhigang case (see, for example, Huang and He 2003).

According to Chinese estimates, more than 120 million Chinese citizens (nearly 10 percent of the population) are HBV carriers. Although many of these carriers have not developed full Hepatitis B infections and are not a threat to those around them, they have been systematically excluded from civil service positions and frequently suffer discrimination in education, marriage, and other areas (see generally Chen 2004c; *China Law and Governance Review* 2004). In April 2003, a man named Zhou Yichao, who had been denied a civil service position because of his HBV status, entered a government office in Zhejiang Province, killed a local official, and seriously injured another. Although Zhou was eventually sentenced to death and executed, the case attracted significant and somewhat sympathetic media attention. The case also prompted commentators to debate the appropriateness of the discriminatory hiring practices that led Zhou to commit this desperate act (Chen 2003; Guo 2004).

Shortly after Zhou's trial, other Chinese citizens took steps to challenge HBV discrimination through legal channels. In November 2003, a man from Anhui Province named Zhang Xianzhu filed a groundbreaking lawsuit in a basic level court in the city of Wuhu challenging the decision of the Wuhu municipal government to deny him employment because of his HBV status. The lawsuit argued that such discrimination violated both Zhang's right to participate in the affairs of the state (through government employment), and his right to equal protection, as enshrined in Articles 2 and 33 of the Constitution respectively. Zhang was represented by Zhou Wei, a well-known law professor and public interest lawyer. Zhou, who had previously filed other antidiscrimination lawsuits based on similar constitutional arguments, was hoping to use this case not only to push for antidiscrimination reforms but also more broadly to promote constitutional consciousness and judicial application of the Constitution (*China Law and Governance Review* 2004; see also *Sichuan xinwen wang* 2003).

At the same time, a group of HBV carriers submitted a constitutional Review Proposal to the NPCSC on the HBV discrimination issue. The proposal challenged the constitutionality of a large set of national, provincial, and municipal regulations that systematically excluded HBV carriers from public employment. The proposal, which was circulated and discussed on an Internet site devoted to HBV carriers, was eventually signed by more than 1,611 citizens and formally submitted to the NPCSC in December 2003 (*Xinjing bao* 2003).

Both the court cases and the proposal received national media coverage and generated sustained constitutional discussion among the public. A commentary on the Web site of China's central television network noted that, like the Sun Zhigang case, the Hepatitis B cases had the potential to promote a systemic change that would affect all Chinese citizens. The report also noted that reformers were pursuing legal strategies to deal with the problem that resembled those in the Sun Zhigang incident (*CCTV.com* 2004; see also Chen 2003; Guo 2004). The Zhang court case ended in a technical but hollow victory for legal reformers. The Wuhu court overturned the local government decision to disqualify Zhang, but it grounded its decision in an evidentiary issue and dodged the constitutional question that Zhang had raised. (It also declined to order the Wuhu government to employ him, noting that the recruiting season had already ended; see *China Law and Governance Review* 2004.)

Collectively, however, the Zhou killings, the Zhang lawsuit, the constitutional review proposal, and related public discussion helped to catalyze a series of broader legal reforms on HBV discrimination. In the wake of these events, at least six provinces announced that they would no longer exclude noninfectious HBV carriers from public employment (Yan 2004). In August 2004, the NPC passed revisions to the Law on the Prevention and Control of Infectious Diseases (*Zhonghua renmin gongheguo chuanranbing fangzhi fa* 2004) that banned discrimination against disease carriers (see Art. 17). And in early 2005, the personnel and health ministries finalized new health standards confirming that HBV carriers who do not show symptoms of the disease are eligible for public employment (see Article 7 of the Civil Service Employment Physical Examination General Standards (Provisional) (*Gongwuyuan luyong tijian tongyong biaozhun (shixing)* 2005)). Officials from the Ministry of Personnel noted that they had received proposals in the past on this issue and had been working on modifications to the civil service health standards for some time, an indication of government policy flexibility. However, the officials noted that public opinion "provided the impetus for the new amendment" (Chen 2004c). Subsequently, both the Ministry of Labor and Social Security (see Ministry of Labor and Social Security 2007) and the NPCSC (see *Xinhuanet* 2007) have taken steps to begin addressing the problem of HBV discrimination in the private sector.

D. Discriminatory Injury Compensation Standards

In 2006, legal activists built on their experience in the Hepatitis B cases and applied similar constitutional strategies to challenge discriminatory compensation standards for accident-related injuries. Subsequent to the filing of constitutional review proposals and related media coverage, both local and national authorities took steps to limit the impact of the discriminatory standards. The case provides a recent example of constitutional claims that appear to have contributed to a positive legal reform dynamic.

The death of three students in a traffic accident in Chongqing Municipality in early 2006 brought the issue of injury compensation standards to national attention (Yardley 2006). Pursuant to a Supreme People's Court legal interpretation (SPC 2003, Art. 29), many local courts in China determine compensation in part on the basis of whether accident victims hold an urban or rural residence registration (see generally Cheng, Zhou, and Li 2006). Based on this standard, the party responsible for the Chongqing accident provided the families of two students with urban residence registrations more than twice the compensation it agreed to provide the family of a third student with a rural residence registration, despite the fact that the family of the third, supposedly "rural" victim had lived in Chongqing for almost fifteen years. As in the Sun Zhigang and Hepatitis B cases, domestic media reported widely on the case and the controversy surrounding the disparate compensation standard (see, for example, *Zhengyi wang* [undated]; *Renmin wang* (2003); see generally Hand 2006, 191).

This controversy prompted several legal reformers to file constitutional review proposals with the NPCSC challenging the constitutionality of the Supreme People's Court (SPC) interpretation. In April 2006, Zhou Wei, the lead lawyer in Zhang Xianzhu's Hepatitis B litigation, filed a proposal on behalf of the Chongqing family with the rural residence registration. The proposal challenged the constitutionality of Article 29 of the SPC interpretation, citing the equal protection clause of the Constitution and offering detailed arguments for why the compensation distinction in the SPC interpretation was constitutionally impermissible. Zhou Wei noted that NPC delegates had raised questions about the compensation standard at the 2006 NPC meetings and, drawing on official rhetoric, argued that such legal discrimination against rural residents "violated constitutional principles of building a socialist rule of law society," and was "not in accord with aim of building a harmonious society" (Cheng, Zhou, and Li 2006).

The Zhou Wei proposal was one in a series of citizen proposals on the issue. Beijing activist Hu Xingdou (2006) and Chongqing labor lawyer Zhou Litai (2004) also filed constitutional review proposals challenging the SPC interpretation. Subsequently, PRC citizens sent additional constitutional review proposals and suggestions on the interpretation both to the NPCSC and directly to the SPC. All of these proposals took advantage of political conditions favorable to policy movement, as the controversy arose at a time when senior leaders had been actively promoting new policies designed to narrow China's urban-rural income gap (see, for example, Wen 2006). As discussion of the Chongqing case and the constitutional review proposals circulated in the media, SPC officials indicated that the issue of compensation disparity had been under discussion for several years and that there was broad agreement on the need for a uniform standard (*Xinjing bao* 2006).

Since the filing of the constitutional review proposals, both local and national authorities have announced changes to injury compensation standards. In mid-2006, the Henan High People's Court issued an opinion that brought injury compensation standards for migrants meeting certain conditions into line with compensation standards for urban residents. According to domestic reports, Anhui Province, Guangxi Province, and Chongqing Municipality have all adopted similar measures (*Congressional-Executive Commission on China Virtual Academy* 2006b; *Fazhi ribao* 2006). After accepting public suggestions on revision of the interpretation in 2006, SPC President Xiao Yang announced in March 2007 that the interpretation would be revised sometime after the close of the 2007 NPC session (*People's Daily Online* 2007; *Xinjing bao* 2007). Reporting on the SPC interpretation in government mouthpieces such as the *Workers Daily* and *Xinhua* acknowledged the role that this robust constitutional debate was playing in discussions on the revision of the discriminatory standard (Cheng 2006; *People's Daily Online* 2007).

IV. Concluding Observations

What does popular engagement in constitutional interpretation and challenge tell us about China's constitutional development? Despite the reform enthusiasm that followed the repeal of the C&R Measures in 2003, the record of the past three years provides significant ammunition for critics (see, for example, *Nanfang dushibao* 2004; Lin 2005; Cai 2005b; see also Pils, this volume). Following the Sun Zhigang incident, authorities took small steps to build up the NPCSC's constitutional review capacity and related procedures. However, as explanations of the Law on Legislation published by the NPC Legal Affairs Commission indicate, the NPC intended the proposal right established under Article 90(2) to serve primarily as a safety valve for citizen complaint and as an information collection mechanism, rather than as an enforceable right to constitutional review (see Zhang 2000, 265–268). Under the current system, citizens have no right to a response to their constitutional review proposals. Indeed, not only has the NPCSC yet to issue a formal answer to a single proposal, but also it seems to be taking great pains to avoid doing so even on relatively benign issues, such as with regards to the collection of road maintenance fees (see *Xinhua News Agency* 2006). Moreover, the details of the review process do not appear to have been made readily available to the public,[5] and the mechanism cannot be used to challenge the constitutionality of national statutes passed by the NPC or the concrete behavior of administrative officials in specific cases. Finally, as noted in Section II of this chapter, authorities have explicitly ruled out the possibility of constitutional litigation in the people's courts.

Why then do Chinese citizens continue to raise constitutional arguments under the Law on Legislation review procedure? Several reasons might be offered. First, in some cases, constitutional review proposals appear to provide reformers with a useful tool for promoting modest legal and policy reforms. Filing a constitutional review proposal with the NPCSC generates media coverage and social discussion of reform issues. Engaging what is at least superficially the proper legal forum for constitutional complaints also gives activists a way to cloak their reform arguments in legal and constitutional legitimacy. The RTL and Aegean Sea examples suggest that when constitutional review proposals challenge fundamental party or state interests, the short-term impact of constitutional arguments may be limited or even nonexistent. However, the Sun Zhigang and antidiscrimination examples suggest that when there is policy flexibility on the part of the government, constitutional review proposals may help to nudge authorities in the direction of reform. Given the lack of any official NPCSC responses and the opaque nature of leadership decision making in China, it is difficult to establish a cause (a constitutional review proposal) and effect (movement on specific reforms) relationship with any degree of certainty.

Nevertheless, the fact that Chinese citizens continue to file constitutional review proposals tells us that even if the NPCSC review mechanism remains deficient as a *legal process*, reformers view these proposals as one of a number of useful tools, including media coverage and individual cases of injustice, to attract public attention and build political momentum for legal and policy reforms.

More importantly, many of the citizen activists who are filing such proposals are doing so in a long-term effort to make constitutional review meaningful as a legal process. Although flawed in numerous respects, the NPCSC review mechanism remains the one existing legal forum that Chinese authorities have authorized as an acceptable forum for constitutional challenges. By occupying this space, activists help to consolidate the symbolic citizenship gains that the creation of the constitutional review proposal mechanism represents. They also challenge China's authorities to live up to their rule of law rhetoric and make the existing review process meaningful in practice (see, for example, Teng 2004a; Yang 2004; Shang and Zhang 2005). Finally, filing proposals and exposing the limitations of the current mechanism gives citizen activists leverage from which to pry open space for enhanced constitutional review. By generating public discussion of legal issues, stimulating new government rhetoric that can be used as further political cover by reformers, establishing precedents, and creating patterns of and expectations for government responsiveness to citizen action, citizen constitutional challenges can push reform discussions to new levels and build foundations for more dramatic constitutional change should political conditions be more conducive to such change in the future (see also *Radio Free Asia* 2006j).

Viewed from this perspective, citizen constitutional review proposals are part of a dynamic process of constitutional development, one shaped not only by top-down decision making but also by interactions between the government and ordinary citizens (see Fu, this volume; Dowdle this volume). The Sun Zhigang incident illustrated this dynamic. Discussion by government leaders and state-run media of constitutional enforcement and the rule of law provided a source of (perhaps unintended) legitimacy for the initial scholar demands for review of C&R. However, it was media and Internet coverage of the citizen challenge to C&R, more than the government's planning and more general rhetoric on constitutionalism, that generated a sense of citizen empowerment and strengthened public consciousness of constitutional rights and enforcement mechanisms. Reformers not only capitalized on official legal rhetoric and existing legal institutions, but also created a legal story of their own. This story attracted public attention and, amplified by media and Internet coverage, provided legal activists with an opportunity to disseminate and reinforce messages of their choosing. The government's response to these pressures in turn generated further publicity on the issue, a flurry of new constitutional review proposals, and an expectation that NPCSC's December 2005 procedures for handling constitutional review proposals were "just the beginning of the establishment of constitutional review" (*Xinjing bao* 2005a).

In sum, the Sun Zhigang incident and government rule of law rhetoric legitimized a self-reinforcing cycle of citizen action, reform pressures, and further publicity that promoted constitutional development. Similar observations might be made about the Hepatitis B cases, challenges to the SPC injury compensation standard, and even to some degree the challenges to RTL.

Whether these constitutional claims will prove successful in prompting the creation of a more robust mechanism for constitutional review in China remains to be seen. Given the sensitive political dynamics that surround this issue and the present reluctance of the NPCSC to issue public decisions in response to constitutional review proposals, the establishment of such a mechanism seems unlikely in the near term. In the current political environment, however, reformers do not have many effective alternatives for promoting constitutional development. Unrealistic reform demands, politicized appeals, unauthorized organization and collective action, and demonstrations all hold significant risks for legal reformers and, as some in China have noted, may actually set the reform process back (see Eva Pils' chapter in this volume).[6] Constitutional review proposals offer citizens the limited but nonetheless significant opportunity to bolster arguments for specific legal reforms and to keep pressure on the state to breathe life into constitutional review. To the extent that the party and the government increasingly rely on constitutionalism and rule of law as sources of legitimacy, and on legal institutions to address growing instability (see also He, this volume), such long-term movement seems plausible.

Notes

1. The author has collected thirty-six examples of citizen proposals filed under the Law on Legislation review mechanism. The actual number of proposals are almost certainly much higher. Not all such proposals cite the Constitution specifically, but are nevertheless "constitutional" in a broader sense.
2. Except as otherwise indicated, the account presented in this subsection is based on Chen and Wang (2003). See also Yun (2003).
3. Both interpretations of the second argument appear to be controversial (see Deng 2003; Jiang 2003).
4. It is unclear if the proposal was ever formally sent to the NPC Legislation Filing and Review Office.
5. The author has been able to identify only one obscure Internet source for the full text of the procedures and has been unable to locate any published NPCSC decision on a review proposal. When last visited in August 2007, the Web site that had earlier posted the procedures had become inoperable.
6. See, e.g., Kahn (2005). In discussions with the author, other rights lawyers have made similar comments.

CHAPTER FOURTEEN

Rights Activism in China: The Case of Lawyer Gao Zhisheng

EVA PILS

I. Introduction: The Debate among Chinese "Rights Defenders"

In late 2005, a Chinese lawyer named Gao Zhisheng decided to address a particularly "sensitive" political issue in a particularly provocative way. He published an online call, addressed to China's leadership, to stop the torture of Falungong practitioners, substantiating his appeal by detailed descriptions of individual cases of torture, which he claimed to have received from the tortured victims themselves (Gao 2005a). Within days, his Beijing law firm's license to practice was suspended and he was put under surveillance by the secret police. However, these were not the only consequences. Following his public call for a hunger strike to oppose state violence, launched a few months later, he was also subjected to vehement criticism by other Chinese lawyers and rights activists, who advised, implored, or even angrily demanded of him to stop. At one point, he narrowly escaped being imprisoned in a *yaodong* cave by his own brothers in his home village in the province of Shaanxi.

His experience, while unique, is in many ways characteristic of the current situation of many Chinese rights activists engaged in what in China now is often described as "rights defence *[weiquan]*" (see also Fu and Cullen 2008). Despite remarkable successes in the past thirty years of reform, Chinese law and civil society remain weakened by party and personal autocracy, and by contradictions between rules and principles recognized in different parts of the law and actual political practices. This weakness shapes the experiences of those engaged in using the law to fight injustices. Rights defenders not only record and protest the denial of legal rights to Chinese citizens, but in doing so, they also expose and challenge the inner contradictions of the legal and political system; in particular, the contradiction between the PRC Constitution's new commitment to constitutional rights, and its old commitment to party rule and democratic centralism. The need to choose strategies in this difficult situation has proved divisive among Chinese rights defenders, pitting those more cautious against those who could be called more "radical." Some of these more radical activists now take on cases of political persecution that have no prospect of institutional success. From the perspective of people working toward institutional reform, it can seem risky to expose rights violations and other wrongs when there is no chance of redress, and every chance of persecution for political activism, or even of escalation into violence on both sides of the dispute.

However, from the perspective of the more radical side, it would be wrong not to speak up for those most in need of solidarity, sympathy, and protection. According to this view, the case for speaking out against wrongs does not rest on predictable consequences (success). It rests instead on the idea of rights-defending as a strict moral obligation toward the victims of abuses, as well as toward society and oneself. Rights activism, according to this view, can therefore not always be well understood as a constructive contribution to the reform of an existing legal system. At some point, "radical" rights defenders stop appealing to the existing system's legal institutions; and as they stop taking that system seriously, they start calling for the creation of a new system.

This article engages with both sides of the still ongoing debate between these two kinds of rights defenders, on the basis of interviews conducted in the summer of 2006 in Beijing.[1] It describes the experience of one prominent rights defender, Gao Zhisheng, in his efforts to try to "play by the system" for a Falungong practitioner in 2004; the difficulties he encountered in trying to play by that system; and the increasing radicalization of his and others rights-defense strategies, strategies that involved the breaking of certain "pragmatic silences" that up until then had been largely kept by China's legal profession, including its rights defence community. Finally, it discusses the debates about the "politicization" of the work of *weiquan* lawyers that has been triggered by Gao Zhisheng's actions, in an effort to connect these debates with the wider debate about the relationship between rights activism and rule of law reform.

II. Lawyer Gao Zhisheng Tries to "Play by the Rules" for a Falungong Practitioner

Gao Zhisheng was born in the early 1960s, one of seven children of a poor rural family in the province of Shaanxi. He lost his father early (Kahn 2005), and obtained his legal education and a lawyer's license by attending evening classes. He began practicing law in the 1990s. At that time, the law held out many promises to many people, not least because of the intense party-state propagation of the idea of "ruling the country in accordance with law (*yifa zhiguo*)" (see, for example, *Xinhua News Agency* 2002). As a lawyer, Gao was successful in winning compensation for his clients in a number of cases that attracted media attention, and this made him one of China's most famous young lawyers—a respected and envied public figure. Beginning in the late 1990s, Gao also began taking on suits against government authorities and persons with strong links to government institutions, thereby assuming a place among China's so-called "(human) rights defense lawyers" or *weiquan lushi* (see also Fu and Cullen 2008). From around 2003, partly as a consequence of his earlier involvement in cases of Christian persecution, he began receiving many letters from Falungong adherents asking him to take on their cases.[2] In the winter of 2004, Gao took on the case of a Falungong practitioner named Huang Wei, who was challenging his administrative detention (Gao 2004b).

Falungong, or Falun Dafa, is a group—often called a cult or sect, and in Chinese official language referred to as a "crooked teaching [xiejiao]"—of people practicing particular forms of meditation and qigong. After years of ruthless persecution by the party-state, this group is also one of the driving forces of propaganda and information directed against the party, especially from abroad. One of its major campaigns has focused on encouraging party members to quit the party.

Huang Wei had been accused of distributing material propagating Falungong in his native Shijiazhuang, in Hebei province, and had consequently been assigned by the police to a Re-education through Labor (RTL) labor camp. After an application for administrative reconsideration of the decision against Huang Wei had been unsuccessful (the administrative authority that was supposed to review the decision simply did nothing), Huang, represented by Gao Zhisheng, tried to challenge the decision through administrative litigation. Huang's complaint alleged, among other things, that the protocol of his "interrogation" in May 2004 was falsified before Huang Wei's eyes by an officer, who faked Huang Wei's signature. He also complained about various procedural violations. Lastly, he argued that the Regulations regarding Re-education through Labor (*Guanyu laodong jiaoyang buchong guiding* (1979), the legal regulations upon which the RTL system is built, violated Article 37 of the Constitution, which says that citizens can only be arrested upon approval of a People's Procuracy or by decision of a People's Court (see also the discussion of Article 37 by Keith Hand in his chapter to this volume). Neither courts nor the procuratorates are involved in a decision to impose RTL, which is made exclusively by a committee internal to the police. Moreover, the administrative regulations and administrative decisions upon which the system is built do not meet new standards imposed by Articles 8 and 9 of the Law on Legislation (*Zhonghua Renmin Gongheguo Lifa Fa* 2000) and by Article 9 of the Administrative Punishment Law (*Zhonghua Renmin Gongheguo Xingzheng Chufa Fa* 1996), both of which hold that only a "statute (*falu*)" created by the National People's Congress can restrict the right to personal freedom (see also Hand, this volume).

In his effort to get legal protection, Huang encountered two difficulties. One was that there is currently no effective mechanism to subject statutes, administrative regulations, and a large number of other official decisions to legal scrutiny through an adjudicative process, even if they are unconstitutional. This is the subject of the section that immediately follows, which by exploring how Huang Wei's case was hopeless as a case of potential litigation, throws some light on the institutional limits of rights protection and constitutionalism in China's environment of fragmented law. The other difficulty concerns what the complaint in Huang Wei's case did *not* mention, and is discussed later.

III. Challenging the Lessons of Institutional Reform Pragmatism

Huang Wei's attempt to get justice from the courts should be compared to the now famous Sun Zhigang case in 2003 (see generally Hand, this volume). Sun Zhigang had been wrongly detained as a "vagrant" under China's Custody and Repatriation (C&R) system, and during this detention had been beaten to death under order of the police. This case was widely reported on, and caused the C&R system, with its various rampant abuses, to come under attack from academics and the public. After petitions to strike down this system had been presented to the National People's Congress by prominent scholars, it was repealed by the authority that had created it, the State Council. Importantly, Sun had been an educated university graduate, whereas the multitude of other victims of the C&S system were already socially-marginalized, rural "peasant" migrant workers. In Chinese society, he was an intensely sympathetic figure. The success of the campaign to get rid of the the S&R system was all the more remarkable because the review procedure for citizen proposals filed under Article 90 of the Law on Legislation is generally speaking not public: the National People's Congress has no clear duty even to acknowledge receipt of such proposals; and complaints are often sorted out through informal negotiation with the legislating authority, rather than decided as a matter of (constitutional) law (see Wang 2004). The Sun Zhigang case the most well-known case of effective utilization of the new review mechanism. It appeared to have established in the public mind the idea that a law can be bad even on the lawgiver's own terms, and in that sense represented an important breakthrough.

Only a few weeks later, a similar proposal challenging the constitutionality of the RTL system, the system that Huang Wei would later seek to challenge in court, failed. The arguments used in that proposal almost identical to those used against the C&R system (see Hu 2003c; Hand, this volume). They were no less good in the case of RTL. However, the complaint against RTL was quickly suppressed in the media and on the Internet. The National People's Congress did not even bother to acknowledge receipt of the proposal. The issue died down, and the legal and constitutional deficiencies of the RTL system remain unaddressed to this day. As described by Keith Hand elsewhere in this volume, most observers thought that RTL was not, at that time, a mechanism that the party wanted to or perhaps even could dispense with. The pragmatist lesson from this experience was that if one wished to push for legal reform through the available institutional mechanisms, in order to strengthen such institutions and mechanisms, one had to accept the limitations set by the institutions.

By the end of 2004, Gao Zhisheng was becoming aware of these limitations. He chose to take his client's case to court, asking it to address the case in a correct and constitutional manner. Yet in technical terms, the mechanism of administrative litigation before ordinary courts is even more limited as a means for challenging the constitutionality of administrative regulations. According to Article 12 of the Administrative Litigation Law (*Zhonghua Renmin Gongheguo Xingzheng Susong Fa*, 1989), only challenges to "concrete" administrative acts (i.e., actual actions of administrative enforcement) are allowed before the courts. So-called "abstract" administrative acts, by contrast, are excluded (SPC 1999b; see also Liu 2007). This means that statutes (*falu*) and administrative regulations issued in the name of the State Council cannot be challenged in court for being inconsistent with other legislation or with the Constitution, (Jiang 2002b, 173). At the same time, administrative litigation also cannot be used to obtain judicial scrutiny of the so-called "red-letterhead documents (*hongtou wenjian*)" that are commonly issued by party institutions and that direct much local governmental activity in China (Zhou Qingzhi 2004).

In the shadow of the People's Republic of China's (PRC's) express commitment to "democratic centralism" in Article 3 of its Constitution, narrow interpretation of the above mentioned rule prohibiting judicial review of "abstract administrative acts" makes some sense. According to democratic centralism, a decision once made is to be obeyed unconditionally, and this makes it difficult to address the problem of inconsistency among different rules, (Angle 2005). It seems that the only model on which a review of existing rules can work under democratic centralism is one in which rules are invalidated by subsequent act of fiat, by new political decision made by the "democratic" the norm-giver. By contrast, constitutional complaints against rules in other jurisdictions have as their unspoken premise that rules found to be unconstitutional *must* be invalidated independent of some subsequent recognition of invalidity by the original norm-giver.

So, as a potential court case, the case of Huang Wei was basically hopeless. Insofar as Gao was complaining that the RTL system was not in accordance with the Constitution and other laws, or that the rules against Falungong practitioners were unconstitutional, his complaint was very unlikely to be considered because of the judiciary's inability to sit in judgement of "abstract administrative acts." Moreover, in 1999, the Supreme People's Court issued directives to all lower courts further limiting these courts' authority to accept cases brought by Falungong petitioners contesting confiscations of their "illegal" materials (Peerenboom 2002, 99).

However, Gao also argued in terms of rights and duties, rather than simply in terms of legal formality. He insisted that the government had a duty to annul its public security bureau's illegal administrative decision, and that consequently Huang Wei had a right to a favorable decision by the courts. Of course, he did not expect the court to decide as he argued it ought to. And so, to help his client further, he published several open letters describing Huang Wei's case and making some broader observations about the persecution of members of Falungong more generally (see Gao 2004a; Gao 2005a; Gao 2005b). He also published the complaint he had drafted on behalf of Huang (Gao 2004b). Ultimately, Huang was released on health grounds six months after Gao Zhisheng got involved in his case, and after serving fourteen months of his three-year administrative sentence.

However, what neither the complaint in Huang Wei's case nor Gao's open letters mentioned was that, according to Gao Zhisheng's information, Huang Wei had been repeatedly subjected to torture while in detention.[3] The effects of torture were still perceptible when Huang Wei came forward to seek legal advice from Gao. The complaint also did not mention the fact that apart from being twice subjected to formal administrative detention, Huang had been detained at other times without any legal basis at all—again according to information that Gao said he had from his client. Gao explained that his strategy at the time was to address the illegality of persecuting Falungong generally, rather than to address the specific issue of torture in this case. It must be noted, of course, that detailed and concrete allegations of torture would also have amounted to an allegation of a concrete crime against his client.

It was only after Huang's case had been handled with some success—at least Huang Wei had been released—that Gao broke his silence on these other issues.

IV. Protesting the System: Open Letters and "Relay Hunger Striking"

What changed Gao's attitude was his confrontation with more and more victims of and witnesses to torture. He decided to conduct his own small-scale "investigation" into the torture of Falungong practitioners. On October 18, 2005, he published another open letter (his second) online. It addressed the cases of eleven persons who described various forms of torture they had suffered (Gao 2005a). On December 13 of that year, Gao published a third open letter, similar in content to the second (Gao 2005b). As they stand, these open letters should be regarded as accusations and demands for further investigation, in themselves very possibly insufficient as evidence in court trials, if such trials ever happened.

In an interview, a friend who accompanied Gao on his second "investigative trip" commented on the specific targeting of prisoners' genitalia during torture, a practice described to them during their "investigation." This description conveys how difficult it is to talk about such torture (Gao 2005b), which has been characterized by Elaine Scarry as an "illusory spectacle of power" (Scarry 1985, 27). For investigators trying to gather information from these victims about their extreme pain and humiliation, there are the problems of voyeurism and shame, and of interacting with victims whose rationality and judgment may have been impaired by their experience (see also *Radio Free Asia* 2006b).

It has, however, been persuasively argued that despite various efforts to address the problem, torture remains widely used by the Chinese police (see United Nations Commission on Human Rights 2006; Amnesty International online library 2004), and there is little doubt that it is used in particular against Falungong practitioners. The availability of various administrative detention mechanisms outside the criminal justice system (such as RTL); the lack of an explicit right to silence during interrogation of a criminal suspect (see especially Article 93 of the Criminal Procedure Law of the PRC (*Zhonghua Renmin Gongheguo Xingshi Susong Fa* 1996)); and the lack of basic protections in criminal procedure (especially of the right to the presence of a lawyer); are at the root of this problem (*Open Constitution Initiative* 2006). Torture is at the same time prohibited and punished by China's criminal law and by various rules on discipline (for example, those governing the police) (see United Nations Commission on Human Rights 2006), as well as by the 1984 Convention against Torture and Other Cruel, Inhuman or Degrading Treatment or Punishment, which China ratified in 1988.

Gao's experience with his own investigations suggests that being confronted with others' experience of torture can change one's assessment of what matters. In an interview, rights defender Guo Feixiong (aka "Yang Maodong"), described Gao as having entered into a "big psychological mode (*weida zhuangtai*)" after his investigation trips. Asked to clarify what he meant by this, Guo said that only this mode allowed Gao to speak up on the issue of Falungong persecution, when nobody else would (Radio Free Asia 2006a). Gao himself wrote that "all individual private interests and immediate individual needs had become entirely irrelevant." He announced his decision to quit the party (Radio Free Asia 2006b).

As a consequence of these actions, he was unable to continue working formally as a lawyer, as his law firm, the Shengzhi Law Firm, was suspended from practice for one year and he was put under surveillance. So he plunged into a series of novel "rights-defense" actions. In early February 2006, Gao and some fellow rights defenders, including Zhao Xin and Hu Jia, announced a "Relay Hunger Strike Movement to Oppose Violence." It was to be staged by rights defenders and sympathizers all across the country (Radio Free Asia 2006d). The "strikers" would not eat for one day, and they would perform the strike in their own homes or workplaces. The declared aim of the hunger strike was to "oppose violence and rights violations in government; to defend human rights, democracy and rule of law (*kangyi hei'e baoli qinquan, hanwei renquan minzhu zhengzhi*)" (Radio Free Asia 2006d). Participants' names would be published and hunger strikers could write down their views, feelings, and individual experiences of cases of injustice; some of these notes were later published online.

This low-key action could only be noticed in the unique conditions of communication and information transfer now created by the Internet and its various uses. As a congregation of passive fasters in a new virtual space, highly visible but not really tangible as a group, this was the kind of action that the state would find it hard to "get at" using its laws and regulations on maintaining social order. Teng Biao, a constitutional scholar and rights activist then already well-known due to his involvement in the Sun Zhigang case, explained:

> Nor do I think that this is a very "activist" political movement, this is a nonviolent way of expressing oneself, everybody hunger-strikes in their own home and then writes up their feelings and thoughts about the hunger-strike [experience], showing their concern for Chinese politics. I think that it is entirely in accordance with the law, as well as with reason. (Radio Free Asia 2006d)

Yet, as the discussion in the previous section has shown, China does not currently have a legal system that would allow for certain civil rights demands to be gradually absorbed into legal practice. Neither does it have a media that is able to report on movements like a "relay hunger strike," nor, consequently, a reasonably well-informed and politically influential wider public that can pressure for policy change. Efforts to strengthen the role of the courts from within the judiciary are at best described as "modest" by Western observers (Cohen 2006). Even if many individual judges are asserting a desire to judge independently, this will not necessarily strengthen the judiciary as an institution.

The vagueness of the "relay hunger strike"—the fact, in particular, that there was no condition upon which the strike would be ended—seems to be as much an expression of the vagueness of the rights defenders' best hopes as a response to a repressive political system. It is not any particular act that was the focus of this movement, as was the case, for example, with the Civil Rights Movement of the 1960s in the United States challenging specific governmental acts such as social discrimination and an unjust and possibly unconstitutional war. What was targeted, instead, could be understood as a vague and largely extra-legal exaction of "pragmatic silences" regarding certain matters of legal, moral, and political principle. From the perspective of the organizers of the "hunger strike," it might be said that the right way to capture this kind of vague exaction has to be itself vague, and that the right way to challenge the imposition of this silence has to be itself silent.

By 2006, several of these rights defenders confided to the author of this chapter that one could no longer "put hope in institutional reform." They came to view their work as embedded in a political system and dependent upon wider civil society activities and attitudes that challenged state injustices. Their efforts shifted to "raising the power of civil society" rather than restricting themselves to strengthening the role of legal professionals, and included publicizing representative cases of rights abuse and suggesting to ordinary people, including rural peasants, the possibility of nonviolent means of rights protection. One such rights defender made a specific reference to the work of Václav Havel, the Czech author, dissident, and later President of the Czech Republic. He cited Havel's important idea of "living in truth," which explores a possibility that Havel (1987, 120–121) says reflects and constitutes the "power of the powerless" through pursuit of the negative condition of not engaging in telling lies. The government soon responded to the "relay hunger strikes," which had been reported in Chinese-language media, and in American and European media (albeit not in media legally distributed in China, of course). Surveillance of Gao and his family was increased, his home and work phone lines were cut off, and his Internet connection was disrupted. A number of arrests followed, and more and more people supporting the strike "disappeared" for varying lengths of time (Radio Free Asia 2006e).

V. Consequences and Responsibilities

If "rule of law" is regarded as the ultimate goal of state reform, then judgments regarding the rightness or wrongness of actions taken within an *existing*, but imperfect, legal framework may have to be subordinated to this ultimate end goal. For this reason, reformers who believe in this model will reject as "wrong" actions that promote individual legal rights but nevertheless do not further the overall goal of institutional reform. Considerations restraining rights-assertion in this way may be categorized as both consequentialist and pragmatic. These terms require some brief explanation.

Consequentialists argue that the moral rightness of an act is determined by its good consequences. Deontological moral theories, on the other hand, claim that there is an obligation to "do the right thing" regardless of the consequences. According to a deontological account, it is not possible to determine what the right thing is, merely by looking at the consequences of a course of action one is contemplating (Singer 1972).

Institutional reform thinking is also often associated with pragmatism. William James explained that pragmatism was "the attitude of looking away from first things, principles, 'categories', supposed necessities; and of looking towards last things, fruits, consequences, facts" (James 1995). In that sense, pragmatism is connected to consequentialism. Yu Xingzhong, in his insightful discussion of legal pragmatism in contemporary China, characterized the Chinese version of this school of thought as "the resort to ad hoc measures, the separation of legal doctrines from practice, the overemphasis of instrumental facets of law, and the placement of policy before law" (Yu 1989, 30).

The core argument against consequentialism in moral argument is that it distorts one's judgment of moral obligation. As Bernard Williams (1973, 99–100, 116–117) put it, the point of a "deontological restriction" on conduct is that you *yourself* should not engage in that conduct. Indeed, the law itself can be understood to track distinctly deontological forms of restriction and permission by protecting fundamental legal rights largely irrespective of the concrete consequences of these protections.

Consequentialism and pragmatism seem to be the dominant modes of thinking amongst Chinese legal professionals to date. This has to be attributed to the repressive system they live in. As the previous discussion has shown, such repression manifests itself importantly in silences—for instance, silences about torture in administrative detention, especially that of Falungong practitioners; or about certain inconsistencies between the Constitution and laws supposed to conform to the Constitution. We mentioned above attitudes of "pragmatic silence" about certain matters of legal, moral, and political principle. Such silences are not directly state-imposed, so much as they are simply observed by a community of pragmatically oriented reformers and professionals. If the party-state can be said to encourage those silences, it does so not merely by the things it does to those who break them, but also indirectly, by creating social environments in which the breaking of silences is "punished" by experiences of guilt and estrangement brought on by those whose welfare and whose attitudes matter most to one.

The party-state's reactions to Gao's open letters and his involvement in the "relay hunger strike movement" were not legal in every respect; but they were partly given a legal form. We can discern a dualistic strategy. On the one hand, there was a legal process at work, that began with a one-year suspension of Gao's Shengzhi law firm by the Beijing Bureau of Justice under the Ministry of Justice (see Beijing Municipal Bureau of Justice 2005a; Beijing Municipal Bureau of Justice 2005b; Shengzhi Law Firm 2006a; Ministry of Justice 2006; Shengzhi Law Firm 2006b). It went through the formal stages of administrative decision, administrative reconsideration, and—unsuccessfully—administrative litigation. The suspension was imposed, first because the firm had failed to register its new address with the supervising bureau under the Ministry of Justice when it moved offices in June 2005, and second because the firm had failed to satisfy the requirements for authorizing external lawyers, and for the use of standardized forms for mandates received from clients in a criminal defense case (see Beijing Municipal Bureau of Justice 2005a).

The Shengzhi law firm contested both points, arguing that, among other things, the firm had tried several times to register the change of address, but had not been allowed to do so (*Radio Free Asia* 2005a). The two lawyers working on this case claimed that the suspension of Shengzhi Law Firm was motivated by the desire to "get at" Gao Zhisheng (*Radio Free Asia* 2005b; *Radio Free Asia* 2005c). The Beijing Bureau of Justice, in November and December 2005 respectively, issued warning statements dismissing these accusations, and addressed to all Beijing law firms. To quote from the first, dated November 8, 2005:

> All of the city's law firms and lawyers ought to take a high-minded attitude, conscientiously acknowledge the true account, and raise their ability to discern right from wrong in this affair. Do not accept untruthful and distorted reports from foreign media and illegal organizations. Do not participate in any instigating or organizing activities by foreign media or by individuals with ulterior motives. If you receive reports regarding Shengzhi Law Firm or Lawyer Gao from foreign media or illegal organizations, report them directly to this Bureau. (Beijing Municipal Bureau of Justice 2005b)

The suspension of the Shengzhi law firm's license to operate exemplifies a wider tendency in recent years to strengthen the supervision of legal professionals in China through legal regulation. Faced with new legislation that, from their perspective, violates higher-ranking legal norms either facially or as applied, lawyers find that the obstacles to challenging such legislation now suddenly affect themselves, not only their clients. As various lawyers observed in conversations with the author, this has produced the need to "defend the rights defenders;" and one rights defender commented on the trend to "legalize" control of the profession as follows:

> Now they can with just one law render several thousand people unable to make any move! And where are these techniques coming from? From the West, from a large number of cadres who received their education in the West. It is like the law was in Germany, formerly, exercising control through the law. You know, China did not use to be like that. It used to have just arbitrary rule. But now that control relies on law, the degree

of "legality" has increased and so they can now say that they are entirely "doing things according to law."[4]

But, Gao was not only subjected to these "legal" measures. He was also, on the other hand, subject to persecution by plainclothes police and special agents. What these officers and hired agents did was in part grossly illegal. Not only were his phone connections cut off or frequently disrupted, but also his Internet access was effectively suspended (*Radio Free Asia* 2006b; *Radio Free Asia* 2006d). He was followed everywhere by special agents; in one case even when he was meeting Manfred Nowak, the Special Rapporteur on Torture for the United Nations Commission on Human Rights, during Nowak's mission to China at the end of November 2005 (Nowak mentioned the incident in his report, see United Nations Commission on Human Rights 2006, 52). Gao Zhisheng added that as they tried to take pictures of the special agents who were seeking to monitor their conversation, these "irate" agents complained that taking their pictures against their will was "seriously violating their human rights." By August 2006, Gao had also suffered several physical attacks by the people following him around (*Radio Free Asia* 2005b).

There were also "costs" of rights-defending that were borne primarily by others, especially by his family and his friends and colleagues. Gao Zhisheng's thirteen-year old daughter, for instance, was reported to have been routinely followed and occasionally molested on her way to school and back (*Radio Free Asia* 2005b). From the moment the system decided to persecute Gao in earnest, the entire family led an anxious and at times unbearably restricted life. References to consequences affectiong family, friends, and colleagues run like a thread through the interviews of Gao conducted by the Radio Free Asia (RFA) journalist Zhang Min, and through conversations with other Chinese lawyers (see, for example, *Boxun Xinwen Wang* 2005).

In my interviews, some rights defenders described themselves as uniquely lonely. The moment, one of them said, that one decided to speak out against certain kinds of injustice—in the language used in earlier sections of this chapter, to break a "pragmatic silence"—the people "in one's back," meaning those normally supporting and cooperating with oneself, ceased to understand one. One was left, he said, with "no one to talk to." Even if they did not become one's opponents, they could themselves be victimized. Persons involved in this way included one's immediate family, colleagues in one's law firm and other fellow lawyers, one's neighbors, and even members of the general public. A lawyer's clients, too, might be adversely affected by the lawyer's politically sensitive "rights defender" status. Describing such a constellation, another lawyer remarked bitterly that rights defenders were "really the most selfish people of all," because they "put their own notions of justice and morality above everything else," making others suffer for them (see also Ma 2006).

One's responsibility to persons occupying these special roles in one's life, and especially to one's immediate family, might not be adequately defined by what could be called one's public rights and obligations. It seems instead to be defined by the special relationship one has with them, for instance with one's children while they are minors. That relationship seems far removed from considerations about constructing the rule of law for a population of 1.3 billion. Yet as observed earlier on, to identify a conflict between different goals or values does not imply that the right way for resolving the conflict is to *weigh up* the different consequences a particular course of action has. It does not require that we think of the unwelcome consequences in terms of a moral "cost" incurred to achieve morally-desired consequences. Even less are we required to think of rights activism as catering to a mere personal preference, a kind of moral taste one indulges in. It is important at least to recognize that there is a rational alternative to this form of consequentialist thinking. It consists of assigning responsibility for particular consequences, not according to the question of who caused them, but rather according to who intended them.

In China, different activists take different attitudes to this issue. Even as one lawyer attributed the actions of other activists to a kind of moral "selfishness," another rights defender said that the difference between more radical and more moderate rights defenders could "be summed up in one single character: 'fear'."

Gao's own attitude, it soon became clear, appeared provocative and dangerous to some, although it earned the admiration of others. Family in his home village in Shaanxi were frightened into opposing him, as he discovered during a trip home in late January 2006 to spend Spring Festival with his family (on this trip, he managed to elude the special agents) (*Radio Free Asia* 2006b). While there, he was rung up by the RFA journalist Zhang Min for another interview. He told her that his wider family had suggested to his brothers to lock him up in a cave, and that his brothers were now discussing this option (*Radio Free Asia* 2006c). This would be done to prevent him from going on with his dangerous political activities, which, they thought, might endanger the entire family or even village. During this interview, Zhang Min also spoke to Gao Zhisheng's eldest brother Gao Zhiyi.

Q: What did you say to him?
A: We told him he should listen to the party and go with the party. And that he should not "pick fights" with the Communist Party.
Q: Do you know in what way he is "picking fights" with the party?
A: I don't know. The Communist Party is fairly evil (*gou hei*). They would do anything.
Q: And who has told you that Gao Zhisheng is "fighting" with the Communist Party?
A: The police did not come to us. They came to people in our village. So of course we would be hearing a couple of things. But they didn't

come to me personally. They just investigated indirectly (*ce mian diaocha*).

Q: So who told you, then?

A: Whomever they investigated indirectly, that's who told us. (*Radio Free Asia* 2006c)

It is clear that in the mind of Gao Zhiyi, detaining his brother for the sake of the safety of the community, the family, and for his and Gao Zhisheng's own safety, would have been right. No less plainly, the conversation shows a local community in fear of the ruling party-state, however distant its actual representatives. In Gao Zhisheng's view, the most important reason why the villagers were opposed to his "picking fights" with the party was that as peasants, they had experienced the party's arbitrary rule at a level different from that of most urban residents. Gao Zhisheng's brother Gao Zhiyi remarks that the party is "fairly evil (*gou hei*)" but that nevertheless the family is hoping that his brother will "listen to the party and go with the party." His attitude could be described as "pragmatic" in a colloquial sense—he insists, ultimately, on the need to protect oneself and one's people, and therefore to be submissive in what he perceives to be conditions of arbitrary rule and lawlessness.

In the end, Gao "escaped" from his home village by means of a ruse (*Radio Free Asia* 2006d). It was back in Beijing that the decision to announce a "relay hunger strike" was taken. The relay hunger strike began on February 4, 2006 and was supported by a number of prominent rights activists and academics. However, back in Beijing, Gao's action was also vehemently opposed by other rights activists.

VI. "Politicization"

Criticism came most prominently from "Tiananmen Mother" Ding Zilin, an academic at Renmin University whose teenage son was among those killed on June 4, 1989, and who has for many years been vocal in demanding justice for these cases. Her criticism was important, not only because she derived authority from the fact of her suffering, but also because of her own courageous efforts over the years to seek justice. Her open letter to the hunger strikers was written on February 23, 2006, and as usual nowadays, placed on the Internet. In it, she wrote:

> My abhorrence of this evil government is a hundred times as deep as yours; my craving for a free China is a hundred times as strong as yours; and my sympathy for the weak and persecuted in our society cannot be any smaller than yours. I know the cruelty of this government very well,

> and I feel the suffering and persecution you and your friends have experienced as though they had happened to my own body, because I have come the same way as you since the' 90s of the last century. But even so, I want to persuade you to stop the hunger strike because I don't know what will happen if you persevere with it. What is the point of acting like a fish that dies trying to break through the net! Have you thought about this? In case something like the calamity of sixteen years ago [i.e., the violence of the Tiananmen crackdown] happens again, how are we going to face the mothers and wives of the victims?
>
> ...In my view, a politicized method of rights protection ought not to be adopted. It might result in almost unbearable dangers to the people engaged in rights activism, and you yourself would only be distancing yourself further and further from those masses at the lowest stratum [of society] who need your help. You say that you are acting the way you do in order to "reduce" the "moral decline" and "shame" of the "rights protection heroes." But in my view, those honorable lawyers who bring all their intelligence and wisdom to bear in their proper work as lawyers, and wholeheartedly throw themselves into every individual case of rights protection, deserve general admiration. Sometimes perhaps they may not be successful; but at least they contribute a few bricks and tiles to the process of the construction of rule of law. A concrete rights protection activity on the part of honorable lawyers is a wonderful triumph of publicity for awakening people's legal consciousness and rights consciousness. From a long term perspective, a people which lacks in respect for the law has no future. (Ding 2006)

Ding's alternative to hunger striking is pragmatic and "constructive" reform work, evoked by the metaphor of "bricks and tiles." However, she regards Gao as erring not only in his apparent failure to be constructive in this sense; but she also attributes hypothetical responsibility for "another calamity" like June 4, 1989 to him. On a consequentialist reading, Gao's hunger strike could make him responsible for any violent consequences (such as people being locked up, beaten, or killed) if things escalated. Such an attribution of responsibility would only be meaningful in a consequentialist sense, if the bad consequences in fact outweighed the good consequences, and if the hunger strikers had some ability to prevent these bad consequences. The implication in what Ding Zilin says is that both might be the case.

So according to Ding's criticism, the responsibility of lawyers and other rights activists must also be understood on consequentialist terms. It must be made intelligible in terms of "constructing" the rule of law regime of the future. Even though she explicitly endorses Gao Zhisheng's right to express his concern for persecuted Falungong members, Ding Zilin infers from the consequence of illegal political oppression that to demand basic rights for the "politically" persecuted is unlawyerly. According to this view, then, Falungong adherents will have to wait for demands for justice to be made by rights defenders, until the system has got better.

Ding Zilin won strong public support for her criticisms, voiced on overseas Web sites. In "Why I am not hunger striking," Liu Di, a prominent Internet dissident better known as "the Stainless Steel Rat (*buxiugang laoshu*)" emphasized effectiveness as a necessary attribute of politically meaningful action, saying that in her own situation of felt-powerlessness, participating in the strike would be like "a child refusing to eat to annoy his parents." She could not, she said, distinguish such a "hunger strike" action from nervous anorexia ("Buxiugang laoshu" 2006). Li Jianqiang, nother prominent rights defender who published under the name of "Liu Lu," said that hunger-striking and rights-defending were two completely different things, and that "of course" the hunger strike initiated by Gao Zhisheng was not conducted for the purpose of rights protection.

> Liu: The protection of rights is just the protection of legal rights. If in advocating rights protection you insult the government, you are acting like a rogue. To deny the legality of the government at its most basic level means to deny the . . . laws . . . constituting that government. So what kind of "rights" are you then still protecting? It almost amounts to fighting for power or grasping power. I believe that this rights protection hunger strike movement is in reality a political demonstration. Especially since overseas all kinds of political forces have separately joined in and blown the matter up, this problem has become even more obvious.
>
> (. . .)
>
> [Journalist] Ying: And so what is the boundary of rights-defending?
>
> Liu: The law. What is defended by "rights-defending" are the legal rights of the ordinary people, their real and concrete interests. That is why rights-defending is a form of conduct in accordance with law. Rights-defending is subject to the standards contained in the paragraphs of the law. The central and local government cannot, at least not in theory, deny the legitimizing value of the rights-defense movement, because that movement is in accordance with law. And just because this is so, rights-defending must take the law as its boundary. Once it exceeds this boundary, it has lost its legal justification. (Ying 2006; see also "Liu Lu" 2006.)

"Liu Lu"'s comment here suggests that he finds some comfort in thinking of restrictions on political action as "legal." Yet China has no written, certainly no statutory, national law setting out clear boundaries of political speech in terms of authors, topics, or means of communication. There are formal and informal commands, such as those issued by the Central Propaganda Department; however, these do not reach the level of statutory law, and the constitutional status of such commands is unclear. Anticipation and guesswork and indirect instructions are the tools of both censorship and self-censorship.

It seems that a consequentialist or pragmatic focus on consequences and results, as opposed to "first principles," urges for the acceptance of, for instance, "laws" violating basic constitutional guarantees—unjust laws that in less repressive circumstances might be recognized as not being law at all, especially when the violations of such basic constitutional or moral requirements are severe and pervasive. It invites cautious action "challenging" only those bad elements of the system, which the rulers find they can dispense with. Could not the constructivist picture of bricks and tiles used by Ding Zilin turn out to be misleading? In the worst case, the "rule of law" being built in China would become a mere façade, as would be the case where it did not offer any—not even the most basic—protection to some people, like Falungong adherents or other religious believers.

Among those who supported Gao's position, there was much anxiety about exactly how "bad" the law might become, and about one's responsibility toward current victims of injustice. One such supporter, Yuan Hongbing (2006), said:

> If you want the people to put their trust in this kind of legal system when they defend their rights, to put their trust in this bad kind of law, that is really like wanting them "to ask the tiger for his skin." (...) The "rules of the game," as prescribed by the brutal political regime of the Chinese Communist Party, deprive people of their human rights, of their basic rights, and they protect the "ten thousand families" at the top stratum of society. They follow a rule of protecting the interests of the powerful elite. The crucial point is that we should not respect such rules of the game.

Yuan Hongbing appears to have a point. If law protects only some but not others in society it seems at least less worth having than if it protected all. A legal system entrenching inequality could ultimately become a victim of its own partial success if there were more social crises (instigated, inevitably, not by those most oppressed, however, but by those who are disadvantaged yet still able to protest). Yet although neither side might agree, it is important that there is such communication between reformist and more radical critics. In this way, and to a degree that would have appeared unimaginable ten years ago, persons working "within" the system—as ordinary lawyers and academics, and (it may be surmised) public officials—can be informed about the legal and political challenges facing reform by more radical critics on the edges of the system. These critics, moreover, consist in part of professional lawyers, technical experts with experience in legal practice, who, as this chapter hopes to have shown, initially tried to take the legal system as it is seriously and to reform it "from within." The discussion among the more "radical" rights defenders, freer and more daring, can be expected to exert influence back on the more cautious rights defenders, and on people established in state and academic institutions, even if such influence is unacknowledged.

One rather more cautious lawyer, who was highly critical of Gao Zhisheng, observed in private conversation with the author that the party-state could at any point decide to strike harder. "And if he goes too far, all he will achieve is being locked up. Then who will have heard of Gao Zhisheng?" However, when Gao Zhisheng was forcefully taken from his sister's home in Shandong by plainclothes agents of the Beijing Public Security Bureau only two weeks later (on August 15, 2006) (*China Daily* online edition 2006b; see also *Radio Free Asia* 2006h), that lawyer was among the first to sign a public letter of commitment to join Gao's legal support team, along with over one hundred other Chinese lawyers (*Boxun Xinwen Wang* 2006).

In September 2007, Gao Zhisheng, then under house arrest with orders not to publish, addressed an open letter to the U.S. Congress, complaining about further human rights violations in China, and appealing for help. He was abducted a few days later, brutally tortured for two weeks, and sent back into house arrest in November 2007. Due to the unbearable treatment they had received at the hands of the authorities, Gao's wife and two children fled from China in January 2009. Gao Zhisheng was taken away by the police shortly after their departure, on 4 February 2009, and has since been "disappeared." The story of his detention and exposure to threats and to torture, of his criminal trial, conviction for "plotting to subvert the political power," and subsequent "release" into continued strict surveillance at the end of 2006, and subsequent abduction, torture and "disappearance," continues to be told by reports in the news media and on related web sites.[5] However, it is no longer a story that Gao can tell for himself.

Notes

1. Conversations were conducted in June and July 2006 in Beijing, with eight anonymous rights defenders, all of whom were at the center of the events covered in this chapter.
2. Interview with Rights Defender in Beijing, China (July 15, 2006).
3. Information in this paragraph comes from the author's personal interviews with someone acquainted with Gao's handling of the Huang Wei case.
4. Interview.
5. For updated information on Gao Zhisheng, see China Human Rights Lawyers Concern Group [undated].

CHAPTER FIFTEEN

Epilogue: Virtual Constitutionalism in the Late Ming Dynasty

PIERRE-ÉTIENNE WILL

I. Introduction

Any historian of China knows that speaking of a Constitution, or of constitutionalism, or of constitutional control in Imperial China (late or otherwise), as I do, can only be by analogy. There was no such thing in Imperial China as a coherent legal text that would impose itself upon the holders of political power as well as on the ordinary citizens, and that would have to be referred to in order to verify the legality of the decisions and actions of the government and the regulations it promulgated.

However, analogies and approximations may be acceptable, and may help explain things, provided that one is always aware of where one stands and does not get carried away by the force of the analogy. As I try to suggest in this chapter, I believe it is possible, even legitimate, to ask whether there might not exist, beyond the strict definitions of modern law, not only notions and texts playing a role similar to that of a constitution, but also institutions and procedures whose aim would be comparable with that of constitutional control in our own systems. It is a valid question to ask, "Did the imperial system admit of the possibility that the actions of the emperor, or of the state, or of its officials, be legally controlled?"

I think it can be argued that, to an extent that needs to be carefully delineated of course, such was the case—at least under certain dynastic regimes. I draw this conclusion primarily from research I did on the political life of the late Ming in the late sixteenth and early seventeenth centuries, particularly the long reign of the Wanli emperor (from 1573 to 1620) (see also Jie 2002). Political life during these years was profoundly hostile and contentious, both within the officialdom and the larger political society beyond, and between large segments of the bureaucracy on the one hand and the emperor and his close associates on the other. In particular, certain members of the bureaucracy opposed what they denounced as the emperor's excesses of absolutism with what could be termed, as we shall see, "quasi-constitutional" arguments. Adding to this quasi-constitutional character is a peculiar quality of late-Ming political life, what we might call its openness and flamboyance, that gave this censure a distinctive *publicity* and that itself could be politically exploited. Indeed, the fierce competitiveness of political factions, the unrestricted political communication, and the weakness of the throne have led not a few modern scholars, especially in China, to claim that this period featured certain "democratic" characteristics that might have developed, independently from Western influence, into something significant if they had not been cut short by the Manchu conquest of China in 1644 (see Huang 1988; Huang 1981).

In what follows, I first examine what I think to be a kind of virtual "dynastic constitution" in Ming China. I then say a word about the powers and tasks of China's controlling institution par excellence—the Censorate. Finally, I discuss the political conditions that seemed to determine the exercise and efficiency of censure. It is in this last respect that the late Ming period offers a very special pattern in which I think we can detect a kind of pre-constitutional *thinking*.

II. The Dynastic "Constitution" of the Ming

So, I begin with what in my view can be thought of as an equivalent to a "Constitution," in the sense that it set limits on the actions and decisions of both the emperor and the bureaucracy and ruled their relations with the population. It seems to me that, in the Ming dynasty especially, this consisted of three distinct elements. These were, in order of eminence: (1) the values and precedents embodied in *The Classics*; (2) the so-called ancestral institutions of the dynasty; and (3) the administrative constitution as embodied in certain official treatises, and in a body of penal and administrative law, constantly revised and enlarged, which controlled the activities of the bureaucracy. All these elements, as I see it, composed together what was called the *guoti*, or what I call "the ordered form of the state"—"ordered" in the sense that authority was carefully allocated. The "affairs of the state," or *guoshi*, were supposed to be decided in such a way as to be in conformity with the *guoti*.

Let us examine these three elements with a little more detail.

The Classics—which were, so to speak, "co-opted" by every new dynasty—had no direct legal or administrative application. However, they had important political implications, because they constituted a sort of superior orthodoxy and because the ones who considered themselves to be in charge of interpreting *The Classics* and protecting the orthodoxy were the literati. The intellectual power the literati derived from their social position made them, in a way, the functional equivalents of guardians of the "constitution"—except that in this case it was not a legal document that they guarded, but the scriptures with which dynastic policies were supposed to be in conformity. Still, inasmuch as *The Classics* were constantly quoted or alluded to in the conflicts that erupted during the late Ming between the emperors and parts of the bureaucracy, the role of what we might call "literati power" in the political (constitutional) ordering cannot be overlooked. It was only later that the Manchu emperors managed to monopolize for themselves the right to interpret the scriptures and establish the orthodoxy.

The ancestral institutions are of course something very different. There is in fact no clear definition of what these consist of. They were comprised of a variable combination of pronouncements emanating from the dynastic founder—or sometimes from the first few emperors of a dynasty—along with certain institutions or regulations that had been created by these early emperors. What distinguished these particular pronouncements, institutions, and regulations as ancestral institutions was that it was considered impossible, or very difficult, to change them, or at least change them openly, without risking an accusation of lack of filial piety. In the case of the Ming, the ancestral institutions consisted of, first and foremost, several texts emanating from the Hongwu emperor, the dynastic founder. These began with the *Ancestral Instructions of the August Ming* (*Huang Ming Zuxun*) (Farmer 1995), which are a kind of familial constitutionalism centered on the rights and duties of the royal princes. Other such texts included three series of *Grand Pronouncements* (*Dagao*), whose extremely harsh and repressive recommendations were not enforced under subsequent emperors, but which were typically still supposed to be memorized by public officials alongside the penal code, and which continued to possess a very high symbolic authority. The Penal Code itself, which in its final form was published in 1397 at the end of the Hongwu reign, should also be considered one of these ancestral institutions. Beyond this, we have a number of institutional structures created by the Ming founder that also constituted part of the ancestral institutions. These included, above all, a central governmental structure characterized by the *absence* of a prime minister and of a central secretariat, offices that Hongwu had abolished in 1380 in order to concentrate executive power in the emperor's own hands.

As is well known, the situation created by the absence of a prime minister and central secretariat could not be sustained for long. The reigns of Hongwu's first few successors saw the emergence of a new institution, albeit one that was *not* part of the "Constitution" built by Hongwu, called the

Grand Secretariat (the *Neige*). This was originally simply supposed to assist the emperor in his everyday chores. But by the 16th century it had developed into a powerful cabinet whose head secretary was commonly referred to as the "prime minister (*zaixiang*)"—because this was exactly what he was. The constitutional contradiction created by this development was the source of much conflict between the Grand Secretariat and the rest of the bureaucracy. A similar contradiction infected a whole set of other institutions and rules that had been invented by the dynastic founder, and that therefore enjoyed a kind of constitutional status, but that nevertheless had to be progressively ignored because they were no longer attuned to the socioeconomic realities of the empire.

Finally, we have what I have dubbed the "administrative constitution," but which one might also call the "institutional description" of the dynastic regime. This was found in a variety of treatises, the most comprehensive and authoritative of which was the *Collected Institutions of the Great Ming* (*Da Ming Huidian*). Basically, the *Collected Institutions* was a systematic and hierarchized enumeration of all the organs and offices that comprised the state—from the imperial household at the top to the local administrations at the bottom, each with a list of its statutory personnel and an indication of its main tasks and rules of operation. Although the first *Collected Institutions* was only published in the beginning of the 16th century, its content was mostly based on treatises going back to the reign of the dynastic founder; and for this reason it possessed the strong flavor of an "ancestral instruction" that could only be very sparingly revised, whatever the reality of institutional change in the empire might be. For example, the Grand Secretariat, which was the actual seat of central power during much of the dynasty, is not even mentioned in the two surviving versions of the *Collected Institutions.*

In contrast to a "real" Constitution, as we generally understand the term, the *Collected Institutions* was not a *juridical* document enunciating general laws in conformity with which new institutions had to be built and new laws had to be created. It was, as I said, no more than an *administrative* constitution. Moreover, it featured what we might call a "double articulation": on the one hand, it provided a basic institutional description of the state dating from the first reign, which could not be subject to much change; on the other, it also articulated what are called "precedents." These precedents consisted of subsequent administrative practices that had accumulated as of the time of publication of that particular edition of the *Collected Institutions*, and whose totality constituted a kind of "living law" of administrative control.

At this point, it may be asked how this complicated set of nonjusticiable texts and rules—which formed, as I see it, a kind of virtual Constitution—could be used to control abuses on the part of the state and its representatives, including those of the emperor himself. Succinctly, I would propose they presented three kinds of control, relating to the state, the emperor, and the bureaucracy, respectively.

The first form of control, that relating to "the state," derives from the fact that there was in fact no conception of "the state" as an autonomous legal entity in Imperial China. The imperial "state" was simply an aggregate of the particular moral personalities and moral and legal responsibilities of those men who happened to occupy its administrative positions.

So, how about the emperor himself? Deriving from our observation above, one might very well have said that "the emperor was the state" (or, if you use the first person, "*l'État, c'est moi*"). And I would say (and this is my second proposed kind of constitutional control) that while in theory at least, the emperor could be censured for his personal behavior, including for personal behavior that supported or allowed particular policies, such censure could not derive from the laws themselves because (in theory again) the emperor was not bound by any laws—he was the one who promulgated them, or at least sanctioned them with a rescript, they were *his* laws. However, officials could still remind him, respectfully of course, of those laws and other usages that had been established by himself and by his predecessors, and which possessed by this very fact the value of a dynastic precedent (rather than simply that of positive legislation). And the fact is that in many cases the Ming and Qing emperors indeed felt compelled *not* to act against what were called "established precedents (*dingli*)."

The fact that these ancestral rules and precedents (not to mention the transcendent teachings in *The Classics*) made it possible, despite all the risks involved, to attack an emperor's decisions or actions—even though the attack was political or moral rather than legal—seems to me to bring us very close to the domain of constitutionalism, but with the important caveat that the efficiency of such "constitutional control" was entirely dependent upon the general political situation. Ming officials did attack their emperors, and attacked them publicly, by brandishing the *Ancestral Instructions of the August Ming*, with varying results both with regards to the situation and to themselves. And the fact is that some of these episodes had an immense impact on the development of political life in the second half of the Ming. (But let me also add, importantly, that if the emperor could be criticized, in no case could he be *punished*, nor could the measures he had taken be legally rescinded.)

Finally, my third proposed kind of constitutional control concerned bureaucratic officials. They could be censured and controlled, and punished, based on a wide array of criminal and administrative legislation. Some of this legislation, such as the many statutes (*lu*) in the Penal Code dealing with crimes or misdemeanor by officials acting in their official capacities, had, I would say, a constitutional flavor, because they were inseparable from the "*Ur*-Code" promulgated by the dynastic founder. However, most were part of what I have called the "living law" of administrative control. The important distinction between "public" and "private" offences by officials, which was present in the formal Penal Code, was further refined in this secondary legislation, especially under the Qing.

III. The Censorate

Without entering into detail, however, one thing of particular interest to us here is *who* could prosecute an official for public offences. Such prosecution could only come from within the bureaucracy itself. The notion of an independent judge or court whose role it would be to arbitrate between the state (or rather, its agents) and the citizenry was absent in Imperial China. Evaluating and controlling administrators (and, as the case might be, censuring and punishing them) was a procedure entirely internal to the bureaucracy: either in the form of the hierarchy controlling itself; or in the form of a body of officials external to that bureaucratic hierarchy but still a part of the state apparatus—that is, the Censorate (Hucker 1966; Mu 1982).

However, ordinary citizens were *not* allowed to submit complaints directly to the Censorate. At one point, the Ming founder, the Hongwu emperor, who was extremely distrustful of his own bureaucracy, did actually encourage commoners to come straight to the capital and denounce corrupt officials. However, this, as far as I know, is a unique example in the history of Imperial China. Although remaining within the formal dynastic regulations, this procedure was rapidly subjected to such controls and conditions that in effect it was almost impossible to resort to. Criticism and denunciation were the particular province of the censors, and therefore analyzing their role is important for our purpose.

Institutionally, censors were protected against outside pressures. They also enjoyed the added, symbolic protection that stemmed from their reputation for courage and integrity. This independence, plus the fact that the Censorate was supposed to control not just individuals but also administrative decisions in general, might seem to bring it closer than any other institution in Imperial China to a modern constitutional court. However, in reality such a comparison needs all sorts of qualifications, beginning with the fact that *in theory*, the Censorate investigated problems and denounced people always on its own initiative.

Generally speaking, the censors had three sorts of functions. The first was to check on the formal and legal conformity of any document or decision issued by the central administration. The Censorate was also supposed to keep watch over the professional and personal behavior of officials everywhere in the empire. Although when censors toured provinces they had almost unlimited powers to investigate everything they wanted, this was certainly a formidable—actually an impossible—task given the very modest means the Censorate could mobilize, primarily in terms of personnel. And finally, the third function of the censors involved remonstrating the emperor regarding his own conduct and commenting on the government's policies in general.

I could discuss at length the fascination that the Chinese Censorate exerted on Western observers (beginning with the Jesuits in the seventeenth and eighteenth centuries), who knew of the role of this powerful and secretive body through its denunciations published in the *Peking Gazette* (an official bulletin that circulated everywhere in the empire). To cite just one example, one British consular official, Thomas Meadows—to whom we owe quite penetrating observations on Chinese administration in the mid-nineteenth century—did not hesitate to claim that the Censorate assumed at least one of the functions of the English Parliament, namely that of controlling the operation of public administration. This was perhaps a bit far-fetched, but certainly some of the Censorate's traditional missions partook of the general idea of entrusting the control of the actions of the government and even of the emperor himself to a body of officials whose independence was protected at the same time by the law, by established custom, and by their reputation for integrity.

This reputation, as it happened, was a symbolic asset that they tended to overuse during the political controversies of the Wanli reign. And indeed, politics appears to have been absolutely central to the actual operation of the Censorate and to its effectiveness (or the lack of it) in fulfilling its functions. One reason for this has to do with the power and impact of the emperor.

As we already saw, the emperor was, in a way, the keystone of Imperial China's "constitutional" structure as I have sketched it. To begin with, he embodied the continuing dynastic legitimacy that had been established by his ancestors. He was also the formal source of what I have called "living" legislation, since the latter had only legal value insofar as it was sanctioned by an imperial rescript (however routinized that rescript procedure might be). To sum up, the entire system revolved around his person and his actions. In particular, it was through him that that system was connected with the dynastic legitimacy of the government and, beyond that, with the legitimacy of "civilization" as embodied in *The Classics*.

All of this means that even while control of a constitutional nature could exert itself on a fairly wide range of issues in Imperial China, it was always functioning in the shadow of the emperor. Consequently, the character of the relations between the throne and the bureaucracy (and the educated elite in general) was a crucial factor in determining the circumstances, quality, and intensity of the constitutional control exerted by an institution like the Censorate. It is in this respect that the last few reigns of the Ming dynasty display an exceptional pattern, because the highly contentious relations between the emperor and officialdom that characterize that period favored the emergence of a particular critique of autocracy whose arguments were, in many cases, constitutional arguments.

IV. "Constitutional" Conflicts during the Late Ming

It would be much too long to recount the history of these conflicts, whose causes were both institutional and personal. As far as personal causes were concerned, it is well known that many members of the Ming ruling house were, to say the least, obstinate persons who did not like to have high-minded officials in the way when they wanted to satisfy some whim. On more than one occasion, their idiosyncrasies led to political and institutional stalemates that had profound consequences on the functioning of the state and on relations between the throne and the bureaucracy.

The institutional causes were closely intertwined with those deriving from the character of the individual emperors. As I have already said, one of the fateful decisions of the Hongwu emperor had been the elimination of the Secretariat and of the office of the prime minister, and the concentration of the totality of executive power in his own hands. This was not a sustainable solution, even in the relatively simple circumstances of the early Ming. Hongwu's successors, who were not always as dedicated as he was to the tasks of everyday governance, soon found themselves facing an incredibly heavy workload, for which they needed assistance. This was of course the origin of the Grand Secretariat; it also explains the increasingly important role played by the eunuch bureaucracy in the palace. All of this is well-known; however, it is important to insist on the fact that, although the grand secretaries during most of the period were extremely powerful and controlled much of the government, they were also politically vulnerable because, as we have seen, they were a *constitutional anomaly* (insofar as the Grand Secretariat itself was not regarded as an ancestral institution) and thus owed their positions only to the continuing favor of the emperor.

During certain reigns, notably in the fifteenth century, the political system managed, more or less, to accommodate this constitutional anomaly. But at other times, the conjunction of this anomaly with problems posed by the caprices of the emperors created unmanageable situations and much disorder. Some of the decisions or demands of the emperors were viewed as provocations by the bureaucracy at large, and in many of these cases the bureaucracy would respond by directing their attacks at the Grand Secretariat—and especially its head secretary—whose legitimacy could easily be disputed on constitutional grounds. Particularly in the sixteenth century, some of those head secretaries—those ersatz "prime ministers"—came to exert almost total control over the government. Yet some of them were still compelled to resign by the ferocity of bureaucratic opposition and the resulting administrative stalemate.

Another sort of constitutional problem that was a cause of much conflict between the emperor and bureaucracy during the same period concerned the mode of imperial succession—and there of course the ancestral institutions were even more relevant than they were with regards to the Grand Secretariat. I cannot dwell on the two major crises of that sort that marked the sixteenth century. In both cases the emperor, still a young man, attempted to tinker with the rules of succession set by the dynastic founder and frontally opposed the advice of the specialists of ritual who were brandishing the *Ancestral Instructions of the August Ming* to criticize him. In the latter of these two cases, which poisoned political life during the 1580s and 1590s, the Wanli emperor (who wanted to designate as heir apparent a son who was not entitled to it according to the rules) yielded in the end, but grudgingly, but thereafter remained in constant conflict with his bureaucracy.

As a matter of fact, this latter dispute and its aftermath are especially interesting for our purpose, because the attacks against the behavior and initiatives of the Wanli emperor soon extended beyond the problem of imperial succession itself, and in some cases evolved into lengthy arguments that the emperor was overstepping what one could very well have called his "constitutional" powers. And for reasons, I will shortly explain, these attacks were widely and, in a sense, quite "officially" publicized. In other words, the attacks of the Wanli period—which involved much more than the succession affair—were not only distinctly "constitutional" in content, they were also distinctly public in presentation.

The bureaucrats actually had much to reproach the Wanli emperor for. After the first decade of his reign, during which he had been strictly tutored by the last of the all-powerful head secretaries, the emperor started to behave in ways that were capricious, violent, irresponsible, and extravagant. Although in theory regular court assemblies should have been held to discuss problems of government—this was a custom that was handed down by the dynastic ancestors and thus of "quasi-constitutional" status so to speak—in effect the Wanli emperor reduced direct contact with the bureaucracy, including the grand secretaries he had himself chosen, to almost nothing. And he refused to answer most of the numerous memorials with which he was bombarded by his officials on every sort of subject—including those that dealt at length with the officials' own disputes, which he found to be very obnoxious, and those that involved subjects that he truly hated to see publicly discussed, such as, for instance, his designs for choosing his heir apparent, or his health problems.

Indeed, one of the points of contention between the Wanli emperor and much of the bureaucracy was his habit of "keeping memorials in the palace"—in other words, as I earlier noted, not answering them, when in many instances it would have entailed no more than writing a rescript of two or three characters. I think it is fair to say that this practice of not returning memorials was taken by the opposition as being a kind of *constitutional breach*, because by behaving this way the emperor denied the bureaucracy its right to be informed about government business. If the "ordered form of the state" (the *guoti*) was to be preserved, these memorials needed to be returned to the Censorate with a rescript. From there, they could be fed into the bureaucracy's communication machinery, which irrigated not only the entire administrative structure but also, beyond that, the political public of the literati, who believed that they too had a right to be informed about government activities. In response to this constitutional breach, the censors in charge of supervising the *Peking Gazette* began committing their own "constitutional breach" by allowing documents—including memorials that criticized the emperor very harshly—to be published in the *Gazette* without his approval.

Another important consequence of the dispute over the designation of the imperial heir apparent was the formation of political factions that soon evolved into the equivalent of political parties openly competing for power. The most famous of these was, of course, the Donglin party, established in 1604. Its members were mostly former officials who had left the government during the time of the dispute over succession and who lived in Jiangnan in the south. Their explicit goal was to overthrow the government in Peking, which they eventually did in 1620, only to themselves fall victim to a bloody purge a few years later at the hands of the eunuch dictator Wei Zhongxian.

Now in a sense, partisan politics was also a sort of constitutional problem. It had always been a controversial question whether or not it was legitimate to assemble an association of politically like-minded people, who might consider themselves to be gentlemen (*junzi*) devoted to the common good, but who were usually considered by their opponents to be simply a bunch of small-minded individuals (*xiaoren*) pursuing their own selfish interests. Although, the Ming emperors strictly forbade the formation of any kind of political faction (or any kind of horizontal grouping) and considered that the only valid loyalty for an official was that to the throne, the last half century of the Ming certainly was the golden age of partisan politics in China. Even the censors openly joined in the politics of factionalism—and in a sense this too could be described as yet another constitutional breach of the period, since the censors were supposed to be the guardians of objectivity and neutrality.

Two other important constitutional themes emerged from the bitter controversies that raged during the reign of Wanli, and I will briefly discuss them as a way of conclusion. They were, first, the question of what we can only call the "freedom of expression"; and second, the question of the behavior and rights of the emperor.

What I call freedom of expression concerns, more accurately, the right to remonstrate and to denounce, in memorials sent to the throne, abuses of power. The question was, who possessed this right, and what were its limits? In the Ming, in principle, the laws enacted by the dynastic founder allowed any official to issue such a remonstration, but the Ming State did much to discourage officials from freely exercising this right to criticize. And the risks could be very high, especially when the emperor was the target of the criticism: one could be brutally beaten on order of the emperor, thrown in one of the central governmental jails to die, or at a minimum lose all of one's ranks and titles. But nevertheless, one *had* such a right and one could always choose to exercise it. And moreover, doing so could bring one much political prestige.

What we see in the last half century of the Ming is that more and more lower officials felt entitled to bombard the throne with memorials protesting this or that decision, or attacking this or that person. And interestingly, when there was the occasional backlash (because the emperor had actually read the memorial and become infuriated), it would trigger a public argument about the *right* of remonstration as guaranteed by the early dynastic regulations. In one particularly remarkable example (dating to 1586), three recently appointed doctors doing an internship in Nanking jointly memorialized a ferocious attack on a high official. For this they were deprived of their rank for having "overstepped their position." The interesting thing in the campaign of protest that ensued is that at least one well-known member of the faction who supported the doctors, a certain Shen Shixiao, quoted entries in the *Collected Institutions* and in the Penal Code that indeed supported the right of "even workers and artisans" to address the throne on problems concerning the country and the population in general. And he summarized the situation in terms I find rather striking. According to him, while the censors had the *duty* (*ze*) to express themselves in protest, it was still "not forbidden" (*bu jin*) for other officials and indeed for the literati and people in general to also express themselves in this way. Therefore these other people *ought to* (*de*, meaning, morally) and *were allowed to* (*ke*, meaning, legally) do so. Such was, he said, the "system" (*zhi*) established by the dynastic ancestors. He also gave examples of students who had sent memorials of denunciation in the past without encountering the least problem. In other words, in advancing his claim, he appealed to the authority both of what we might call a "constitutional" rule and of what we might call that rule's particular, "constitutional" jurisprudence.

What is also important to note in these debates is that nobody would go so far as to insist on a right of expression for his political enemies. In fact, in asserting the scope of this right, one almost always drew an explicit distinction between those who should enjoy the right of remonstration, whom they referred to as "righteous people" (*zhengren*) and who invariably agreed with their particular position, and those who should not, whom they referred to as "heterodox people" (*xieren*) and who generally consisted of their political enemies. In other words, the idea underlying this right was not that the entire citizenry should be considered equals in terms of their right to express themselves publicly. Rather, the memorialists merely claimed that it was only a scandal when this right was denied to those who forwarded the "pure opinions (*qingyi*) expressed in the empire." Finally, Shen Shixiao and other authors claimed in effect that freedom of expression was a protection against tyranny, in the sense that if public opinion were not allowed to be conveyed to the throne by anybody who deemed it his duty to do so, one day some "powerful traitor" (read: a prime minister or eunuch) might very well seize the reality of power without the emperor even being aware of what was happening.

Finally, there was the problem of the emperor's personal conduct. As I said, the emperor was the keystone of the entire constitutional construct, so that if he were not up to the task the whole thing would be in risk of collapsing. What is extremely striking in the case of the Wanli emperor is the number of scathing memorials that criticized *both* his personal behavior and his public policies and that were circulated nationwide. In other words, even the polite fiction of the sage-ruler simply being led astray by a bad entourage was no longer being maintained.

Concerning his personal behavior I could cite, for example, certain memorials during the 1580s that reproached the emperor for drinking too much, for being prone to lose his temper, for being unable to control his women, and for similar personal failings that resulted in the low level of attention he was able to devote to public affairs. More important to mention here, however, are the incredibly vehement attacks that were motivated by his infamous mining and fiscal policies in the years before and after 1600. Again, some of these attacks were very close to constitutional arguments.

The policies in question consisted in sending to the provinces palace eunuchs with large staffs who had been given full power to open silver mines wherever they wanted, and in general to take control of commercial taxation (the Wanli emperor needed lots of money for various purposes involving the imperial palace and family). The result was widespread turmoil and much loud protest from officials both in the capital and in the provinces. One of the most vocal of these protestors was a rather colorful ally of the Donglin leaders, a certain Li Sancai, who in 1599 had become governor of the Huai region in Central China and in 1604 became a political star by resisting the eunuch sent by Wanli to open mines and levy taxes in his region, to the point of driving that enuch to commit suicide. In 1600, he sent to the emperor several memorials that, resorting to a well-balanced and forceful rhetoric, accused the emperor of misusing the position that had been entrusted to him by Heaven and the empire and that he had inherited from his ancestors. In essence, Li's point was that the emperor is not the owner of the empire and its riches, and that by seeking to monopolize them for his own selfish purposes, and thus driving his people to suffer hunger and to "wander in the wilderness," he was in effect betraying his ancestors and behaving against what I can only call his constitutional position.

Of course, these memorials were to no avail, and we do not even know if the Wanli emperor ever read them. In a way, the emperor had become "out of control"—constitutionally or otherwise. Li Sancai was far from being the only one during these years to toy with the theme, going back to Mencius, of what I would call "twin sovereignty": the ruler is the master of men, but the people are "the master of the master of men (*renzhu zhi zhu*)." This concept, which a little later would be famously developed by Huang Zongxi in his *Waiting for the Dawn* (*Mingyi Daifang Lu*)—a work that was enthusiastically resuscitated by the late Qing constitutionalists and revolutionaries, meant that the people's sovereignty is a *given*, whereas the ruler's sovereignty is conditional (see De Bary 1993; Balazs 1968, 235–246). In times of crisis, the people's sovereignty would express itself in the negative forms of resistance and rebellion. In contrast, the ruler's sovereignty could only be established and sustained through proper and positive attitudes and actions through which the empire was able to enjoy peace and prosperity in accordance with the Heavenly way. What I have discussed in this chapter are the "constitutional" elements that conceptually framed these proper attitudes and actions: the precedents found in *The Classics*, the *Ancestral Instructions*, the administrative Constitution, and the administrative and penal jurisprudence that governed the concrete life of the government. This pattern is not specific to the Ming dynasty. However, as far as I know, never was it so explicitly, and so polemically, expressed in the debates and conflicts that ran through the body politic. In some ways, which I leave to my colleagues to evaluate, all this seems to me to connect with Chinese constitutional thought as it has been playing itself out in the twentieth and now twenty-first centuries.

BIBLIOGRAPHY

Books, Chapters and Articles

21 shiji jingji baodao [21st Century Business Herald]. 2003. Sheping: shourong zhidu cun liang nan, weixian shencha you keneng [Editorial: two difficulties with the custody and repatriation system, constitutional review possible]. May 26.

A Ji. 2002. "Min gao guan," youyu "xing gongtang"—xingzheng fuyi fa chutai beijing toushi ["Civil court" and now also the "new tribunals"—a new perspective on the Administrative Reconsideration Law]. In *Jianzheng—shiji zhi jiao de gongheguo lifa, zhifa baogao*, 390–413. Beijing: People's Press.

Abraham, Henry J. 1998. *The judicial process, an introductory analysis of the courts of the United States, England, and France*. 7th ed. Oxford: Oxford University Press.

Ackerman, Bruce. 1991. *We the people*, Vol. 1, *Foundations*. Cambridge, MA: Belknap Press.

Ackerman, Bruce. 1992. *The future of liberal revolution*. New Haven: Yale University Press.

Alford, William. 1986. The inscrutable occidental? Implications of Roberto Unger's uses and abuses of the Chinese past. *Texas Law Review* 64:915–972.

Amnesty International online library. 2004. People's Republic of China: executed "according to law"?—The death penalty in China. March 22. http://www.amnesty.org/en/library/asset/ASA17/003/2004/en/dom-ASA170032004en.html.

An Chen. 2007. The failure of organizational control: changing party power in the Chinese countryside. *Politics and Society* 35:145–179.

Angle, Stephen C. 2005. Decent democratic centralism. *Political Theory* 33:518–546.

Angle, Stephen C., and Marina Svensson. 2001. *The Chinese human rights reader: documents and commentary 1900–2000*. Armonk: M.E. Sharpe.

Arendt, Hannah. 1998. *The human condition*. 2nd ed. Chicago: Chicago University Press.

Aristotle. 1968. *Aristotle's Poetics: translation and commentary for students of literature*. Trans. Leon Golden. Englewood Cliffs, NJ: Prentice-Hall.

Asimow, Michael. 2005. Popular culture and the American adversarial ideology. In *Law and popular culture*, ed. Michael Freeman, 606–637. Oxford: Oxford University Press.

Balazs, Etienne. 1968. *La bureaucratie céleste*. Paris: Gallimard.

Balme, Stéphanie. 2005. The judicialisation of politics and the politicisation of the judiciary in China (1978–2005). *Global jurist frontiers*. www.bepress.com/gj/frontiers/vol5/iss1/art1/.

Balme, Stéphanie. 2009. Local courts in western China: the question for independence and dignity. In *Judicial independence in China: a comparative developmental approach*, ed. Randall P. Peerenboom. Oxford: Oxford University Press, 2009.

Baum, Richard and Alexei Shevchenko. 1999. The "state of the state." In *The paradox of China's post-Mao reforms*, ed. Merle Goldman and Roderick MacFarquhar, 33–60. Cambridge, MA: Harvard University Press.

BBC News (online edition). 2004. China internet dissident arrested. February 17. http://news.bbc.co.uk/1/hi/world/asia-pacific/3494969.stm.

Beijing Municipal Bureau of Justice. 2005a. Guanyu dui Beijing shi Shengzhi Lushi Shiwusuo de chufa jueding [Decision regarding the punishment of the Beijing Shengzhi Law Firm]. November 30.

Beijing Municipal Bureau of Justice. 2005b. Guanyu Gao Zhisheng de tonggao [Announcement regarding Gao Zhisheng]. November 8.

Beijing Municipal Bureau of Justice. 2006. Xingzheng chufa zhixing gaozhi shu [Executory notice of administrative punishment]. November 30.

Beijing qingnian bao [Beijing Youth Daily]. 2003. Huludao laoba pan sixing, Luo Gan, Zhou Yongkang, Zhang Fusen zuo zhongyao pishi [Huludao prison bully sentenced to death, Luo Gan, Zhou Yongkang, Zhang Fusen issue important orders]. December 16.

Beijing Review. 1980a. Front Cover. No. 48: Front cover. December 1

Beijing Review. 1980b. Trial of Lin-Jiang cliques begins. No. 48: 3–5. December 1.

Beijing Review. 1980c. Indictment of the Special Procuratorate. No. 48: 9–28. December 1.

Beijing Review. 1980d. Wang and Yao admit: Jiang Qing was chief instigator of the Changsha false charges. No. 48: 30–31. December 1.

Beller, Elisa T. 2004. The headscarf affair: the *Conseil d'Etat* on the role of religion and culture in French society. *Texas International Law Journal* 39:581–623.

Bentley, Eric. 1964. *The life of the drama*. New York: Atheneum.

Berger, Peter L., and Thomas Luckmann. 1966. *The social construction of reality: a treatise in the sociology of knowledge*. Garden City, NY: Anchor Books.

Bodde, Derk, and Clarence Morris. 1967. *Law in imperial China*. Philadelphia: University of Pennsylvania Press.

Bodeen, Christopher. 2004. China's "BMW collision affair" draws out anger, suspicions against newly wealthy. *The Seattle Times*. April 7.

Bork, Robert H. 1990. *The tempting of America: the political seduction of the law*. New York: Simon and Schuster.

Bourgon, Jérôme. 1998. De quelques tendances récentes de la sinologie juridique américaine. *T'oung Pao* 84:380–414

Boxun Xinwen Wang [Boxun News Online]. 2005. RFA Zhang Min: Gao Zhisheng lushi suifanglu (zhi yi): ma bu ting ti—dedao lushishiwusuo bei tingye yi nian koutou tongzhi hou . . . [Zhang Min of Radio Free Asia: Gao Zhisheng interview series (no. 1): The horse keeps on walking—after being orally informed of one year suspension of law firm . . .]. November 24. http://www.peacehall.com/news/gb/china/2005/11/200511241241.shtml.

Boxun Xinwen Wang [Boxun News Online]. 2006. 102 ge ge jie renshi zucheng "Gao Zhisheng falu hou yuan tuan" [102 people from different groups in society form a legal support team for Gao Zhisheng]. August 25. http://peacehall.com/news/gb/china/2006/08/200608250429.shtml.

Braithwaite, John. 2006. Accountability and responsibility through restorative justice. In *Public accountability: designs, dilemmas and experiences*, ed. Michael W. Dowdle, 33–51. Cambridge: Cambridge University Press.

Brands, H. W. 2006. *Andrew Jackson: his life and times*. New York: Random House.

Braud, Philippe. 1997. *Penser l'etat*. Paris: Seuil.

Bugaric, Bojan. 2001. Courts as policy-makers: lessons from transition. *Harvard International Law Journal* 42:247–288.

"Buxiugang laoshu [Stainless-steel mouse]" (pseudonym of Liu Di). 2006. Wo wei shenme bu jueshi [Why I am not hunger-striking]. *Boxun Xinwen Wang*, February 27. http://www.peacehall.com/news/gb/china/2006/02/200602270330.shtml.

Cai Dingjian. 2005a. The development of constitutionalism in the transition of Chinese society. *Columbia Journal of Asian Law* 19:1–29.

Cai Dingjian. 2005b. Zhongguo xiang weixian shencha wanbu [China strides forward toward constitutional review]. *Nanfang zhoumo*, December 22.Cai Dingjian. 2006. *Xianfa jingjie [An intensive reading of the constitution]*. Beijing: Falu chubanshe.

Cai, Yongshun. 2004. Managed participation in China. *Political Science Quarterly* 119: 425–451.

Cao Lin. 2003. Feichang zeren weihu xianfa quanwei [Special responsibility to uphold the authority of the constitution]. *Guangming ribao*, June 6.

Cardozo, Benjamin. 1921. *The nature of the judicial process*. New Haven: Yale University Press.

Cassels, Jamie. 1989. Judicial activism and public interest litigation in India: attempting the impossible? *The American Journal of Comparative Law* 37:495–519.

CCTV.com. 2004. Shehui jilu: yigan qiashi diyian [Social record: the first Hepatitis B discrimination case]. January 15. http://www.cctv.com/news/china/20040115/100200.shtml.

Ceng Xianwen. 2005. Fangwu chaiqian: ruhe baohu sichan [Housing demolition: how to protect private property]. *Procuratorial Daily* (online edition), September 29. http://www.jcrb.com/n1/jcrb221/ca134880.htm.

Central Political-Legal Cadres School, State Law Teaching and Research Office (Zhongyang zhengfa ganbu xuexiao gujiafa jiaoyanshi), ed. 1957. *Zhonghua renmin gongheguo xianfa xuexi cankao ziliao [Reference materials for the study of the PRC Constitution]*. Beijing: Falu chubanshe.

Central Political-Legal Cadres School, State Law Teaching and Research Office (Zhongyang zhengfa ganbu xuexiao guojiafa jiaoyanshi), ed. 1957. *Zhonghua renmin gongheguo xianfa jiangyi [Teaching materials on the PRC Constitution]*. Beijing: Falu chubanshe.

Central Political-Legal Cadres School, Theory of State and Law Teaching and Research Office (Zhongyang zhengfa ganbu xuexiao guojia he fa de lilun jiaoyanshi), ed. 1957. *Guojia he fa de lilun jiangyi [Teaching materials on the theory of the state and law]*. Beijing: Falu chubanshe.

Ch'ien Mu. 1982. *Traditional government in imperial China: a critical analysis*. Hong Kong: The Chinese University Press.

Chang, Alberto and Cesar Calderon. 2000. Causality and feedback between institutional measures and economic growth. *Economics and Politics* 12:69–81.

Chang, Carsun. 1952. *The third force in China*. New York: Bookman.

Chen, Albert. 1999–2000. Toward a legal enlightenment: discussions in contemporary China on the rule of law. *UCLA Pacific Basin Law Journal* 17:125–165.

Chen, Albert. 2004a. *An introduction to the legal system of China*. 3rd ed. Hong Kong: LexisNexis/Butterworths.

Chen Binghui. 2004b. Minzhu yu duoshu de huanzhi: jiedu Tuokewei'er de minzhu lilun [Democracy and tyranny of the majority: an interpretation of Tocqueville's theory of democracy]. *Xiamen Daxue Xuebao*, no. 2:29–34.

Chen Chao. 2004c. Public opinion defeats HBV discrimination. *China Internet Information Center*, September 23. http://www.china.org.cn/english/2004/Sep/107886.htm.

Chen Feng and Wang Lei. 2003. Bei shourongzhe Sun Zhigang zhisi [The death of detainee Sun Zhigang]. *Nanfang dushibao [Southern Metropolitan Daily]*. April 25.

Chen Feng. 2003a. Women gao shourong jiu shi yao gao qian [We engage in custody and repatriation to make money]. *Nanfang dushibao [Southern Metropolitan Daily]*. June 19.

Chen Hanbo. 1954. *Yingjie zuguo di yi bu xianfa [Meet the motherland's first Constitution]*. Beijing: Zhongguo qingnian chubanshe.

Chen Jiansheng. 2004d. Lun Tuokewei'er "Yi Shehui Zhiyue Quanli" sixiang [Regarding Tocqueville's idea of "Restriction of Power by Society"]. *Hainan Daxue Xuebao Shehui Kexue Ban* no. 2:188–192.

Chen Qiqiang. 2003b. Zhejiang daxue xuesheng sharenan yinfa gongzhong dui gongwuyuan luyong biaozhun zhiyi [Zhejiang University student murder case causes public to call into question civil service employment standards]. *Fazhi ribao [Legal Daily]*, October 27.

Chen Xiwen. 2007. Speech by Chen Xiwen, Deputy Director of the Office of Central Financial Work Leading Group. *Zhongguo wang*, February 23. http://china.org.cn/e-news/news060222.htm.

Chen, Leslie H. Dingyan. 1999. *Chen Jiongming and the Federalist movement: regional leadership and nation building in early republican China*. Ann Arbor: University of Michigan Center for Chinese Studies.

Cheng Denlan, Zhou Wei, and Li Cheng. 2006. Guanyu qingqiu dui zuigao renmin fayuan "Guanyu shenli renshen sunhai peichang anjian shiyong falü ruogan shenti de jieshi" di ershijiu tiao jinxing weixian shencha de jianyishu [Proposal on requesting constitutional review of Article 29 of the Supreme People's Court's "Interpretation on Several Problems in Applying the Law in Adjudicating Bodily Injury Compensation Cases"]. Submitted March 25, 2006. Reprinted at http://www.xianzheng.com/xzxk/details.asp?perID=601&classId=5&typecat=%E6%96%B0%E4%BD%9C%E9%80%89%E5%88%8A.

Cheng Ming. 2006. Huozhe de bu gong yu sihou de butong [Unfairness in life and difference in death]. *Gongren ribao [Workers Daily]*, July 7.

Chesneaux, Jean. 1966. Le mouvement fédéraliste en Chine, 1920–1923. *Revue Historique* October–December:347–384.

Chevrier, Yves. 1993. Anarchisme, Maoïsme et culture politique chinoise. *Historiens et géographes* no. 340:193–202.

Chi'en, Tuan-sheng. 1961. *The government and politics of China*. Cambridge, MA: Harvard University Press.

Chi'en, Tuan-sheng [Qian Duansheng]. 1950. *The government and politics of China, 1912–1949*. Cambridge, MA: Harvard University Press.

China Daily (online edition). 2006a. Official: China's poverty line too low. August 23. http://www.chinadaily.com.cn/china/2006-08/23/content_672510.htm.

China Daily (online edition). 2006b. Beijing police detains Gao Zhisheng. August 18. http://www.chinadaily.com.cn/china/2006-08/18/content_668137.htm.

China Daily. 2004a. "BMW Case" reinvestigation ends. March 28.

China Daily. 2004b. New NPC body to address law conflicts. June 21.

China Human Rights Lawyers Concern Group [Zhongguo weiquan lushi guazhuzu]. Undated (last accessed May 8, 2008). Weiquan gean: Gao Zhisheng [Rights defense cases: Gao Zhisheng]. http://www.chrlcg-hk.org/?cat=8.

China Law and Governance Review. 2004. Voices against discrimination: Chinese citizens challenge discriminatory regulations and practices. Issue 2: 1–9.

China Society for Politics and Law [Zhongguo zhengzhi falü xuehui], ed. 1954. *Xianfa fenjie cankao ziliao [Analytical reference materials on the constitution]*. Beijing: Renmin chubanshe.

Chinese Communist Party (CCP) and the State Council (PRC). 2006. Zhonggong Zhongyang Guowuyuan guanyu tuijin shihui zhuyi xin nongcun jianshe de ruogan yijian [Several opinions of the Central Committee of the Chinese Communist Party and the State Council on promoting the building of a new socialist countryside]. *Zhonghua Renmin Gongheguo Nongyebu Gongbao* no. 2: 4–12.

Chinese Communist Party (CCP). 1945. *Zhongguo Gongchandang Zhangcheng [Charter of the Chinese Communist Party]*. Issued June 11.

Chinese Communist Party (CCP). 1956. *Zhongguo Gongchandang Zhangcheng [Charter of the Chinese Communist Party]*. Issued September 26.

Chinese Communist Party (CCP). 2007. *Zhongguo Gongchandang Zhangcheng [Charter of the Chinese Communist Party]*. Issued October 21.

Choate, Allen C. 2000. Legal aid in China. *The Asia Foundation Working Paper Series (Working Paper #12)*. San Francisco: The Asia Foundation.

Christodoulidis, Emilios. 2003. Constitutional irresolution: law and the framing of civil society. *European Law Journal* 9:401–432.

Chu, Tung-tsu. 1961. *Law and society in traditional China*. Paris: Mouton.

Cohen, Jerome A. 2006. China's legal reform at the crossroads. *Far Eastern Economic Review* no. 169 (March): 23–28.

Congressional-Executive Commission on China Virtual Academy. 2006a. Groups petition government to review constitutionality of internet news rules. June 25. http://www.cecc.gov/pages/virtualAcad/index.phpd?showsingle=54921.

Congressional-Executive Commission on China Virtual Academy. 2006b. Henan to use same compensation standards for urban residents, qualified migrants. August 31. http://www.cecc.gov/pages/virtualAcad/index.phpd?showsingle=64979.

Congressional-Executive Commission on China Virtual Academy. 2006c. Petition on behalf of the Aegean Sea web site et al. [sic] to repeal provisions on the administration of Internet news information services (CECC full translation). September 22. http://www.cecc.gov/pages/virtualAcad/index.phpd?showsingle=47693&PHPSESSID=c2295d454c9f3f4afe807b7f4111c4b9.

Congressional-Executive Commission on China Virtual Academy. 2006d. Authorities arrest Gao Zhisheng supporters for inciting subversion. December 3. http://www.cecc.gov/pages/virtualAcad/index.phpd?showsingle=76342.

Congressional-Executive Commission on China. 2005. *China's household registration system: sustained reform needed to protect china's rural migrants*. Washington, DC: Congressional-Executive Commission on China.

Congressional-Executive Commission on China. 2004. *Annual Report: 2004*. Washington, DC: US Government Printing Office.

Congressional-Executive Commission on China. 2005. *Annual Report: 2005*. Washington, DC: US Government Printing Office.

Corrado, Michael Louis. 2004. *Comparative constitutional review: cases and materials*. Durham, NC: Carolina Academic Press.

Cui Li. 2003. San gongmin shangshu renda jianyi dui shourong banfa jinxing weixian shencha [Three Chinese citizens submit an appeal to the National People's Congress proposing that the NPC conduct constitutional review of the custody and repatriation measures]. *Zhongguo qingnian bao [China Youth Daily]*, May 16.

Daniels, Ronald J., and Michael J. Trebilcock. 2004. The political economy of rule of law reform in developing countries. *Michigan Journal of International Law* 26:99–140.

Davidson, Donald. 1973. Radical interpretation. *Dialectica* 27:314–28.

De Bary, William Theodore. 1993. *Waiting for the dawn: a plan for the Prince*. New York: Columbia University Press.

Deng Shaoling. 2003. Sun Zhigang an yu weixian shencha xueshu yantaohui zongshu [The Sun Zhigang case and constitutional review: summary of an academic symposium]. *Zhongguo faxüe [China Legal Science]* no. 4: 189–192.

Deng Xiaoping. 1994. *Deng Xiaoping xuanji [Selected readings of Deng Xiaoping]* 2nd ed. Beijing: Renmin chubanshe.

Deng Zhenglai. 2002. *Hayeke falu zhexue de yanjiu [Studies in Hayek's legal philosophy]*. Beijing: Falu chubanshe.

Deng Zhenglai. 2004. *Guize, zhixu, wuzhi [Rules, order, and ignorance]*. Beijing: Sanlian Shudian.

Deng Zhenglai. 2006. *Zhongguo faxue xianghe chu qu [Where is China's jurisprudence going]?* Beijing: Shangwu Yinshuguan.

Diamant, Neil J., Stanley B. Lubman, and Kevin J. O'Brien, eds. 2005. *Engaging the law in China: state, society, and possibilities for justice*. Stanford: Stanford University Press.

Dicey, A.V. [Albert Venn]. 1981. *Introduction to the study of the law of the constitution*. Indianapolis: Liberty Classics.

Ding Zilin. 2006. Ding Zilin zhi Gao Zhisheng gongkaixin: qing huidao weiquan de hanglie zhong lai [Open letter from Ding Zilin to Gao Zhisheng: please return to the job of rights-defending]. *Epoch Times (online edition)*, February 23. http://peacehall.com/news/gb/china/2006/02/200602232225.shtml.

Dong Biwu. 2001. *Dong Biwu faxue wenji [Legal works of Dong Biwu]*. Beijing: Falu chubanshe.

Dong Boyu. 1989. Zhongguo xianfa si shi nian [Forty years of China's constitutional jurisprudence. *Zhengfa Luntan* no. 5: 20–26.

Dongfang Zaobao. 2008. Wei Shenmo Gaoxueli Faguan Ling Ren Huai Yi [Why Should Highly Educated Judges Make People Suspicious]? September 22. B7.

Dowdle, Michael W. 1997. The constitutional development and operations of the *National People's Congress. Columbia Journal of Asian Law* 11:1–125.

Dowdle, Michael William. 2002. Of parliaments, pragmatism, and the dynamics of constitutional development: the curious case of China. *New York University Journal of International Law and Politics* 35:1–200.

Dowdle, Michael William. 2004. Of "socialism" and "socialist" constitutional transformations in China and Vietnam. In *Asian socialism and legal change: the dynamics of Vietnamese and Chinese reform*, ed. John Gillespie and Pip Nicholson, 21–44. Canberra: Asia Pacific Press.

Du Chengming. 2005. 1954 nian xianfa de jichu—"gongtong gangling" de lishi diwei ji qi fansi [The foundation of the 1954 Constitution—rethinking the historical position of the "common program"]. In *1954 nian xianfa yanjiu*, ed. Zhang Qingfu and Han Dayuan, 22–35. Beijing: Zhongguo renmin gong'an daxue chubanshe.

Du Xiaolin. 2003. Rang xianfa yishi chengwei gongmin renge xinli zhong de zhuti yishi [Make constitutional consciousness the principal consciousness in the hearts and character of citizens]. *Zhongguo pufa wang [China legal publicity net]*, December 1. http://www.legalinfo.gov.cn/zt/2005-12/01/content_228381.htm.

Duara, Prasenjit. 1993. Deconstructing the Chinese nation. *The Australian Journal of Chinese Affairs* no. 30:1–26.

Duara, Prasenjit. 1995. *Rescuing history from the nation: questioning narratives of modern China*. Chicago: University of Chicago Press.

Dworkin, Ronald. 1977. *Taking rights seriously*. Cambridge, MA: Harvard University Press.

Dworkin, Ronald. 1986. *Law's empire*. Cambridge, MA: Harvard University Press.

Eckholm, Erik. 2003. Petitioners urge China to enforce legal rights. *New York Times*, June 2. A1.

Ellmann, Stephen. 1990. Lawyers for justice in a flawed democracy: review of *Lawyers and Justice: An Ethical Study* by David Luban. *Columbia Law Review* 90:116–190.

Epp, Charles R. 1998. *The rights revolution: lawyers, activists, and supreme courts in comparative perspective*. Chicago: University of Chicago Press.

Escarra, Jean. 1936. *Le droit chinois. conception et évolution, institutions législatives et judiciaires, science et enseignement*. Paris: Librairie du Recueil Sirey.

Ewald, William. 1994. The American Revolution and the evolution of law. *American Journal of Comparative Law* 42:1–14.

Farmer, Edward L. 1995. *Zhu Yuanzhang and early Ming legislation: the reordering of society following the era of Mongol rule*. Leiden: Brill.

Fazhi ribao [Legal Daily]. 2006. Chongqing gao yuan toulu you guan "tong ming bu tong jia" zhidao yijian yunniang guocheng [Chongqing High Court reveals preparation process for the guidance opinion on "Different Prices for a Life"]. October 26.

Fazhi Wang [Legal Daily Online Edition]. 2006. Dangjin Zhongguo Sifa Xingzheng Renyuan Gongzuo Zhuangkuang Diaocha [Survey on the working situation of judicial administrative workers in contemporary China]. July 18. http://big5.xinhuanet.com/gate/big5/www.gx.xinhuanet.com/misc/2006-07/18/content_7547107.htm.

Fehrenbacher, Don E. 1978. *The Dred Scott case: its significance in American law and politics*. New York: Oxford University Press.

Fei Anling. 2004. Lun siquan linian yu chengshi sifang chaiqian de lifa [The ideas of private rights and the legislation of urban private housing demolition]. *Zhengfa Luntan* no. 5.

Fei Xiaotong. 1988. *Huangquan he Shenquan [The emperor's power and the power of the gentry class]*. Tianjin: Tianjin renmin chubanshe.

Fewsmith, Joseph. 2003a. China's response to SARS. *China Leadership Monitor* No. 7.

Fewsmith, Joseph. 2003b. The sixteenth National Party Congress: the succession that didn't happen. *China Quarterly* no. 173: 1–16.

France, Anatole. 1900. In *Le Figaro*, November 14.

Fu Hualing. 2003. Putting China's judiciary into perspective: is it independent, competent, and fair? In *Beyond common knowledge: empirical approaches to the rule of law*, ed. Eric G. Jensen and Thomas C. Heller, 193–219. Stanford, CA: Stanford University Press.

Fu Hualing. 2004. Cong xiangcun falü zhidu de jianshe kan falü yu fazhan: jiufen de jiejue yu jingji fazhan [Law and development from the perspective of the rural legal system]. *Hongfan Pinglun* no. 1: 110–139.

Fu Hualing. 2007. When lawyers are prosecuted: the struggle of a profession in transition. *Journal of Comparative Law* 2:95–132.

Fu Hualing and Richard Cullen. 2008. Weiquan (rights protection) lawyering in an authoritarian state: building a culture of public-interest lawyering. *The China Journal* no 59: 111–128.

Fuller, Lon L. 1964. *The morality of law*, rev. ed. New Haven: Yale University Press.

Fung, Edmund S.K. 2000. *In search of Chinese democracy: civil opposition in nationalist China, 1929–1949*. Cambridge: Cambridge University Press.

Fung, Edmund S.K. 2006. The idea of freedom in modern China revisited. *Modern China* 32:453–482.

Galanter, Marc. 1974. Why the "haves" come out ahead: speculations on the limits of legal change. *Law and Society Review* 9:95–160.

Galanter, Marc. 1983. The radiating effects of courts. In *Empirical theories about courts*, ed. Keith O. Boyum and Lynn M. Mather, 117–142. New York: Longmans.

Gallagher, Mary E. 2005. Use the law as your weapon! institutional change and legal mobilization in China. In *Engaging the law in China: state, society, and possibilities for justice*, ed. Neil J. Diamant, Stanley B. Lubman, and Kevin J. O'Brien, 54–83. Stanford: Stanford University Press.

Gallagher, Mary E. 2006. Mobilizing the law in China: "informed disenchantment" and the development of legal consciousness. *Law and Society Review* 40:783–813.

Gao Zhisheng. 2004a. Lushi zhi Quanguo Renda de gongkai xin [Lawer Gao Zhisheng's open letter to the National People's Congress]. *The Epoch Times* (online edition), December 30. http://news.epochtimes.com/gb/4/12/30/n764897.htm.

Gao Zhisheng. 2004b. Shijiazhuang falungong xueyuan Huang Wei de xingzheng qisushu [Huang Wei's Complaint]. December 31, 2004. Published at http://minghui.org/mh/articles/2004/12/31/92504p.html.

Gao Zhisheng. 2005a. Gao Zhisheng kaixin: tingzhi pohai ziyou xinyangzhe, gaishan tong Zhongguo renmin de guanxi [Gao Zhisheng open letter: stop the persecution of persons freely adhering to a faith, improve your relationship with the Chinese people]. *Boxun Xinwen Wang*, October 18. http://www.peacehall.com/news/gb/china/2005/10/200510190023.shtml.

Gao Zhisheng. 2006. Gao Zhisheng guanyu Ding Zilin nushi gongkaixin de huiying [Gao Zhisheng answers Madam Ding Zilin's open letter]. *Epoch Times (online edition)*, February 24. http://www.epochtimes.com/gb/6/2/24/n1236006.htm.

Gao Zhisheng. 2005b. Gao Zhisheng wei falungong san zhi zhongguo dangju gongkai xin—bixu liji tingzhi miejue women minzu liangzhi he daode de yeman xingjing [Gao Zhisheng third open letter to china's leadership on behalf of Falungong—must immediately stop our barbarous behavior before we completely loose our innate democratic understanding and democratic morality.] *Epoch Times* (online edition), December 13. http://news.epochtimes.com/gb/5/12/13/n1151842.htm.

Gény, François. 1954. *Méthodes d'interprétation et sources en droit privé positif: essai critique.* 2nd ed. Paris: LGDJ.

Gong Qun. 2005. Lun baohu shaoshu de quanli [The rights of minority]. *Zhongguo Renmin Daxue Xuebao* no. 3: 95–101.

Gongfa Pinglun. 2002. Dewojin, "Ziyou Zhuyi Falun linian yu Meiguo xianzheng chuantong" xueshu zuotanhui jiyao [Symposium summary of Dworkin, "Taking Rights Seriously and the American tradition of constitutionalism"]. May 21. http://www.gongfa.com/dewojinyantaohui.htm.

Goodnow, Frank J. 1915. Reform in China. *American Political Science Review* 9:209–224.

Grieff, Thomas E. 1985. The principle of human rights in nationalist China: John C. H. Wu and the ideological origins of the 1946 Constitution. *The China Quarterly* 103:441–461.

Grimheden, Jonas. 2004. Themis v. Xiezhi: assessing judicial independence in the People's Republic of China under international human rights law (Lund University Doctoral Dissertation). Lund: Intellecta DocuSys. Published at http://www.lu.se/o.o.i.s?id=12588&postid=21659.

Guo Guoseng. 2003. Members of the CPPCC Guangdong provincial committee point out that the country's reeducation through labor system lacks legal basis. *Nanfang zhoumo [Southern Weekend]*, trans. Foreign Broadcast Information Service [FBIS], September 4.

Guo Junwang. 2004. Guanyu Sun Zhigang anjian de falü sikao [Legal reflections on the Sun Zhigang case]. *Falü sixiang wang*, October 14. http://www.fatianxia.com/review_list.asp?id=314.

Guo Yanjun. 2006. Difang "yiba shou" ying renzhen kandai gongmin xianfa quanli—ping qin zhong fei bianfa duan xin bei juan de qi luo ["Local heads" should take citizens' constitutional rights seriously—comments on the qin zhongfei's tele-messaging case]. *Faxue* no. 11: 3–10.

Guo Yunsheng and Song Gongde. 1997. Kongji—pingheng lun—jianlun xiandai xingzhengfa de lishi ming [From the power control theory to the balance theory: a discussion on the historic mission of modern administrative law]. *Zhongguo Faxue* no. 6: 48–56.

Guo Zi. 2004. Dismantling discrimination. *China Daily*, March 9.

Halmai, Gabor, and Kim Lane Scheppele. 1997. Living well is the best revenge: the Hungarian approach to judging the past. In *Transitional justice and rule of law in new democracies*, ed. A. James McAdams, 155–184. Notre Dame: University of Notre Dame Press.

Han Dayuan and Hu Jinguang, ed. 2004. *Zhongguo xianfa fazhan yanjiu baogao [Research report on the development of China's Constitution].* Beijing: Falu chubanshe.

Han Dayuan and Mo Jihong, ed. 2005. *Waiguo xianfa panli [Cases of foreign constitutions].* Beijing: Zhongguo renmin daxue chubanshe.

Han Dayuan, Lin Laifan, and Zheng Xianjun. 2004. *Xianfaxue zhuanti yanjiu [Researching constitutional law].* Beijing: Zhongguo renmin daxue chubanshe.

Han Dayuan. 2004. *1954 nian xianfa yu xin zhongguo xianzheng [The 1954 constitution and constitutionalism in new China].* Changsha: Hunan renmin chubanshe.

Han Dayuan. 2006. Liang qian ling wu nian xianfa xueshu yanjiu huigu [Constitutional scholarship in 2005]. *Faxuejia* no. 1.

Hand, Keith J. 2006. Citizens engage the constitution: the Sun Zhigang incident and constitutional review proposals in the People's Republic of China. *Columbia Journal of Transnational Law* 45:114–147.

Hao Tiechuan. 1997. Zhongguo jindai faxue liuxuesheng yu fazhi jindaihua [Returned law students in modern China and the modernization of the legal system]. *Faxue yanjiuno* no. 6: 3–26.

Hao Tiechuan. 2000. Zhongguo jindai faxue liuxuesheng yu xin Zhongguo chuqi de fazhi jianshe [Returned law students in modern China and the construction of the legal system in the early years of new China]. *Faxue yanjiu* no. 2: 136–153.

Havel, Václav. 1987. The power of the powerless. In *Václav Havel, or living in truth*, ed. Jan Vladislav, trans. P. Wilson, 36–122. London: Faher and Faher.

Hayek, Friedrich A. 1944. *The road to serfdom*. London: Routledge.

Hayek, Friedrich A. 1960. *The constitution of liberty*. Chicago: Chicago University Press.

He Haibo, ed. 2005. *Fazhi de jiaobu sheng: zhongguo xingzheng fada shiji: 1978–2004 [The footsteps of rule of law: chronicle of events of administrative law in China: 1978–2004]*. Beijing: Zhongguo zhengfa chubanshe.

He Qinhua. 2004a. Fake liuxuesheng yu zhongguo jindai faxue [Returned law students in law departments and the study of law in modern China]. *Faxue luntan* no. 6: 82–90.

He Qinhua. 2004b. Xifang faxue guan zai jindai zhongguo de chuanbo [The dissemination of Western legal concepts in modern China]. *Faxue* 12:3–16.

He Qinhua. 2004c. Zhongguo jindai xianfa xue de dansheng yu chengzhang [The birth and growth of Modern Chinese Constitution]. *Dangdai Faxue* no. 5: 141–154.

He Weifang, Shen Kui, He Haibo, Xiao Han, and Shen Hong. 2003. Qingqiu quanguo renda changweihui jiu Sun Zhigang an ji shourong qiansong zhidu shishi zhuangkuang qidong tebie diaocha chengxu de jianyi shu [Proposal submitted to the Standing Committee of the National People's Congress on initiating procedures for a special investigation into the Sun Zhigang case and the implementation of the custody and repatriation system]. May 22.

He Weifang, et al. 2004. Wanshan wo guo xianfa renquan baohu tiaokuan de jianyi [Proposals for perfecting our country's constitutional protections for human rights]. *CNCASKY.Com*, April 11. http://www.cncasky.com/get/lltt/fxll/000610917.htm.

He Weifang. 1997. Zhongguo sifa guanli zhidu de liangge wenti [Two problems of the administration of justice in China]. *Zhongguo Shehui Kexue* no. 6: 116–129.

He Weifang. 1998. Fuzhuan junren jin fayuan [Discharged military officers come to the courts]. *Nanfang Zhoumo*, January 2..

He Weifang. 2002. *Yunsong zhengyi de fangshi [The way of transferring justice]*. Shanghai: Sanlian shudian chubanshe.

He Weifang. 2008a. Sifa geige de nanti yu chulu [Problems and pathways to judicial reform]. *Nanfang Zhoumou* (Internet addition), September 17. http://www.infzm.com/content/17280/1.

He Weifang. 2008b. Sifa shenmihua gai ruhe qiqu [The judicial process needs to be demystified]. September 26. http://blog.sina.com.cn/s/blog_488663200100b3s7.html.

He, Xin. 2003. Regulating rural-urban migrants in Beijing: institutional conflicts and ineffective campaigns. *Stanford Journal of International Law* 39:177–206.

He Xin. 2004. Difang de xingqi he "zhengzhi shuanggui" de yusai, zhongdu Fei Xiaotong de *Xiangtu chongjian* [The rise of the regions and the clogging of "two-track politics." a critique of Fei Xiaotong's *Village reconstruction*]. *Xianggang Shehui Kexue Xuebao* 27:27–40.

He, Xin. 2007. Why did they not take on the disputes? Law, power and politics in the decision-making of Chinese courts. *International Journal of Law in Context* 3 203–225.

Hellman, Joel S., Geraint Jones, and Daniel Kaufmann. 2000. *Seize the state, seize the day: state capture, corruption and influence in transition (World Bank Policy Research Paper, no. 2444)*. Washington, DC: World Bank.

Henaff, Marcel. 2002. *Le prix de la vérité : le don, l'argent, la philosophie*. Paris: Seuil.

Henne, Thomas. 2003. [Review essay on] *Controlling environmental policy: the limits of public law in Germany and the United States* (Susan Rose-Ackerman, Yale University Press, 1995). *The American Journal of Comparative Law* 51: 207–228.

Holmes, Oliver Wendell, Jr. 1992. John Marshall. In *The essential Holmes: selections from the letters, speeches, judicial opinions, and other writings of Oliver Wendell Holmes, Jr.* ed. Richard A. Posner, 206–209. Chicago: University of Chicago Press.

Horsley, Jamie P. 2004. Shanghai advances the cause of open government information in China. *Freedominfo.org*, April 20. http: //www.freedominfo.org/news/20040420.htm.

Hu Angang, Wang Shaoguang, and Zhou Jianming. 2003. *Guojia ahidu jianshe [Building state institutions]*. Beijing: Qinghua daxue chubanshe.

Hu Jianmiao, ed. 2002. *Gongfa yanjiu [The study of public law]*. Beijing: Shangwu yinshuguan.

Hu Jintao. 2003. Quanmian guanche shishi xianfa, wei quanmian jianshe xiaokang shehui tigong jianshi falu baozhang [Fully enforce the constitution to provide solid legal guarantee for full construction of a society with minimum satisfaction]. In *Dangzheng ganbu xianfa jiaoyu duben*, ed. Gu Angran and Qiao Xiaoyang, 1–5. Beijing: Zhonggong zhongyang dangxiao chubanshe.

Hu Xingdou. 2003a. Dui laodong jiaoyang de youguan guiding jinxing weixian weifa shencha de jianyishu [Proposal for constitutional and legislative review of reeducation through labor and relevant regulations]. June 21. http://www.huxingdou.com.cn/weixianshencha.htm.

Hu Xingdou. 2003b. Qianfu suo zhi de laojiao zhidu [Everyone condemns the reeducation through labor system]. *Gongmin weiquan wang*. November 3. http://www.gmwq.org/web/news_view.asp?newsid=100.

Hu Xingdou. 2003c. Guanyu feichu laodong jiaoyang zhi zhonggong zhongyang de jianyishu [Proposal to the Party Central [Committee] to abolish the reeducation through labor system]. November 9. Published at http://www.huxingdou.com.cn/feichulaojiao.htm. Accessed June 12, 2008.

Hu Xingdou. 2006. Guanyu xiaochu chengxiang chabie duidai, tongyi renshen sunhai peichang biaozhun de gongmin jianyishu [Citizen proposal on eliminating different treatment of cities and towns, and a uniform standard for bodily injury compensation]. March 12.

Hu, Yunteng. 2002. Application of the death penalty in Chinese judicial practice. In *The implementation of law in the People's Republic of China*, ed. Jianfu Chen, Yuwen Li, and Jan Michiel Otto, 247–275. The Hague: Kluwer Law International.

Huang Guangming and He Qing. 2003. Wo shi yigan huanzhe, dan wo bushi yideng gongmin [I suffer from Hepatitis B, but I'm not a second-class citizen]. *Nanfang Zhoumo,* December 25.

Huang Songyou. 2001. Xianfa sifahuan jiqi yiyi [The judicialization of the constitution and its significance]. *Remnin Fayuan Bao*, August 13.

Huang, Ray. 1981. *1587, a year of no significance: The Ming Dynasty in decline*. New Haven, Yale University Press.

Huang, Ray. 1988. The Lung-ch'ing and Wan-li reigns, 1567–1620. In *The Ming Dynasty, 1368–1644*, ed. Frederick W. Mote and Denis Twitchett. Vol. 7 of *The Cambridge history of China*, 511–584. Cambridge: Cambridge University Press.

Hucker, Charles O. 1966. *The censorial system of Ming China*. Palo Alto: Stanford University Press.

Human Rights in China. 1999. *Not welcome at the party: behind the "clean-up" of China's cities—a report on administrative detention under "custody and repatriation."* New York: Human Rights in China.

Hung, Veron Mei-Ying. 2003. Improving human rights in China: should reeducation through labor be abolished? *Columbia Journal of Transnational Law* 41:303–326.

Hung, Vernon Mei-ying. 2004. China's WTO commitment on independent judicial review: impact on legal and political reform. *American Journal of Comparative Law* 52:77–132.

Israël, Liora. 2007. Quand des professionnels de justice revendiquent leur engagement. In *La fonction politique de la justice*, ed. Jacques Commaille and Martine Kaluszynski, 122–147. Paris: La Découverte.

Jacob, Herbert, Erhard Blankenburg, Herbert M. Kritzer, and Doris Marie Provine. 1996. *Courts, law, and politics in comparative perspective*. New Haven: Yale University Press.

James, William. 1995. Lecture II: what pragmatism means. In *Pragmatism*. Unabridged ed., 17–32. New York: Dover.

Jeans, Roger B., ed. 1992. *Roads not taken: the struggle of opposition parties in twentieth century China*. Boulder: Westview Press.

Ji Shuoming and Wang Jianmin. 2005. Zhongguo weiquan lüshi fazhi xianfeng [China's rights defense lawyers the vanguard of rule of law]. *Yazhou zhoukan*, December 21.

Ji Weidong. 1993. Falu chengxu de yiyi—dui Zhongguo fazhi jianshe de lingyi zhongsi kao [The significance of legal procedures: further reflection on China's construction of a legal system]. *Zhongguo Shehui Kexue* no. 9: 83–103.

Ji Weidong. 2001. What can IT do for judicial reform? Reorganization of the net of justice in the digital age in China. *The Sociology of Law* (The Japanese Association of Sociology of Law) 54: 222–235.

Ji Weidong. 2002. Judicial independence and the values of procedure. *Social Sciences in China,* English ed., no.2: 96–106.

Ji Weidong. 2004a. Different layers of public sphere in China. In *The public opinion taking shape in East Asia*, ed. Hiroshi Mitani, 245–278. Tokyo: The University of Tokyo Press.

Ji Weidong. 2004b. *The composition of the Chinese judicial system.* Tokyo: Yuhikaku Press.

Ji Weidong. 2006. Falu chengxu de xingshi xing yu shizhi xing—yi dui chengxu lilun de pipan he pipan lilun de chengxu huawei xiansuo [The formality and substance of legal procedure—toward a critique of process theory and a process of critical theory]. *Beijing Daxue Xuebao (Zhexue Shehui kexue Ban)* no. 1: 109–131.

Jiang Bikun. 1957. *Zhonghua renmin gongheguo xianfa mingci jianshuo [Brief explanation of the terms used in the PRC Constitution].* Wuhan: Hubei renmin chubanshe.

Jiang Dehai. 2003. Weixian haishi weifa [Unconstitutional is still illegal]. *Faxüe* 6: 16–18.

Jiang Jinsong. 2002a. *The National People's Congress of China.* Beijing: Foreign Languages Press.

Jiang Ming'an. 1993. *Xingzheng Susong Faxue [Studies in the Administrative Litigation Law].* Beijing: Beijing daxue chubanshe.

Jiang Ming'an. 2002b. *Xingzhengfa yu xingzheng susong fa [Administrative law and Administrative Litigation Law].* Beijing: Beijing daxue chubanshe.

Jiang Shigong. 2001. Falu Gongtong tixuanyan [Manifesto of the Community of Jurists]. *Zhong Wai Faxue* no. 3: 1–5.

Jiang Shigong. 2004. Wukelan xianzheng weiji yu zhengzhi jueduan [The constitutional crisis in ukraine and political decision]. *21 Shiji Jingji Baodao,* December 15.

Jie Zhao. 2002. A decade of considerable significance: late Ming factionalism in the making, 1583–1593. *T'oung Pao* 88:112–150.

Jingji guancha. 2003. Guanzhu Sun Zhigang anjian yiyi zhongda [Attention to Sun Zhigang case has important implications]. June 2.

Kahn, Joseph. 2004. China detains 3 who criticized government. *New York Times*, December 14. A10.

Kahn, Joseph. 2005. Rebel lawyer takes China's "unwinnable" cases. *International Herald Tribune*, December 12. A1

Kelliher, Daniel. 1997. The Chinese Debate Over Village Self-Government. *The China Journal* no. 37:63–86.

Kelly, David. 2006. Public intellectuals and citizen movements in China in the Hu-Wen era. *Pacific Affairs* 79:183–204.

Kirby, William C. 2001. Renshi 20 shiji zhongguo [Understanding 20th century China]. *Ershiyi shiji*, October, 114–124.

Kottman, Paul A. 2003. Memory, mimesis, tragedy: the scene before philosophy. *Theatre Journal* 55:81–97.

Krymov, A. G. and M. A. Shafir, ed. 1959. *Konstitutsiya i osnovnye zakonodatelnye akty Kitaiskoi Narodnoi Respubliki, 1954–1958 [Constitution and basic legislative acts of the Chinese People's Republic, 1954–1958].* Moscow: Inlitizdat.

Kuhn, Philip A. 1999. *Les origines de l'etat chinois moderne.* Paris: Éditions de L'Ecole des Hautes Études en Sciences Sociales.

Kui, Shen. 2003. Is it the beginning of the era of the rule of the constitution? Reinterpreting China's "first constitutional case." *Pacific Rim Law and Policy Journal* 12:199–232.

Kuomintang [KMT]. 2005. *Zhongguo Guomindang Zhangcheng [Charter of the Kuomindang]*. Issued October 8.

Lan Hai. 2005. Weixian shencha: ezhi "e fa" de "gongqi" [Constitutional review: a "citizen weapon" to constrain "evil law"]. *Zhongguo renda wang*, December 26. http://www.zzrd.gov.cn/news.asp?newsid=1116.

Lee, Ching Kwan. 2007. What was socialism to Chinese workers? Collective memories and labor politics in an age of reform. In *Re-envisioning the Chinese revolution: the politics and poetics of collective memories in reform China*, ed. Ching Kwan Lee and Guobin Yang, 141–165. Washington, DC: Woodrow Wilson Center Press.

Leu, Siew Ying. 2003. Scrapping of migrant laws praised, but academics who pushed for the easing of police powers are upset that the NBC will not address the issue. *South China Morning Post*, June 20, at 6.

Li Buyun. 1978. Jianchi gongmin zai falu shang yilu ping deng [Adhere to the principle of equality under the law. *Renmin Ribao*, December 9.

Li Buyun. 1999. Shishi yifa zhiguo zhanlue lungang [An outline for implementing the strategy of governing the country in accordance with law]. *Xuexi Yu Tansuo* no. 3: 65–71.

Li Buyun. 2002. Xianfa xue de jige lilun wenti [Some theoretical problems concerning the study of constitutional law]. *Zhongguo Shehui Kexueyuan Yanjiu Shengyuan Xuebao* no. 6: 19–25.

Li Da. 1956. *Zhonghua renmin gongheguo xianfa jianghua [Introduction to the PRC Constitution]*. Beijing: Renmin chubanshe.

Li Lianjiang and Kevin J. O'Brien. 1996. Villagers and popular resistance in contemporary China. *Modern China* 22: 28–61.

Li Qiang. 1999. Gongsidang yu xiandai ziyou zhuyi [Benjamin Constant and modern liberalism]. In *Gudai ren de ziyou yu xiandai ren de ziyou: Gongsidang zhengzhi lunwen xuan [Liberty of the ancients and of the moderns: the political theory of Benjamin Constant]*, by Benjamin Constant, 1–12. Beijing: Shangwu yinshuguan.

Li Shi. 2004. New findings in income inequality in China at the beginning of the new millennium. Paper presented at The Chinese University of Hong Kong, Universities Service Centre for China Studies, 40th anniversary reunion conference: *The state of contemporary China*. Hong Kong: January 6..

Liang Qichao. 1986a. Zhongguo liguo dafangzheng [The central axis for constructing the Chinese state] (April 1912). Reprinted in Liang Qichao, *Yinbingshi heji-wenji [Collected writings from the Ice-Drinker's Studio]*, by Liang Qichao. Vol. 10, 46–62. Beijing: Zhongguo jianzhu gongye chubanshe.

Liang Qichao. 1986b. Yi zai suowei guoti wenti zhe [Another view on the so-called state-structure problem] (August 1915). In *Yinbingshi heji-wenji [Collected writings from the Ice-Drinker's Studio]*, by Liang Qichao. Vol. 10, 90–95. Beijing: Zhongguo jianzhu gongye chubanshe.

Liang Zhiping. 1987. Zhongguo fa de guoqu, xianzai yu weilai: yige wenhua de jiantao [The past, present, and future of Chinese law: an exploration from a cultural perspective.] *Bijiaofa Yanjiu* 17:21–36.

Liang Zhiping. 1991. *Xunqiu ziran zhixu zhong de hexie: Zhongguo chuantong falu wenhua yanjiu [Seeking harmony in the natural order: research into China's traditional legal culture]*. Shanghai: Shanghai renmin chubanshe.

Liang Zhiping. 1997. Xiangtu shehui zhong de falu yu zhixu [Law and order in the peasantry society]. In *Xiangtu shehui de zhixu, gongzheng yu quanwei*, ed. Wang Mingming and Wang Sifu, 415–487. Beijing: Zhongguo Zhengfa Daxue chubanshe.

Liaowang Dongfang Zhoukan. 2003. 2003 nian Zhongguo zaoyu shangfang hongfeng, xin lingdao ren mianlin feichang kaoyan [A flood peak of petitions appears in China in 2003, the new leadership faces serious challenges]. December 28.

Liebman, Benjamin L. 1999. Legal aid and public interest law in China. *Texas International Law Review* 34:211–286.

Liebman, Benjamin L. 2005. Watchdog or demagogue? The media in the chinese legal system. *Columbia Law Review* 105:1–157.

Lin Laifan. 2005. Xianfa buneng quanran meiya [The constitution can't be toothless forever]. *Faxüe* no. 6: 90–91.

Lin Lin. 2006. Shixing jin wushinian falü yiju bu chongfen? Laojiao zhidu zao zhiyi [Legal basis inadequate after nearly fifty years of implementation? The reeducation through labor system called in question]. *Gongren ribao*, February 20.

Lin Mu, et al. 2006. Dui canhai Gao Lushi baoli xingwei de gongmin lianshu kangyishu [Citizens protest violence against Lawyer Gao]. August 2. http://hk.epochtimes.com/6/8/4/28714.htm.

Link, Perry. 2005. Mad, Bad Mao. *Times Literary Supplement*, July 20, 2005.

Liu Denggao. 2003. *Pinwei faguan [A judge with taste]*. Beijing: Renmin fayuan chubanshe.

Liu Feng. 2002. Zhengzhi wu shenxue de pingxing xing [The parallel of politics and theology]. In *Shimite [Carl Schmitt] yu Zhengzhi Faxue*, ed. Liu Xiaofeng, 384–396. Shanghai: Sanlian shudian chubanshe.

"Liu Lu" (pseudonym of Li Jianqiang). 2006. Yi ge gean shan huo zhe de ling yun ba qi—Yuan Hongbing "wei Gao Zhisheng bian" [The reckless remarks of an inflammatory troublemaker—Yuan Hongbing's "defence of Gao Zhisheng"]. *Boxun Xinwen Wang*, February 25. http://www.peacehall.com/news/gb/pubvp/2006/02/200602252004.shtml.

Liu Qing. 1954. *Xianfa changshi jianghua [Introduction to general knowledge about the constitution]*. Beijing: Gongren chubanshe.

Liu Xiaofeng. 2002. Bianzhe Qianyan [Editor's foreword]. In *Shimite [Carl Schmitt] yu Zhengzhi faxue*, ed. Liu Xiaofeng, 1–59. Shanghai: Sanlian shudian chubanshe.

Liu Xin. 2007. Jianlun chouxiang xingwei de tezheng [A short discussion of peculiarities of abstract administrative acts]. *Fazhi Ribao* (online edition), February 2. http://www.legal-daily.com.cn/gb/content/2001-07/29/content_21642.htm.

Long Li and Liu Liantai. 2003. Feichu "liufa quanshu" de huigu yu fansi [Looking back at and reconsidering the abrogation of the "Complete Book of the Six Codes"]. *Henan sheng zhengfa guanli ganbu xuexiao xuebao* no. 5: 39–50.

Lott, John R., Jr. 2005. The judicial confirmation process: the difficulty with being smart. *Journal of empirical legal studies* 2:407–447.

Lou Bangyan. 1955. *Zhonghua renmin gongheguo xianfa jiben zhishi [Basic knowledge about the PRC Constitution]*. Shanghai: Xin zhishi chubanshe.

Lu Sheng. Undated (2004?). Wenbu guize yu shehui zhixu—Zhongguo chengshi fangwu chaiqian zhidu yanjiu [Rules in the context and social order—research into processes of urban housing demolition in China]. *Gongfa Pinglun (online journal)*, http://www.gongfa.com/tudichaiqian.htm.

Luban, David. 1988. *Lawyers and justice: an ethical study*. Princeton: Princeton University Press.

Luo Haocai, ed. 1997. *Xiandai xingzhengfa de pingheng lilun [The balancing theory of modern administrative law]*. Beijing: Beijing Daxue chubanshe.

Lusky, Louis. 1982. Footnote redux: a *Carolene Products* reminiscence. *Columbia Law Review* 82:1093–1109.

Ma Lianzhang and Ji Mengqun. 1955. *Woguo de guojia jiegou [Our country's state structure]*. Beijing: Tongsu duwu chubanshe.

Ma Wendu. 2006. Yinan xian pangting Chen Guangcheng an jishi [Notes on the hearing of Chen Guangcheng in Yinan County]. *Boxun Xinwen Wang*, August 5. http://www.peacehall.com/news/gb/pubvp/2006/08/200608022128.shtml.

Ma, Josephine. 2003. Inmate's death prompts calls for revamp of "reform-through-labor" system. *South China Morning Post*, July 24, 6.

Maltz, Earl M. 2000. *The chief justiceship of Warren Burger, 1969–1986*. Columbia, SC: University of South Carolina Press.

Maltz, Earl M., ed. 2003. *Rehnquist Justice: understanding the court dynamic*. Lawrence, KS: University Press of Kansas.

Mao Shoulong. Undated. Lun *Meiguo de Minzhu* "Xuyan" Daodu [Introduction to the Preface of *Democracy in America*]. http://article.chinalawinfo.com/article/user/article_display.asp?ArticleID=30265.

Mao Zedong. 1975. On correcting mistaken ideas in the Party. In *Selected works of Mao Tse-Tung*, by Mao Zedong. Vol. 1, 105–116. Beijing, Foreign Language Press, 1975.

Mao Zedong. 1991a. Xin minzhu zhuyi de xianzheng [New democratic constitutionalism] (February 20, 1940). In *Mao Zedong xuanji*, by Mao Zedong. Vol. 2, 676–677. Beijing: Renmin chubanshe.

Mao Zedong. 1991b. Lun lianhe zhengfu [On coalition government] (April 24, 1945). In *Mao Zedong xuanji*, by Mao Zedong. Vol. 3, 1056. Beijing: Renmin chubanshe.

Mao Zedong. 1991c. Guanyu shiju de shengming [Statement on the present situation] (January 14, 1949). In *Mao Zedong xuanji*, by Mao Zedong. Vol. 4, 1389. Beijing: Renmin chubanshe.

Mao Zedong. 1991d. Xianfa qicao gongzuo jihua [Plan for constitutional drafting work] (January 15, 1954). In *Mao Zedong wenji*, by Mao Zedong. Vol. 6, 320. Beijing: Renmin chubanshe.

McCubbins, Mathew D., Roger G. Noll, and Barry R. Weingast. 1987. Administrative procedures as instruments of political control. *Journal of Law, Economics, and Organization* 3:243–277.

Meili, Stephen. 1998. Cause lawyers and social movements: a comparative perspective on democratic change in Argentina and Brazil. In *Cause lawyering, political commitments and professional responsibilities*, ed. Austin Sarat and Stuart Scheingold, 487–522. Oxford: Oxford University Press.

Meng Guang. 1955. *Renmin xianfa jianghua [Introduction to the people's constitution]*. Guangzhou: Huanan renmin chubanshe.

Michelson, Ethan. 2006. Connected contention: social resources and petitioning the state in rural China. *Social Sciences Research Network*. http://ssrn.com/abstract=922104.

Michelson, Ethan. 2007. Justice from above or justice from below? Lessons from rural China from the study of disputing. *The China Quarterly* 192:43–64.

Michelson, Ethan. 2008. "Dear Lawyer Bao." every day problems, legal advice, and state power in china. *Social Problems* 55:43–71.

Miller, H. Lyman. 2003a. China's leadership transition: the first stage. *China Leadership Monitor* no. 5.

Miller, H. Lyman. 2003b. The Hu-Wen leadership at six months. *China Leadership Monitor* no. 8.

Ming Pao. 2003a. Liaoning reeducation-through-labor center inmates torture and kill inmate. Trans. World News Connection (http://wnc.fedworld.gov/sources.html). July 13.

Ming Pao. 2003b. Scholar warned for appeal to abolish reeducation-through-labor system. Trans. World News Connection (http://wnc.fedworld.gov/sources.html). July 14.

Ministry of Higher Education and Ministry of Justice (PRC). 1957. *Zhonghua renmin gongheguo gaodeng jiaoyubu, sifabu tuijian zhonghua renmin gonghehuo xianfa jiaoxue dagang (zonghe daxue falüxi ji zhengfa xueyuan yong) [Teaching plan for the PRC Constitution recommended by the PRC Ministries of Higher Education and Justice (for use by the law departments of comprehensive universities and institutes of law and politics)]*. Beijing: Falu chubanshe.

Ministry of Justice, Legal Aid Center. 2005. *Falü Yuanzhu Gongzuo Baogao 2004 [Annual Working Report 2004]*. Beijing: Legal Aid Center of the Ministry of Justice.

Ministry of Justice. 2006. *Zhonghua renmin gongheguo sifabu xingzheng fuyi jueding shu [Notice of judgment of administrative reconsideration]*. Issued March 17.

Ministry of Labor and Social Security (PRC). 2007. *Guanyu weihu yigan biaomian kangyuan xiedaizhe jiuye quanli de yijian [Opinion on safeguarding the employment rights of Hepatitis B carriers]*. Issued May 18.

Minzner, Carl F. 2006. Xinfang: an alternative to formal Chinese legal institutions. *Stanford Journal of International Law* 42:103–79.

Mo Jihong. 2004. *Xianfa xue [Constitutional law studies]*. Beijing: Shehui kexue wenxian chubanshe.

Montlake, Simon. 2008. Critics slam Thailand's activist judges: judges increasingly are calling the shots in a tumultuous political situation. Are they playing fair? *The Christian Science Monitor*, October 6.

Mu, Ch'ien. 1982. *Traditional government in imperial China: a critical analysis*. Hong Kong: The Chinese University Press.

Nadeau, Jean-Benoît, and Julie Barlow. 2005. *Sixty million Frenchmen can't be wrong: what makes the French so French*. London: Robson Books.

Nanfang dushibao [Southern Metropolitan Daily]. 2003a. Yi ge 27 sui de daxue biyesheng zhisi yinqi le women de guanzhu [The death of a 27-year-old university graduate attracts our concern]. April 25.

Nanfang dushubao [Southern Metropolitan Daily]. 2003b. Yi daxue biyesheng yin wu zanzhuzheng bei shourong bing zao ouda zhisi [A university graduate detained because he did not have a temporary residence card is beaten to death]. April 25.

Nanfang dushibao [Southern Metropolitan Daily]. 2003c. Gongmin, ni you quan zhuanggao weifa zhi "fa" [Citizens, you have the power to file suit on unlawful "laws"]. May 29.

Nanfang dushibao [Southern Metropolitan Daily]. 2004. Fagui beian shencha bushi weixian shencha [Putting laws and regulations on file for review is not constitutional review]. July 9.

Nanfang dushibao [Southern Metropolitan Daily]. 2006. Pengshui shi an de san da chuangxin [The three breakthroughs of the Pengshui poetry case]. October 22.

Nanfang zhoumo [Southern Weekend]. 2003a. Xianzheng zhilu: cong zunzhong xianfa kaishi [The path of constitutional government begins with respect for the constitution]. March 13.

Nanfang zhoumo [Southern Weekend]. 2003b. Jujiao weixian shencha diyi xuan'an [Focusing on the first unsettled case of constitutional review]. May 22.

Nathan, Andrew J. 1976. *Peking politics 1918–1923: factionalism and the failure of constitutionalism*. Berkeley: University of California Press.

Nathan, Andrew J. 1996. China's constitutional option. *Journal of Democracy* 7:43–57.

Nathan, Andrew J. 1997. *China's transition*. New York: Columbia University Press.

Nie Longyun. 2003. "Sun Zhigang shijian" yu weixian shencha zhidu [The "Sun Zhigang incident" and China's constitutional review system]. *Liaowang zhoukan [Outlook Weekly]*, June 5.

Nussbaum, Martha C. 1996. Emotion in the language of judging. *Saint John's Law Review* 70:23–29.

O'Brien, Kevin J. 2002. Villagers, elections, and citizenship. In *Changing meanings of citizenship in modern China*, ed. Merle Goldman and Elizabeth J. Perry, 212–231. Cambridge, MA: Harvard University Press.

O'Brien, Kevin J., and Lianjiang Li. 2006. *Rightful Resistance in Rural China*. Cambridge: Cambridge University Press.

Oi, Jean. 1992. Fiscal reform and the economic foundations of local state corporatism in China. *World Politics* 45:99–126.

Open Constitution Initiative. 2006. Lushi zaichangquan xiangmu: fangtan Tian Wenchang lushi [The Lawyers' rights project: an interview with lawyer Tian Wenchang]. April 26, 2006. http://www.gongmeng.cn/sub_r.php?zyj_id=497.

Pan, Philip P. 2003. China releases 3 Internet writers, but convicts 1 other. *Washington Post*, December 1. A14.

Pang De [Roscoe Pound]. 2005. Lun zhongguo xianfa [On the Chinese constitution]. In *Yang Zhaolong faxue wenji*, ed. Ai Yongming and Lu Jinbi, 544–548. Beijing: Falu chubanshe.

Pangalangan, Raul. 2004. The Philippine "People Power" constitution, rule of law, and the limits of liberal constitutionalism. In *Asian discourses of rule of law: theories and implementation of rule of law in twelve Asian countries, France and the U.S.*, ed. Randall Peerenboom, 371–384. New York: RoutledgeCurzon.

Pasquino, Pasquale. 1998. *Sieyes et l'invention de la constitution en France*. Paris: Odile Jacob.

Peerenboom, Randall P. 2002. *China's long march toward rule of law*. Cambridge, MA: Cambridge University Press.

Peerenboom, Randall P. 2004a. Show me the money: the dominance of wealth in determining rights performance in Asia. *Duke Journal of Comparative and International Law* 15:75–152.

Peerenboom, Randall. 2004b. Out of the pan and into the fire: well intentioned but misguided recommendations to eliminate all forms of administrative detention in China. *Northwestern University Law Review* 98:991–1104.

Peerenboom, Randall. 2005. Assessing human rights in China: why the double standard? *Cornell International Law Journal* 38:71–172

Peerenboom, Randall. 2007a. *China modernizes: threat to the west or model for the rest?* Oxford: Oxford University Press.

Peerenboom, Randall. 2007b. Are China's legal reforms stalled? In *Rule of law in China publications*. Vol. 2, *Is China trapped in transition? Implications for future reforms*, ed. Randall Peerenboom, Policy Brief no. 5. Oxford: Foundation for Law, Justice and Society.

Pei, Minxin. 2006. *China's trapped transition: the limits of developmental autocracy*. Cambridge: Harvard University Press.

Peng Zhen. 1990a. Zai Zhongyang Zhengfa Weiyuanhui kuoda huiyi shang de jianghua [Speech before enlarged meeting of the Central Political–legal Committee]. In *Zhonghua Renmin Gongheguo Quanguo Renmin Daibiao dahui wenxian ziliao huanbian 1949–1990*, ed. National People's Congress Standing Committee General Office Research Department, 582586. Beijing: Zhongguo minzu fazhi chubanshe.

Peng Zhen. 1990b. Bujin yao kao dang de zhengce, erque yao yi fa banshi [Not only follow party principles, also work according to the law]. In *Zhonghua Renmin Gongheguo Quanguo Renmin Daibiao dahui wenxian ziliao huanbian 1949–1990*, ed. National People's Congress Standing Committee General Office Research Department, 590–592.Beijing: Zhongguo minzu fazhi chubanshe.

People's Daily (online edition). 2002. Number of lawyers rapidly rising in China. July 8. http://china.org.cn/english/Life/36430.htm.

People's Daily (online edition). 2005. China holds environment hearing over disputed project in imperial garden. April 14. http://english.people.com.cn/200504/14/eng20050414_181007.html.

People's Daily Online. 2007. China to revise controversial death compensation rule, judge says. June 12. http://english.peopledaily.com.cn/200703/15/eng20070315_357698.html..

People's University Constitutional and Administrative Law Research Center, ed. 2004–2007. *Xianzheng yu xingzhen fazhi pinglun [Comments on constitutional government and the rule of administrative law]*. 3 Volumes. Beijing: Zhongguo renmin daxue chubanshe.

People's University Law Department, State Law Teaching and Research Office [Zhongguo renmin daxue falüxi guojiafa jiaoyanshi], ed. 1964. *Zhonghua renmin gongheguo xianfa jiangyi (chugao) [Teaching materials on the PRC constitution (draft)]*. Beijing: Zhongguo renmin daxue chubanshe.

People's Daily book materials group [*Renmin ribao* tushu ziliao zu], ed. 1954. *Xianfa wenti cankao ziliao [Reference documents on constitutional questions]*. Beijing: Renmin chubanshe.

Piant, Hervé. 2006. *Une justice ordinaire: Justice civile et criminelle dans la Prévôté royale de Vaucouleurs sous l'Ancien Régime*. Rennes: Presses Universitaires de Rennes.

Pils, Eva. 2007a. Asking the tiger for his skin: rights activism in China. *Fordham International Law Journal* 30:1209–1287.

Pils, Eva. 2007b. China's other citizens: the legal status of its nine hundred million peasants and internal peasant migrants. In *Zhidu, fazhan, hexie*, ed. Xiangmin Liu et al., 173–243. Hong Kong: Ming Pao Press.

Plato. 1961. The sophist. In *The sophist and The statesman*. Trans. A. E. Taylor; ed. Raymond Klibansky and Elizabeth Anscombe. London: T. Nelson.

Pomfret, John. 2003. China orders halt to debate on reforms. *Washington Post*, August 27.

Posner, Richard A. 2001. *Breaking the deadlock: the 2000 election, the constitution, and the courts*. Princeton: Princeton University Press.

Pound, Roscoe. 1948a. *Some problems of the administration of justice in China*. Nanking: National Chengchi University.

Pound, Roscoe. 1948b. Development of a Chinese constitutional law. *New York University Law Quarterly* 23:375–392.

Powe, Lucas A., Jr. 2000. *The Warren Court and American politics*. Cambridge, MA: Harvard University Press.

Qian Duansheng. 1949. Tongyi zhanxian, renmin zhengquan, gongtong gangling [The united front, the people's regime and the common program]. *Guancha* 6, no. 1: 6–8.

Qin Hui. 1999. *Wenti he zhuyi [Problems and ideologies]*. Jilin: Changchun Press.

Qingnian zaixian [China Youth Online]. Lun gongmin qianxi ziyou he xianzheng jianshe [Citizen freedom of residence and building constitutionalism]. April 7. http://www.people.com.cn/GB/guandian/29/173/20030407/964833.html.

Quentin Skinner. 1989. The state. In *Political innovation and conceptual change*, ed. Terence Ball, James Farr, and Russell L. Hanson, 90–131. Cambridge: Cambridge University Press.

Radio Free Asia. 2005a. Gao Zhisheng lushi suifang lu: er, "tingzhenghui"—muqian muhou [Gao Zhisheng interview series: no. 2, "public hearing"—what is in front of and behind the veil]. Broadcast November 19.

Radio Free Asia. 2005b. Gao Zhisheng lushi suifang lu: san, zai jingcha genzong jiankong xia [Gao Zhisheng interview series: no. 3, under police persecution and surveillance]. Broadcast November 26.

Radio Free Asia. 2005c. Gao Zhisheng lushi suifang lu: si, Gao Zhisheng shuaidiao genzong qu banan sifaju chufa juedingshu songda [Gao Zhisheng interview series: no. 4, local justice bureau serves notice of punishment regarding Gao Zhisheng escaping surveillance to handle a case]. Broadcast December 12.

Radio Free Asia. 2006a. Gao Zhisheng lushi suifang lu: liu, tan "jiyi," "shenpan" yu "quanmin hejie" [Gao Zhisheng interview series: no. 6, discussing "memory," "trial," and "harmonious reconciliation among the entire people"]. Broadcast January 7.

Radio Free Asia. 2006b. Gao Zhisheng lushi suifang lu: qi, shiwusuo bei tingye xiang Sifabu shenqing fuyi, Gao Zhisheng yu xian xing wu yang hui xiang ji mu [Gao Zhisheng interview series: no. 7, after his law firm closes following a review by the Ministry of Justice, Gao Zhisheng escapes danger by returning to his native village and visits his mother's grave]. Broadcast January 21.

Radio Free Asia. 2006c. Gao Zhisheng lushi suifang lu: ba, jia xiang xing [Gao Zhisheng interview series: no. 8, travelling home]. Broadcast January 28.

Radio Free Asia. 2006d. Gao Zhisheng lushi suifang lu: jiu, jieli jueshi, weiquan kang bao—changyi yu fanxiang [Gao Zhisheng interview series: no. 9, relay hunger-striking, rights defending and protesting violence—the project and reactions]. Broadcast February 11.

Radio Free Asia. 2006e. Gao Zhisheng lushi suifang lu: shiyi, dawen—chujing—jueshizhemen [Gao Zhisheng interview series: no. 11, answers from—and the situation of—the hunger-strikers]. Broadcast February 18.

Radio Free Asia. 2006f. Gao Zhisheng lushi suifang lu: shiwu, sifabu "Fuyi Jueding" weichi tingye yi nian—chufa jeili jueshi di qi zhou—canjiazhe zai tan jueshi yiyi. [Gao Zhisheng interview series: no. 15, Ministry of Justice "Review Decision" to close law firm for one year—hunger strike enters its seventh week—participants discuss the idea behind the strike]. Broadcast March 25.

Radio Free Asia. 2006g. Gao Zhisheng bei bianyi ouda jieshou ben tai zhuanfang [Gao Zhisheng gives an interview after having been roughed up by plainclothes officers]. Broadcast July 31.

Radio Free Asia. 2006h. Gao Zhisheng bei juliu shencha, hai nei wai yunniang huyu shifang [Gao Zhisheng detained for investigation, calls for his release are being prepared in China and abroad]. Broadcast August 18.

Radio Free Asia. 2006j. Zhongguo weiquan yundong he gongmin shehui de fazhan (si) [The development of China's rights defense movement and civil society (4)]. Broadcast September 5, 2006.

Ramseyer, Mark. 1994. The puzzling (in)dependence of courts. *Journal of Legal Studies* 23:721–747.

Redish, Martin H., and Elizabeth J. Cisar. 1991. "If angels were to govern." the need for pragmatic formalism in separation of powers theory. *Duke Law Journal* 41:449–506.

Ren Bo. 2003. Chaiqian zi su [Litigating housing demolition]. *Caijing* no. 13: 24–28.

Renda yu Shehui Wang. 2003. 1611 gongmin yaoqiu dui zhongguo 31 sheng gongwuyuan luyong xianzhi yigan xiedaizhe guiding [1611 citizens make demands on regulations in china's 31 provinces that restrict civil service employment for Hepatitis B carriers]. December 22. http://www.yihuiyanjiu.org/oldweb/jdlt_d.asp?id=1305.

Renmin ribao [People's Daily]. 1954a. Canjia xianfa cao'an taolun shi gongmin de zuida rongyao [Participating in the discussions of the draft constitution is the greatest honor for a citizen]. July 28.

Renmin ribao [People's Daily]. 1954b. Zhongyang ge jiguan ganbu shenru taolun xianfa cao'an, ge minzhu dangpai jiguan ganbu relie jinxing xuexi he taolun [Cadres of every central organ thoroughly discuss the draft constitution, cadres of every organ of the democratic parties enthusiastically carry out study and discussion], August 2.

Renmin wang [People's Daily Net]. 2003. He Weifang: cong Sun Zhigang shijian kan zhongguo fazhi fazhan [He Weifang: viewing china's rule of law development from the Sun Zhigang case]. June 10. at http://www.jcrb.com/zyw/n131/ca72252.htm.

Renmin wang [People's Daily Net]. 2003. Tebie cehua: "tongming butong jia" kaowen falü gongping [Special synopsis: examining the legal fairness of "different prices for a life"]. July 20. http://legal.people.com.cn/GB/42731/4608947.html.

Renmin wang [People's Daily Net]. 2004. Wo guo you renda jiandu xianfa shishi, xianfa reng buneng chengwei susong genzhu [In China, the NPC supervises implementation of the constitution, the constitution still cannot constitute a basis for litigation]. December 2. http://www.people.com.cn/GB/shehui/1060/3028137.html.

Reporters without Borders. 2004. Press Release: Du Daobin's sentence confirmed on appeal. August 11. http://www.rsf.org/article.php3?id_article=10598.

Rigobon, Roberto and Dani Rodrik. 2005. Rule of law, democracy, openness, and income: estimating the interrelationships. *Economics of Transition* 13:533–564.

Sager, Lawrence G. 1990. The incorrigible constitution. *New York University Law Review* 65:893–961.

Scarry, Elaine. 1985. *The body in pain.* Oxford: Oxford University Press.

Schmemann, Serge. 1993. Compromise or no, rivals of Yeltsin still seek ouster. *New York Times.* March 25.

Schneiderman, David. 1998. A.V. Dicey, Lord Watson, and the law of the Canadian Constitution in the late nineteenth century. *Law and History Review* 16:495–526.

Selden, Mark. 1995. *China in revolution: the Yenan way revisited.* Armonk, NY: M.E. Sharpe.

Shang Wei and Zhang Chen. 2005. Women dou cheng shangshu quanguo renda [We have all petitioned the National People's Congress]. *Qingnan zaixian [China Youth Online]*, December 22. http://zqb.cyol.com/gb/zqb/2005-12/22/content_110005.htm.

Shang Zhiyong. 2000. Guanyu qingqiu quanguo renda changweihui du "nongmin chengdan feiyong he laowu guanli tiaoli" jinxing weixiang shencha bing yu chexiao de falü jianyi [Legal proposal requesting the National People's Congress Standing Committee to conduct constitutional review and repeal the regulations on the management services and fees borne by peasants]. Dated August 2000.

Shao Junwu. 2001. Renmin fating cunfei zhi zheng [The debate on the retention and abolition of people's court branches]. *Xiandai Faxue* 23:146–151.

Shapiro, Martin and Alec Stone Sweet. 2002. *On law, politics, and judicialization.* Oxford: Oxford University Press.

Shapiro, Martin. 1981. *Courts: a comparative and political analysis.* Chicago: University of Chicago Press.

Shengzhi Law Firm. 2006a. Xingzheng fuyi shenqing shu [Application for administrative reconsideration]. January 19.

Shengzhi Law Firm. 2006b. Xingzheng qisu shu [Application for administrative Litigation]. March 30.

Shue, Vivienne. 1988. *The reach of the state.* Stanford, CA: Stanford University Press.

Shyu, Lawrence N. 1977. China's "wartime parliament": The People's Political Council, 1938–1945. In *Nationalist China during the Sino-Japanese war, 1937–1945*, ed. Paul K.T. Sih, 273–313. Hicksville, NY: Exposition Press.

Sichuan xinwen wang. 2003. Chuanda jiaoshou "beifa" yigan qishi, yi xianfa de mingyi qisu [A Sichuan university professor sets out against HBV discrimination, and files litigation in the name of the constitution]. November 13. http://news.sina.com.cn/s/2003-11-13/05422124292.shtml.

Singer, Peter. 1972. Famine, affluence, and morality. *Philosophy and Public Affairs* 1:229–243.

Spence, David B. 1999. Managing delegation ex ante: using law to steer administrative agencies. *Journal of Legal Studies* 28:413–459.

State Council (PRC). 1957. *Guanyu laodong jiaoyang wenti de jueding [Decision regarding the question of reeducation through labor].* Issued August 3.

State Council (PRC). 1999. *Guanyu quanmian tuijin yifa xingzheng de jueding [Decision to comprehensively implement administration in accordance with the law].* Issued November 8.

State Council (PRC). 2004a. *Quanmian tuijin yifa xingzheng shishi gangyao [Outline for comprehensively implementing further administration in accordance with the law].* Issued March 22.

State Council (PRC). 2004b. *Guanyu kongzhi chengzhen fangwu chaiqian guimo yange chaiqian guanli de tongzhi [Notice regarding constraining the management of urban housing demolition].* Issued June 17.

State Council General Office (PRC). 1998. *Notice of the General Office of the CCP Central Committee and the State Council General Office on Thoroughly Implementing the System of Transparent and Democratic Management of Village Affairs in the Countryside [Zhonggong Zhongyang Bangongting Guowuyuan Bangongting Fachu tongzhi zai nongcun pubian shixing cunwu gongkai he minzhu guanli zhidu].* Zhongbanfa [1998] no. 9. Issued April 18, 1998.

State Council General Office (PRC). 2003. *Guanyu zuohao nongmin jincheng wugong jiuye guanli he fuwu gongzuo de tongzhi [Notice on effectively doing the work of managing and serving migrant laborers who come into the cities to work].* Issued January 1.

State Council Information Office (PRC). 2006. White paper: building political democracy. *China Reports* 42:101–115.

Stone Sweet, Alec. 1992. *The birth of judicial politics in France: the constitutional council in comparative perspective.* Oxford: Oxford University Press.

Suli [Zhu Suli]. 1996. *Fazhi jiqi bentu ziyuan [Rule of law and its local resource]*. Beijing: Zhongguo zhengfa daxue chubanshe.

Suli [Zhu Suli]. 1999. *Yuedu zhixu [Reading process]*. Jinan: Shandong jiaoyu chubanshe.

Suli [Zhu Suli]. 2004. *Daolu tongxiang chengshi—zhuanxing zhongguo de fazhi [all roads lead to cities—rule of law in china's transformation]*. Beijing: Falu chubanshe.

Suli [Zhu Suli]. 1998a. Renzhen dui dairen zhi—Weibo "*Jingji yu Shehui*"de yige dushu biji [taking rule of man seriously: notes on Weber's "*Economy and Society*"]. *Huadong Zhengfa Xueyuan Xuebao* 12:8–13.

Suli [Zhu Suli]. 1998b. "*Ziyou Zhixu Yuanli*" dushu biji [Notes on "*The Constitution of Liberty*"]. *Zhongguo Shehui Kexue Jikan (Hong Kong)* Spring Issue.

Sun Yatsen. 1986. Guomin zhengfu jianguo dagang [A constitutional program of the national government]. In *Sun Zhongshan quanji [Complete works of Sun Yat-sen]*, by Sun Yatsen. Vol. 9, 126–129. Beijing: Zhonghua shuju.

Sunstein, Cass R., and Richard A. Epstein, eds. 2001. *The vote: Bush, Gore, and the Supreme Court*. Chicago: University of Chicago Press.

Supreme People's Court (PRC). 1955. *Zuigao Renmin Fayuan guanyu zai xingshi panjue zhong buyi yinyong xianfa zuo lunzui kexing yiju de pifu [Reply of the Supreme People's Court on not citing the constitution as the basis for determining guilt or sentences in criminal judgments]*. Issued July 30. Reprinted In *Xin zhongguo sifa jieshi daquan*, 420–421 Beijing: Zhongguo jiancha chubanshe.

Supreme People's Court (PRC). 1986. *Zuigao Renmin Fayuan Guanyu Renmin Fayuan zhizuo falu wenshu ruhe yinyong falu guifanxing wenjian de pifu [Reply concerning how People's Courts are to cite legally normative documents when producing legal documents]*. Issued October 28.

Supreme People's Court (PRC). 1991. *Guanyu guanche zhixing : "honghua Renmin Gongheguo Xingzheng Susongfa" ruogan wenti de yijian [Opinion on several questions related to implementing the PRC Administrative Litigation Law]*. Issued June 11.

Supreme People's Court (PRC). 1999a. Renmin Fayue Wunian gaige gangyao [A five-year programme for the reform of the People's Courts]. *Zhonghua Renmin Gongheguo Zuigao Renmin Fayuan Gongbao [Gazette of the Supreme People's Court]* no. 6:185–196.

Supreme People's Court (PRC). 1999b. *Guanyu zhixing xingzheng susong fa ruogan wenti de jieshi [Interpretation regarding questions relating to the application of the Administrative Litigation Law]*. Issued November 24.

Supreme People's Court (PRC). 2001. *Guanyu yi qingfan xingmingquan de shouduan qingfan xianfa baohu de gongmin shoujiaoyuquan de jiben quanli shifou ying chengdan minshi zeren de pifu [Response regarding whether one who violated the constitutionally protected basic right to education of the citizen should bear civil obligation]*. Reprinted in *Zuigao Renmin Rayuan Gongbao [Gazette of the Supreme People's Court of the People's Republic of China]* no. 5:158–161.

Supreme People's Court (PRC). 2003. *Guanyu shenli renshen sunhai peichang anjian shiyong falü ruogan wenti de jieshi [Interpretation regarding several problems in applying the law in adjudicating bodily injury compensation cases]*. Issued December 4.

Supreme People's Court (PRC). 2005. *Guanyu dangshiren da bucheng chaiqian buchang anzhi xieye jiu buchang anzhi zhengyi tiqi minshi susong renmin fayuan pishouli wenti de pifu [Response to whether the People's Courts shall take the litigation on housing demolition compensation filed through civil procedure]*. Issued August 11.

Supreme People's Court (PRC). 2006. *Guanyu shenli sheji nongcun tudi chengbao jiufen anjian shiyong falv wenti de jieshi [Interpretation regarding applicable legal issues for hearing cases about rural land contracting disputes]*. Fashi No. 6.

Supreme People's Court Research Office (PRC). 2001a. *Guanyu renmin fayuan dui nongcun jiji jingji suo de shou yi fenpei jiufen shi fou shuoli wenti de Dafu [Response to the question of whether people's courts shall accept the disputes over distributing the income of rural collective economic organization*. Fayan No. 51.

Supreme People's Court Research Office (PRC). 2001b. *Guanyu cunmin ying tudi buchang fei, an buzhufei wenti yu cunmin weiyuanhui fasheng jiufen renmin fayuan yingfou shouli wenti de dafu [Response to the question of whether a people's court shall accept suits on the disputes over land compensation fees and resettlement subsidies between villagers and a villagers committee].* Fayan No. 116.

Supreme People's Court (PRC). 2008. *Zuigao Renmin Fayuan guanyu feizhi nian di yiqian fabu de youguan sifa jieshi (di qi pi) de jueding [Decision regarding the anullment of judicial interpretations issued prior to the end of 2007].* Fashi No. 15. Issued December 25.

Taipei Times (Online edition). 2003. Mafia kingpin dies in execution van. December 23. http://www.taipeitimes.com/News/world/archives/2003/12/23/2003084622.

Tan Baiqiao. 2006. Gao Zhisheng jijin ma? [Is Gao Zhisheng radical?]. *Boxun Xinwen Wang*, February 25. http://www.peacehall.com/news/gb/pubvp/2006/02/200602251250.shtml.

Tanner, Murray Scot. 1994. Organizations and politics in China's post-Mao law-making system. In *Domestic law reforms in post-Mao China*, ed. Pittman Potter, 56–96. Armonk, NY: M. E. Sharpe.

Tate, C. Neal, and Torbjorn Vallinder, ed. 1995. *The global expansion of judicial power.* New York: New York University Press.

Ten Kate, Jan and Peter J. Van Koppen. 1994. Judicialization of politics in the Netherlands: towards a form of judicial review. *International Political Science Review* 15:143–151.

Teng Biao. 2002. Huayu, shijian yu zhidu bianqian: dangdai Zhongguo sifa de guanjianci fenxi (1949–2002) [Discourse, practice, and systemic changes: analysis of key judicial terms in contemporary China (1949–2002)]. Peking University School of Law Ph.D. dissertation.

Teng Biao. 2003a. Rao buguo de weixian shencha [Unavoidable constitutional review]. *Falü sixiang wang*, July 6. http://law-thinker.com/show.asp?id=2168.

Teng Biao. 2003b. Sun Zhigang shijian: bei taolun de he bei huibi de [The Sun Zhigang case: what was discussed and what was evaded]. *Falü sixiang wang*, September 23. http://www.huayilawyers.com/Website/index.php?ChannelID=9&NewsID=268.

Teng Biao. 2004a. Jihuo xianfa [Activating the constitution]. *Boxun.com*, July 7. http://www.boxun.com/hero/tengb/18_1.shtml.

Teng Biao. 2004b. Sun Zhigang shijian: zhishi, meijie yu quanli [The Sun Zhigang incident: knowledge, media, and rights]. Unpublished manuscript dated October 25.

Teng Biao. 2005. Shenghuo shi weiquan yundong de yuantou huoshui [Life is the fountainhead of the rights defense movement]. *Boxun.com*, May 30. http://www.boxun.com/hero/tengb/22_1.shtml.

Terrill, Ross. 1999. *Madame Mao: the white-boned demon.* Rev. ed. Palo Alto: Stanford University Press.

The Economist. 1997. Peru: court crisis. May 24.

Thwaites, Richard. 1986. *Real life China 1978–1983.* Sydney: William Collins.

Tong Zhiwei. 2003. *Ziyou, chengxu, guize—Sun Zhigang an de fali sikao [Freedom, procedure, and rules—reflections on legal issues in the Sun Zhigang case]. Faxüe* no. 7:3–6.

Tribe, Laurence H. 1985. *Constitutional choices.* Cambridge, MA: Harvard University Press.

Tulloch, H.A. 1977. Changing British attitudes towards the United States in the 1880s. *The Historical Journal* 20:825–40.

Tuokewei'er [Alexis de Tocqueville]. 1988. *Lun Meiguo de Minzhu [Democracy in America].* 2 vols., trans. Dong Guoliang. Beijing: Shangwu yinshuguan.

Tyler, Tom. 1990. *Why people obey the law.* New Haven: Yale University Press.

Unger, Roberto Mangabeira. 1976. *Law in modern society: toward a criticism of social theory.* New York: Free Press.

United Nations Commission on Human Rights. 2006. *Civil and political rights, including the question of torture and detention: report of the special rapporteur on torture and other cruel, inhuman or degrading treatment or punishment, Manfred Nowak—mission to China.* E/CN.4/2006/6/Add.6. Issued March 10.

Upham, Frank K. 2005. Who will find the defendant if he stays with his sheep? Justice in rural China. *The Yale Law Journal* 114:1675–1718.

Vernant, Jean-Pierre. 1992. Myth and Tragedy. In *Essays on Aristotle's Poetics*, ed. Amelie Oksenberg Rorty, 33–50. Princeton: Princeton University Press.

Visiting Delegation of Chinese Justice Workers to the Soviet Union [Ministry of Justice?]. 1955. *Sulian sifa gongzuo fangwen ji guanyu shenpan sifa xingzheng gongzuo bufen [Visitor's journal of Soviet judicial work—section on adjudication and judicial administration work]*. Beijing: Zhongguo sifa gongzuozhe fangsu daibiaotuan.

Visiting Delegation of Chinese Justice Workers to the Soviet Union [Ministry of Justice?]. 1956. *Sulian sifa gongzuo fangwen ji guanyu jiancha gongzuo bufen [Visitor's journal of Soviet judicial work—section on procuratorial work]*. Beijing: Zhongguo sifa gongzuozhe fangsu daibiaotuan.

Volcansek, Mary L. 1990. Judicial review in Italy: a reflection of the United States. *Policy Studies Journal* 19:127–139.

Walsh, Brian. 1987. 200 years of American constitutionalism—a foreign perspective. *Ohio State Law Journal* 48:757–771.

Wang Chaoguang. 2000. *Zhonghua minguo shi [History of the Republic of China]*. Vol.3, *Cong kangzhan shengli dao neizhan baofa qianhou [From the victory in the Sino-Japanese war to the beginning of civil war]*. Beijing: Zhonghua shuju.

Wang Chenguang. 1998. Falü de kesuxing: xiandai fazhi guojia zhong falü de tezheng zhiyi [Justiciability of law: one characteristic of a modern rule of law country]. *Faxue* 8:18–22.

Wang Hanbin. 1989. Zhonghua Renmin Gongheguo Xingzheng Susong Fa (caoan) de shuoming [Explanation of the draft Administrative Litigation Law of the PRC]. Reprinted in *Renmin Ribao*, April. 10.

Wang Jian. 2002. Xifa dongjian: zhongxi falu gainian duiying guanxi zaoqi lishi de kaocha [Legal transplantation from the West to the East: a study of the corresponding meaning of legal concepts between the West and China in the late Qing Dynasty]. In *Qinghua Fazhi Lunheng*, ed. Gao Hongjun. Vol. 2, 296–359. Beijing: Qinghua daxue chubanshe.

Wang Lin. 2005. Chongfen renshi falu yuanzhu de zhanlue yiyi [The strategic importance of legal aid]. *Renmin Wang*, March 21. http://cppcc.people.com.cn/GB/34961/45560/45563/3258847.html.

Wang Shengjun. 2008. Sifa buyao gao shenmihua [Justice should not cause mystery]. *Xinhua Wang [Xinhua Net]*, August 28. http://news.xinhuanet.com/politics/2008-08/28/content_9725432.htm.

Wang Xianzhi. 1990. Kangzhan shiqi Guomindang zuzhi jianshe yu zuzhi fazhan de jige wenti [Issues on the Kuomintang's organizational construction and development during the Anti-Japanese war]. *Jindaishi Yanjiu* 2:230–250.

Wang Xinyou. 2008. Yingxiangxing susong: yi gean tuidong minzhu fazhi [Impact litigation: using individual cases to promote democracy and rule of law]. *Zhengyi wang*, November 21. http://www.jcrb.com/zyw/n7/ca435792.htm.

Wang Yi. 2003. 2003: "xin minquan yundong" de faren he caolian [2003: the beginning and practice of the "new citizens rights movement"]. *Guancha*, December 19.

Wang Zhenmin. 2004. *Zhongguo weixian shencha zhidu [China's constitutional review system]*. Beijing: Zhongguo zhengfa daxue chubanshe.

Wang, Ke-wen. 1998. Constitutional orthodoxy: *fatong*. In *Modern China: an encyclopedia of history, culture, and nationalism*, ed. Ke-wen Wang, 77–78. London: Taylor and Francis.

Wang, Shaoguang. 2006. Regulating death at coal mines: changing mode of governance in China. *Journal of Contemporary China* 15:1–30.

Wen Jiabao. 2006. Report on the work of the government (March 5, 2006). Trans. State Council (PRC). http://english.gov.cn/official/2006-03/14/content_227248.htm.

Wen Zhengbang. 1994. *Gongheguo xianzheng licheng [The trajectory of constitutionalism in the republic]*. Zhengzhou: Henan renmin chubanshe.

Wilkinson, Michael A. 2003. Civil society and the re-imagination of European constitutionalism. *European Law Journal* 9:451–472

Williams, Bernard. 1973. A critique of utilitarianism. In *Utilitarianism: for and against*, ed. J.J.C. Smart and Bernard Williams, 77–150. Cambridge: Cambridge University Press.

Wong, R. Bin. 1999. The political economy of agrarian empire and its modern legacy. In *China and imperial capitalism: genealogies of sinological knowledge*, ed. Timothy Brooks and Gregory Blue, 210–245. Cambridge: Cambridge University Press.

Wong, Young-Tsu. 1993. The fate of liberalism in revolutionary China. *Modern China* 19:457–490.

Wood, Gordon S. 1993. *The Radicalism of the American Revolution*. New York: Random House.

World Bank. 2005. *Global Monitoring Report (2005)*. Washington DC: The World Bank.

World Bank. 2006. China Testing New Approach to Poverty Alleviation. June 1. http://go.worldbank.org/5SFKLXF8L0.

Wu Defeng. 1954. *Zhonghua renmin gongheguo xianfa jianghua [Introduction to the PRC Constitution]*. Zhengzhou: Henan renmin chubanshe.

Wu Jialin. 1954. *Xianfa jiben zhishi jianghua [Introduction to basic knowledge about the constitution*. Beijing: Zhongguo qingnian chubanshe.

Xia Yong, ed. 1999. *Gonfa [Public law]*. Beijing: Falu chubanshe.

Xia Yong. 1992. *Renquan gainian qiyuan [Origin of the conception of human rights]*. Beijing: Zhongguo zhengfa daxue chubanshe.

Xia Yong. 2005. Piaohu de fazhi—Qing mo Minchu Zhongguo de bianfa sixiang yu fazhi [Uncertain rule of law—rule of law and the transformation of thought during the end of the Qing Dynasty and the beginning of the Republic of China]. *Bijiao Fa Yanjiu* no. 2:1–19.

Xianfa cao'an chugao taolun yijian huiji [Collected opinions from discussions of the draft constitution]. 1954. 25 vols. Beijing: Zhonghua renmin gongheguo xianfa qicao weiyuanhui ban'gongshi.

Xiang Chunyi. 1991. Dang de lingdao yu fazhi jianshe [Party leadership and the construction of the legal system]. *Zhongguo faxue* no. 4:4–13.

Xianzheng yu xingzheng fazhi fazhan baogao [Report of the development of constitutional and administrative law in China]. 2005. Beijing: Zhongguo renmin daxue chubanshe.

Xiao Han. 2003. Dang e fa bei feichu de shihou [When an evil law was repealed]. *Zhongping wang*, June 18. http://www.china-review.com/everyday/everyday-79.htm.

Xiao Yang. 2003. Weihu xianfa de zhishang quanwei [Defending the supremacy of the constitution]. In *Dangzheng ganbu xianfa jiaoyu duben [A constitutional reader for the party and government cadres]*, ed. Gu Angran and Qiao Xiaoyang, 268–274. Beijing: Zhonggong zhongyang dangxiao chubanshe.

Xie Weiyan. 2004. *Cong xianfa dao xianzheng [From constitutions to constitutionalism]*. Jinan: Shandong Renmin chubanshe.

Xinhua News Agency. 2002. Yi fa zhiguo, yi de zhiguo [Ruling the country in accordance with law and ruling the country in accordance with virtue]. *Xinhua.net*, September 6. http://news.xinhuanet.com/newscenter/2002-09/06/content_552721.htm.

Xinhua News Agency. 2003a. Twelve people sentenced for beating death of a young man . Trans. http://russian.china.org.cn/english/government/66584.htm. Dated June 10.

Xinhua News Agency. 2003b. China adopts draft regulation on vagrants, beggars. Trans. Foreign Broadcast Information Service. June 18.

Xinhua News Agency. 2003c. China adopts draft regulation on vagrants, beggars. Trans. Foreign Broadcast Information Service. June 18.

Xinhua News Agency. 2003d. China vows to look after vagrants and beggars. Trans. Foreign Broadcast Information Service. June 27.

Xinhua News Agency. 2004. More Chinese province discontinues Hepatitis discrimination in civil service. Trans. Foreign Broadcast Information Service. May 17.

Xinhua News Agency. 2005. Supreme People's Court Work Report for 2005. Trans. http://lawprofessors.typepad.com/china_law_prof_blog/files/spc_work_report.html. Submitted April 1.

Xinhua News Agency. 2006. Youguan fuzeren dawen: zhengshou gonglu yanglu fei fuhe falü guiding [Responsible persons answer questions: collection of public road maintenance fees conforms to the law]. November 24.

Xinhuanet. 2003a. Zhengxie weiyuan jianyan: shourong yisong buneng chengwei duifu mingong de shouduan [CPPCC Committee member advises: custody and repatriation cannot be a tool against migrants]. March 5. http://past.people.com.cn/GB/shizheng/252/10307/10316/20030305/936948.html.

Xinhuanet. 2003b. Sun Zhigang zhisi jingdong zhongyang, 13 ming xianyiren quanbu bei jibu guan [The death of Sun Zhigang disturbs the center, 13 suspects are all seized and brought to justice]. May 13. http://news.xinhuanet.com/legal/2003-05/13/content_867553.htm.

Xinhuanet. 2004. Renda shi weixian shenchazhi, renhe gongmin ke tiqing weixian shencha [The NPC explains the constitutional review system, any citizen may call for constitutional review]. December 2. http://news.xinhuanet.com/legal/2004-12/02/content_2284651.htm.

Xinhuanet. 2007. Jiuye cujinfa caoan zhunbei ba gongping jiuye zuowei zhuanmen yizhang [Employment promotion law draft to make equal employment a special chapter]. July 13. http://news.xinhuanet.com/employment/2007-07/13/content_6371382.htm.

Xinjing bao [Beijing News]. 2003. 1611 ren qingqiu weixian shencha, huyu xiugai gongwuyuan zhaokao jinling [1611 people appeal for constitutional review, call for amendment of civil service admission prohibitions]. November 26.

Xinjing bao [Beijing News]. 2004. Wo guo shouxian chengli zhuanmen jigou jinxing fagui weixian shencha [China for the first time establishes a special mechanism to engage in constitutional review of laws and regulations]. June 19.

Xinjing bao [Beijing News]. 2005a. Quanguo renda mingque weixian shencha chengxu [NPC clarifies constitutional review procedure]. December 20.

Xinjing bao [Beijing News]. 2005b. Weixian shencha: jian gongmin quanli luodao shiqu [Constitutional review: put citizen rights into practice]. December 21.

Xinjing Bao [Beijing News]. 2006. Renshen sunhai peichang jiang chutai xin guiding [A new provision to emerge on bodily injury compensation]. March 21.

Xinjing bao [Beijing News]. 2007. Zhongguo jinqi jiang gaibian "tongming bu tongjia" [China will soon change "different prices for a life"]. March 15.

XinSheng.net. 2006. Yuan Hongbing ping Ding Zilin zhi Gao Zhisheng gongkaixin [Yuan Hongbing criticizes Ding Zilin's open letter to Gao Zhisheng]. February 25. http://xinsheng.net/xs/articles/gb/2006/2/25/36002.htm.

Xu Chongde, et al., eds. 1996. *Zhongguo Xianfa [The Chinese Constitution].* Beijing: Beijing daxue chubanshe.

Xu Chongde, et al., eds. 2004. *Zhongguo Xianfa [The Chinese Constitution].* 2nd ed. Beijing: Beijing daxue chubanshe.

Xu Panqiu. 1954. *Xianfa changshi [General knowledge about the constitution].* Shanghai: Xin zhishi chubanshe.

Xu Yiguan. 1955. *He nongmin tantan xianfa [Talking about the constitution with peasants.* Beijing: Tongsu duwu chubanshe.

Xu Yinghui. 2004. Cong "dunwei" dao "guiwei"—dui chengshi fangwu chaiqian buchang moshi de tantao [From "dunwei" to "guiwei"—an exploration of models for urban housing demolition compensation]. *Zhongwai Faxue* no. 5:556–570.

Xuexi xianfa ruogan wenti jieda [Answers to certain questions in studying the constitution]. 1955. Beijing: Tongsu duwu chubanshe.

Yan Xiaohu. 2003. Shourong zhidu ruogan wenti de falü fenxi, [Legal analysis on several issues with custody and repatriation]. *Faxüe* no. 7:10–21.

Yan, Alice. 2004. Hunan lifts ban on hiring Hepatitis B carriers. *South China Morning Post*, March 4, 6.

Yang Chengwu. 1987. *Yang Chengwu huiyilu [Memoirs of Yang Chengwu]*. Beijing: jiefangjun chubanshe.

Yang Tao. 2004. Wo weishenma xian quanguo renda ti jianyi [Why I want to raise proposals to the National People's Congress]. *Zhengyi wang*, August 8. http://news.xinhuanet.com/legal/2005-08/04/content_3307229.htm.

Yang, Zhaolong. 2005. Xianzheng zhi dao [The road to constitutionalism] (1944). In *Yang Zhaolong faxue wenji*, ed. Ai Yongming and Lu Jinbi, 455–465. Beijing: Falu chubanshe.

Yarbrough, Tinsley E. 2001. *The Rehnquist court and the constitution*. Oxford: Oxford University Press.

Yardley, Jim. 2005. A judge tests China's courts, making history: unintentionally opens debate on autonomy. *The New York Times*, November 28, at A1.

Yardley, Jim. 2006. 3 deaths in China reveal disparity in price of lives. *New York Times*, April 14.

Ying Chunzi. 2006. Liu Lu jiu jueshi shijian fangtan lu [Interview with Liu Lu on the hunger-strike]. *Boxun Xinwen Wang*, February 28. http://www.peacehall.com/news/gb/china/2006/02/200602280026.shtml.

Yu Jiang, Teng Biao, and Xu Zhiyong. 2003. Guanyu shencha "chengshi liulang qitao renyuan shourong qiansong" de jianyishu [Proposal to examine the "Measures for the Custody and Repatriation of Vagrants and Beggars in Cities"]. Dated May 14.

Yu Jianrong. 2004a. Dangqian nongmin weiquan huodong de yi ge jieshi kuangjia [A framework for analyzing the rights protection movement of today's peasants]. *Shehuixue Yanjiu* no. 2: 49–55.

Yu Meisun. 2004b. Cong Jiaoyubu dang beigao de liangan, kan zhaosheng zhidu chuangxin de poqiexing [On the exigency of renovating the college recruiting system, judging from the two cases where the Ministry of Education is the defendant]. *Epoch Times* (online edition), April 23. http:// www.epochtimes.com/gb/4/4/23/n519496.htm.

Yu Xingzhong. 1989. Legal pragmatism in the People's Republic of China. *Journal of Chinese Law* 3:29–52.

Yuan Hongbing. 2006. Wei Gao Zhisheng bian [In defense of Gao Zhisheng]. *Boxun Xinwen Wang*, February 24. http://www.peacehall.com/news/gb/pubvp/2006/02/200602242309.shtml.

Yun Xiang. 2003. Sun Zhigang's death and reform of [sic] detention system. *Human Rights* 2, no. 5:19–26.

Zhang Chunsheng, ed. 2000. *Zhonghua renmin gongheguo lifa fa shiyi (Zhonghua renmin gongheguo falü shiyi congshu, quanguo renmin daibiao dahui changwu weihui fazhi gongzuo weiyuanhui pian), [Interpretation of the China's Law on Legislation (People's Republic of China Legal Interpretation Series, edited by the Commission on Legislative Affairs of the National People's Congress Standing Committee)]*. Beijing: Falu chubanshe.

Zhang Geng and Gong Xiaobing, eds. 1998. *Zhongguo falu yuanzhu zhidu dansheng de qianqian houhou [The birth of China's legal aid system]*. Beijing: Zhongguo Fangzheng Press

Zhang Hengshan. 1989. Fa de zhongxin hezai?—Ping "quanli benwei" shuo [What is the focus of Law?—A critique of the "rights-orientation" thesis]. *Zhengzhi yu Falu* no. 1:6–9.

Zhang Hong. 2005. Xingzheng qiangzhi lüelun [A brief theory of administrative coercion]. *Zhongguo renda wang*, December 29. http://www.npc.gov.cn/cwh/common/zw.jsp?label=WXZLK&id=343996&pdmc=hyjc.

Zhang Jinfan. 1986. *Zhongguo fazhi shigang [An outline of China's legal system]*. Beijing: Zhongguo zhengfa daxue chubanshe.

Zhang Jing. 1999. Xiang gui min yue ti xian de cun zhuang zhi quan [Governance of village in the view of village pacts and social agreements]. *Beida Falu Pinglun* no. 1:4–48.

Zhang Qingfu and Ren Yi. 2005. *1954 nian xianfa—xianxing xianfa de jichu [The 1954 Constitution—the foundation of the current constitution]*. In *1954 nian xianfa yanjiu*, ed. Zhang Qingfu and Han Dayuan, 7–14. Beijing: Zhongguo renmin gong'an daxue chubanshe.

Zhang Qingfu. 1989. *Xianfaxue yanjiu shulue [Review of constitutional research]*. Tianjin: Tianjin jiaoyu chubanshe.

Zhang Qingfu. 2001. *Xianfa luncong [Constitutional collections]*. Beijing: Falu chubanshe.

Zhang Wenxian. 2002. Cong yiwu benwei dao quanli benwei shi fa de fazhan guilu [The Developmental Pattern of Law: From Obligations to Rights]. *Zhongguo Lilun faxue yanjiu xinwen wang [Legaltheory.com.cn]*, December 24, 2002. http://www.legaltheory.com.cn/info.asp?id=854. Accessed May 9, 2008.

Zhang Wenxian. 1987. *Dangdai xifang fazhexue [Contemporary western legal philosophy]*. Jilin: Jilin renmin chubanshe.

Zhang Yue and Ding Xiguo. 2003. Democracy and the legal system: descending from heaven to earth. *Xinhua News Service*. Trans. Foreign Broadcast Information Service. March 11.

Zhao Ling and Shen Ying. 2003. Liu qi jiuzhu banfa juece guocheng [Policymaking process for the aid measures for vagrants and beggars]. *Nanfang Zhoumo*, June 26.

Zhao Xiao. 2002. The two faces of the People's Tribunals in rural China. *Perspectives* 3, no. 4.

Zhengyi wang. [undated]. Chengzhen tongming butong jia, sunhai peichang biaozhun ying tongyi [Different prices for a life in cities and countryside, injury compensation standards should be unified]. http://www.jcrb.com/zyw/pcbzty/index.htm.

Zhong Sheng and Tang Sengshu. 1999. Shilun Nanjing guomin zhengfu xunzheng qianqi (1928–1937) de difang dangzheng jiufeng [Local party-government conflicts during the early tutelary period (1928–1937) of the Nanjing national government]. *Shixue Yuekan* no. 2:53–58.

Zhongguo Falu Nianjian 1997 [China Legal Yearbook 1997]. 1998. Beijing: Zhongguo falu nianjian chubanshe.

Zhongguo Falu Nianjian 1998 [China Legal Yearbook 1998]. 1999. Beijing: Zhongguo falu nianjian chubanshe.

Zhongguo Falu Nianjian 2000 [Law Yearbook of China 2000]. 2000. Beijing: Zhongguo falu nianjian chubanshe.

Zhongguo Falu Nianjian 2006 [Law Yearbook of China 2006]. 2006. Beijing: Zhongguo falu nianjian chubanshe.

Zhongguo lüshi wang. 2003a. Qingdao: gongmin xianfa quanli sifa baohu yantaohui [Qingdao: conference on judicial safeguards for citizen constitutional rights]. January 14. http://www.acla.org.cn/article/200301146166.html.

Zhongguo lüshi wang. 2003b. Sun Zhigang: tiantanli bu xuyao zanzhuzheng [Sun Zhigang: you don't need a temporary residence permit in heaven]. June 9. http://www.acla.org.cn/pages/2003-6-9/s8129.html.

Zhongguo xinwen wang. 2002. Hu Jintao qiangdiao jinyibu shuli xianfa yishi yu quanwei [Hu Jintao stressed progressively establishing constitutional consciousness and authority]. December 4. http://www.chinanews.com.cn/2002-12-04/26/250121.html.

Zhou Litai. 2004. Guanyu jianyi dui Zuigao Renmin Fayuan *(Fashi <2003> 20 hao)* weixian guiding jinxing shencha de shenqing [Application for review of unconstitutional provisions of the "*Legal Interpretation <2003> no. 20*" by the Supreme People's Court]. Dated December 7.

Zhou Qingzhi. 2004. *Zhongguo xianji xingzheng jiegou ji qi yunxing—dui "W" xian de shehui xuekao [County level government organization and operation in China—a sociological study of County "W"]*. Guiyang: Guizhou renmin chubanshe.

Zhou Wei. 2006. *Xianfa jiben quanli: yuanli·guifan·yingyong [Fundamental constitutional rights]*. Beijing: Falu chubanshe.

Zhou Zhenxiang, et al., eds. 1990. *Xin Zhongguo fazhi jianshe sishi nian yao lan [New China's forty years of establishing a legal system]*. Beijing: Qunzhong chubanshe.

Zhou Zhitai. [undated]. Nongcun shanyang jiufen zengduo de yuanyin fenxi yu duice sikao [Reflection on the reasons of the increase in maintenance disputes in rural areas and the counter-measures]. *Chongqing Fayuan Wang*. http://www.cqcourt.gov.cn/chinese/infos/index.asp?items=3&newsid=3879&scid=31.

Zhu Suli. 2000. *Song fa xiaxiang: Zhongguo jiceng sifazhidu yanjiu [Sending law to the countryside: research on China's basic-level judicial system]*. Beijing: Zhongguo zhengfa daxue chubanshe.

Zi Yue. 2003. Bid an eternal farewell to the Sun Zhigang tragedy. *Nanfang dushibao,* trans. Foreign Broadcast Information Service, June 19.

Zou Tang. 1994. *Ershi niandai de Zhongguo zhengzhi: cong hongguan lishi yu weiguan xingdong jiaodu kan [China's politics in the 20th century: from a macro historical and micro behavioral perspective]*. Hong Kong: Oxford University Press.

Treaties and Legislation

Chengshi Fangwu Chaiqian Guanli Tiaoli [Demolition Provisions]. Issued by the State Council (PRC), June 13, 2001.

Chengshi Liulang Qitao Renyuan Shourong Qiansong Banfa [Measures on Custody and Repatriation of Vagrants and Beggars in Cities]. Issued by the State Council (PRC), May 12, 1982.

Chengshi Shenghuo Wuzhuo De Liulang Qitao Renyuan Jiuzhu Guanli Banfa [Measures on the Administration of Aid to Indigent Vagrants and Beggars]. Issued by the State Council (PRC), June 18, 2003, effective August 1, 2003.

Convention against Torture and Other Cruel, Inhuman or Degrading Treatment or Punishment. G.A. res. 39/46, [annex, 39 U.N. GAOR Supp. (No. 51) at 197, U.N. Doc. A/39/51 (1984)]. Entered into force June 26, 1987.

Draft Treaty Establishing a Constitution for Europe. CONV 850/03. Submitted July 18, 2003.

Falu Yuanzhu Tiaoli [Legal Aid Regulation]. Issued by the State Council (PRC), July 16, 2003.

Gongwuyuan Luyong Tijian Tongyong Biaozhun (shixing) [Civil Service Employment Physical Examination General Standards (Provisional)]. Issued by the State Council (PRC), January 17, 2005.

Guanyu Laodong Jiaoyang Buchong Guiding [Regulations regarding Reeducation through Labor]. Issued by the State Council (PRC), November 29, 1979.

Guojia Gongwuyuan Zanting Tiaoli [Provisional Regulations for the State Civil Service]. Issued by the State Council (PRC), August 14, 1993.

Hulianwang Xinwen Xinxi Fuwu Guanli Guiding [Provisions on the Administration of Internet News Information Services]. Issued by the State Council (PRC) and the Ministry of Information Industry (PRC), September 25, 2005.

Laodong Jiaoyang Shixing Banfa [Re-education through Labor Provisional Measures]. Issued by the State Council (PRC), January 21, 1982.

Susong Feiyong Jiaona Banfa [Measures on the Payment of Litigation Fees]. Issued by the State Council (PRC) December 19, 2006, effective April 1, 2007.

Xingzheng Fuyi Tiaoli [Administrative Reconsideration Rules]. Issued by the State Council (PRC), June1989; effective January 1, 1990.

Zhonghua Renmin Gongheguo Chuanranbing Fangzhi Fa [Law on the Prevention and Control of Infectious Diseases]. Adopted 2004.

Zhonghua Renmin Gongheguo Cunmin Weiyuanhui Zuzhi Fa [Organic Law of the Villagers Committees of the People's Republic of China]. Adopted 1998.

Zhonghua Renmin Gongheguo Funu Quanyi Baozhang Fa [Law of the People's Republic of China on the Protection of Women's Rights and Interests]. Adopted 1994.

Zhonghua Renmin Gongheguo Lifa Fa [Law on Legislation of the People's Republic of China]. Adopted 2000.

Zhonghua Renmin Gongheguo Minfa Tongze [General Principles of the Civil Law of the Peoples Republic of China]. Adopted 1986.

Zhonghua Renmin Gongheguo Minshi Susong Fa [Civil Procedure Law of the People's Republic of China]. Adopted 1991.

Zhonghua Renmin Gongheguo Nongcun Tudi Chengbao Fa [Law of the People's Republic of China on Land Contract in Rural Areas]. Issued 2002, effective 2003.

Zhonghua Renmin Gongheguo Renmin Faguan Zuzhi Fa [Organic Law of the People's Courts of the People's Republic Of China]. Adopted 1979, amended 1983.

Zhonghua Renmin Gongheguo Wuquan Fa [Property Law of the People's Republic of China]. Adopted 2007.

Zhonghua Renmin Gongheguo Xingshi Fa [Criminal Law of the People's Republic of China]. Adopted 1979, amended 1997.

Zhonghua Renmin Gongheguo Xingshi Susong Fa [Criminal Procedure Law of the People's Republic of China]. Adopted 1979, amended 1996.

Zhonghua Renmin Gongheguo Xingzhong Chufa Fa [Administrative Punishment Law of the People's Republic of China]. Adopted 1996.

Zhonghua Renmin Gongheguo Xingzheng Susong Fa [Administrative Litigation Law of the People's Republic of China]. Adopted 1989.

Zhonghua Renmin Gongheguo Xingzheng Xuke Fa [Administrative Licensing Law of the People's Republic of China]. Adopted 2004.

Cases

Bush v. Gore. 2000. 531 U.S. 98.

Dred Scott v. Sandford. 1856. 60 U.S. 393.

Kress v. France. 2001. European Court of Human Rights. No. 39594/98, § 48, ECHR 2001-VI.

Marbury v. Madison. 1803. 5 U.S. (1 Cranch) 137.

Myers v. United States. 1926. 272 U.S. 52.

Planned Parenthood of Southeastern Pennsylvania v. Casey. 1992. 505 U.S. 833.

United States v. Carolene Products Co. 1938. 304 U.S. 144.

Worcester v. Georgia. 1832. 31 U.S. (6 Pet.) 515.

INDEX